Cross-Border Taxation of Permanent Establishments

Series on International Taxation

VOLUME 59

Series Editors

Introduction & Contents

The Series on International Taxation deals with a wide variety of topics in the global tax arena. The authors include many of the field's leading experts as well as talented newcomers. Their expert views and incisive commentary has proven highly useful to practitioners and academics alike.

Objective

The volumes published in this series are aimed at offering high-quality analytical information and practical solutions for international tax practitioners.

Readership

Practitioners, academics and policy makers in international tax law.

Frequency of Publication

2-3 new volumes published each year.

The titles published in this series are listed at the end of this volume.

Cross-Border Taxation of Permanent Establishments

An International Comparison

Andreas Waltrich

Wolters Kluwer

Published by:
Kluwer Law International B.V.
PO Box 316
2400 AH Alphen aan den Rijn
The Netherlands
Website: www.wklawbusiness.com

Sold and distributed in North, Central and South America by:
Wolters Kluwer Legal & Regulatory U.S.
7201 McKinney Circle
Frederick, MD 21704
United States of America
Email: customer.service@wolterskluwer.com

Sold and distributed in all other countries by:
Turpin Distribution Services Ltd
Stratton Business Park
Pegasus Drive, Biggleswade
Bedfordshire SG18 8TQ
United Kingdom
Email: kluwerlaw@turpin-distribution.com

ISBN 978-90-411-6832-0

About the Author

From 02/2016	Consultant at the Tax Department of EnBW (German Energy Supplier)
01/2015-02/2015	Research Stay, International Bureau of Fiscal Documentation (IBFD), Amsterdam
09/2011-12/2015	Scientific Assistant at the Chair of Business Administration and Taxation II, Prof. Dr Christoph Spengel
09/2008-12/2008	Semester Abroad at the University of Jyväskylä (Finland)
09/2006-06/2011	Study of Business Administration, University of Mannheim
10/2005-06/2006	Compulsory social service
06/2005	Abitur, Lessing-Gymnasium, Karlsruhe

Table of Contents

Foreword

The taxation of permanent establishments is a complex topic, especially from a cross-border point of view. From my understanding, despite various existing academic literature, a detailed and combined analysis of both the definition and the allocation of business profits to a permanent establishment which provides feasible proposals for reform, is still missing. Consequently, numerous qualification conflicts and situations of double taxation and double non-taxation still exist. The doctoral thesis of Andreas Waltrich provides a comprehensive contribution to close these gaps.

Mr Waltrich has assessed the taxation of permanent establishments based on economic and legal criteria. The analysis presents the status quo and reform proposals of current OECD tax policy regarding permanent establishments. In addition, the thesis includes an in-depth analysis of the taxation of permanent establishments in national and tax treaty law, from the perspective of Germany, the United States, Brazil, Russia, India and China. The choice of these six countries forms a basis for an elaborated systematization of the concept of the permanent establishment from an international perspective. Finally, the thesis identifies qualification conflicts and discusses proposals for reforming the cross-border taxation of permanent establishments.

The doctoral thesis of Mr Waltrich is a diversified and sound work which fulfils economical as well as tax law requirements. It constitutes a valuable contribution to the tax implications of the use of the permanent establishment in the selected countries as well as to the systematic evaluation of current OECD practice. The presented results are not only of importance for international researches in this field, but also for policy makers in the OECD and non-OECD member countries dealing with this issue, as well as for tax practitioners who need an overview of the taxation concepts for permanent establishments. I therefore strongly recommend the doctoral thesis of Mr. Waltrich to this audience.

Prof. Dr Christoph Spengel
Mannheim, April 2016

List of Figures

List of Tables

List of Abbreviations

AAR	Authority for Advanced Rulings
ABB	ASEA Brown Boveri
AmtshilfeRLUmsG	*Amtshilferichtlinienumsetzungsgesetz*
AO	*Abgabenordnung* (German General Tax Code)
AOA	Authorised OECD Approach
APA	Advance Pricing Agreement
Art.	Article
Arts	Articles
AStG	*Außensteuergesetz* (Foreign Tax Act)
BEPS	Base Erosion and Profit Shifting
BFH	*Bundesfinanzhof* (German Federal Fiscal Court)
BIAC	Business Industry Advisory Committee
BMF	*Bundesministerium der Finanzen* (German Federal Ministry of Finance)
BRIC	Brazil, Russia, India, China
BRICS	Brazil, Russia, India, China, South Africa
BsGaV	*Betriebsstättengewinnaufteilungsverordnung*
BStBl.	*Bundessteuerblatt*
CCCTB	Common Consolidated Corporate Tax Base
CCTB	Common Corporate Tax Base
CEN	Capital Export Neutrality
CIN	Capital Import Neutrality
CON	Capital Ownership Neutrality
COPESUL	*Companhia Petroquímica do Sul* (Brazilian petroleum company)
CTC	German Corporate Tax Code (*Körperschaftsteuergesetz*)

DBA	*Doppelbesteuerungsabkommen*
Dem.	Democratic
DStJG	*Deutsche Steuerjuristische Gesellschaft*
DTA	Double Taxation Agreement
e.g.	*Exempli gratia* (for example)
e.V.	*eingetragener Verein* (registered association)
EC	European Commission
ECI	Effectively connected income
Ed.	Editor
Eds	Editors
EFG	*Entscheidungen der Finanzgerichte*
EStÄR	*Einkommensteueränderungsrichtlinien*
Et al.	*Et. alii*
EU	European Union
f.	Following
FA	Formula apportionment
FDAP	Fixed or Determinable Annual or Periodic income
FG	*Finanzgericht*
FIFA	*Fédération Internationale de Football Association*
Fn.	Footnote
FTA	Foreign Tax Act (*Außensteuergesetz*)
GDP	Gross Domestic Product
GTC	German General Tax Code (*Abgabenordnung)*
i.a.	*Inter alia* (among other things)
i.e.	*Id est* (that is)
IBFD	International Bureau of Fiscal Documentation
ICT	Information and communication technologies
IFA	International Fiscal Association
IFRS	International Financial Reporting Standards
ifst	*Institut Finanzen und Steuern*
IMF	International Monetary Fund
IRC	Internal Revenue Code
IRS	Internal Revenue Service
ITAT	Income Tax Appellate Tribunal
ITC	German Income Tax Code (*Einkommenssteuergesetz*)
JStG	*Jahressteuergesetz*
JTPF	Joint Transfer Pricing Forum

KStG	*Körperschaftsteuergesetz*
M&A	Merger and Acquisitions
MA	*Musterabkommen* (Model Convention)
MAP	Mutual agreement procedure
MC	Model Convention
NATO	North Atlantic Treaty Organization
No.	Number
NV	*Nicht veröffentlicht* (not published)
n. F.	*Nach Fassung*
OECD	Organisation for Economic Co-operation and Development
p.	Page
PAN	Permanent Account Number
Para.	Paragraph
PE	Permanent establishment
PGFN	*Procuradoria Geral da Fazenda Nacional* (Brazilian National Treasury Attorney's General Office)
pp.	Pages
PPP	Purchasing-Power-Parity
PwC	PricewaterhouseCoopers
R&D	Research and Development
Rep.	Republic
RRIL	Rolls Royce Indian Limited
SAT	State Administration of Taxation
SEC	US Securities and Exchange Commission
Sec.	Section
Sent.	Sentence
SEStEG	*Gesetz über steuerliche Begleitmaßnahmen zur Einführung der Europäischen Gesellschaft und zur Änderung weiterer steuerrechtlicher Vorschriften*
SET	Sony Entertainment Television
Suppl.	Supplementary
SUB	Subsidiary
TD	Toronto-Dominion
TP	Transfer Pricing
TRE	Tax Resident Enterprises
TT	Tax Treaty
UN	United Nations
USCIB	US Council for International Business

V.	Versus
Vol.	Volume

List of Abbreviations of Countries

AT	Austria
BE	Belgium
BG	Bulgaria
BR	Brazil
CN	China
CY	Cyprus
CZ	Czech Republic
DE	Germany
DE	Germany
DK	Denmark
EE	Estonia
ES	Spain
FI	Finland
FR	France
GR	Greece
HR	Croatia
HU	Hungary
IE	Ireland
IN	India
IT	Italy
LT	Lithuania
LU	Luxembourg
LV	Latvia
MT	Malta
NL	Netherlands
PL	Poland

PT	Portugal
RO	Romania
RU	Russia
SE	Sweden
SI	Slovenia
SK	Slovakia
UK	United Kingdom
US	United States
USA	United States of America

Acknowledgements

This doctoral thesis was developed while I was working at the Chair for Business Administration and Taxation II of Prof. Dr Christoph Spengel at the University of Mannheim. This dissertation was accepted in March 2016 by the University of Mannheim Business School.

First, I would like to thank my supervisor Prof. Dr Christoph Spengel. All the time he has been an academic and personal mentor for me and I am especially indebted to him for supporting me in my academic goals, actively encouraging and contributing to the success of this work and, in general, for guiding me and still letting me handle it ‘my own way’.

In addition, I would like to thank Prof. Dr Ulrich Schreiber for being the second supervisor of my thesis and for his supportive remarks. I also would like to thank the research and library staff of the International Bureau of Fiscal Documentation (IBFD) in Amsterdam who supported me during my academic research stay. The excellent working atmosphere and fruitful discussions with other researchers helped me a lot while working on my thesis. In this context, I also would like to acknowledge the support of the Julius Paul Stiegler Memorial Foundation. Special thanks go to Prof. Dr Dieter Endres and his team of tax experts and partners of PricewaterhouseCoopers (PwC) who supported the thesis by providing detailed and professional answers in a country-specific questionnaire. Their additional advisory and practical experience also considerably contributed to the success of this work.

Of course, I also would like to thank all my colleagues of the chair, the Area of Accounting and Taxation, the Centre for European Economic Research (ZEW) and the Mannheim Business School gGmbH for the constructive and harmonious working environment. In particular, I would like to thank Dr Sven-Eric Bärsch, Hannah Nusser, Ina Meier and Sören Bergner for their ongoing friendly support and technical as well as non-technical conversations.

Finally, I am most grateful to my parents and my beloved fiancée Kristina who always supported and encouraged me not only during my time at the chair but during my whole life. Without you, this work could not have been finished.

Andreas Waltrich
Mannheim, March 2016

CHAPTER 1
Introduction

As a general rule, international business operations can be conducted in two ways: direct business and direct investment activities. While direct business activities are rather short-term and are not linked to a certain degree of intensity in the source country, direct investment activities generally require a sufficient nexus in the source country.[1] Cross-border direct investment distinguishes between the establishment of two legal forms: the subsidiary as separate legal entity held by the multinational parent or the permanent establishment (PE) as integrating part of the foreign investor.

Apart from the subsidiary, the PE has traditionally been the connecting factor of taxation in the country of source. It guarantees taxation at source if the basic requirements are met, such as a fixed place of business and a sufficient degree of permanence in the source country.[2] Due to a more globalized world with a higher intensity and complexity of international business relations, the taxation of business profits becomes even more important. Especially in relation to the states of Brazil, Russia, India, China (BRIC states), which are traditionally considered as more or less opposed to the goal-settings of the Organisation for Economic Co-operation and Development (OECD), the PE question is a highly debatable topic.[3] Against this background, the development of the PE definition is one of the major topics to be discussed. Although the wording of Article 5 of the OECD MC remained constant over time, considerable changes in the OECD MC Commentary with regard to significant PE features such as the clear meaning of the requirement of disposal, the implementation of a service PE proposal, discussions considering the existence of a construction site PE established by subcontractors, and several international decisions considering the possible existence of an agency PE, all give the impression of a shrinking taxable

1. See Endres/Spengel (2015) p. 281.
2. See Lehner/Reimer (2005a) p. 547.
3. See Sheppard (2006) p. 1455.

threshold in the source country.[4] This is also topic of the OECD Revised Public Discussion Draft from 19 October 2012 about the interpretation and application of Article 5 of the OECD MC which examines an adapted version of the PE provision under a revised OECD MC. Also Action Plan 7 of the current OECD project on Base Erosion and Profit Shifting (BEPS) discusses the prevention of the artificial avoidance of the PE status, especially with regard to the avoidance of the agency PE through commissionaire arrangements.[5] At the same time, the OECD Report on the Attribution of Profits to PE from 2010 basically indicates the fiction of the PE as a separate legal entity for the allocation of business profits under Article 7 of the OECD MC, thereby following the Authorized OECD Approach (AOA).[6]

In fact, multinational companies and fiscal authorities are thus faced with the condition that, for border cases, reliable statements considering the existence of a PE in another state can hardly be given.[7] This is especially true for international business organizations nowadays which use global management teams and mobile personnel travelling around the world.[8] In addition, the functionally separate entity approach of the OECD MC can bear significant conflict potential with regard to the adequate allocation of business profits to the PE which actually determines the effective tax amount levied at source.[9] Qualification conflicts and thus double and non-taxation situations can occur for the multinational investor being subject not only to PE provisions of the OECD (and/or the UN) MC under a valid tax treaty but also to national statutes considering the existence of a PE and the allocation of relevant business profits. Even if the national tax legislations make efforts to implement the AOA in their national tax provisions such as established in Germany under the Tax Amendment Act 2013, further questions of practicability and feasibility will arise.[10] This is also true for treaty cases, as due to the non-simultaneous implementation of the AOA, at least two different concepts of profit attribution between the head office and the PE will co-exist under national and tax treaty statutes.[11]

Against this background, the goal of this work is to illustrate and compare the OECD statutes with the country-specific source taxation rules of selected countries focusing on specific requirements of the PE concept and the allocation of relevant business profits. Existing double and non-taxation issues due to qualification conflicts are analysed, evaluated and a reform proposal is worked out.

The structure of the dissertation follows the overall objective. Chapter 2, 3 and 4 present the PE as source taxation threshold and justification for the allocation of business profits under the OECD standards which are compared with country-specific source taxation rules of business profits in Germany, the US and the BRIC states.

4. See OECD MC Commentary (2014) Article 5, No. 4.2 ff., pp. 95 ff., No. 42.11 ff., pp. 115 ff., See e.g. for the *Rolls Royce* case Munoz (2010) p. 390, for the *Morgan Stanley* case Yang (2010) pp. 249 ff.
5. See OECD Discussion Draft BEPS Action 7 (2014) p. 4.
6. See OECD Report on the Attribution of Profits to PE (2010) Part I, No. 8 f., pp. 12 ff.
7. See Ditz/Quilitzsch (2012) p. 493.
8. See Collier (2013) pp. 639 ff.
9. See Jacobs (2011) p. 667.
10. See Brunsbach/Endres/Lüdicke/Schnitger (2012) pp. 63 ff.
11. See Andresen/Busch (2012) pp. 451 ff.

Chapter 3 revises the relevance of the PE concept from an OECD point of view by illustrating the status quo, the considered changes of the PE definition and the allocation of business profits under the AOA. In addition, special PE cases such as the construction site, agency and service PE are separately taken into account. Chapter 4 presents in detail the country-specific source taxation rules of business profits of Germany, the US and the BRIC states. Provisions regarding the fiscal nexus under national and treaty law as well as national rules on the attribution of business income between head office and PE are described. The different rules are then compared and systematized so that taxable implications upon the country-specific PE concepts can be derived.

Chapter 5 analyses the national PE concepts and the rules on the attribution of business income and identifies qualification conflicts in simulated cross-border national and treaty cases. Resulting double and non-taxation situations due to insufficient clarifications of terms and definitions are illustrated and confronted with the arising complexity of source taxation of business profits.

Chapter 6 derives further reform proposals in order to avoid the described qualification conflicts and to cope with guiding tax criteria, such as the avoidance of double and non-taxation and the achievement of feasibility and transparency during the compliance process. Reform proposals regarding the PE concept as such and the attribution of business income between the head office and PE are discussed from the viewpoint of the countries under consideration and from an OECD perspective. It is examined if the trend of enlargement of the PE concept is justified in practice and if it still contributes to the goals of reducing complexity and increasing harmonization of international taxation. It is further derived if and how the AOA can be actually implemented in taxation practice, especially with regard to growing economies such as the BRIC states. In addition, possible tax system changes beyond the current status quo are discussed and a recommendation is proposed. Finally, the topic is considered from a company perspective and a checklist is derived as how to avoid the risk of unintentionally establishing a PE for the given cases if no changes occur.

Chapter 7 concludes the illustrated findings in brief statements.

CHAPTER 2
Fundamentals and Objective

2.1 CLASSIFICATION OF THE PE CONCEPT AS OBJECT OF INVESTIGATION

The PE concept is an integrating part of international business taxation. The PE also plays a role in a purely national case where it basically works as connecting factor for local taxation of different states on a regional level, e.g., in Germany for purposes of determining the adequate trade tax base.[1] However, in the context of this work, only the cross-border case is considered at which a resident investor conducts business activities in a foreign country. In an international context, depending on the intensity of the business activity in the country of source, the PE effectively works as a '*tool*' in order to:

(1) establish a taxing right for the country where the business activities are conducted;[2] and
(2) allocate the business profits achieved between the residence country of the investor and the country where the investment takes place.[3]

Thus, the PE term signals a type of economic activity in the source country whose intensity is indeed larger than a pure short-time export activity, but which is still not incorporated. In contrast to the regular parent-subsidiary structure which involves at least two different legal persons from a private and tax law perspective (*separate legal entity approach*), the attribute shared by all existing PEs is the legal integration, i.e., being part of the overall business.[4] Being a dependent part of the investing company, contractual relations between the parent and the PE or between several PEs of the same

1. See Kumpf (1989) p. 401, Lüdicke (2008) p. 116.
2. See Skaar (1991) p. 1.
3. See Puls (2005) p. 4.
4. See Heinsen (2011) No. 1, p. 1.

company cannot exist. Still, the PE determines a heterogeneous business entity which can be established i.a. by the pure existence of an advertising pillar,[5] the placing of cleaning equipment in a certain storeroom,[6] the market stand of a greengrocer,[7] as well by financing institutions holding donation capital of several million Euros.[8]

When choosing between the direct investment alternatives of the establishment of a subsidiary or the constitution of a PE, a multinational investor has several reasons to prefer the structure of the PE. One non-fiscal reason is the intention of the investor to invest only temporarily and not on a permanent basis. If the direct investment is limited with regard to knowledge, time or place, the establishment of a PE is often considered as more useful and more straightforward than the possibility of incorporation.[9] This is especially true for mobile global management, sales or consultancy services conducted all over the world. In fact, especially for occasional mobile services or construction activities for which the establishment of a corporation at source is typically not compulsory, investors usually perform those business activities in the source state as long as it takes and thus end up more or less automatically in the field of PE taxation.[10] Specific PE forms which play a role here, are the construction site, agency or service PE. On the other side, if the investor wants to achieve a limitation of liability in the source country, e.g., due to unpredictable product liability risks, the establishment of a corporation as separate legal entity can indeed be the better choice.[11] Other operational factors which favour the establishment of a PE are a high degree of economic interdependence of the different national entities, a flat structure and hierarchy of the corporation and a high immediacy of implementation of corporate directives and guidance.[12]

From a tax perspective, the multinational investor has to account for different cost factors of the direct investment alternatives including not only the comparison of the effective tax burden but also compliance and administration costs. Apart from formal costs of registration, as to terms of reference and articles of incorporation, the establishment of a subsidiary can additionally lead to capital-dependent founding taxes in the source country which usually do not occur for the constitution of a PE.[13] Another fiscal reason for choosing the form of a PE are changes in domestic tax law of the source country or specific supporting tools like tax holidays, lump-sum taxation, favourable taxation of capital gains resulting from liquidation of the PE, loss-compensation with the head office's business income, tax deferral in case of transfer of assets between head office and PE, or simplified tax assessment which can make the establishment of a PE more attractive in an inbound case.[14]

5. See BFH, 13 May 1958, I B 49/58 U, BStBl. III 1958, p. 379.
6. See FG Hessen, 26 March 1982, VIII 326/78, EFG 1983, p. 34.
7. See BFH, 28 July 1993, I R 15/93, BStBl. II 1994, p. 148.
8. See BFH, August 23, 2000, I R 98/96, BStBl. I 2002, p. 207. See for a non-exhaustive list of German jurisdiction considering PE case law, Puls (2005) pp. 26 ff.
9. See Skaar (1991) p. 8.
10. See Skaar (1991) p. 8.
11. See Grotherr (2001) pp. 182 ff.
12. See Friedrichsen (2013) p. 184.
13. See Schoss (2011) pp. 52 ff.
14. See Heinsen (2011) No. 10, pp. 3 ff., Schoss (2011) p. 57.

In general, an optimal solution whether to choose a PE or subsidiary is hard to find and depends on several non-fiscal and fiscal reasons which have to be evaluated on case-by-case basis.[15] One intuitive way is the comparison of the effective tax burden of the two direct investment alternatives (casuistic assessment simulation).[16] This calculation basically includes all current taxation aspects of PE and subsidiary taxation, such as i.a. the legal form of the investing head office, the level of the tax rates in the two involved countries, the methods to avoid double taxation in the residence state, the possibility of retention or redistribution of business profits, the existence of withholding taxes and incurring additional local profit taxes.[17]

If a subsidiary is not given, the question whether certain economic activities constitute a PE or not is of central importance for the head office, especially in a cross-border case. While the national PE definition basically pursues the goal of separating foreign from domestic business income, the PE definition of tax treaties aims for an adequate allocation of business income and represents the different fiscal interests of the contracting states.[18] However, as treaty law solely determines which country is allowed to impose a tax on a certain amount of taxable income, the pure existence of limited liability to tax regularly depends on domestic tax statutes. Treaty law rather works as a '*stencil paper*' in a descriptive way:[19] While it constrains or '*lets pass*' domestic tax law, it never actively imposes a taxing right. In relation to the PE concept, the interpretation and analysis of the national PE definition of the involved countries is therefore decisive for the understanding and evaluation of the PE term from a cross-border perspective, also in case of a valid tax treaty.

Apart from the question of the PE existence and the establishment of a taxing right in the country of source, the allocation of business profits between the head office and the legally dependent PE is another debatable topic. According to the OECD, the functionally separate entity approach is favoured which treats the PE as a fictitious independent entity for the allocation of profits and transactions between the head office and its legally integrated PE (dealings) and with regard to external parties (transactions), thereby following the arm's length principle for the valuation of the dealings, similar to the general transfer pricing regulations between associated companies.[20] The allocation of business profits is not only necessary for the purpose of determining the tax base of the PE in the source country. It also has an effect on the impact of the method relieving from double taxation applied by the residence state.[21] Apart from the amount of taxable income allocated to the country of residence, the attribution of taxable profits to the source country has an influence on the level of the tax credit granted in case of a limited tax credit method or on the progressive tax rate of the

15. See Schoss (2011) p. 74.
16. See in detail for Germany i.a. Andresen (2010) pp. 1 ff., Grotherr (2001) pp. 182 ff., Jacobs (2011) pp. 931 ff., Scheffler (2007) pp. 446 ff.
17. See Grotherr (2001) p. 186.
18. See Wassermeyer (2009) Article 5, No. 8, p. 40.
19. See Reimer (2014) OECD MC, p. 6.
20. See OECD MC Commentary (2014) Article 7, No. 16, p. 136.
21. See Baker/Collier (2006) p. 25.

residence country in case of the exemption method including progression. However, in this work, the focus is on the inbound case looking at the fiscal treatment of the PE in the country of source.

In summary, there are two controversial fields of international PE taxation which are discussed in this context as they are undoubtedly interconnected: the establishment of a taxing right in the country of source depending on the definition of the PE and the allocation of business profits in order to determine the exact amount of tax levied at source.

2.2 STATE OF LITERATURE

On a normative-jurisdictional level, several country analyses, compiled research studies and practical manuals exist which deal with the PE definition and the profit allocation between head office and PE.[22]

A paper by *Hilbert* and *Engel* compares the aspects of the OECD PE Reform Proposal 2012 in relation to German national tax rules.[23] Another piece of work by *Puls* includes a detailed analysis of the single PE requirements especially from a German perspective.[24] Other German monographs, e.g., by *Plansky*[25] and *Mödinger*[26] pick up the OECD PE income allocation rules and analyse the different attribution rules in a detailed way.

The work presented here integrates both: questions of PE definition and income allocation. The current OECD policy is compared with the national viewpoints of the BRIC states on a normative basis, also in order to derive potential hypotheses for further reform proposals in the area of international PE taxation. In this context, the study explicitly focuses on a comparison of OECD and non-OECD policy while taking into account not only the basic PE but also specific PE cases, such as the construction site, agency and service PE. This can eventually contribute to the generality of the overall results and the thoroughness of the further analysis.

2.3 PROBLEMS CONSIDERED IN THIS WORK

The primary purpose of this work is to clarify the PE concept in international business taxation. Therefore, the first question raised is whether there is a trend towards increased source taxation derived from an analysis of the PE definition and rules on the attribution of business profits of the OECD MC and selected countries. The analysis focuses on specific interpretable requirements of the PE definition on the one hand and the future interpretation of the PE as fictitious separate legal entity on the other hand and identifies if the premises of the principle of single taxation and the reduction of

22. See i.a. IFA (2006), IFA (2009), Gutiérrez/Perdelwitz (2013), Reimer/Schmid/Orell (2014), Williams (2014).
23. See Hilbert/Engel (2012).
24. See Puls (2005).
25. See Plansky (2010).
26. See Mödinger (2012).

complexity are still valid for the given cases. The focus is on border PE cases for which a fully integrated organizational structure and substance can usually be neglected, e.g., for the provision of services, representations through agents or sent personnel. It is examined if the current status quo can lead to higher uncertainty and higher risk of qualification conflicts in international PE taxation, both under the general PE provision as well as for the establishment of special PE cases (construction site PE, agency PE and service PE). In addition, it is analysed if a double and non-taxation risk arises under the AOA, e.g., for the recognition of internal dealings between head office and PE, or for the application of the arm's length principle regarding the valuation of such cross-border dealings, also with regard to special PE cases. In addition, the analysis critically discusses if the current PE interpretation is still consistent with the goal of decreasing compliance and administration costs for multinational investors and the countries affected.

For the analysis, the PE interpretation of the OECD MC with regard to the definition and the attribution of business profits is taken as internationally justified standard model. In this context, the PE concept included in the OECD MC and its interpretation in the OECD MC Commentary shall work as '*guidance*' for treaty negotiations of several OECD and also non-OECD countries worldwide.[27]

On this basis, due to the various deviations and characteristics, domestic law still remains relevant in the context of cross-border PE taxation.[28] This is especially true for the interpretation of special PE cases such as the construction site, agency PE or service PE. Despite the fact that Articles 5 and 7 of the OECD MC and the OECD MC Commentary include most definitions of PE taxation which factually disregards domestic PE interpretation for treaty purposes, domestic PE statutes are still relevant for determining the final tax liability of the foreign investor in the country of source.[29] In addition, country-specific case law and court decisions indicate how the respective PE requirement is interpreted by the countries under consideration.

Against this background, the goal of this study is not only to consider the provisions of the OECD MC but also to include the national and country-specific treaty perspective of selected countries. Hereby, especially the BRIC states seem to be interesting, on the one hand due to the increasing economic power and the continuous influence in OECD policy, and on the other hand due to the domestic PE understanding which differs from OECD standards in several points.[30] The analysis thus poses the question if the AOA in its current form is also realizable with regard to countries like the BRIC states and if the existence of different profit attribution methods in domestic law, tax treaty law and OECD MC is consistent with the goal of reducing double and non-taxation risks and complexity.

27. See already Debatin (1989) p. 1692. In fact, over 3000 tax treaties worldwide follow the OECD MC. See OECD (2012) Current Tax Agenda, p. 114. Of course, from a legal perspective, statements and definitions of the OECD are legally not binding for the contracting states. See e.g. Heinsen (2011) p. 4.
28. See Reimer (2012) OECD MC, p. 5.
29. See Reimer (2012) OECD MC, p. 6.
30. See section 4.1.

What is not covered in this work, is the PE issue with regard to the establishment of partnerships. If a partnership is in line with Article 5 of the OECD MC and is qualified as being transparent for tax purposes, the transparent partnership is classified as PE in the country of source for each single partner which is also relevant with regard to the attribution of business profits under Article 7 OECD MC.[31] Qualification conflicts can occur if one of the involved countries applies the transparency principle and the other country treats the partnership as separate legal entity for tax purposes so that the partnership is taxed like a company and not similar to a PE.[32] Still, in this work, taxation of partnerships is disregarded.[33]

Another field of PE taxation which is not considered is the question of a PE establishment in the context of e-commerce. Electronic business activities like electronic communication networks, online shops, electronic sales of software, downloads of videos and music are all virtualized and conducted solely via electronic markets.[34] These changes in international company structures also have an effect on the traditional system of corporate taxation, especially in the context of the PE concept. Apart from PE attributes of an internet server which has been discussed to a considerable extent in tax law and literature,[35] nowadays new forms of electronic information and communication technologies (ICT) like cloud computing, hosting or software application (apps) let international borders blur and make it harder to apply the traditional PE definition and the rules on the attribution of profits to virtualized markets.[36] Also in the context of the OECD BEPS discussion, the taxation of the digital economy and the possible establishment of a virtual PE threshold in order to circumvent aggressive tax planning structures of IP companies is a debatable issue.[37] However, in this work, the focus is on the traditional company structures including the distribution and sales channels of the '*old economy*' where something '*tangible*' happens in the source state, such as a place of management, a branch, a factory or an office.[38] The study therefore focuses on the installation of a construction site, the usage of agents or the cross-border provision of services which all are supposed to be conducted with real personnel.

In this context, what is also not considered, are further special PE cases, for instance of banks,[39] financial institutions and insurance companies.[40] These industries

31. See Bendlinger (2009) pp. 206 ff.
32. See OECD Partnership Report (1999) No. 12, p. 9.
33. See for an elaborated overview on cross-border taxation of partnerships, Wehrße (2011).
34. See Tappe (2011) p. 870.
35. See i.a. for Germany Strunk/Wichmann (2001) pp. 409 ff., Pinkernell/Ditz (2001) pp. 1193 ff., Kahle/Ziegler (2009) pp. 834 ff.
36. See i.a. Bal (2012) pp. 335-339, Cicconi (2012) pp. 715-723, Choudhary (2011) pp. 33 ff., Heinsen/Voß (2012) pp. 1231 ff., Singh (2014) pp. 325 ff.
37. See i.a. Sheppard (2013) pp. 297 ff., Gaoua (2014) pp. 10 ff., Hellerstein (2014) pp. 346 ff., Pinkernell (2014).
38. See for detailed overview on PE taxation in the context of e-commerce, i.a. Brunsbach (2003), Jacobs (2011) pp. 321 ff., Jacobs/Spengel/Schäfer (2003) pp. 214 ff.
39. See for a detailed work considering the attribution of PE profits to banks, Henkes-Wabro (2009), Greier/Persch (2012), pp. 1318 ff.
40. See e.g. Förster (2008), pp. 800 ff.

often include special attributes and characteristics due to their intangible character which is focused on monetary transactions and is therefore excluded in this work.[41]

Before taking into account the specific national tax statutes and treaty policy of each selected single country, the PE provisions of the OECD MC are considered in detail.

41. See for OECD instructions on the attribution of PE profits, OECD Report on the Attribution of Profits to PE (2010) Part II, III, IV.

CHAPTER 3

Source Taxation of Business Profits according to the OECD Model

3.1 THE BASIC PE DEFINITION OF THE OECD MC

This section presents the characteristics of the basic PE definition included in Article 5 (1) of the OECD MC. It refers to the current understanding of the general PE criteria and also includes selected proposals of the OECD Discussion Draft of 2012 considering the interpretation of important PE attributes in the OECD MC Commentary.[1]

3.1.1 Current Status[2]

The *basic definition* of the PE is included in Article 5 (1) of the OECD MC. This treaty definition of the PE generally stands on its own and cannot be transferred to the national tax law perspective of the contracting states.[3] The PE definition is especially important for the allocation of taxing rights for business profits (Article 7 OECD MC), for capital gains from moveable assets which is attributed to a PE (Article 13 (2) OECD MC), as well as for source taxation of dividends (Article 10 (4) OECD MC), interest (Article 11 (4) OECD MC), royalties (Article 12 (3) OECD MC) and other income (Article 21 (2) OECD MC), which guarantees a taxation in the PE state if the underlying value of the mentioned types of income can indeed be allocated to the PE.[4] Furthermore, in case an employer constitutes a PE in the working state of the employee, the

1. See OECD Revised Proposals (2012).
2. The following sub-section refers to the 2014 version of the OECD MC and the OECD MC Commentary from 15 July 2014.
3. See Wassermeyer (2009) Article 5, No. 8, p. 40.
4. See Wassermeyer (2009) Article 5, No. 12(e), p. 44, Heinsen (2011) No. 121, p. 55.

designated income earned is allocated to the PE and is taxable in the source country being independent of any duration of stay of the employee at source (Article 15 (2c) OECD MC).

Article 5 (2) OECD MC provides a non-concluding list of various examples of prima facie PEs such as a place of business, a branch, an office, a factory, a workshop and several examples of places of extraction of natural resources like a mine, a gas or oil well, a quarry or similar activities. This enumeration does not extend the scope of the PE definition in Article 5 (1) OECD MC but has to be understood as list of PE examples which still have to meet the general PE criteria of Article 5 (1) OECD MC.[5]

Article 5 (4) OECD MC, on the contrary, contains a negative catalogue of auxiliary or preparatory activities which are a priori excluded from being a PE, such as the usage of any fixed place of business or maintenance of stock for the purpose of storage, purchase, processing, merchandise, display or delivery of goods. Even if they meet the PE criteria of a fixed place of business, those activities are definitely excluded from PE status.[6]

Article 5 (3) OECD MC enlarges the PE definition to building and construction sites. Similar to the auxiliary activities listed in Article 5 (4) OECD MC, this article has to be understood as '*lex specialis*' rule which determines a construction site PE solely based on the fulfilment of the timing requirement of twelve months independent of the achievement of any PE criteria of Article 5 (1) OECD MC.[7]

Article 5 (5) determines a PE of an agent who can establish a PE of its principal given that certain criteria are met such as acting on behalf and concluding contracts in the name of the represented principal unless the activities are of auxiliary or preparatory nature (Article 5 (4) OECD MC) or the agent is considered as being independent (Article 5 (6) OECD MC). Again, the fulfilment of a fixed place of business criterion is not necessary.[8] In this context, Article 5 (7) OECD MC clarifies that in case a principal-agent relationship exists between the represented enterprise and its subsidiary, the mere fact of control is not decisive to determine a PE of the enterprise. Still, if the additional criteria of Article 5 (1) OECD MC are fulfilled, it is possible that a controlling subsidiary can also constitute a PE of the principal.[9]

According to Article 5 (1) of the OECD MC, a PE is defined as '*fixed place of business through which the business of an enterprise is wholly or partly carried on*'.[10] This definition indicates that several criteria have to be fulfilled in order to constitute

5. See OECD MC Commentary (2014) Article 5, No. 12, p. 100.
6. See OECD MC Commentary (2014) Article 5, No. 21, p. 103. In fact, according to the ongoing OECD BEPS revised discussion draft considering the prevention of PE avoidance, the auxiliary and preparatory-condition is a separate condition to be checked additionally for all business activities of the negative catalogue of Article 5 (4) OECD MC. See OECD Revised Discussion Draft BEPS Action 7 (2015) pp. 22 ff.
7. See Wassermeyer (2009) Article 5, No. 95, pp. 84 ff.
8. See Wassermeyer (2009) Article 5, No. 4, p. 39.
9. See Reimer (2014) OECD MC, No. 355, p. 108.
10. This section only deals with the characteristics and specific criteria of the basic PE definition included in Article 5 (1) OECD MC. The concept of a construction site PE (Article 5 (3) OECD MC) and agency PE (Article 5 (5)-5 (7) OECD MC) together with the proposal of a service PE in the OECD MC Commentary are treated separately in section 3.2.

a PE under the OECD MC. First of all, a '*place of business*' has to exist. According to a definition of *Skaar*, a place of business can constitute all '*physical objects that are commercially suitable to serve as the basis of a business activity*'.[11] The place of business has to be tangible. Intangible assets such as a mailing address or the holding of shares are thus not able to constitute a PE.[12] The emphasis in the place of business-criterion is on the business purpose: Any place which can qualify for performing business activities of the enterprise, from the home office to substantial machinery, is principally able to be interpreted as place of business under Article 5 (1) of the OECD MC.[13] However, the mere owning of any tangible place in the source country without any visible business indication, such as holding real estate, does not establish a PE of the owner.[14] The presence of any staff or other personnel is not necessary under the criterion of fixed place of business.[15]

Another criterion of the OECD PE term is the location requirement. The place of business has to be '*fixed*' in the source state which includes a local and a timing character. Locally, the place of business of the PE needs to have a non-temporary nexus or link to a specific geographical point at source.[16] Although it does not have to be tied or installed to the ground, business vehicles which move along different places and whose only purpose is the constant change of its position, do not fulfil the criterion of a fixed place.[17] However, in case the business activities are conducted at several places located in the source state and moving between them is necessary for business reasons (e.g., inside a marketplace), the standard of fixation is modified.[18] In order to establish one single place of business in this context, the OECD demands a business activity which is considered as being '*a geographical and commercially coherent*' entity.[19] Both connections between the business units, the geographical and the commercial one, have to be fulfilled in order to determine one single place of business of the taxpayer. If the business activities lack of a commercial coherence, e.g., for a manufacturer which performs his activities geographically at one location but for several unrelated clients, one single place of business is not given.[20] On the other side, locally separated units which are spread throughout the source country, cannot be pooled as one single place of business if they are commercially coherent with respect to technical, organizational and economic reasons.[21]

Another important factor in this context is the requirement of timing in the sense of an adequate degree of permanence in the source country. The OECD MC

11. See Skaar (2012) p. 9.
12. See Sasseville/Skaar (2009) p. 23, Wassermeyer (2009) Article 5, No. 30, p. 50.
13. See Sasseville/Skaar (2009) p. 24.
14. See Skaar (2012) p. 9.
15. See Sasseville/Skaar (2009) p. 24.
16. See OECD MC Commentary (2014) Article 5, No. 5, p. 96.
17. See Wassermeyer (2009) Article 5, No. 37, p. 56.
18. See Reimer (2014) OECD MC, No. 47 f., pp. 45 ff.
19. See OECD MC Commentary (2014) Article 5, No. 5.1, p. 96.
20. The OECD MC Commentary uses again the example of a painter. See OECD MC Commentary (2014) Article 5, No. 5.3, pp. 96 ff.
21. See OECD MC Commentary (2014) Article 5, No. 5.4, p. 97, Wassermeyer (2009) Article 5, No. 37, p. 56. See for another opinion Kumpf (1982) p. 31.

Commentary therefore requires a place of business which exists not only on a '*purely temporary nature*'.[22] In contrast to construction sites which do not constitute a PE until a minimum period of twelve months has passed (Article 5 (3) OECD MC), a clear minimum time threshold is principally not given for the basic PE case under Article (5) (1) OECD MC. The only fact which has been actually observed according to the OECD MC is that a PE has not been established in practice yet if business activities are conducted at source for a length of less than six months.[23] In case business activities are conducted solely in the source state, a short period of time can indicate a fixed place of business due to the stronger connection and the exclusive character of the business activities.[24] In general, the fulfilment of the time criterion does not depend on the actual time period, but on the intention of the investor.[25] A place of business which has been planned initially on a temporary basis becomes a fixed PE if the investor retrospectively decides to use the place of business permanently. The other way around, a fixed place of business remains a PE if the intention to use it existed from the beginning, even if the place of business has been abandoned right after the instalment of the PE.[26] Special rules apply for recurrent activities which include temporary interruptions, so that for each single consideration, the permanence requirement of the place of business is not fulfilled, but still forms one comprehensive entity. According to the OECD MC Commentary, in this case, each time period is supposed to be considered including the number of times of usage of the place of business.[27]

In fact, the permanence test in connection with the requirement of a fixed place of business is closely related to another PE criterion, namely the disposal or right to use test. Similar to the permanence test, the disposal requirement is not directly included in the wording of Article 5 (1) OECD MC but is still a crucial criterion of the basic PE. According to the OECD MC Commentary, the investor needs to have a certain degree of disposal over the place of business in order to establish a PE at source.[28] A certain level of control is needed so that the investor can use the place of business at his own choice at any time for his own business purposes.[29] A formal legal right of the investor to use the place of business is not required.[30] The necessary degree of control is indicated by the words '*through which*' in Article 5 (1) OECD MC which basically mean

22. See OECD MC Commentary (2014) Article 5, No. 6, p. 97.
23. See Sasseville/Skaar (2009) pp. 29 ff.
24. See OECD MC Commentary (2014) Article 5, No. 6, p. 97.
25. See Skaar (2012) p. 23.
26. See Wassermeyer (2009) Article 5, No. 37, p. 57.
27. See OECD MC Commentary (2014) Article 5, No. 6, pp. 97 ff. Technically, the number of days can either be multiplied with the number of periods in case the duration of each period is the same or added together in case the duration of each single period differs. See Reimer (2014) OECD MC, No. 82, p. 53. However, due to the vague wording in the OECD MC Commentary, it is still unclear if the reference time is the proposed six months or another case-driven period. See Skaar (2012) p. 24.
28. See OECD MC Commentary (2014) Article 5, No. 4.1, p. 95. See for another opinion which lays the focus on the permanence requirement, Wassermeyer (2009) Article 5, No. 42a, pp. 62 ff.
29. See Reimer (2014) OECD MC, No. 106, p. 58.
30. See OECD MC Commentary (2014) Article 5, No. 4.1, p. 95. If a legal right to use is granted to the investor, the fulfilment of the time criterion depends on the factual time period in which the place of business was at the disposal of the investor and not on the duration of any legal right to use. See Sasseville/Skaar (2009) p. 28.

that the investor conducts his business by directly using the place of business as an instrument for his business activities.[31] According to the OECD MC Commentary, this '*functional integration*', as *Reimer* calls it, has to be understood on a rather wide basis so that in principle, the performance of business activities '*in*' or '*at*' a controlled fixed place of business can also constitute a PE for the investor.[32] An illustrative example is the '*painter example*' included in the OECD MC Commentary:[33] From the OECD's point of view, a painter who works several days a week at the premises of his client, establishes a PE as he performs the significant part of his business, namely painting, while he is present in the building of the client. From the perspective of the OECD MC, the painted building is both, the object of the business activity and the place of business of the painter where he is bound by working contract and which is supposed to be at his disposal in the formulated example.[34]

The last basic PE requirement is the business activity criterion. The investor has to use the place of business actively for his business operations.[35] The business activity needs to be functionally integrated to the place of business in the sense of conducting the activity '*through*' the place of business. However, in accordance with the OECD painter example, this can be understood on a wide basis. In addition, the activity performed needs to represent a business activity according to domestic law of the involved source country and according to the respective treaty law.[36] If the business activity qualifies as auxiliary or preparatory activity, the PE status is explicitly excluded under Article 5 (4) OECD MC.

3.1.2 OECD Reform Proposals[37]

The following section describes several reform proposals conducted by the OECD Working Party I with regard to the definition of the PE and its interpretation in the OECD MC Commentary. In the course of the preparation of a revised OECD MC Commentary, the OECD recommended a change to several points of the Commentary to Article 5 OECD MC which was published for discussion.[38]

One of the recommended proposals, which has a decisive influence on the understanding and interpretation of basic PE attributes of Article 5 (1) OECD MC, is the introduction of additional explanations to the meaning of *disposal* over the PE.[39] The OECD proposes that the establishment of a place of business for the investor at source shall depend on the '*effective power to use that location*' and on the '*extent of the*

31. See Reimer (2014) OECD MC, No. 121, p. 61.
32. See OECD MC Commentary (2014) Article 5, No. 4.6, p. 96.
33. See OECD MC Commentary (2014) Article 5, No. 4.5, p. 96.
34. Domestic law of several countries, i.a Germany, demands apart from the character of the place of business as object of business activity, also a certain power over this place of business in the form of a qualified disposal and explicitly distinguishes this fact in domestic law.
35. See Sasseville/Skaar (2009) p. 38.
36. See Skaar (2012) p. 26.
37. The following sub-section refers to selected bullet points of the OECD Revised Proposals (2012) concerning the interpretation and application of Article 5 (PE) of the OECD MC.
38. See OECD Revised Proposals (2012).
39. See OECD Revised Proposals (2012) pp. 5 ff.

presence' of the investor in the country of source.[40] Considering the work of an enterprise at the premises of a client, the OECD proposal clarifies that an '*exclusive legal right to use*' the location only for business purposes of the enterprise clearly indicates a sufficient degree of disposal over the place of business. The disposal requirement is also fulfilled if the enterprise has the admission to use the premises of its client and indeed carries on its business at the location '*on a continuous basis during an extended period of time*'. If the presence of the enterprise at the location is considered as incidental and discontinuous, e.g., in case of insufficient working time of employees at external premises, a place of business is not established under Article 5 OECD MC. The OECD Working Party I thus clarifies that an exclusive legal possession is adequate for achieving the disposal requirement. In addition, it is proposed that the fulfilment of the disposal criterion is set in relation to the achievement of a further time requirement. However, further explanations with regard to the necessary degree and interpretation of disposal are still missing. Especially, it is not clearly determined whether the requirement of disposal over a place of business is understood on a wide basis or if it can also be constricted by, e.g., having the possibility of excluding others from the access and usage of the premises.

The revised OECD proposal also recommends clarifying changes to the time requirement included in the OECD MC Commentary.[41] Although no fixed duration period is set for constituting a fixed place of business, the case of recurrent activities is given a more detailed interpretation. Therefore, an example of a drilling rig is introduced which is operated for three months each year for an overall time period of five years.[42] Despite the non-achievement of the practical minimum duration of six months of each working slot, the OECD supports the existence of a PE in this case. Still, the proposal emphasizes to consider the '*specific nature*' of the relevant business so that shorter recurrent periods other than mentioned in the example can also theoretically fulfil the time requirement of a basic PE.

In this context, the OECD proposal also names an example of so-called *short-term* business activities which are concluded solely in the source country.[43] In case the business is performed exclusively in the source state on opportunity, which means that it is operated by a person who is generally not involved in that business in any other state, and the business is terminated after the considered time period, which is also a short-time period, can indicate a fixed place of business and therefore a PE in the country of source.[44]

In general, the different PE requirements on OECD level are clearly defined. Still, criteria which are not explicitly mentioned in the wording of Article 5 OECD MC, like the necessary degree of disposal or the time threshold, can offer scope for discussions despite the explanations in the OECD MC Commentary and the additional examples and further clarifications in the OECD Reform Proposal (see Table 3.1).

40. See OECD Revised Proposals (2012) No. 11, p. 6.
41. See OECD Revised Proposals (2012) pp. 12 ff.
42. See OECD Revised Proposals (2012) No. 33, p. 14.
43. See OECD Revised Proposals (2012) No. 33, p. 14.
44. *Skaar* calls this business operations conducted on special opportunities '*on-off projects*'. See Skaar (2012) p. 24.

Table 3.1 Basic PE Article 5 (1) OECD MC

Current Status	*OECD Reform Proposal*
- Clearly defined criteria - Place of business: Fixed in the source country and functional integration of business activity - Additional criteria not included in the wording: Permanence test and disposal requirement	- Additional explanations to disposal criterion: Exclusive legal possession and fulfilment of time threshold as additional indicators for achievement of necessary degree of disposal

3.2 SPECIAL PE CASES

Apart from the basic PE case of Article 5 (1) OECD MC, the following section refers to the PE attributes and definitions of special PE cases including the specific characteristics of a construction site PE (Article 5 (3) OECD MC), the distinctive features of an agency PE (Article 5 (5) OECD MC) and the status quo of a service PE in the OECD MC. However, this section will not include every detail of each specific PE attribute. Instead, selected issues are considered which are worthwhile for discussion in an international context. Again, selected points of the OECD Reform Proposal on Article 5 of the OECD MC are also included.

3.2.1 Construction Site PE

3.2.1.1 Current Status

The construction site PE is a special form of the basic PE which refers to building sites, construction and installation projects and is thus mentioned in a separate paragraph of the OECD MC. One of the decisive attributes of the construction site PE is the time requirement of twelve months as crucial criterion of the PE existence.[45] Article 5 (3) OECD MC is considered as '*lex specialis*' rule: Construction and installation projects which qualify for the establishment of a PE under Article 5 (3) OECD MC do not have to meet the criteria of the basic PE rule under Article 5 (1) OECD MC such as a fixed place of business or a necessary degree of disposal.[46] The OECD MC Commentary emphasizes that also for deemed forms of PE of Article 5 (2) OECD MC, such as an office or a workshop which is installed and thus effectively '*belongs*' to the construction

45. See Reimer (2014) OECD MC, No. 165, p. 70.
46. See Wassermeyer (2009) Article 5, No. 95, pp. 84 ff., Reimer (2014) OECD MC, No. 175, p. 72. However, the consideration of Article 5 (3) OECD MC as '*lex specialis*' rule is not given for every country. See for an overview with regard to this discussion Kahle/Kindich (2016) pp. 83 ff.

or installation site, the twelve months time requirement has to be fulfilled.[47] The reason for the focus on the duration test for a construction site PE is of practical nature as the intensity of the business activities in the country of source is supposed to be given for construction or installation projects.[48]

In order to apply the time threshold under Article 5 (3) OECD MC, the activities which constitute a construction or installation site have to be identified. According to the OECD MC Commentary, the construction and installation term shall exemplary include the construction and renovation of '*buildings, roads, bridges or canals, the laying of pipe-lines, excavating and dredging*'.[49] In general, these activities have to be carried out '*on-site*' where the building, construction or installation project is located.[50] Apart from any physical work of construction, installation and renovation which does explicitly exclude any work of maintenance or redecoration, further activities of on-site planning and supervision are included as well.[51] These can also be performed by a subcontractor who works on behalf and by order of the general contract.[52] To prevent the circumvention of the establishment of a construction site PE by artificially splitting construction sites and projects in order to stay below the time requirement of twelve months, Article 5 (3) OECD MC demands as further requirement a geographical and commercial coherence of the different projects, similar to the attributes of the basic PE case under Article 5 (1) OECD MC.[53] Considering the calculation of the twelve-month period, the OECD MC Commentary actually does not give any detailed instructions. Therefore, it can be concluded that the necessary time threshold shall be calculated according to domestic law of the contracting states following Article 3 (2) OECD MC.[54] The OECD MC Commentary only determines the point of time of existence and the end of a construction site and indicates, again similar to the basic PE rule, that temporary interruptions can be ignored under certain circumstances when considering the period of existence of the PE at source, e.g., due to '*shortage of material*', '*labour difficulties*' or other external factors, such as bad weather conditions.[55] In addition, the commentary considers that the time requirement also counts for subcontractors working for the general contractor who transfers a part of the construction or installation project to other subcontract partners. In this case, the working period of the subcontractor is effectively assigned to the time of the general contractor in case the general contractor is also physically present in the source state, either by himself or through employees.[56]

47. See OECD MC Commentary (2014) Article 5, No. 16, p. 101.
48. See Wassermeyer (2009) Article 5, No. 94, p. 84.
49. See OECD MC Commentary (2014) Article 5, No. 17, p. 101.
50. See Skaar (2012) p. 37.
51. See OECD MC Commentary (2014) Article 5, No. 17, p. 102.
52. See Reimer (2014) OECD MC, No. 195, p. 76.
53. See OECD MC Commentary (2014) Article 5, No. 18, p. 102.
54. See Wassermeyer (2009) Article 5, No. 126, p. 98. See for a critical opinion Gassner/Lang/Lechner (1998) pp. 66 ff.
55. See OECD MC Commentary (2014) Article 5, No. 19, p. 102.
56. See Perdelwitz (2013) Chapter 2, p. 46.

3.2.1.2 OECD Reform Proposals

The OECD Reform Proposal also deals with specific potential changes regarding the construction site PE.[57] One aspect concerns the case of a general contractor transferring not only a part, but all of his work of a comprehensive construction or installation project to subcontractors.[58] In general, the checking of basic PE requirements of Article 5 (1) OECD MC also has to be necessary if the non-resident conducts business activities through other employees such as subcontractors.[59] In this case, a general contractor can also constitute a basic PE if all the other PE criteria are fulfilled, especially with regard to the necessary degree of disposal.[60] If the enterprise does not send own personnel who are present at the construction site, the OECD Reform Proposal determines that the disposal criterion depends on other factors such as legal possession, control of access and use and a certain *'overall responsibility for what happens at that location'*.[61] In summary, from an OECD perspective, the requirement of physical presence of the general contractor is substituted by the disposal criterion, or as *Perdelwitz* calls it, the *'legal responsibility'*.[62] Thus, a construction site PE can be established for the general contractor without being physically present in the state where the construction site is located (see Table 3.2).

Table 3.2 Construction Site PE Article 5 (3) OECD MC

Current Status	*OECD Reform Proposal*
- *Lex specialis* rule: focus on time threshold of twelve months - Inclusion of planning and supervision activities on-site - Partial delegation of work to subcontractor involves additional checking of basic PE requirements	- Total delegation of work can lead to PE without physical presence of general contractor

57. In this study, the focus is on the total delegation of functions to a subcontractor. Other bullet points of the OECD Revised Proposals which marginally address Article 5 (3) OECD MC are not considered in more detail. See i.a. for the case of the application of the construction site PE rules to joint ventures and partnerships, OECD Revised Proposals (2012), No. 51 f., pp. 19 ff., and for the question of including additional work on a construction site in the calculation of the time threshold, OECD Revised Proposals (2012), No. 65 f., pp. 23 ff.
58. See OECD Revised Proposals (2012) No. 44, pp. 17 ff.
59. See OECD Revised Proposals (2012) No. 46, p. 17.
60. See OECD Revised Proposals (2012) No. 47, p. 18.
61. See OECD Revised Proposals (2012) No. 47, p. 18.
62. See Perdelwitz (2013) Chapter 2, p. 51.

3.2.2 Agency PE

3.2.2.1 Current Status

Article 5 (5) of the current OECD MC determines an agency PE for the investor in case business activities are conducted in the source state via a dependent agent. Similar to the '*lex specialis*' rule of the construction site PE, the agency PE basically constitutes a separate provision whereby the establishment of a fixed place of business is not necessary.[63] In case the requirements of the basic PE rule under Article 5 (1) OECD MC are already met, such as a fixed place of business, the agency PE provision under Article 5 (5) OECD MC principally becomes non-relevant.[64] Still, the criterion of a certain permanency and the exclusion of preparatory and auxiliary activities under Article 5 (4) OECD MC shall also hold for the agency PE.[65] According to Article 5 (5) OECD MC, the constitution of an agency PE has the following requirements: The person performing the business activities at source has to be a dependent agent who acts on behalf of the principal and generally has the authority to conclude contracts actively and habitually in the name of the latter. A person according to Article 5 (5) OECD MC is defined as such in Article 3 (1a) of the OECD MC and thus can comprise natural persons, companies and other corporate forms such as partnerships.[66] Associated companies can also be persons in the context of Article 5 (5) OECD MC concluding that a controlled subsidiary can become an agent of its parent company and vice versa.[67]

One of the crucial criteria of the agency PE of Article 5 (5) OECD MC is the '*authority to conclude contracts in the name of the enterprise*'. This power to conclude contracts in the name of the principal cannot only be understood in a direct legal way but can also be conducted on a wider factual or economic basis according to the OECD MC Commentary. Contracts which bind the principal in a certain sense but which are not explicitly concluded '*in the name of*' the enterprise can thus be considered under the agency PE rule.[68] The OECD MC Commentary further states that the authority to conclude contracts is generally given if the agent in charge is delegated to '*negotiate all elements and details of a contract*' so that the principal enterprise is bound, independent of the person who officially signs the contract or of any other formal power of

63. See OECD MC Commentary (2014) Article 5, No. 31, p. 107.
64. See Sasseville/Skaar (2009) p. 50.
65. See Skaar (2012) p. 39.
66. See OECD MC Commentary (2014) Article 3, No. 2, p. 80.
67. See Wassermeyer (2009) Article 5, No. 197, p. 121. However, following Article 5 (7) OECD MC, the mere fact of controlling is not sufficient to constitute a PE.
68. See OECD MC Commentary (2014) Article 5, No. 32.1, pp. 107 ff. This conclusion is discussable as the OECD initially introduced this provision in order to include the undisclosed principal of 'common law' in the agency PE sphere. See i.a. Pijl (2013b) pp. 83 ff. However, the wording in the Commentary is not that clear and still offers room for interpretation. See i.a. Pleijsier (2001) p. 177.

representation.[69] Thus, the OECD determines the power to conclude contracts not explicitly on a pure legal basis but rather on a wider economic basis.[70]

Independent agents under Article 5 (6) OECD MC, such as a broker or a general commission agent, are explicitly excluded from the PE sphere of Article 5 (5) OECD MC as long as they act '*in the ordinary course of their business*'. Several factors exist which indicate the independence of the agent at source. In general, the business activities of an independent agent do not have to be bound by '*detailed instructions or comprehensive control*'.[71] In addition, it is considered whether the entrepreneurial risk is held by the agent or the principal. *Reimer* exemplarily names some additional independence indicators, such as the preference of profit- or revenue-based remuneration or the performance of business activities for several principal enterprises.[72] Acting in the ordinary course of business basically indicates that the independent agent has to focus primarily on his own business interests and not on the interest of the principal.[73] Following Article 5 (7) of the OECD MC, all the mentioned rules including the features of an agency PE can also be applied for subsidiaries of an associated group of companies whereby the agency PE criteria have to be checked separately for each member of the company group.[74]

3.2.2.2 OECD Reform Proposals

With regard to specific characteristics of the agency PE, the OECD Working Party I made several arrangements to the OECD MC Commentary.[75] One of them is related to the '*wide*' view of the OECD considering the agency PE feature of concluding contracts in the name of the enterprise. According to the OECD MC Commentary, concluding contracts shall also be possible on a factual and economic basis if significant reasons exist that the agent concludes the contract for the principal even if it is not literally '*in the name*' of the enterprise.[76] The OECD recommends the inclusion of an additional example to the commentary which illustrates that principals can also be bound under national law of some countries, in case the agent does not mention the name of the enterprise in the contract and does not '*formally disclose that it was acting for the enterprise*'.[77] Obviously, the intention of the example is to clarify that the concept of an

69. See OECD MC Commentary (2014) Article 5, No. 33, p. 108.
70. See Wassermeyer (2009) Article 5, No. 201a, p. 122.
71. See OECD MC Commentary (2014) Article 5, No. 38, p. 109.
72. See Reimer (2014) OECD MC, No. 339, p. 104.
73. See Wassermeyer (2009) Article 5, No. 229, p. 135.
74. See OECD MC Commentary (2014) Article 5, No. 41.1, pp. 111 ff.
75. Other aspects of the OECD reform proposal of Article 5 OECD MC which are not considered in this work, deal with clarifications on which activities are included under the concept of an agency PE and the disapproved further explanation of entrepreneurial risk as requirement of an independent agent under Article 5 (6) OECD MC. See OECD Revised Proposals (2012) No. 113 f., pp. 36 ff.
76. See OECD MC Commentary (2014) Article 5, No. 32.1, pp. 107 ff.
77. See OECD Revised Proposals (2012) No. 109, p. 34. In fact, the origin of this rule is based on influence of 'common law' understanding of the agent principle (e.g., in the UK or US): If only agents which literally perform business activities in the name of the principal constitute an agency PE, a 'common law' agent not revealing his principal according to an 'undisclosed

undisclosed principal following '*common law*' of certain Anglo-Saxon countries also falls under the OECD agency PE provision.[78] However, even though an additional example is provided, the wording of the OECD MC Commentary is formulated too generally, thus still offering room for interpretation: It is not clear whether the OECD determines the obvious and legal authority to conclude contracts for the principal as only PE-establishing criterion or whether a factual and wider economic approach is followed.[79] Thus, the OECD Reform Proposal of 2012 does not find a common solution for all Member States as determined in the OECD MC Commentary but rather emphasizes the application of national law of the considered countries with regard to the interpretation of the authority to conclude contracts.[80] The example in the OECD Reform Proposal does not give further clarifications with regard to the degree of the authority to conclude contracts. In the course of Action Plan 7 of the OECD BEPS project which should prevent the avoidance of agency PEs through '*artificial*' commissionaire structures the OECD changed the wording of Article 5 (5) of the OECD MC.[81] In the first discussion draft of 2014, the OECD developed four different versions (A to D) of a new wording of the agency PE concept which specifically addresses the degree of authority to conclude contracts for the principal.[82] In fact, two of the proposals (A and B) reduced the agency PE threshold by determining that an agency PE does not only exist by acting in the name of the enterprise but also by the transfer of ownership of property, or for the provision of the principal's services by the agent.[83] In a revised discussion draft of 2015, the OECD decided to choose option B which determined that an agency PE could exist if an agent habitually concludes contracts, or negotiates material elements of a contract, in the name of the enterprise, for the transfer of ownership or the granting of a right to use the principal's property, or for the provision of services by the principal.[84] Thus, the question whether the principal has to be legally or economically bound by the principal should not play a major role anymore when deciding about the existence of an agency PE (see Table 3.3).[85] Instead, the future focus

principal' contract, is actually never considered as agency PE. This is why the OECD introduced the 'wide' view in the OECD MC Commentary. See BIAC Response (2013) No. 40 f., p. 10.

78. See i.a. Welbers/Schulz (2012) p. 323.
79. See Pleijsier (2001) p. 177.
80. See Staringer (2010) p. 410.
81. See OECD Discussion Draft BEPS Action 7 (2014) p. 4, Parillo/Sheppard (2014) p. 483.
82. See OECD Discussion Draft BEPS Action 7 (2014) p. 11.
83. See OECD Discussion Draft BEPS Action 7 (2014) pp. 11 ff. The other two proposals (C and D) exclude the phrase of 'concluding contracts in the name' of the principal from the beginning and replace it with concluding contracts which are on the 'account and risk' of the enterprise.
84. See OECD Revised Discussion Draft BEPS Action 7 (2015) p. 13. Apart from Article 5 (5), the OECD also proposed to change Article 5 (6) and formulated that an independent agent does not avoid the existence of a PE if this agent is acting exclusively for one or more connected enterprises for which the beneficial interest is larger than 50%. Another indicator of dependence, e.g., for a sales agent, is that this agent's sales activities to independent parties are less than 10% of all sales conducted. See OECD Revised Discussion Draft BEPS Action 7 (2015) p. 20. On 5 October 2015, the OECD published a final report on Action Plan 7 which is similar in the content. Still, two specific formulations of Article 5 (5) and (6) are changed, i.e., 'negotiates the material elements of a contract' is replaced by ' plays the principal role leading to the conclusion of contracts' and the term of 'connected' enterprises is replaced by 'closely related' enterprises. See OECD Final Report BEPS Action 7 (2015) p. 16.
85. See Pleijsier (2015) pp. 148 ff.

of the OECD lies on the independence criterion, which takes into account whether the agent is concluding contracts solely for one or more connected principals.[86]

Table 3.3 Agency PE Article 5 (5) & (6) OECD MC

Current Status	*OECD Reform Proposal & BEPS Report on Action 7*
- Basic PE requirements not necessary - Crucial criteria of acting on behalf of the principal, holding the authority to conclude contracts actively and habitually in the name of the enterprise - Authority to conclude contracts can be determined on legal and (effectively) on an economic basis	- Additional example with regard to the power to conclude contracts in case the principal is bound economically - OECD BEPS proposal indicate that authority to conclude contracts can be determined on an economic basis - Focus on independence criterion of agent

3.2.3 Service PE

3.2.3.1 Current Status

In contrast to the special PE cases of a construction site and an agency PE, a provision considering a service PE is not included in the OECD MC.[87] Still, with respect to the interests of certain service-importing countries that benefit from source taxation of services, the OECD introduced an optional service PE provision in the OECD MC Commentary.[88]

According to this optional provision, service activities of a resident of one state performed in another state are supposed to qualify for a service PE if they are rendered:

> a) through an individual who is present in that other State for a period or periods exceeding in the aggregate 183 days in any twelve month period, and more than 50 per cent of the gross revenues attributable to active business activities of the enterprise during this period or periods are derived from the services performed in that other State through that individual, or
> b) for a period or periods exceeding in the aggregate 183 days in any twelve month period, and these services are performed for the same project or for connected projects through one or more individuals who are present and performing such services in that other State.[89]

The OECD service PE alternative applies notwithstanding Article 5 (1) and (2) of the OECD MC which indicates, similar to the other special PE cases, that the provision

86. See OECD Revised Discussion Draft BEPS Action 7 (2015) pp. 17 ff.
87. In contrast, the UN MC includes a deemed service PE provision under Article 5 (3b) UN MC. Since 2000, income from professional services (former Article 14 OECD MC) is also allocated to business profits Article 7 OECD MC. Negotiated OECD tax treaties shall follow that rule from then on. See OECD MC Commentary (2014) Article 14, p. 255.
88. See OECD MC Commentary (2014) Article 5, No. 42.14, p. 116.
89. See OECD MC Commentary (2014) Article 5, No. 42.23, pp. 117 ff.

is not valid in case the requirements of a basic PE are met, such as a fixed place of business.[90] Qualifying services have to be explicitly rendered to third parties meaning that internal activities such as service provisions of an employee abroad towards his employer or parent company in the residence country are not included.[91] In addition, outsourcing activities where one company transfers its service units to another company (secondment of employees) only creates a service PE of the transferring company if the services are performed '*under supervision, direction or control*' of the latter enterprise.[92] The qualifying business income from services has to be taxed on a net basis so that economically connected expenses are considered for tax purposes.[93]

In detail, the service PE proposal tries to cover both, the taxation of business income from services provided by individuals and by enterprises. The first alternative (a) deals with service provisions of single individual persons such as sole proprietors or partners of a partnership.[94] For the establishment of a service PE it requires, first, a 183-days minimum period of physical presence of the service-providing person in the source country. In addition, at least 50% of the gross revenues of active business activities of the service performer have to be derived from the rendered services in the source country while this can also be substituted by 50% of the particular business profits.[95] The second alternative (b) addresses in particular service-providing companies which can perform their activities either as an own proprietor or through one or more shifting employees who do not have to be permanent workers but also act as persons that are bound by instructions.[96] In addition, the time limit of 183 days in this case refers to the days of economic activity of the company in the source country, not to the physical presence as stated in the first alternative.[97] In addition, the service activities have to be conducted for the same or for connected projects whereas the decisive factor which describes these qualifying connected projects is the commercial coherence of the projects.[98]

Apart from this '*active*' service PE option in the OECD MC Commentary which can determine a taxation right in the country where the services are provided without the existence of a fixed place of business, there also has been a tendency in OECD policy to give room for a '*passive*' service PE, especially with regard to the crucial criterion of disposal as proof of existence of a fixed place of business in the source country. In general, this OECD view is expressed by the controversial painter example where the OECD considers a building in and at which a painter performs his painting

90. See OECD MC Commentary (2014) Article 5, No. 42.25, p. 118.
91. See OECD MC Commentary (2014) Article 5, No. 42.30, pp. 119 ff. Still, this does not exclude service activities between associated enterprises (e.g. contracts for services) where a seconded employee is conducting services at the premises of a subsidiary. See Rautenstrauch/Binger (2009) p. 625.
92. See OECD MC Commentary (2014) Article 5, No. 42.43, p. 123.
93. See OECD MC Commentary (2014) Article 5, No. 42.47, p. 125.
94. See Rautenstrauch/Binger (2009) p. 622.
95. See OECD MC Commentary (2014) Article 5, No. 42.37, p. 121.
96. See OECD MC Commentary (2014) Article 5, No. 10, pp. 99 ff., No. 42.32, p. 120, No. 42.39, p. 122, No. 42.43, p. 123.
97. See Bendlinger (2009) p. 59.
98. See OECD MC Commentary (2014) Article 5, No. 42.41, pp. 122 ff.

services as PE of the painter.[99] Given that the permanence threshold is fulfilled, this '*passive*' service PE can enable countries to establish a PE even though the service PE provision is not included in the tax treaty if services are performed at the premises of a client without an own fixed place of business.[100]

3.2.3.2 OECD Reform Proposals

One element of the OECD Reform Proposal of Article 5 OECD MC which can be related to the OECD service PE option, deals with the question of the establishment of a PE by employees of a foreign company that work for another company in the source country (cross-border secondment of employees).[101] According to the current OECD MC Commentary, services which indicate a service PE do not have to be performed by own employees but can also be rendered by '*other personnel engaged by the enterprise*'.[102] Whether such personnel is allocated to the host company at source which hires the personnel or to the non-resident company which actively lends the workforce (or to another third party manpower company eventually), depends on '*the supervision, direction and control*' of the respective company.[103] To clarify the PE issue in case of secondment arrangements, the OECD Working Party I proposes to amend the commentary by further explanations to this topic. If employees are seconded to another company in a source country and effectively conduct the business of this host company, they cannot constitute a service PE for the non-resident parent.[104] This is also the case if due to administrative reasons the employment contract cannot be changed and remains between the formally employing non-resident parent company and the hired workers. Decisive in this case is the '*economic*' employer which can be identified by reference to the OECD MC Commentary regarding Article 15 OECD MC.[105] Thus, in case personnel of a parent company is seconded to a host company and provides services there, economic factors such as the authority of instruction, the control over the place of work or the character of remuneration are crucial when deciding about the PE establishment through service activities provided by hired employees located at the host company (the actual place of work) irrespective from the legal employer.[106] In fact, the concept of the economic employer provides a further clarification with regard to the secondment of employees. The interpretation of the

99. See section 3.1.1.
100. See e.g. Munoz (2010) p. 382. See critically Nitikman (2009) pp. 249 ff.
101. See OECD Revised Proposals (2012) No. 35 f., pp. 15 ff.
102. See OECD MC Commentary (2014) Article 5, No. 10, pp. 99 ff., No. 42.32, p. 120.
103. See OECD MC Commentary (2014) Article 5, No. 42.43, p. 123.
104. See OECD Revised Proposals (2012) No. 37, p. 15.
105. See OECD Revised Proposals (2012) No. 42, p. 17. In fact, the original purpose of the 'economic' employer concept in the commentary of Article 15 OECD MC is the definition of the remuneration of the host company for services provided by the seconded employee. This payment can either be regarded as employment income (contract of services) or business income for services conducted by the parent company (contract for services). See OECD MC Commentary (2014) Article 15, No. 8.1, p. 265, No. 8.12 f., pp. 267 ff. See for further explanation Portner (2014) pp. 437 ff.
106. See in detail for the criteria of an 'economic' employer, OECD MC Commentary (2014) Article 15, No. 8.13-8.15, pp. 267 ff.

respective factors of the economic employer concept is decisive in order to decide whether the OECD Reform Proposal provides for a clarification or a possible enlargement of the PE term. If the PE decision is based mainly on economic factors and not on the legal working contract, a certain scope of interpretation still remains. In general, an increased fiscal nexus at source is given for secondment cases if a service PE provision is included in the respective tax treaty.

Therefore, the service PE option represents an enlargement of the PE term in the country of source from an OECD perspective, as a PE can also be constituted without the establishment of a fixed place of business. The additional differentiation between legal and economic employer in case of hiring out service-providing personnel generally provides for more clarification but can also introduce another level of interpretation in the OECD service PE approach which can make a further contribution to the enlargement of the PE term (see Table 3.4).

Table 3.4 OECD MC Commentary Service PE Option

Current Status	*OECD Reform Proposal*
- Basic PE requirements not necessary - Crucial criteria: Timing requirement of 183 days and 50% of gross revenue/ profit earned by service activities - Service PE also possible for secondment as long as employees are under supervision, direction or control of transferring enterprise	- Introducing the concept of economic employer in case of secondment of employees

3.3 ATTRIBUTION OF BUSINESS PROFITS UNDER THE OECD MC

A correct and congruent interpretation of the PE definition in Article 5 of the OECD MC forms the basis for the adequate allocation of taxing rights between the residence and the source country. The next step in this process is to identify the concrete tax on the business profits each country levies from the international investor. As legal or contractual relations are generally not possible between head office and PE, business profits which are earned by the enterprise have to be allocated between the head office and the PE located in another state.

This attribution of business profits is generally set by Article 7 of the OECD MC. In its current version of 2010, Article 7 (1) OECD MC (which effectively remained unchanged during the last decades) states that business profits shall be taxable exclusively in the country of residence of the profit-generating company except for the fact that a PE according to Article 5 OECD MC exists in another country.[107]

With the publication of the OECD MC 2010, Article 7 of the OECD MC was modified in its wording and in the number of paragraphs in order to represent the

107. See OECD MC Commentary (2014) Article 7, No. 1, p. 132.

functionally separate entity approach or AOA which had been developed over the past years – actually having started development in 1993-1994.[108]

As several tax treaties worldwide still apply the *'old'* version of Article 7 OECD MC, the following section briefly illustrates and describes the pre-2010 version (hereby referred to as *'old view'* later on) in order to identify differences to the current version and the AOA.

3.3.1 The *'Old View'* of the OECD considering the Attribution of Business Profits

The following section refers to the OECD MC and OECD MC Commentary before the implementation of the AOA in 2010. However, the functionally separate entity approach already started to expand in the OECD MC Commentary of 2008, so that similarities of the *'old'* view and the AOA of 2010 exist.[109]

The *'old'* Article 7 of the OECD MC consisted of seven paragraphs.[110] Before the implementation of the AOA in the MC and in the Commentary, the concrete wording of Article 7, in fact, had not changed from 1977 until 2010.[111] Similar to the AOA, Article 7 (1) of the *'old'* OECD MC determined the principle taxing right with regard to the business profits which can be allocated to a PE established in the country of source.

Article 7 (2) of the *'old'* OECD MC limited the taxing right with regard to the amount of taxes which can only be levied upon profits the PE *'might be expected to make if it were a distinct and separate enterprise engaged in the same or similar activities under the same or similar conditions and dealing wholly independently with the enterprise of which it is a permanent establishment'*.[112] The goal was to allocate the relevant part of the business profits earned by the total enterprise to the PE under the basic assumption that these business profits have been earned under the arm's length principle, similar to Article 9 OECD MC.[113] This means that the PE as dependent, integral part of the single enterprise was hypothetically set equal to a separate legal entity in order to determine the PE tax base.[114] Therefore, the OECD MC Commentary proposed a two-step approach similar to the OECD Transfer Pricing Guidelines for

108. See for instance OECD Attribution of Income to PE (1993), p. 2 which complains about the insecurities concerning the fiscal treatment of PE. See for further discussions on OECD level until 2010, OECD Discussion Draft on the Attribution of Profits to PE (2001), OECD Discussion Draft on the Attribution of Profits to PE (2004), OECD Report on the Attribution of Profits to PE (2006), OECD Report on the Attribution of Profits to PE (2008).
109. See Hemmelrath/Kepper (2013) pp. 38 ff. In fact, the OECD Report on the Attribution of Profits to PE (2008) already included the ideas of the AOA. See OECD MC Commentary (2014) Article 7, No. 5, p. 133. Tax treaties which were ratified before 17 July 2008 are supposed to follow the OECD MC Commentary of 2003 or older. Tax treaties with the 'old' wording of Article 7 which were ratified after 17 July 2008 shall follow the OECD MC Commentary of 2008 which is referred to in this work. See Andresen (2013) pp. 324 ff.
110. See for an overview Bendlinger (2009) p. 125.
111. See Russo (2006) pp. 96 ff.
112. See OECD MC Commentary (2014) Previous Version Article 7, No. 2, p. 157.
113. See Bendlinger (2009) p. 126.
114. See Wassermeyer (2009) Article 7, No. 323, p. 178.

associated enterprises:[115] First, under a functional and factual analysis, the relevant economic activities and responsibilities of the PE have to be identified. Then, in a second step, the arm's length principle applies in order to identify the adequate transfer price considering the external transactions with third parties and the internal dealings of the PE with its head office or other associated entities.[116] Still, the *'old view'* also considered the dependent status of a PE which is not able to conclude contracts with the head office or other associated enterprises in a company group. In general, any profit mark-up on internal rental or licence payments for the temporary use of tangible or intangible assets was not considered, as head office and PE form a single enterprise which is not allowed to conclude any contracts with itself.[117]

From an OECD perspective, the *'old view'* was interpreted as *'relevant business activity approach'*.[118] Only the *'relevant business activities'* in which the PE actively participates could thus be allocated to the PE.[119] The total result of the enterprise which is considered as one individual profit-earning unit had to be allocated among its different associates.[120] The major aspect of this approach was that only profits which have been generated by the head office or the PE from transactions with third parties or associated enterprises were considered for the attribution of business profits.[121] Internal dealings between the head office and the PE were thus principally considered at cost.[122] However, exceptions have been developed: The arm's length principle had to be applied for the transfer of tangible goods to the PE for the purpose of resale. A profit margin was also justified in case of internal services provided by the PE to the enterprise in case providing such services is the major business activity of the PE and the services account for a main part of the overall costs of the enterprise which, in addition, benefits from it.[123] Therefore, under the relevant business activity approach, the crucial point was to differentiate between those internal transactions which can include a profit mark-up following the separate entity approach of Article 7 (2) OECD MC, or dealings which are exclusively considered without any charge of profit.[124]

The *'old'* Article 7 (3) OECD MC determined as deductions from the profits of a PE *'expenses which are incurred for the purposes of the permanent establishment, including executive and general administrative expenses so incurred, whether in the State in which the permanent establishment is situated or elsewhere'*.[125] This provision indicated that the allocation of expenses to the PE is independent of any place of emergence or factual

115. In fact, this approach of the 'old' OECD view is similar to the new AOA for the determination of PE profits, but not in that detail.
116. See OECD MC Commentary (2014) Previous Version Article 7, No. 18, pp. 162 ff.
117. See Bendlinger (2009) p. 128. See Van Raad (2000) p. 164 for a descriptive list of income categories which is regarded on a cost basis.
118. See OECD Report on the Attribution of Profits to PE (2008) No. 62, p. 23.
119. See OECD Report on the Attribution of Profits to PE (2008) No. 61, p. 23.
120. See Plansky (2010) p. 106.
121. See Baker/Collier (2006) p. 30.
122. With regard to the internal transfer of assets between head office a PE, however, the application of arm's length prices is possible according to the OECD. See Plansky (2010) p. 112.
123. See OECD MC Commentary (2014) Previous Version Article 7, No. 36, p. 167.
124. See Van Raad (2000) p. 164.
125. See OECD MC Commentary (2014) Previous Version Article 7, No. 3, p. 158.

accounting between head office and PE.[126] However, it still depended on the rules in domestic law of the country of source whether incurring expenses were indeed considered as deductible business expenses.[127] Except for specific PE of banks or other financial institutions, fictitious interest payments on internal loans of the head office granted to the PE were generally disregarded as deductible PE expense.[128] Differences only existed for interest which occurred due to an external loan agreement entered into by the enterprise for the purpose of financing the PE. Under given circumstances, these interest expenses could be deducted from PE profits.[129] However, in order to determine the level of deductible external interest, at first, a certain amount of PE equity capital, the donation or endowment capital, had to be allocated to the PE.[130] This amount of allocated donation capital had a direct influence on the amount of external interest which could be allocated to the PE.[131] Still, the OECD MC Commentary did not indicate a fixed method of determining the amount of donation capital. It only emphasized that the attribution of donation capital should be *'capable of giving an arm's length result'*.[132]

In general, Article 7 (3) of the *'old'* OECD MC referred to the application of the direct method for the allocation of business profits between head office and PE. Following the direct method, the outcome of the PE business is determined by the compilation of a separate PE accounting.[133] For each business unit of the single enterprise, head office and PE, a separate accounting entity exists which considers every single business case for each PE separately.[134] *Debatin* calls it descriptively a *'separation of spheres'* between head office and PE.[135] Article 7 (4) of the *'old'* OECD MC additionally allowed the indirect method of profit allocation: As long as it has been *'customary'* in the source country *'to determine the profits to be attributed to a permanent establishment on the basis of an apportionment of the total profits of the enterprise to its various parts'* and given the condition, that this attribution method followed the principles of Article 7 OECD MC, the total business profit of a multinational enterprise was allocated to each single part of the enterprise on the basis of an adequate allocation formula.[136] Thus, the amount of business profits allocated to head office and PE depended on two factors: the total amount of business profits earned by

126. See Ditz (2004) pp. 119 ff. for a discussion whether the 'old' Article 7 (3) OECD MC is supposed to be considered as constraint to the arm's length principle under Article 7 (2) OECD MC or as concretion of the allocation of expenses.
127. See Bendlinger (2009) p. 129.
128. See OECD MC Commentary (2014) Previous Version Article 7, No. 41, p. 168.
129. See OECD MC Commentary (2014) Previous Version Article 7, No. 43, p. 168. However, in this case, the OECD MC Commentary does not determine on a concrete basis how to allocate the external interest expenses to the PE. See Plansky (2010) p. 174.
130. See Jacobs (2007), pp. 631.
131. See Jacobs (2007), pp. 632 ff., Plansky (2010) p. 175.
132. See OECD MC Commentary (2014) Previous Version Article 7, No. 46, p. 169. See section 3.3.2 for a more detailed description of the different capital allocation methods.
133. See Wassermeyer (2009) Article 7, No. 189, p. 117.
134. See Plansky (2010) p. 142.
135. See Debatin (1989) p. 1739.
136. In fact, the indirect method of the OECD MC resembled the 'Common Consolidated Corporate Tax Base' approach as proposed by the European Commission in 2011. See European Commission (2011).

the overall enterprise and the chosen allocation formula.[137] With regard to the allocation method, the OECD MC Commentary listed three major categories upon which the method can be based. This was either the revenue earned, such as turnover of the enterprise, or the earnings paid, such as wages paid to the employees, or the working capital of the overall enterprise.[138] One crucial point of the indirect method is that the determination of total business profits of the overall enterprise has to be adapted to the national rules of profit determination of the PE state.[139] Although a comparison to the direct method of Article 7 (2) OECD MC is difficult, the result of the indirect method has to approximate the amount which could have resulted from the application of separate accounts '*as closely as possible*'.[140] In practice, the indirect method especially applied for construction site PEs which are usually existent on a temporary basis and where the relations between PE and head office are generally considered as being interdependent and entangled.[141]

As a result, both methods of profit allocation were allowed under the previous version of Article 7 of the OECD MC.[142]

Considering the special PE forms, such as the construction site, agency and service PE, the '*old*' OECD setting actually did not include any concrete regulations or references. With regard to the construction site PE, the '*old*' OECD MC Commentary only referred to the importance of clear allocation of business profits to the PE which was especially problematic for constructions sites as several parties were usually involved in the construction process.[143] Thus, the indirect method of profit allocation was accepted as alternative solution for the allocation of profits to a construction site

137. See Plansky (2010) p. 153.
138. See OECD MC Commentary (2014) Previous Version Article 7, No. 54, p. 171.
139. See Bendlinger (2009) p. 133.
140. See OECD MC Commentary (2014) Previous Version Article 7, No. 54, p. 171.
141. See Plansky (2010) p. 157. Another industry which uses the indirect method of profit allocation between head office and PE is the bank and insurance industry. See Bendlinger (2009) p. 133.
142. Still, following Article 7 (6) of the 'old view', the chosen method of allocation shall not be switched annually but has to be used consistently and on a continuous basis in order to guarantee certainty for the states involved. See OECD MC Commentary (2014) Previous Version Article 7, No. 58, p. 172. Article 7 (5) of the 'old' OECD MC determined that profits resulting from purchase activities shall generally not be allocated to a PE. Despite the fact that Article 5 (4d) OECD MC excluded purchase activities from the PE establishment right from the beginning, Article 7 (5) dealt with the case of a PE which conducts several business activities in the country of source where one of them consisted of purchasing goods for the head office. In this sense, the purpose of the provision was to circumvent a fictitious increase of the overall business profits allocated to the PE by additionally adding profits from purchase activities. See OECD MC Commentary (2014) Previous Version Article 7, No. 57, p. 172. Article 7 (7) of the 'old' OECD MC included a subsidiary clause: Profits which are considered by other provisions shall thus be not affected by Article 7 OECD MC. This basically implied a preferential treatment of other provisions of the OECD MC in relation to Article 7 of the 'old' OECD MC given that certain types of income, such as dividends, interest payments, royalties or capital gains could eventually be allocated to both Article 7 and another provision, such as Article 10, 11, 12 or 13 of the OECD MC. In principle, this means that the special articles shall be preferred in relation to the general Article 7 for business profits. Still, if the type of income can be clearly identified as PE income, provisions such as Article 10 (4), Article 11 (4), or Article 12 (3) of the OECD MC re-point to Article 7 OECD MC as provision to be applied. See Wassermeyer (2009) Article 7, No. 354, p. 188.
143. See OECD MC Commentary (2014) Previous Version Article 7, No. 24, p. 164.

PE. Regarding the agency PE under Article 5 (5) OECD MC, the *'old'* OECD MC Commentary explicitly stated that the *'functional and factual'* analysis as proposed under Article 7 (2) of the *'old'* OECD MC also had to be valid for agency PEs.[144] With respect to the service PE, the sole reference which could be allocated to the service PE sphere was the determination of the *'old'* OECD MC Commentary to propose a recognition of internal service charges at cost, while only in exceptional cases a profit mark-up was included.[145]

3.3.2 The Authorised OECD Approach

In 1993, the OECD already recognized that the *'old view'* of the allocation of business profits to a PE actually led to a lack of consensus among the member countries.[146] Mostly, this resulted from the two-sided approach of the *'old'* Article 7 OECD MC which basically treated the PE as a fictitious separate legal entity and applied the profit-mark-up approach towards external transactions with third parties but still included several exceptions which did not allow for a recognition of profit, especially for internal dealings between head office and PE.[147] From an international perspective, this duality led to the risk of double or non-taxation as the inclusion of a profit mark-up upon the transfer of goods involving a PE was not clear but often a question of interpretation.[148]

Against this background, the OECD finally developed the AOA and changed not only the content of the OECD MC Commentary but also the wording of Article 7 OECD MC.[149] In addition, the OECD MC Commentary continues to refer in a separate part to the provisions of the *'old'* OECD view before 2010, which continued to be relevant in relation to tax treaties concluded before the implementation of the AOA.[150] Therefore, despite the fact that the OECD usually applies a dynamic approach and includes revisions of the OECD MC Commentary in the interpretation of already existing treaties, the AOA is supposed to be an exclusive guideline for tax treaties which integrate the new wording of Article 7 OECD MC.[151]

Article 7 (1) of the OECD MC is almost unchanged in comparison to the former version: Paragraph 1 still determines the distributive provision under which business profits are generally taxed in the residence state except for those which can be allocated to a PE established in the source country *'in accordance with the provisions of paragraph 2'*. Article 7 (2) of the OECD MC now includes the *'functionally separate entity approach'* which determines the amount of profits being allocated to the PE: These are the profits the PE:

144. See OECD MC Commentary (2014) Previous Version Article 7, No. 26, pp. 164 ff.
145. See OECD MC Commentary (2014) Previous Version Article 7, No. 31, pp. 165 ff.
146. See OECD Attribution of Income to PE (1993) p. 2 which was reassessed in 2001 under the OECD Discussion Draft on the Attribution of Profits to PE (2001) No. 3, pp. 6 ff.
147. See Kobetsky (2011) p. 195.
148. See OECD Attribution of Income to PE (1993) No. 2(b), p. 2.
149. See Plansky (2010) pp. 39 ff. for a historical overview regarding the change of the OECD MC and the OECD MC Commentary.
150. See OECD MC Commentary (2014) Previous Version Article 7, pp. 157 ff.
151. See OECD MC Commentary (2014) Introduction, Nos 35 & 36, pp. 15 ff., Article 7, No. 7, p. 131.

> might be expected to make, in particular in its dealings with other parts of the enterprise, if it were a separate and independent enterprise engaged in the same or similar activities under the same or similar conditions, taking into account the functions performed, assets used and risks assumed by the enterprise through the permanent establishment and through the other parts of the enterprise.

Under the functionally separate entity approach, the allocation of profits is neither limited by the relevant business activity nor the overall profit of the enterprise.[152] In contrast to the *'relevant business activity approach'* the arm's length principle has to be applied to all transactions of a PE, considering dealings with external parties and internal dealings between the PE and the head office or other parts of the enterprise (see Table 3.5).[153]

Table 3.5 Comparison – Relevant Business Activity versus Functionally Separate Entity Approach

Relevant Business Activity Approach	*Functionally Separate Entity Approach*
- Allocation of profits according to relevant business activity participated in - External transactions with third parties or associated enterprises recognized including a profit mark-up - Internal dealings between head office and PE considered at cost - Exceptions for transfer of tangible goods for purpose of resale, internal services as major business activity	- Allocation of profits according to functions performed - External transactions and internal dealings between head office and PE recognized including a profit mark-up according to the arm's length principle

Although the PE formally remains a non-independent part of the single enterprise, it has to be fictitiously treated comparable to a separate legal entity for purposes of profit allocation.[154] In order to reach this goal, the AOA proposes two steps: First, under a *factual and functional analysis*, profits are attributed to the PE which is supposed to perform functions, use assets and assume risks just like a regular legal, independent entity such as the parent company or a subsidiary.[155] Thus, even if the total corporation does not achieve any profits, it is still possible under the AOA that certain profits are attributed to the PE. In fact, this was not possible under the old *'relevant business activity approach'*.[156] Following a detailed functional and factual analysis of the facts of the case on-site, the AOA thus first checks for functions which are performed by people working for the single enterprise and the PE itself and then

152. See Plansky (2010) p. 106.
153. See OECD MC Commentary (2014) Article 7, No. 15, p. 136.
154. However, the degree of independence of the PE is not widened to the maximum by the application of the AOA. Differences to independent companies still occur with regard to the credit rating (which is always similar to the head office for a PE), the non-qualification as resident person for treaty purposes and the exclusion of withholding taxes on internal dealings between head office and PE. See Bernales (2013) Chapter 6, p. 152.
155. See Nouel (2011) p. 7 for an illustrative diagram explaining the basics of the AOA.
156. See OECD MC Commentary (2014) Article 7, No. 17, p. 136.

tries to identify which functions are decisive for profit-making of each single unit of the enterprise including the PE.[157] In this context, it is important to consider several factors when identifying the functions in order to hold up the fiction of the PE as a separate legal entity, such as the '*characteristics of the specific property or service performed, contractual terms, economic circumstances and business strategies*'.[158] After having determined the '*significant people functions*', it should be possible to identify the economic ownership of the assets and the risk between the sphere of the head office and the PE.

In accordance with the OECD Transfer Pricing Guidelines which also formulate a functional analysis for separate legal entities, the AOA demands an identification of all tangible and intangible assets which can be attributed to the PE on the basis of the significant people functions, in short '*assets follow functions*'.[159] For that purpose, it is necessary to follow an '*economic ownership*' approach as the assets of the overall enterprise cannot be allocated to the legally non-independent PE.[160] Following the arm's length principle, the head office or the PE can only be taxed upon allocated profits if the responsible and significant people are also able to control the asset.[161] In principle, economic ownership implies that the resulting revenues and costs are attributable to the part of the enterprise which bears the benefits and risks considering the change in value of assets.[162] Whereas for tangible assets, the place of use is decisive, the attribution of intangible assets between the head office and the PE is more complex.[163] In accordance with Chapter VI of the OECD Transfer Pricing Guidelines which deals with the transfer of intangibles between separate enterprises, intangible property can be differentiated between marketing intangibles and other internally developed and acquired trade intangibles.[164] Self-developed as well as acquired intangible assets are generally allocated to the significant people who actively take part in the decision-making process in the different development stages and who are actively involved in the management of the risks occurring when creating or acquiring the intangible property.[165] The same criteria apply for marketing intangibles, such as the name, brand or logo of the overall enterprise. Those significant people of the enterprise who are in charge of developing, protecting and controlling the marketing intangibles, fulfil the function of active decision-making and managing of involved risks and are thus considered as economic owners of the intangible property.[166]

157. See OECD Report on the Attribution of Profits to PE (2010) Part I, No. 62, p. 25.
158. See OECD Report on the Attribution of Profits to PE (2010) Part I, No. 63, p. 26.
159. See Bendlinger (2008) p. 511.
160. See OECD Report on the Attribution of Profits to PE (2010) Part I, No. 72, p. 28. See also Jacobs (2011) pp. 684 ff.
161. See Kosch (2010) p. 43.
162. See Kahle/Mödinger (2010) p. 760.
163. See OECD Report on the Attribution of Profits to PE (2010) Part I, No. 75 f., p. 29.
164. See OECD Report on the Attribution of Profits to PE (2010) Part I, No. 79, pp. 29 ff. Against the background of the current BEPS discussion, the OECD revises the Transfer Pricing Guidelines, especially for intangible assets. See OECD Discussion Draft BEPS Action 8, 9 & 10 (2015).
165. See OECD Report on the Attribution of Profits to PE (2010) Part I, No. 91 & No. 94, p. 32.
166. See OECD Report on the Attribution of Profits to PE (2010) Part I, No. 97, p. 33.

Taking into account the functions performed by the people of the PE and the assets which are allocated to those functions, it is possible to derive a certain risk profile of the PE ('*risk follows functions and assets*').[167] Different forms of risk, such as inventory, currency or product warranty risk, are usually allocated between independent enterprises based on contractual agreements. As such contractual relations are not possible between the head office and the PE, risk is basically allocated depending on the people who perform the related functions and thus actively decide about and manage those risks.[168]

On the basis of the risk attribution, it should then be possible to allocate an adequate amount of free capital or donation capital to the PE whereby it is generally assumed that the creditworthiness of the head office and the PE is the same ('*capital follows risk*').[169] Sufficient free capital has to be attributed to the PE so that it is able to finance the allocated assets and the assumed risks.[170] However, the OECD MC does not fix a method of how to exactly measure the risks and the value of the assets in order to allocate an exact amount of donation capital to the PE although different methods of asset valuation are described.[171] The OECD MC only indicates that the valuation method has to be chosen on a continuous basis.[172] With regard to the risk profile of the PE, it is considered that more free capital is allocated to the PE the more risk is involved, such as for instance the risk of market success in order to come up for possible downturns.[173] Several approaches exist for the determination of free equity capital allocated to the PE. Under the capital allocation approach, the donation capital allocated to the PE takes into account the structure of assets and risks of the overall enterprise. Thus, if the PE holds a certain percentage of the enterprise's assets and risks, the same percentage will be allocated as free capital.[174] Another method described by the OECD is the thin capitalization approach. This method uses a comparability approach: It allocates the amount of free capital to the PE which an independent enterprise being resident in the PE state has by performing '*the same or similar activities under the same or similar conditions*'.[175] In detail, considering this approach, it will be necessary to compare the total funding of the PE derived under the functionally separate entity approach with the debt-equity ratio of a comparable enterprise of the PE state in order to identify the amount of free PE equity capital.[176]

167. See Bendlinger (2008) p. 511.
168. See OECD Report on the Attribution of Profits to PE (2010) Part I, No. 24, p. 17.
169. See Bendlinger (2008) p. 511.
170. See OECD Report on the Attribution of Profits to PE (2010) Part I, No. 107, p. 35.
171. See OECD Report on the Attribution of Profits to PE (2010) Part I, No. 108 f., p. 35.
172. See OECD Report on the Attribution of Profits to PE (2010) Part I, No. 110, p. 36.
173. See OECD Report on the Attribution of Profits to PE (2010) Part I, No. 112, p. 36.
174. See OECD Report on the Attribution of Profits to PE (2010) Part I, No. 121, p. 38. A special method in this context is the economic capital allocation approach which emphasizes the economic risk, e.g. the financing risk in the banking sector, as benchmark for allocating donation capital to the PE. See OECD Report on the Attribution of Profits to PE (2010) Part I, No. 128, p. 39.
175. See OECD Report on the Attribution of Profits to PE (2010) Part I, No. 129, p. 39.
176. See OECD Report on the Attribution of Profits to PE (2010) Part I, No. 131, pp. 39 ff. Another method which is mentioned by the OECD is the quasi-thin capitalization or safe harbour approach which especially addresses PE of the banking industry: It requires the PE to hold the

The amount of allocated equity capital to the PE implies the amount of debt capital of the overall enterprise which can be attributed to the PE. Furthermore, the amount of debt capital determines the amount of interest expense which can eventually be deducted from taxable profit of the PE. Just as for other internal streams of income between PE and head office, it is possible under the AOA that internal interest expenses are recognized at arm's length including a profit mark-up if the PE fulfils a certain treasury function in the enterprise structure.[177]

With regard to the allocation of interest expenses between PE and head office, the OECD describes two optional methods: the tracing and the fungibility approach.[178] Under the tracing approach, the necessary funding of the PE is *'traced back'* to the overall enterprise which raised the loan from an external third party. The interest rate of the debt allocated to the PE equals the interest rate which the enterprise has to pay to the external creditor. According to the fungibility approach, real internal payments between the head office and the PE are basically disregarded. Instead, a weighted average of the external interest rates of the enterprise is formed, based on a certain ratio, which allocates the overall interest amount to each entity in the single enterprise.[179] Thus, under the fungibility approach, any internal interest dealing can be ignored and does not have to be recognized and valued anymore.[180]

After having identified the significant people functions, the respective assets, the assumed risks and the capital of the PE, internal dealings between the head office and the PE have to be recognized and valued. As the functionally separate entity approach calls for a treatment of the PE as fictitious separate legal entity, the PE not only has to be able to carry out internal performance allocations and transactions, such as the transfer of assets, the provision of services, or the use of intangible assets.[181] Under the AOA, internal dealings between the PE and the head office additionally have to be recognized at an arm's length price which is basically the crucial modification of Article 7 (2) OECD MC in comparison with the *'old view'* of the relevant business activity approach.[182] Whereas the dealings are derived from the functional and factual analysis, documentation requirements such as accounting records and other simultaneously documented data can thereby serve as a supporting starting kit.[183] National tax law of considered OECD countries thus has to use relevant documentation as long as the data is in line with the *'economic substance'*, the comparison with independent third party transactions and the allocation of functions, assets, risks and capital under the functional and factual analysis.[184] Similar to the OECD Transfer Pricing Guidelines, the AOA indicates a comparability analysis to the extent that controlled transactions

same amount of free capital which another independent banking enterprise of the PE state holds for certain regulatory purposes. See OECD Report on the Attribution of Profits to PE (2010) Part I, No. 135, p. 40.

177. See OECD Report on the Attribution of Profits to PE (2010) Part I, No. 159, p. 44.
178. See OECD Report on the Attribution of Profits to PE (2010) Part I, No. 154, p. 43.
179. See Hoogterp (2009) p. 399.
180. See OECD Report on the Attribution of Profits to PE (2010) Part I, No. 154, p. 43.
181. See OECD Report on the Attribution of Profits to PE (2010) Part I, No. 177, p. 48.
182. See Kahle/Mödinger (2010) p. 761.
183. See OECD Report on the Attribution of Profits to PE (2010) Part I, No. 177, p. 48.
184. See OECD MC Commentary (2014) Article 7, No. 26, p. 139.

like internal dealings between the head office and the PE can be compared with transactions between independent enterprises in accordance with the arm's length principle.[185] The criterion of comparability is expressed in five factors which have to be checked for the valuation of dealings, namely the characteristics of property or services, a functional analysis, contractual terms, economic circumstances and business strategies.[186]

For four common types of dealings, namely the change in the use of tangible and intangible assets, cost contribution arrangements and the provision of internal services, the AOA describes separate procedures: In case of a change of use of a tangible asset between head office and PE, the fair market value has to be used for the valuation with regard to the arising capital gain and as basis for further depreciation.[187] In case of the allocation of intangible assets, the functional and factual analysis identifies the owner of the intangible property who performs the significant functions, based on the concept of '*economic ownership*'.[188] In addition, the OECD explicitly states that '*fictitious*' royalties for the benefit of the allocation of profits between head office and PE do not form a basis for levying any withholding taxes.[189] Remuneration charged for internal services, mostly conducted by the head office to the PE, such as strategic management, payroll or accounting activities, also has to be consistent with the arm's length principle.[190] Recommended methods to identify the adequate arm's length price for the provision of internal services include two of the traditional transaction methods, i.e., the comparable uncontrolled price and the cost-plus method.[191]

Article 7 (3) of the OECD MC 2010 provides a way to avoid double taxation in case misunderstandings exist between the two involved contracting states with regard to the correct interpretation of the allocation of profits between head office and PE under Article 7 (2) OECD MC. The OECD basically commits one of the states '*to make an appropriate adjustment (...) (...) to the extent necessary to eliminate double taxation*' on profits which the other contracting state already has been adjusted. One field where the OECD recognizes a probable problematic situation with regard to double taxation issues is the allowance of different capital allocation methods which can be used in

185. See OECD Report on the Attribution of Profits to PE (2010) Part I, No. 190, p. 51.
186. See OECD Transfer Pricing Guidelines (2010), No. 1.33, pp. 41 ff.
187. See OECD Report on the Attribution of Profits to PE (2010) Part I, No. 196, p. 52.
188. See OECD Report on the Attribution of Profits to PE (2010) Part I, No. 200 f., pp. 53 ff. For the adequate attribution of intangible property, the OECD refers to Chapter VI of the OECD Transfer Pricing Guidelines which are currently revised under the ongoing BEPS discussion. See OECD Discussion Draft BEPS Action 8, 9 & 10 (2015).
189. See OECD Report on the Attribution of Profits to PE (2010) Part I, No. 203, pp. 53 ff. Apart from licence agreements, it is also possible to attribute profits from intangible assets by applying a profit split method or a cost contribution agreement where the share of cost and risk contributions of head office and PE is consistent with the expected benefits. Royalty payments are thus not necessary anymore as each party is considered at least economically as beneficial owner and not as licensee of the intangible asset. See OECD Transfer Pricing Guidelines (2010), No. 8.3, p. 220. Still, a cost contribution agreement can also be possible for other business activities not involving intangibles, such as for centralizing management or advertising activities. See OECD Transfer Pricing Guidelines (2010), No. 8.7, p. 221.
190. See OECD Report on the Attribution of Profits to PE (2010) Part I, No. 216, p. 56.
191. See OECD Report on the Attribution of Profits to PE (2010) Part I, No. 219, p. 57.

order to attribute donation capital to the PE.[192] In such cases, Article 7 (3) OECD MC comes into play. However, if the state which follows the initial adjustments of the first state, is not able to do so, either because of limitations in domestic law or due to the opinion that the first adjustment is not in line with Article 7 (2) OECD MC, a mutual agreement procedure (MAP) under Article 25 (1) OECD MC shall be used by the taxpayer in order to solve the double taxation problem.[193] In addition to the regular formulation of Article 7 (3) OECD MC, the OECD MC Commentary provides another alternative version of Article 7 (3) which directly leads to the application of the MAP in case the reacting state does not agree with the adjustments of the other contracting state.[194] Independent of the consideration whether the state which adjusted first is in line with the AOA under Article 7 (2) OECD MC, the reacting state is thus not bound to initially agree in contrast to the version of Article 7 (3) included in the wording of the OECD MC.[195] Instead, the MAP under Article 25 (1) OECD MC is obligatory for both contracting states.[196]

Article 7 (4) of the new OECD MC is similar to Article 7 (7) of the *'old'* version of the OECD MC which determines the priority of specific articles over the business profits-article, such as for royalty, interest or dividend income. Still, in case the income can be clearly allocated to a PE, the specific articles include a reference back to Article 7 OECD MC.[197]

The OECD also refers separately to the allocation of profits to an agency PE which shall be applied irrespective from the existence of an agency PE under Article 5 (5) OECD MC.[198] In principle, the functionally separate entity approach also has to work for an agency PE of the head office. Apart from the agent's remuneration, the functional and factual analysis additionally allocates specific assets, risks and capital to the agency PE based on significant people functions. Those can also be provided at the level of the agent on behalf of the head office such as the negotiation with third parties or management of inventory or credit risks.[199] For the internal transfer of assets from the head office to the PE additional costs valued at arm's length can occur at the level of the agency PE.[200] Whether the functional and factual analysis attributes additional risk and thus additional profit to the agency PE apart from the arm's length provision received from the head office depends on the specific facts and circumstances of the case to be considered.[201] This is also the difference to the *'single taxpayer approach'*, an alternative approach with regard to the profit allocation to the agency PE, which states that an arm's length agency fee paid to the agent totally compensates the profits to be

192. See OECD MC Commentary (2014) Article 7, No. 49, p. 146.
193. See OECD MC Commentary (2014) Article 7, No. 56, p. 148. An arbitration procedure under Article 25 (5) OECD MC is possible as well if the two involved parties are not able to agree. See OECD MC Commentary (2014) Article 7, No. 64, pp. 149 ff.
194. See OECD MC Commentary (2014) Article 7, No. 68, p. 151.
195. See OECD MC Commentary (2014) Article 7, No. 69, p. 151.
196. See Kahle/Mödinger (2010) p. 763.
197. See OECD MC Commentary (2014) Article 7, No. 74, p. 152.
198. See OECD Report on the Attribution of Profits to PE (2010) Part I, No. 227, p. 58.
199. See OECD Report on the Attribution of Profits to PE (2010) Part I, No. 232, p. 60.
200. See Ott (2009) p. 87.
201. See OECD Report on the Attribution of Profits to PE (2010) Part I, No. 234, p. 60.

attributed to the agency PE.[202] Basically, this implies that the profit to be allocated to the agency PE is zero as the profit is the same as the remuneration paid by the head office which is allocated as expense to the PE.[203] The OECD rejects the '*single taxpayer approach*' due to fairness reasons and due to redundancy of Article 5 (5) OECD MC since the existence of an agency PE at source becomes rather irrelevant for tax purposes if no taxable profit is allocated to the source state.[204] Still, it is considered that under given facts and circumstances in the functional analysis, a zero profit allocation to the agency PE should nevertheless be possible.[205]

Except for the agency PE, the AOA does not explicitly refer to the allocation of profits to special PE cases, such as for the service PE.[206] The OECD MC Commentary on Article 7 OECD MC also does not mention the construction site PE. More specifically, the indirect method of profit allocation which was possible under the '*old*' Article 7 (4) OECD MC is not allowed anymore under the AOA. Thus, it can be concluded that according to the OECD MC, the functionally separate entity approach generally has to work for the basic PE as well as for the other special PE cases, such as the construction site, agency and service PE.

3.4 INTERIM RESULT

When considering the development of the PE definition and attribution of business profits on OECD level, it can be concluded that in the last decade, the rather fixed PE concept as traditional nexus of source taxation changed to a considerable extent. Although the basic PE definition is actually clearly defined in Article 5 (1) OECD MC, there is room for interpretation with regard to certain PE criteria such as the disposal criterion as one of the necessary requirements of a fixed place of business.[207] Also, the OECD Reform Proposal for a revision of Article 5 of the OECD MC lacks clarity with regard to those PE requirements (see Table 3.1). With regard to the construction site PE, OECD regulations on the delegation of work to subcontractors and the integration of the disposal criterion in case of partial and total delegation of construction work to a subcontractor are discussable (see Table 3.2). The determination of the power to conclude contracts of an agency PE on an economic basis also provides scope for interpretation between the country of residence of the principal and the country of

202. See OECD Report on the Attribution of Profits to PE (2010) Part I, No. 235, p. 60.
203. See e.g. Niehaves (2011) p. 374. Under the 'single taxpayer approach' a profit can still arise if the agent is considered as employee of the principal as the provision to be paid is generally lower in comparison to what an independent agent will earn. See e.g. Ott (2009) p. 82.
204. See OECD Report on the Attribution of Profits to PE (2010) Part I, No. 236 & 239, p. 61.
205. See OECD Report on the Attribution of Profits to PE (2010) Part I, No. 234, p. 60.
206. In fact, the AOA includes recommendations with regard to the provision of internal services between head office and PE which shall follow the principles of the OECD Transfer Pricing Guidelines with respect of finding an adequate arm's length price. See OECD Report on the Attribution of Profits to PE (2010) Part I, No. 216, pp. 56 ff. Still, it is questionable if these specifications are applied to the allocation of income to service PEs which deal with services provided to external parties.
207. In fact, there are several PE requirements for which an interpretation is possible, e.g. with regard to the necessary time threshold. For this work, though, the disposal requirement is determined as being crucial as it provides for the most controversial interpretation possibilities.

residence of the agent. If an undisclosed principal is bound by the actions of the agent under national tax statutes of a *'common law'* country, the OECD Reform Proposal of 2012 obviously indicates that an agency PE can be established for some countries. Still, for a civil law country, an agency PE is not established if the agent does not act legally in the name of the foreign principal.[208] This can lead to misunderstandings among the OECD Member States.[209] It is debatable if the OECD MC in its current status enables the establishment of an agency PE for the principal if the agent has (only) factual power to conclude contracts on behalf of the principal.[210] Still, the OECD MC Commentary at least forms the basis for countries which want to interpret it in this way. In addition, the recent proposals added by the OECD BEPS Discussion Draft on Action Plan 7 indicate that the legal authority to conclude contracts in the name of the principal does not play a major role anymore when deciding about the existence of an agency PE. Actually, the OECD BEPS proposals support the wider *'economic'* authority to conclude contracts as decisive factor for the establishment of an agency PE and focus on the independence criterion as decisive agency PE requirement.[211] However, the inclusion of the rule of acting solely for one or more closely related principals as an exception from the independence character of the agent can indicate an enlargement of the agency PE definition (see Table 3.3). The implementation of the service PE option in the OECD MC Commentary and the introduction of the economic employer as additional criterion in case of the secondment of employees also can trigger further discussions (see Table 3.4).

In general, one can indicate a trend of enlargement of the PE definition on OECD level. Therefore, it can be argued that source taxation rules are extended by the OECD policy considering the definition of the PE due to the given possibilities of interpretation of relevant PE attributes. In fact, this not only affects limited taxation in the source country but has crucial consequences for residence taxation in the country of the head office. Increased taxation at source generally implies less tax revenue in the country of residence, independent of the method to be applied to avoid double taxation (exemption of PE profits or the granting of a tax credit).

Beyond, there is the AOA as guiding regulation considering the attribution of business profits between PE and head office. With regard to revenue implications between residence and source state, the consequences are not clear. It is possible that the extent of deductible expenses from the PE tax base is enlarged by assuming fictitious internal dealings priced at arm's length including a profit mark-up (see Table 3.5). Thus, it can be argued that the AOA supports taxation in the country of residence of the investor. On the other side, this result is not clear as taxable income of internal dealings between head office and PE can flow in both directions so that the amount of business profits allocated to the PE in the country of source can also be increased.

208. See Persico (2000) p. 69.
209. See Fernández (2013) pp. 10 ff., Rasch/Dotterweich (2014) p. 71.
210. See critically i.a. Piltz (2004) pp. 184 ff., Seltenreich (2006) pp. 251 ff., Ditz/Bärsch/Schneider (2013) p. 500, Pijl (2013a) pp. 14 ff.
211. See Kroppen (2005) p. 703. See critically Heußner (2004) p. 163.

As a result, the OECD basically strives for two different taxation policies with regard to PE taxation of cross-border cases. Whereas discussions considering the PE as connecting factor for source taxation clearly indicate an enlargement of source taxation, the allocation of business profits to the PE under the AOA basically shows no clear tendency. It can be assumed though that the AOA is preferred by industrialized capital-exporting countries, not at least since the UN MC representing the interests of mostly capital-importing developing and developed states, clearly refuses the implementation of the AOA in Article 7 UN MC.[212] Still, it can be argued that the OECD as an international association of countries worldwide claims not only a kind of universal validity towards OECD member countries but also at least indirectly towards all states which conclude a tax treaty with an OECD Member State.[213] By considering the national and country-specific treaty regulations of PE taxation and the rules on the attribution of business profits of two industrialized states, Germany and the US, and four emerging countries, Brazil, Russia, India and China (BRIC), a further systematization towards the national PE concepts in comparison to the OECD view is elaborated.

212. See UN MC Commentary (2011) Article 7, No. 1, pp. 139 ff. A reason might be the application of transfer pricing rules in the sphere of PE taxation which leads to a more complex PE income allocation and a higher tax compliance, especially for developing states. See Daurer (2014) p. 68.
213. See Krabbe (2009) Vor Article 1, No. 166, p. 71. Actually, the development of the AOA was based on the differences in profit allocation between OECD and non-OECD countries. See OECD Report on the Attribution of Profits to PE (2010) No. 4, p. 8.

CHAPTER 4

Source Taxation of Business Profits from a National Point of View of Germany, the US and the BRIC States

4.1 BASIC STRUCTURE AND CHOICE OF COUNTRIES

First of all, it has to be argued why it is reasonable to consider the national aspects of source taxation of business profits, the national PE concepts and the attribution of business profits between PE and head office in the first place. It is true that at first sight the PE is actually clearly defined in Article 5 OECD MC. Also, the attribution of business profits seems to be clarified when looking at the wording of Article 7 OECD MC and especially when taking into account the OECD MC Commentary as interpretation guide. Still, this does not mean that national law is irrelevant for further understanding of the PE concept. Treaty law generally assumes that both states initially apply their own tax law and in order to avoid double or non-taxation, restrict domestic taxing rights.[1] Thus, provisions of the tax treaty also have to tie to national tax rules, especially if it is required from the overall context.[2] In addition, there are often various judgments, court decisions and domestic case law which deal with the adequate understanding and interpretation of country-specific tax treaty regulations and definitions.[3] Therefore, a qualitative comparison of national PE concepts and profit attribution rules might help comparing the status quo of the OECD policy with the national trends of PE taxation worldwide.[4]

1. See Vogel/Rust (2015) No. 30, p. 23.
2. See Lang (2011) p. 289.
3. See for an overview on treaty court decisions, IBFD (2015), Tax Research Platform, Tax Treaty Case Law.
4. In fact, the differentiation between the national PE definition and the international approach on OECD level also has to reconsider the different goals which are pursued by national tax authorities on the one hand and the OECD as institution of international cooperation on the other hand. Whereas national tax systems mostly strive for the collection of tax revenue and the protection of

As not all national regulations towards the PE concept of all countries can be analysed in detail, it has to be decided which countries are the most relevant with regard to the extent and variety of evidence. Table 4.1 presents an overview considering the PE definition and profit attribution rules of the EU Member States, the BRIC states and the US. The second column shows whether the PE provision of the national treaty policy of the different countries is comparable with Article 5 of the OECD MC. The third column identifies important deviations from the PE definition under national tax and treaty law. The fourth column presents the national method of allocation of business profits between PE and head office of the different countries.

Table 4.1 PE Definition and Attribution of Business Profits in the EU Member States, BRIC and US

EU Member States	*Treaty PE Definition Compatible with OECD MC (Article 5) X = yes*	*Important Variations under National Tax and Specific Treaty Law*	*Attribution of Business Profits between Head Office and PE under National Tax Law*
AT	X	Varying time threshold for construction sites under treaty law (six to twenty-four months)	- Direct method (separate entity approach) - Indirect method allowed if at arm's length
BE	X	- Varying time threshold for construction sites (thirty days under national law, six to twenty-four months in treaty law) - No negative list under national law	- Direct method (separate entity approach) - Disregard of internal interest, royalty and rent payments
BG	X	Inclusion of a service PE under national and treaty law	- Direct method (separate entity approach) - Disregard of internal interest payments
CY	X	Varying time threshold for construction sites (three months in national law)	Direct method (separate entity approach)

the domestic tax base, including also non-resident taxpayers investing in the source state, tax treaty policy of the OECD, but also of other organizations such as the UN, acquire an equal and fair allocation of taxing rights between contracting states. Double respectively non-taxation situations shall be avoided and international cooperation and trade shall be supported. See i.a. Kobetsky (2011) p. 14, Uckmar (2012) §6.03, p. 164. Vogel/Rust (2015) No. 90, p. 41.

EU Member States	*Treaty PE Definition Compatible with OECD MC (Article 5) X = yes*	*Important Variations under National Tax and Specific Treaty Law*	*Attribution of Business Profits between Head Office and PE under National Tax Law*
CZ	X	Inclusion of a service PE under national and treaty law	- No specific rules - '*No-lower tax base than resident entity*' clause
DE	X	- Variations considering the time threshold for construction sites under national and treaty law (six to twelve months) - Creation of source taxation right also for independent agent under national law (permanent representative)	- Direct method (separate entity approach) - Indirect method alternatively under national law (e.g., for constructions sites) - Disregard of internal interest payments
DK	X	No time threshold for construction sites under national law	- Direct method (separate legal entity approach) - Disregard of internal interest payments
EE	X	- Construction site and service PE included under national law - No time threshold for construction sites under national law - No negative list under national law	- Direct method (separate legal entity approach) - Disregard of internal interest payments - Distribution tax levied (with exceptions)
ES	X	- Varying time threshold for construction sites under treaty law (six to twenty-four months) - No negative list under national law	- Direct method (separate legal entity approach) - Disregard of specific internal interest, royalty, commission payments - Indirect method in exceptional cases
FI	X	Similar to OECD MC	- Direct method (separate legal entity approach) - Disregard of specific internal interest and royalty payments

EU Member States	*Treaty PE Definition Compatible with OECD MC (Article 5) X = yes*	*Important Variations under National Tax and Specific Treaty Law*	*Attribution of Business Profits between Head Office and PE under National Tax Law*
FR	X	- Varying time threshold for construction sites under treaty law (three to eighteen months) - Local branch remittance tax for PE income (often excluded under treaty law)	- Direct method (separate legal entity approach) - Disregard of specific internal interest and royalty payments - Indirect method in exceptional cases
GR	X	- No time threshold under national law	- Direct method (Separate legal entity approach) - Deduction of head office expenses from PE income up to 5% of PE administrative expenses
HR	X	- Consultancy or business services for more than three months indicate PE	- Direct method (separate legal entity approach)
HU	X	- Varying time threshold for construction sites under national law (three months)	- Direct method (separate legal entity approach) - Obligatory inclusion of 5% of foreign head office profits realized with the help of PE as PE tax base under national law - Indirect method in residual cases
IE	X	- PE concept not recognized under national law - Any '*trading activity*' can induce source taxation - Special provisions for supervisory activities in relation to construction sites under tax treaty law	- Negotiation basis under national law - Direct method under treaty law (separate legal entity approach) - Disregard of specific internal interest payments

EU Member States	*Treaty PE Definition Compatible with OECD MC (Article 5) X = yes*	*Important Variations under National Tax and Specific Treaty Law*	*Attribution of Business Profits between Head Office and PE under National Tax Law*
IT	X	- Specific rules for agency PE under national law - Varying time threshold for construction sites under treaty law (three to thirty-six months) - Items on list of Article 5 (2) OECD MC considers a priori a PE under treaty law	- Direct method (force of attraction principle under national law) - Reference to transfer pricing rules
LT	X	Less importance of *'fixed place of business'* criterion under national law	Direct method (separate legal entity approach)
LU	X	Inclusion of permanent representative under national law	Direct method (separate legal entity approach)
LV	X	- Inclusion of service PE under national law	- PE treated as incorporated entity - Disregard of specific internal interest, royalty, commission and rent payments - Simplified income attribution method possible for PE with a time horizon of less than twelve months
MT	X	- No specific national definition - Rules on active income derived by non-resident indicates PE existence under national law	Direct method (separate legal entity approach) based on International Financial Reporting Standards (IFRS)

EU Member States	*Treaty PE Definition Compatible with OECD MC (Article 5) X = yes*	*Important Variations under National Tax and Specific Treaty Law*	*Attribution of Business Profits between Head Office and PE under National Tax Law*
		- Varying time threshold for construction sites under treaty law (six to eighteen months) - Inclusion of service PE under treaty law	
NL	X	- Varying time threshold for construction sites under treaty law (three to eighteen months)	- Direct method (separate legal entity approach) - Disregard of specific internal interest, royalty and rent payments
PL	X	Similar to OECD MC	- No specific regulations under national law - Direct method under treaty law - Indirect method allowed if customary
PT	X	Similar to OECD MC	Direct method (force of attraction principle under national law) (reservation against OECD AOA)
RO	X	Similar to OECD MC	Direct method (separate legal entity approach)
SE	X	- Varying time threshold for construction sites under national and treaty law (three to twelve months) - No negative list	Direct method (separate legal entity approach)
SI	X	- Consulting and management activities constitute PE under treaty law - Supervisory activities related to construction site constitute PE under treaty law	Direct method (separate legal entity approach)

EU Member States	*Treaty PE Definition Compatible with OECD MC (Article 5) X = yes*	*Important Variations under National Tax and Specific Treaty Law*	*Attribution of Business Profits between Head Office and PE under National Tax Law*
SK	X	Concrete time threshold under national law for PE (six months in a twelve-month period)	- Negotiation basis under national law - *No-lower tax base than resident entity*' clause
UK	X	No time threshold for construction sites under national law	- Direct method (separate legal entity approach) - Disregard of specific internal interest, royalty and commission payments
BRIC & US			
BR	X	- No PE definition under national law - Extensive registration process to constitute PE (subject to interpretation) - Varying time threshold for construction sites under treaty law (six months)	- No specific rules - PE treated as incorporated entity - Reference to national transfer pricing rules
CN	X (& UN MC)	- No minimum time threshold under national law - Secondment of personnel can constitute a PE under national law - Inclusion of service PE provision under treaty law	- Direct method (separate legal entity approach) - Disregard of specific internal interest, royalty, rents and commission payments - Alternative application of a '*deemed profit method*' - Indirect method in exceptional cases (e.g., for the provision of services)
IN	UN MC	- Concept of business connection under national law (broader than OECD PE definition)	- No specific methods under national law - Choice of method based on facts and circumstances

EU Member States	*Treaty PE Definition Compatible with OECD MC (Article 5) X = yes*	*Important Variations under National Tax and Specific Treaty Law*	*Attribution of Business Profits between Head Office and PE under National Tax Law*
		- Inclusion of service PE provision under treaty law - Supervisory activities related to construction site constitute PE under treaty law	- Force of attraction principle occasionally under treaty law
RU	X	No minimum time threshold for construction sites under national law	- Direct method (separate legal entity approach) - Indirect method in exceptional cases
US	US MC	- Broader '*engaged in US trade or business*' concept under national law (case law-based) - Specific regulations considering trading activities and the performance of personal services under national law	- Inclusion of all US source income (limited force of attraction principle) under national law - Differentiation between effectively connected income (ECI) and fixed or determinable annual or periodic income (FDAP)

Sources: See IBFD (2015) Country Analyses, IFA (2006), IFA (2009), Reimer et al. (2014) Country Perspectives.

It can be concluded from Table 4.1 that most of the EU countries' individual PE treaty definitions are consistent with the OECD view. Deviations in EU national law mostly occur with regard to the time requirement of the construction site PE and the inclusion of a service PE under national or treaty law. The preferred method of business profit attribution under national law of the EU countries is the direct method including a certain independence fiction of the PE for the allocation of business profits, hereby referred to as '*separate legal entity approach*'. In this context, at first sight, Germany embodies the typical OECD member country which obviously follows OECD policy considering the fiscal treatment of the PE, but not for every PE requirement.

The BRIC countries and the US follow different approaches with regard to many aspects. The US stands for one of the most important non-European OECD countries which under its national tax law and special US MC include its own rulings regarding the PE concept. Still, the US MC is also basically consistent with the OECD MC with regard to the fiscal treatment of a PE. National PE rules of the BRIC states partly deviate to a considerable extent from the OECD position. The BRIC as emerging states are all non-member countries of the OECD and usually take a critical stance towards the application of the OECD regulations as they often are of the opinion that the OECD follows the interests of the industrialized countries.[5] Thus, in several cases, those countries rely on the UN MC for treaty negotiations. Still, despite their non-member status, the BRIC states generally accept the function of the OECD MC as balance of interest between residence and source country.[6] That acceptance is also expressed by the fact that the UN MC builds up on the OECD MC as well.[7] The viewpoints of the BRIC states are also included in the OECD MC Commentary summing up to about thirty non-Member States actually involved in OECD decisions.[8] In fact, Brazil, China and India are key partners of the OECD whereas Russia is even involved in the accession process of becoming an OECD Member State.[9] In addition, the BRIC states are also actively involved in the process of the ongoing OECD BEPS project.[10] Thus, it can be concluded that the national viewpoints of the BRIC states towards the PE concept and the attribution of business profits also interrelate with OECD policy, although they are considerably different with regard to several aspects.

In addition, the increasing economic importance of the BRIC states actively drives the OECD to involve the emerging BRIC states in decision-making and to cover their interests as well.[11] This increasing importance is illustrated by Figure 4.1 which compares the different gross domestic products (GDP) adjusted for purchasing power of the ten largest world economies. In this context, the GDP works as indicator for the economic power of a country.

5. See Lorenzen/Feldtkeller (2012) p. 456.
6. See Wassermeyer (2009) Vor Article 1, No. 54, p. 39.
7. See Mitra/Sen (2012), p. 6.
8. See Palwe/Kumar (2009) p. 237.
9. See OECD's Current Tax Agenda (2012) p. 144.
10. In fact, Brazil, China and India take part in regional network meetings in order to participate in the discussion process of the OECD. See OECD Developing countries and BEPS (2015). In addition, the G20 finance ministers, among them leading executives of the BRIC countries, actively initiated the OECD BEPS Action Plan. See OECD BEPS Action Plan (2013) p. 11.
11. See i.a. starting with O'Neill (2001) pp. 3 f., Owens (2012) p. 687, Dagan (2015) p. 30. Still, the BRIC states differ with regard to structural, economic and political features and circumstances and are therefore not supposed to be considered as a single homogeneous group. See Owens (2015) p. 354.

Figure 4.1 Ten Largest World Economies – Gross Domestic Product based on Purchasing-Power-Parity (PPP) Valuation of Country GDP (Billions USD) (National Statistics for 2013/ International Monetary Fund (IMF) Estimation for 2020)

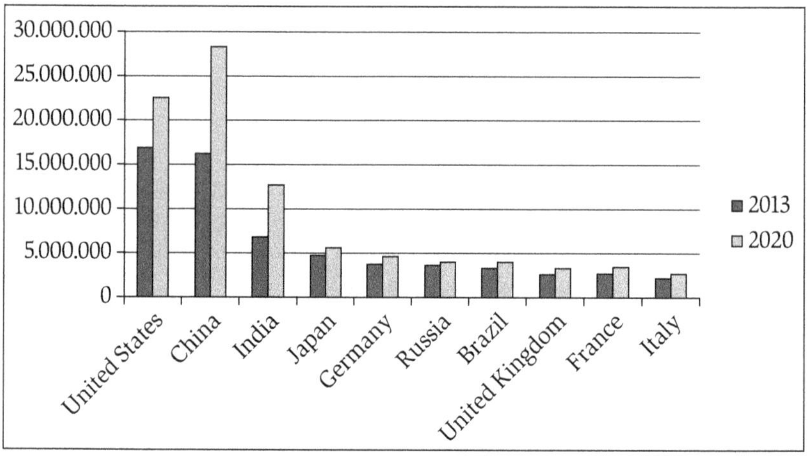

Source: International Monetary Fund – World Economic Outlook Database (April 2015)

Apart from the US which inhabits the highest GDP, China and India's GDP is larger than Germany's whereas Russia and Brazil are close behind. According to IMF prediction, this tendency will also hold until 2020.[12] In fact, according to IMF numbers, the current OECD Member Countries' ratio of the total world GDP only amounts to 63 % in 2013 with a declining trend estimated to 59 % in 2020.[13]

Therefore, it makes sense to integrate the BRIC states in the PE discussion and compare them with two of the most important industrialized countries, Germany and the US. The reason for this comparison is not only the economic importance of the countries under consideration but also the rising influence of the BRIC states in OECD decision-making.[14] The choice of the countries thus not only influences the generality of results but can also work as basis for a more elaborated systematization and identification of conflicts and solution proposals in the further analysis.

12. In 2013, there was a slowdown of real GDP growth for the BRIC in comparison to the rate expected in 2011. See IMF World Economic Outlook (October 2013) pp. 41 ff. Actually, since 2010, there is a decline in growth rates for all BRIC states in comparison to the 1990s. See Owens (2015) p. 354.
13. See IMF World Economic Outlook (April 2015) Database.
14. See i.a. Baistrocchi (2013) p. 763 who names the BRIC states as being members of the '*market leaders for quasi-legal rules*'. See for the influence of the BRIC countries in the OECD BEPS project, OECD BEPS Action Plan (2013) p. 25.

4.2 NATIONAL REGULATIONS CONSIDERING THE TAXATION OF PERMANENT ESTABLISHMENTS OF SELECTED COUNTRIES

4.2.1 Germany

4.2.1.1 Fiscal Nexus under National and Treaty Law

If a non-resident company conducts business activities in Germany, a German *domestic* taxing right is established if these business activities are rendered by a domestic PE (section 12 of the German General Tax Code GTC *Abgabenordnung*) or a domestic permanent agent (section 13 GTC) according to section 1 (4) and 49 (1) No. 2 (a) of the German Income Tax Code ITC (*Einkommensteuergesetz*) in conjunction with section 2 No. 1, section 7 and section 8 (1) of the German Corporate Tax Code CTC (*Körperschaftsteuergesetz*).[15] The PE not only serves as connecting factor for establishing a limited income tax liability in Germany, but it is also a crucial criterion for the imposition of the German local business tax or trade tax.[16]

According to section 12 sentence 1 GTC, a German PE can be '*any fixed place of business or facility which serves the activity of an enterprise*'. Thus, the main criteria of the German PE definition are a fixed place of business including a certain degree of permanence through which the business of the enterprise is carried on.[17] The PE requirements of German tax law actually resemble the OECD formulation and interpretation in Article 5 (1) OECD MC for most cases. The German PE definition also includes a positive non-exhaustive list of PE examples, similar to Article 5 (2) OECD MC. Thus, under domestic German tax law, business activities such as the maintenance of a warehouse or the purchase of goods can establish a PE according to section 12 sentence 2 No. 5 and No. 6 GTC.[18] In fact, these business activities are explicitly excluded from the PE status under Article 5 (4b) and (4d) OECD MC in which they are considered as preparatory or auxiliary activities. Insofar, the PE concept of the OECD is generally stricter and narrower than the German definition.[19] Another important PE requirement of German law is the fact that the non-resident investor needs to have a certain right to use the fixed place not only on a temporal basis, such that it can be considered '*as a place through which the business of an enterprise is wholly or partly carried on*'.[20] The requirement of disposal is also decisive for the possible PE existence

15. See Dehnen/Bacht (2005) pp. 447 f., Jacobs (2011) pp. 283 ff.
16. See Schnorberger (2012) p. 22.
17. See Eckl (2009) pp. 320 f., Jacobs (2011) p. 284.
18. One example of the German national PE list which differs from Article 5 (2) OECD MC, is the place of management. Under German national law, there is only one place of management which can establish a PE (referring to 'the' place of management in section 12 Nr. 1 GTC) whereas according to OECD, there are several places of management (referring to 'a' place of management in Article 5 (2a) OECD MC). See Schnorberger (2012) p. 29.
19. However, when considering the rather 'wide' understanding of the OECD with regard to the PE requirement of disposal in comparison to the German viewpoint, this statement can also be reversed. See section 3.1.
20. See BFH, 17 March 1982, I R 189/79, BStBl. II 1982, p. 625.

under German law in case of services provided at the premises of a client.[21] Apart from the local sphere of the fixed place of business, including a territorial limitation and a local fixation,[22] the German PE definition also requires a certain permanence criterion whereas according to German jurisdiction, the adequate time threshold for the existence of a PE is generally given if the fixed place of business exists for more than six months.[23] In comparison to the OECD regulations which defer the permanence requirement in case of a special economic nature of the business activity, the German PE definition demands a certain degree of permanence in any case.[24] Still, the duration requirement of six months rather works as a guideline and is not considered as definite part of the German PE base case.[25]

The German *tax treaty* policy with regard to the basic PE definition generally follows the concept of Article 5 OECD MC.[26] In German tax treaties, business profits are generally taxed under Article 7 of the OECD MC, meaning that the taxing right upon the business profits is allocated to the residence state, unless a PE according to Article 5 OECD MC exists in the source state. This PE strategy is also confirmed by the German basis for treaty negotiations, published by the German Federal Ministry of Finance on 17 April 2013 which works as a guideline for future German treaty policy.[27] As the PE is defined explicitly in German tax treaties, a reference to the PE definition under German tax law is generally not appropriate with regard to interpretative questions.[28] Still, especially with regard to debatable PE requirements which are not defined in the tax treaty such as the adequate degree of disposal, the German judgments are considered for the interpretation of the PE concept in German tax treaties. Differences to the OECD concept can occur with regard to the number of auxiliary activities in the negative PE list in German treaty law. Some German tax treaties exclude facilities for the use of storage, delivery of goods and merchandise from the '*a priori*' negative list but instead consider those as PE-establishing activities.[29]

For the *construction site PE*, the timing requirement is a crucial criterion under German national law. According to section 12 sentence 8 GTC, a construction site PE is established if the construction or installation project lasts in Germany for at least six months. Apart from the different duration requirement of six months in comparison to twelve months under Article 5 (3) OECD MC, the fiscal treatment of German construction site PEs considering the inclusion of planning and supervisory activities and the use of subcontractors is similar to current OECD provisions.[30] Thus, the work of subcontractors at the construction site without any supervisory or controlling activities

21. See beneath for explanations with regard to the treatment of services in German national and treaty law.
22. See i.a. Haiß (2011) p. 34.
23. See German PE Circular (1999) No. 1.1.1.1, p. 7.
24. See OECD MC Commentary (2014) Article 5, No. 45.8, p. 127.
25. See BFH, 3 February 1993, I R 80-81/91, BStBl. II 1993, pp. 462 ff.
26. See e.g. Endres/Spengel (2012) p. 71.
27. See Ditz/Bärsch/Quilitzsch (2013) pp. 156 ff.
28. See Fresch/Strunk (2012) OECD-MA Article 5, No. 27, p. 49.
29. See Lehner/Reimer (2005b) p. 326.
30. See German PE Circular (1999) No. 4.3.2, pp. 55 ff. Still, this does not include the OECD Reform Proposal of 2012 which deviates from German tax policy in this case.

of the general contractor does not establish a PE for the general contractor under German regulations.[31] Only if the general contractor delegates a part of the work to a subcontractor, supervises the process by its employees on-site, and exhibits a certain degree of disposal over the construction site, a construction site PE will be constituted for the general contractor.[32] In addition, similar to the OECD MC, German rules demand for a geographical and commercial coherence of different construction projects for the purpose of combination.[33]

Considering the fiscal treatment of construction site PEs in German tax treaties, the required minimum time period is often lowered to six to nine months in order to establish a PE at a construction site.[34] Apart from that, the formulation of a construction site PE in German tax treaties principally follows Article 5 (3) OECD MC.

Apart from the basic PE, German law provides another source of limited liability to tax: the *permanent representative* under section 13 GTC. A permanent representative habitually conducts the business activities of the principal from whom he is bound by instructions. This includes business activities such as contract work (concluding and negotiating), procuring mandates and holding and distributing goods.[35] PE requirements of the general PE definition under section 12 GTC do not have to hold for the German permanent representative.[36] Similar to Article 5 (5) OECD MC, the business activity of the permanent representative has to be performed on a continuous and habitual basis which demands a certain regularity of the authority to conclude contracts.[37] In contrast to the OECD, a permanent representative according to German law does not have to conduct the authority to conclude contracts explicitly in the name of the principal.[38] In addition, the German permanent representative does not differentiate between a dependent agent who establishes an agency PE and an independent agent who does not establish a PE under Article 5 (6) OECD MC as long as he acts in the '*ordinary course*' of his business. The activities carried out by the permanent representative on behalf of the principal can be of any kind in order to serve the objectives of the foreign principal.[39] This includes activities which qualify as preparatory or auxiliary activities under Article 5 (4) OECD MC. Therefore, it can be concluded that the German permanent representative under section 13 GTC has a broader scope than the OECD agency PE. Still, in case of a non-existing tax treaty, according to the German Income Tax Guidelines, German tax authorities obviously follow the differentiation between independent and non-independent agents similar to Article 5 (5) and (6) OECD MC.[40] Although German national tax law does not provide for any rules considering the

31. See Eckl (2009) p. 329, Demme (2013) p. 559. See for another opinion Löwenstein (2011) No. 1333, pp. 484 ff.
32. See Schnorberger (2012) p. 36.
33. See German PE Circular (1999) No. 4.3.5, p. 57.
34. See Lehner/Reimer (2005) p. 327.
35. See Schnorberger (2012) p. 45.
36. See Kruse (2003) § 13, p. 54. In fact, a German permanent representative under section 13 GTC is not relevant for the raising of the German trade tax. See Eckl (2009) p. 335.
37. See Kruse (2003) Para. 13, p. 54/2.
38. See Kumpf (1982) p. 47.
39. See Kruse (2003) Para. 13, p. 54/1.
40. See German Income Tax Guidelines (2012), Guideline R 49.1 (1).

possible PE existence of subsidiaries, German tax jurisdiction decided in accordance with OECD regulations that a PE is not established by an affiliated company just by the fact that the parent company owns a certain percentage of participation.[41]

The agency PE provision in German *tax treaties* is principally consistent with Article 5 (5) and (6) of the OECD MC.[42] Similar to the OECD MC Commentary, the German PE Circular determines that a dependent agent is supposed to have the power to conclude contracts in the source state if he is '*authorised to negotiate*' the customer's contract such that the foreign principal is bound legally or economically.[43] An authority to conclude contracts can also be given, if the agent is authorized to negotiate all aspects of the contract bindingly and the principal generally conducts a separate approval.[44] With regard to the wording of the German PE Circular, there is the interpretation that an '*economically*' binding authorization to conclude contracts can usually only be assumed if the power of contract conclusion is conducted legally in the name of the principal.[45] In this context, the German '*Kommissionär*' cannot establish an agency PE in German treaties as he does not conclude contracts in the name of the principal.[46] In fact, the German interpretation is not clear in this case. An updated circular of the Swiss tax legislation in 2014 considering the allocation of profits between German and Swiss principal structures basically implies the establishment of an agency PE in Germany through commissionaire structures which do not legally conclude contracts in the name of the principal.[47] With regard to this interpretation, there are views of the German tax jurisdiction which approve the Swiss interpretation and thus the 'wider' economic authority to conclude contracts.[48]

For *services* to be taxable in Germany the provisions of the general German PE under section 12 GTC have to be fulfilled.[49] This is exemplary given if a non-resident provides services for a certain time through an own office in Germany from which for example consulting services are performed to domestic customers.[50] More critical is the question of PE existence in Germany if services are rendered exclusively in the rooms and buildings of the client himself.[51] In this context, the issue of disposal plays a significant role in German national tax law. The disposal of a company normally

41. See BFH, 29 August 1984, I R 154/81, BStBl. II 1985, pp. 160 ff.
42. See Schnorberger (2012) p. 45.
43. See German PE Circular (1999) No. 1.2.2, pp. 17 f., OECD MC Commentary (2014) Article 5, No. 33, p. 108.
44. See Wassermeyer (2009) p. 128.
45. See Eckl (2009) p. 333, Rasch (2011) p. 12, Hilbert/Engel (2012) p. 474.
46. See also Endres (1996) p. 1, Piltz (2004) pp. 184 f., Niehaves (2010) p. 83.
47. See Krauß (2014) pp. 548 ff.
48. See Morlock (2011) p. 804.
49. See Amann (1998) p. 28. However, disputable cases exist if a foreign company earns income from the provision of services in Germany which can be considered from an isolated point of view as income from independent services according to *49 (1) No. 3* in conjunction with *49 (2) ITC*. That is, the German principle of an isolated view of source income of non-residents, the so-called *isolierende Betrachtungsweise*. In these cases, a PE of the foreign company does not have to be necessary in order to establish a German taxing right. See for more details Amann (1998) pp. 45 f., Kumpf (1982) pp. 191 ff. In fact, it is arguable if this principle actually holds for non-natural persons such as corporations. See Jacobs (2011) pp. 258 ff.
50. See Amann (1998) p. 29.
51. See Rosenberger/Vitali/Ziehr (2010) p. 12.

requires a formal right to use the place of business which cannot be removed or amended without the company's agreement or assistance, such as rental agreements or public legal positions.[52] In addition, a certain local connection or '*rootedness*' of the company has to exist as a factor of an increased relation to the place of its business activities (*Verwurzelung*).[53] In fact, the mere presence of a foreign service provider in the rooms of his client is supposed to be not sufficient to establish a certain disposal over the non-resident company.[54] Against this background, the German case law is rather restricted: While in 2004, a US service contractor who performed services at a US military base in Germany established a PE by fulfilling the right to use test, the German Federal Fiscal Court (*Bundesfinanzhof* BFH) decided in 2008 that, considering a Dutch company which was rendering cleaning services at a North Atlantic Treaty Organization (NATO) airbase in Germany, the activities at the premises of its client did not provide a sufficient degree of disposal, thus denying the existence of a PE.[55] In 2011, the German BFH decided in two judgments that a PE was established by business activities conducted in the rooms of a third person if it could be effectively considered that the third party premises were provided permanently for the use of the service provider.[56] These judgments again identified that a legal right to use was not necessary for the acceptance of an adequate degree of disposal.[57] Still, the principle of '*rootedness*' and the criterion of exclusion possibility continue to represent a strict German interpretation of the disposal requirement.

Business activities performed by seconded employees generally do not constitute a PE for the foreign '*lender*' as the secondment is considered as '*passive*' which means that the employees effectively work for the '*borrower*', the host company, and not for the active workforce-lending company.[58] A PE can only be determined if the workforce-lending company owns an additional place of management from where the secondment arrangements are organized.[59] In addition, an '*active interest*' of the workforce-lending company can be assumed if the reimbursement paid by the host company includes a profit mark-up.[60] In this case, the German domestic basic PE requirements have to be fulfilled in order to create a German taxing right for the services provided by the seconded employees at source.[61]

With regard to the service PE, the *treaty policy* of Germany is rather limited. Nevertheless, Germany concluded a few tax treaties which include a special service PE

52. See Eckl (2009) p. 323.
53. See BFH, 3 February 1993, I R 80-81/91, BStBl. II 1993, pp. 466 ff.
54. See Rautenstrauch/Binger (2009) p. 620.
55. See BFH, 14 July 2004, I R 106/03, BFH/NV 2005, pp. 154 f; BFH, 4 June 2008, I R 30/07, BStBl. II 2008, pp. 922 f; Korff (2009) pp. 231 ff.
56. See BFH, 23 February 2011, I R 52/10, BFH/NV, pp. 1354 f., BFH, August 24, 2011, I R 46/10, BFH/PR 2012, pp. 33 ff.
57. See Kaminski (2012) p. 356.
58. See i.a. Rosenberger/Vitali/Ziehr (2010) p. 6, Buciek (2011) No. 41,§ 12, p. 24.
59. See Bendlinger (2009) p. 46.
60. See German Administrative Principles - Staff Secondment (2001) No. 2.2. p. 4.
61. This does not include the possible German taxing rights on employment income if the secondment is qualified as employment service.

provision only based on a certain permanence condition of the service provider.[62] All of them follow the UN MC which includes a special service PE provision in Article 5 (3b) UN MC.[63] One of the latest tax treaties of Germany including a service PE is the one with Turkey, established in 2011. According to Article 5 (3b) of the tax treaty between Germany and Turkey, the PE definition shall also include *'the rendering of services, including consultancy services, by an enterprise of a Contracting State'* in the other state *'for the same or connected projects'*, but only if the service activity fulfils a certain time threshold, in this case *'more than 6 months within any 12-month period'*.[64] Still, German tax treaty policy usually does not deviate from the traditional PE definition of the OECD MC. In fact, it is slightly more common to extend the scope for royalties in accordance with Article 12 of the UN MC to income from technical or commercial services provided in the source country.[65] One example is Article 12 (1) of the tax treaty of Germany with India which explicitly includes fees for technical, commercial or consulting services in the royalty-article so that those service provisions are taxed at source at a gross amount without the establishment of a PE.[66] Apart from the inclusion of a *'real'* service PE in German tax treaties, German tax treaty policy contains a restricted view with regard to the establishment of a *'passive'* service PE in relation to the interpretation of the basic PE requirement of disposal. In this context, the OECD MC Commentary describes the example of a painter who works for two years every three days in a week at a client's building, thereby fulfilling a certain degree of disposal and establishing a *'passive'* service PE at source although the place of the painter's activity is a fixed place of business of the customer, not of the painter.[67] In accordance with the opinion in national tax jurisdiction, Germany has put an observation in the OECD MC Commentary stating that it does not agree with the OECD understanding of a necessary degree of disposal.[68] Similar to German national law, the secondment of employees providing services at a host company usually does not constitute a PE for the non-resident workforce-lending company as the typical secondment arrangement is considered as *'passive'* business activity of the lending company.[69] However, depending on the requirements of the economic employer of the seconded employees and the character of the reimbursement payment to the workforce-lending company, the secondment arrangement can also be qualified as business-income related service

62. See Mattern/Zimny (2014) Germany, No. 47, pp. 15 ff. These are the tax treaties of Germany with Liberia (1970), Turkey (2011), Taiwan (2012), China (2013) and the Philippines (2013). See Appendix, Table A1. In addition, the tax treaty with South Africa which is not yet in force, also includes the performance of professional services in the PE provision. See Hensel (2012) p. 228.
63. See UN MC Commentary (2011) Article 5, No. 9, pp. 107 ff.
64. See Endres/Freiling (2012) p. 189.
65. See Amann (1998) p. 90, Lehner/Reimer (2005b) pp. 327 ff. See Appendix, Table A1 for a list of German treaties including services in the 'royalties'-Article.
66. See Strauß (1999) Article 12 Indien, pp. 83 ff.
67. See Wichmann (2005) pp. 96 f., OECD MC Commentary (2014) Article 5, No. 4.5, p. 96.
68. See OECD MC Commentary (2014) Article 5, No. 45.7, p. 126. See critically i.a. Müller-Gatermann (2012) p. 1034.
69. See Brunsbach (2012) p. 335.

provision.[70] Thus, a service PE of the workforce-lending company is possible if it is integrated in the respective treaty. Otherwise, the requirements of the basic treaty PE definition have to be additionally fulfilled.

From a domestic and from a treaty perspective, the German PE definition is generally similar to the OECD approach in several cases (see Table 4.2). Major differences exist with regard to the '*strict*' interpretation of the disposal criterion including a certain degree of '*rootedness*' (*Verwurzelung)* and the refusing inclusion of a service PE determining a fiscal nexus without the establishment of a fixed place of business.

Table 4.2 German PE Concept

	National Law	*Treaty Law*
Basic PE	- Similar to OECD MC - Permanence guideline of six months - Strict understanding of disposal	Similar to OECD MC
Construction site PE	Reduced permanence threshold of six months	- Similar to OECD MC - Reduced permanence threshold of six to nine months
Agency PE	Wider permanent representative concept	Similar to OECD MC
Service PE	- Not included - Strict understanding of disposal in case of '*passive*' service PE	- Included in seldom cases - Strict understanding of disposal in case of '*passive*' service PE

4.2.1.2 Attribution of Business Profits between Foreign Head Office and Domestic PE

In principle, German *domestic law* has been ambivalent with regard to the theoretical concept of the attribution of business profits between head office and PE. On the one side, the '*old*' German PE Circular basically followed the relevant business activity approach explicitly stating that profit mark-ups upon internal dealings between head office and PE had to be disregarded.[71] However, the German tax authorities widened the arm's length principle by deleting the prohibition of internal profit mark-ups in the German PE Circular.[72] In fact, this is also consistent with the amendment of section 1

70. See Pickering (2012) p. 52.
71. See German PE Circular (1999) No. 2.2, pp. 22 ff.
72. See Amendment of the German PE Circular (2009) No. 2.2, p. 2. However, this amendment which basically was the start-up for German exit taxation rules including the taxation of hidden reserves in case of the transfer of assets between head office and PE, is discussable. The German

of the German Foreign Tax Act (FTA) in 2013 which implemented the AOA into German domestic law.[73] Section 1 (5) FTA states that the German rules for the implementation of the arm's length principle under section 1 (1), (3) and (4) FTA are applied if the transfer price for dealings between the head office and the PE is not in line with the arm's length principle and domestic profits are otherwise shifted abroad.[74] Dealings between head office and PE are explicitly included as *'assumable contractual transaction'* under section 1 (4) No. 2 FTA. Therefore, a PE has to be treated as separate legal entity for tax purposes. This means that, similar to the AOA, according to section 1 (5) sentence 3 FTA, significant personal functions, adequate business assets, appropriate chances and risks as well as an acceptable donation capital have to be allocated to the PE. In a second step, the type of dealing as well as the corresponding transfer price have to be determined (section 1 (5) sentence 4 FTA).

In general, the current German domestic income allocation rules basically follow the AOA. In accordance with section 1 (6) FTA which officially enables the German Federal Ministry of Finance to release further explanation decrees to the German PE income allocation rules, in October 2014, a decree draft was released with further explanations with regard to the interpretation of the German domestic business profit attribution rules.[75]

Whereas the *'old'* German PE Circular did not adapt the implementation of the functionally separate entity approach, the new PE Decree provides detailed instructions for the introduction of the AOA in German tax law.[76] Similar to the *'old'* circular, the direct method applies for the PE which has to hold and administer own ancillary accounts upon which the business results of the PE can be derived.[77] In contrast, the new PE Decree does not mention the indirect method as possible technique of profit allocation.

The new German PE Decree determines the allocation of personal functions, assets, chances and risk, donation capital, external transactions and internal dealings

---

Federal Fiscal Court decided in 2008 that the taxation of hidden reserves after the transfer of assets to a foreign PE shall also be possible in case of an external sale which basically contradicted the original view of the restriction of the German taxing right in case of a transfer of reserves. See BFH, 17 July 2008, I R 77/06, BStBl. II 2009, pp. 464 ff. See for an overview and discussion Ditz (2009) pp. 115 f., Ditz/Schneider (2010) pp. 81 f., Roth (2011) pp. 75 f., Schnitger (2013) pp. 18 ff.

73. See German Law on the Implementation of the Directive on Mutual Assistance (2013) pp. 36 ff. which finally transcribes the changes in German law of the opposed German Annual Tax Act 2013.
74. See Wilke (2012) p. 274.
75. See PE Decree (2014). This official degree followed the PE Decree Draft from August 2013. See PE Decree Draft (2013).
76. In accordance with the implementation of the AOA in German tax law, the 'old' PE Circular proposed the usage of the direct method based upon separate bookkeeping accounts. See e.g. BFH, 29 July 1992, II R 39/89, BStBl. II 1993, pp. 63 ff. The other method suggested was the indirect method based on certain appropriate ratios which especially applies in the sector of sales or services in relation to the revenues or in the sector of production in relation to wages or material costs. See German PE Circular (1999) No. 2.3.2, pp. 24 ff.
77. See PE Decree (2014) Para. 3 (1), p. 1380.

to the PE in accordance with the AOA.[78] First, personal functions have to be allocated to the PE which include a factual reference to the PE and which are not performed on a short-term basis.[79] Tangible assets have to be allocated according to their place of use, unless the functional analysis comes to another result. In case the usage changes, the tangible asset has to be allocated to the place where it is predominantly used.[80] Intangible assets, self-developed or acquired, are allocated according to the significant personal function responsible for the development or the acquisition.[81] Decisive personal functions for the allocation include the usage, administration, further development, protection and the disposal of the intangible asset.[82]

Chances and risks are allocated directly to an asset in case of a direct relation.[83] If a direct relation does not exist, risk is allocated according to the significant personal function.[84] Decisive personal functions include the administration, regulation and realization of risk as well as the decision power to implement changes with regard to the degree of risk.[85]

Under the new German PE Decree, the donation capital of the German PE has to be determined according to the capital allocation method similar to the AOA.[86] Therefore, the ratio of donation capital allocated to the PE has to be consistent with the PE share of personal functions, assets as well as chances and risks in relation to the residual enterprise.[87] Assets allocated to the head office and the PE generally have to be valued at an arm's length price taking into account the respective chances and risks, unless the enterprise demonstrates that the usage of book values leads to a comparable capital ratio.[88] German enterprises with foreign PE have to show in a credible way that a certain amount of donation capital is necessary which, however, is not allowed to

78. See PE Decree (2014) Para. 1 (2), p. 1379. In general, the basic rule for the allocation of profits between head office and PE under the 'old' German PE approach followed the causation principle or business nexus. See Brüninghaus (2011) p. 830, Schnorberger (2012) p. 61. Income and expenses were supposed to be allocated according to their factual use at the level of the head office or PE. See German PE Circular (1999) No. 2.4, p. 25. However, this part was deleted in the German amendment from 2009. See Amendment of the German PE Circular (2009) No. 2.4, p. 3. The actual circumstances including the structure, organization and the functional purpose of the PE in relation to the overall enterprise were relevant. Another feature was the central function of the head office which determined that certain assets and functions such as the holding of the whole enterprise's capital or of participations, generally had to be allocated to the head office. See German PE Circular (1999) No. 2.4, pp. 25 ff.
79. See PE Decree (2014) Para. 4 (1), p. 1380. A short-term duration is defined as thirty days per year. See Höreth/Zimmermann (2014) p. 745.
80. See PE Decree (2014) Para. 5 (1) and (2), p. 1381.
81. See PE Decree (2014) Para. 6 (1), p. 1381.
82. See PE Decree (2014) Para. 6 (2), p. 1381.
83. See PE Decree (2014) Para. 10 (1), p. 1382.
84. See PE Decree (2014) Para. 10 (2), p. 1382.
85. See PE Decree (2014) Para. 10 (3), p. 1382.
86. See OECD Report on the Attribution of Profits to PE (2010) Part I, No. 121 f., pp. 37 ff. According to the 'old' PE Circular, in order to determine the equity or donation capital of the PE, the part of the external debt capital had to be assigned first which can either be borrowed directly by the PE, or was passed through by another part of the enterprise. See Runge (2001) p. 136.
87. See PE Decree (2014) Para. 12 (1), p. 1383.
88. See PE Decree (2014) Para. 12 (3), p. 1383.

exceed the amount allocated according to the capital allocation method.[89] Similar to the '*old*' PE Circular, external interest expenses from directly acquired, passed through and forwarded debt capital are generally allocated directly to the PE excluding an internal profit mark-up.[90] The function of a treasury PE including the acquisition, administration and investment of financial funds inside the enterprise is considered as internal service so that internal interest dealings are valued on a cost-plus basis.[91] In case of an internal transfer of assets between head office and PE, German national tax rules demand for a taxation of hidden reserves in case the German taxing right is restricted according to section 4 (1) sentence 3 ITC and section 12 (1) CTC.[92] The tax base is the fair market value of the asset less the book value at the point of time of the transfer which effectively leads to taxation of an internal dealing, similar to the AOA.[93] Also for other internal dealings resulting from assumed contractual relations between the PE and the head office, the arm's length principle has to be applied which leads to fictitious profits or expenses, respectively.[94]

Future German *tax treaties* generally have to apply the AOA in accordance with Article 7 of the OECD MC 2010.[95] In fact, only a few German tax treaties already include the AOA in the business profits-article.[96] German tax treaties which apply the rules of the AOA also have to be in line with German domestic law under the new PE Decree draft and section 1 (5) FTA which implements the functionally separate entity approach of the OECD MC. Still, in accordance with the '*old*' German PE Circular, most

---

89. See PE Decree (2014) Para. 13 (2), p. 1383. However, it is possible that the amount of donation capital is higher than determined under the capital allocation approach if non-tax provisions of the foreign state regulate a higher amount by law. See PE Decree (2014) Para. 13 (3), p. 1383.
90. See PE Decree (2014) Para. 15 (1), p. 1384. According to the 'old' PE Circular, the part of internal funding, which was neither donation capital nor external funding, could be assigned as forwarded debt capital which was acquired by the overall enterprise and was allocated to the PE. See for an overview Jacobs (2011) p. 695. The adequate allocation of assets and liabilities to the PE according to the arm's length principle basically implied that the equity or donation capital of the PE was the residual value of the total capital demand minus the liabilities allocated to the PE. See Buchner (2013) p. 228. Other methods applied external comparisons, internal comparisons in relation to functions or equity-asset ratios. See German PE Circular (1999) No. 2.5.1, pp. 27 ff.
91. See PE Decree (2014) Para. 17, p. 1385.
92. However, the justification of this rule is discussed in literature. The implementation of the AOA in German national law is not supposed to work as legal basis for German exit taxation. See Schnitger (2013) pp. 34 ff.
93. See Brüninghaus (2011) p. 851. Still, Germany provides for the realization of a balancing item under section 4(g) ITC in order to defer immediate taxation at the moment of the cross-border transfer. See i.a. Wassermeyer (2008) pp. 430 ff.
94. See PE Decree (2014) Para. 16 (2), p. 1384.
95. This is also consistent with the German basis for treaty negotiations. See Ditz/Bärsch/Quilitzsch (2013) p. 157.
96. These are the tax treaties with Liechtenstein (2011), Luxembourg (2012), the Netherlands (2012), Ireland (2014), Norway (2014) and the UK (2014). See Appendix Table A12. See in detail for the Netherlands Böing/Prang (2012) pp. 2211 ff. Moreover, the German tax treaty with the US also follows the functionally separate entity approach according to the Protocol from 2006 for fiscal years beginning in 2007. See Klein (2009) in Endres DBA USA! No. 2, p. 190. According to the Protocol of the German tax treaties with Spain (2011) and Hungary (2011), the contracting states are at least open to the implementation of the AOA regarding possible future changes of the OECD MC Commentary. See Roser (2013) p. 45. The new tax treaty with Japan is also supposed to introduce the AOA. See Kahle/Kindich (2016) fn. 214, p. 269.

of the German tax treaties treat the PE as separate legal entity for the purpose of income allocation but do not include a profit mark-up for internal cross-border dealings between head office and PE.[97] Considering the relation of the '*new*' German interpretation of the AOA in national tax law to those '*old*' German tax treaties which do not follow the AOA, section 1 (5) sentence 8 FTA provides for a rule of correction. If there are differences in allocation between German domestic law and the rules of a tax treaty between Germany and another state, the income allocation rules of the tax treaty shall hold. This applies under the condition that the taxpayer proves that the other state's taxing right is levied in accordance with the existing tax treaty so that otherwise, a situation of double taxation occurs in case the income allocation under German domestic law applies.[98]

In comparison to the double taxation avoidance-Article of 7 (3) OECD MC, the German basis for treaty negotiations is in line with the alternative version as formulated in the OECD MC Commentary. This demands for an appropriate adjustment under the condition that Germany also agrees with the first adjustment of the other contracting state. Otherwise, a solution has to be found under a MAP.[99]

According to the new German PE Decree, the general income allocation rules following the AOA also have to be applied for *construction site PEs* for which, in contrast to the '*old*' PE Circular, the indirect method of income attribution is generally excluded.[100] Fixed assets which are used at the construction site for the exercise of personal functions are effectively allocated to the PE if the personal functions are interrelated with the acquisition, production or an adequate degree of administration of these assets.[101] The PE Decree refutably presumes that the work of a construction site PE is considered as internal service provided to the residual enterprise and thus has to be priced with the help of a cost-oriented transfer pricing method if the activities performed at the construction site are routine business activities.[102] Still, if the personal functions performed are unique or unique intangible assets are created during the completion of the construction contract, profit-split methods are used for the internal dealings between the head office and a construction site PE.[103]

According to section 1 (5) sentence 5 FTA and the new German PE Decree, the attribution rules under the German implementation of the AOA described above also apply to the German *permanent representative* of section 13 GTC.[104] In general, it is possible that the agency PE profit is minimal in accordance with the '*zero-sum*'-theory

97. See Schaumburg (2013) p. 197.
98. See Schnitger (2012) p. 641.
99. See Lay/Stoecker (2013) p. 369.
100. See PE Decree (2014) Para. 30, p. 1390. In case of complex performance constructs, the 'old' PE Circular allocated the profits according to the performance of activities, functions and the attribution of risk between head office and construction site PE. See German PE Circular (1999) No. 4.3.6, p. 59. In fact, this rule implied the indirect method of profit allocation which is also possible for construction site PE under German domestic law. For a more detailed description of the indirect allocation methods, see Löwenstein (2011) No. 1400, p. 513.
101. See PE Decree (2014) Para. 31 (1), p. 1390.
102. See PE Decree (2014) Para. 32 (1), p. 1390.
103. See PE Decree (2014) Para. 33 (1), p. 1391.
104. See PE Decree (2014) Para. 39, p. 1392.

except for the cases where the permanent representative bears additional considerable business risk.[105] Still, a functional analysis similar to the AOA is generally necessary.

As the *service PE* is not implemented in German domestic law, specific rules with respect to income allocation do not exist. German tax jurisdiction only provides for regulations with regard to internal services performed between head office and PE. According to the *'old'* German PE Circular, those are generally supposed to be recognized at cost, excluding a profit mark-up.[106] However, if the provision of services is a major activity of the PE, the arm's length price is appropriate.[107] Services which are charged at cost are general services of the head office including administration, legal or controlling activities.[108] It is questionable which rules will be applicable to service PEs in the future as the new German PE Decree does not include any provisions with regard to the profit allocation to a service PE.

Given that (future) German *treaty policy* follows the AOA according to the German basis for treaty negotiations, it can be concluded that the general OECD recommendations for income allocation between head office and PE also apply to special PE cases in German tax treaties.[109]

In summary, German national law follows the AOA as implemented in the German Foreign Tax Act and according to administrative law (see Table 4.3). Considering treaty policy, most German tax treaties are still in line with the *'old view'* of the OECD MC whereas the future strategy under the German basis for treaty negotiations implements the AOA as well.

Table 4.3 German Approach of Allocation of Business Profits to PE

National Law	*Treaty Law*
- Allocation of profits similar to AOA under new German domestic law - Allocation of profits according to functions performed - External transactions and internal dealings between head office and PE recognized including a profit mark-up according to the arm's length principle	- Income allocation principally based on the *'old'* OECD MC in most treaties - Future treaties should follow AOA

105. See German *Bundesrat* (2014) p. 141. In fact, it is discussable if the single taxpayer approach or the 'zero-sum theory' should be applied under German national law so that a zero profit is allocated to the agency PE as the income allocated is supposed to be compensated by the costs emerged from business activities provided by the agent for the principal. See Ditz/Bärsch (2013) pp. 411 f., Nientimp/Ludwig/Stein (2014) p. 817, Rasch/Müller (2014) p. 422 supporting the application of the single taxpayer approach. See for another opinion Niehaves (2011) pp. 373 f., Käbisch/Risse (2014) p. 334.
106. See BFH, July 20, 1988, I R 49/84, BStBl. II 1989, pp. 140 ff.
107. See German PE Circular (1999) No. 3.1.2, p. 40.
108. See Schnorberger (2012) p. 64.
109. See e.g. Ditz/Bärsch/Quilitzsch (2013) p. 157.

4.2.2 United States

4.2.2.1 Fiscal Nexus under National and Treaty Law

The US *tax law* does not explicitly contain the term of a PE.[110] According to section 871 (b) and section 882 of the US Internal Revenue Code (IRC) a foreign enterprise which is engaged in business activities in the US, is taxable on the income which is '*effectively connected with the conduct of such trade or business within the United States*'.[111] In this context, basically all income which is earned by doing trade or business within the US, represents '*effectively connected income*' being taxable in the US.[112] In fact, US regulations and statutory law are strongly influenced by US case law and court decisions so that the Treasury Regulations and the IRC on respective terms of US source income often are not defined but constructed on a case-by-case basis.[113]

First, the terms of '*US trade or business*' and '*effectively connected income*' have to be explained in more detail in order to determine the US threshold for a limited liability to tax of business profits. In order to comply with the concept of a '*US trade or business*', a non-resident needs to fulfil the criterion of a certain fixed physical presence in the US.[114] The concrete meaning of this concept can be derived from US case law stating that engaging in US trade or business involves the taxpayer's original motive including qualifying profit and personnel, quantitative aspects such as duration or substantiality of the business activity as well as qualitative aspects such as a real business income in comparison to non-qualifying investment income.[115] In other words, the business activities have to be '*considerable, continuous and regular*' in order to establish a US taxing right.[116]

The next criterion to be fulfilled for US source taxation is the '*effectively connected income*' requirement. Thereby, income is generally '*effectively connected*' to a US trade or business if it can be allocated to a certain office or another fixed place of business in the US. Still, the '*fixed place*' criterion can be considered as connecting factor or signal for US sources and not as definite and exclusive requirement of US source taxation.[117] A US office or fixed place alone (without actively conducting US trade or business) shall thus not be sufficient to constitute a US PE. In addition, two further tests were developed by US Treasury Regulations in relation to applied case law in order to differentiate between effectively connected income and passive investment income,

110. See i.a. Hannes (2006) p. 691.
111. See Tittle (2007a) p. 27.
112. See Puls (2005) p. 161. There is also another US nexus according to section 871 (a) IRC, namely the 'fixed or determinable annual or periodical' income (FDAP income) which includes passive investment income such as interest, dividends, royalties or rents. This income is also taxable in the US but is not 'effectively connected with any US trade or business'. See Djanani/Brähler/Lösel (2005) p. 69.
113. See Djanani/Brähler/Lösel (2005) p. 54.
114. See Avi-Yonah (2007a) pp. 82 ff.
115. See McDaniel/Ault/Repetti (2005) p. 56.
116. See Djanani/Brähler/Lösel (2005) p. 157.
117. See Puls (2005) p. 163.

namely the asset-use and the business-activities test (section 864 (c) (2) IRC).[118] The asset-use test basically asks if the assets that are involved in the US business are actually used for producing the connected income or if they are allocated to passive investment income.[119] A direct relationship between the assets involved and the trade or business within the US has to exist which means that non-residents being located in the US are the ones who produce the effectively connected income and have ultimate control over the investment of the asset.[120] This can be understood as disposal over the intensity and direction of the investment of the business asset in US domestic law used for the differentiation between active US trade and passive investment income. However, the exact interpretation of ultimate control over the asset is not explained further but presumed to be case-driven. The business-activities or material-factor test also determines whether certain passive investment income effectively belongs to the US trade or business.[121] This test identifies the business activities conducted at the fixed place which significantly contribute to the realization of the US income and are performed on a regular basis.[122] In summary, it can be concluded that the US source taxation rules on business profits are wider in comparison to the PE concept of the OECD MC.[123]

In general, the US *treaty policy* is an autonomous one relying on the US Model Convention (US MC) which is still based on the OECD MC in many cases. Thus, also under US treaty policy, the major fiscal connecting factor for US business income is the PE. Similar to the OECD MC, according to Article 5 (1) US MC, a PE exists if there is a '*fixed place of business through which the business of an enterprise is wholly or partly carried on*'. The US MC also includes in Article 5 (2) US MC a non-concluding list of PE examples which shall clarify the definition under Article 5 (1) US MC. In general, the PE definition in US treaty policy is narrower than the domestic fiscal nexus since a number of preparatory and auxiliary business activities are per se excluded from US source taxation under Article 5 (4) US MC.[124] With regard to the interpretation of the relevant PE terms, US treaty policy is often based on court decisions so that the application of the PE attributes are basically interpreted case-by-case without a clear and general rule setting.[125] Thus, according to the Technical Explanation of the US MC, a '*fixed place of business*' shall exist if a building or any other physical location is used by the company for the purpose of its own business while it has to be conceivable that this business activity will be permanent and not only temporary. Following administrative guidance of US domestic law, a certain permanence requirement exists which

118. See McDaniel/Ault/Repetti (2005) p. 59.
119. Assets in this context are generally financial assets producing FDAP income or income from capital gains. See McDaniel/Ault/Repetti (2005) p. 59.
120. See Avi-Yonah (2007a) p. 88, McDaniel/Ault/Repetti (2005) pp. 59 ff.
121. See McDaniel/Ault/Repetti (2005) p. 60.
122. See McCaffery et al. (2011) pp. 214 ff.
123. See Bischel/Levin (2005) p. 713.
124. See Penn/Rinke (2014) United States, p. 10.
125. Apart from the US MC and the Technical Explanation, further guidance upon the interpretation of the PE term is found in decisions of US courts as well as in administrative circulars such as general counsel memoranda, private letter rulings, revenue procedure and further regulations by the US Department of Treasury. See Arnold (2009) pp. 668 ff.

considers the provision of business activities in the US of more than twelve months as being sufficient for the establishment of a PE.[126] Furthermore, a certain degree of regularity and intensity of business operations is necessary so that the business activities provided at the fixed place of business indicate that a profit is achieved within the US.[127]

Corresponding national rules with regard to US source income generated by *construction sites* are not provided by US case law. Due to the broader US nexus, it can be concluded that income resulting from construction sites operated in the US are usually effectively connected to a US trade or business so that the non-resident is taxable under US domestic law if certain connecting factors such as a fixed physical presence are given.[128]

According to Article 5 (3) US MC, similar to the OECD MC, installation projects and construction sites constitute a PE if the activities last in the US for at least twelve months. The US treaty explanations are in line with the OECD MC Commentary. According to the Technical Explanation of the US MC, the permanence requirement of twelve months applies to each construction site, and not to each contract.[129] Geographical and commercial coherence of different construction sites is demanded for the application of the permanence test. Working time of a subcontractor is counted effectively as time of the general contractor spent at the construction site.[130] Some US treaties also differ from the US MC with regard to the time window for the permanence test or with regard to the activities included in the construction site PE clause. As an example, according to Article 5 (3a) of the treaty between the US and China, supervisory or planning activities connected with the construction site are explicitly included as PE-constituting activity if the activities performed at source last for more than six months.[131]

With regard to the specific case of the *agency PE*, the US source taxation rules are similar to OECD standards. Under US domestic rules, a dependent agent can constitute a US trade or business and thus a US agency PE if the agent has the authority to conclude contracts over a regular and continuous period of time in the name of the principal or holds a stock of merchandise belonging to the foreign principal and executes orders for him.[132] In general, a dependent agent performs the business activities of the non-resident in the US as a '*domestic surrogate*' and does not '*run his own business*'.[133] The dependent agent status of an employee working in the office of the principal at source is considered as irrelevant as the office itself indicates a basic PE for the principal.[134] In fact, under US domestic law, the differentiation between dependence and independence of the agent is a crucial criterion when deciding about

126. See Ring (2012) p. 35.
127. See Penn/Rinke (2014) United States, p. 9.
128. See Ring (2012) p. 38.
129. See Ring (2012) p. 38.
130. See US MC Technical Explanation (2006) p. 16.
131. See Ring (2012) p. 38.
132. See Karzon (1999) p. 13, McCaffery et al. (2011) p. 196.
133. See Tittle (2007a) pp. 48 ff.
134. See Parada (2013) p. 61.

the existence of an agency PE.[135] According to section 864 (c) (5a) IRC, business activities conducted by an independent agent, such as a commission agent or a broker who act in the ordinary course of their business are not supposed to be US trade or business income of the non-resident principal. US case law therefore provides suggestions on how to identify an independent agent: Possible criteria which have to be checked to identify the status of an agent are the extent of instructions given by the foreign principal, the degree of control over the work of the agent, the number of non-resident principals the agent works for, the bearing of risks as well as whether the remuneration paid is cost-based or market-based according to the arm's length principle.[136] In contrast to the OECD MC, US domestic case law does not provide for any suggestions considering the question of the necessary degree of authority to conclude contracts of the agent in order to constitute a PE for the principal.[137] The reason for that is that the US as a common law country does not differentiate between legal or economic representation. Thus, also an undisclosed principal can generally be bound under US domestic tax rules.[138] Considering the possible PE constitution at the level of subsidiaries established in the US, US national case law has not included such issues yet.[139] Still, if a US subsidiary regularly concludes contracts and performs business activities on behalf of the non-resident parent company, similar to a dependent agent, an agency PE can be established.[140]

The agency PE provision under Article 5 (5) and (6) US MC is again similar to the OECD MC. Thus, also under US *treaty policy* a dependent agent who regularly concludes contracts and performs business activities which bind the foreign principal, constitutes a PE in the US unless the business activities performed are qualified as being preparatory.[141] Under Article 5 (6) US MC, an independent agent who acts in the ordinary course of his business is not being considered to qualify for the establishment of a PE in the US. Also, according to Article 5 (7) US MC, US treaty policy indicates that ownership and the degree of control between affiliated companies is ignored when it comes to the question of the existence of a PE by one of the companies. With regard to the question of legal or economic authority to conclude contracts, US case law does not provide for any references.[142] Similar to the OECD MC, it is only assumed that the agent has the power to decide and negotiate about key elements of the contract in order to fulfil a necessary degree of authority.[143]

135. See Tittle (2007b) p. 600 & pp. 605 ff. for more details.
136. See Penn/Rinke (2014) United States, No. 51 f., p. 14.
137. See Penn/Rinke (2014) United States, No. 57, p. 15.
138. See Holland (2010) p. 36.
139. However, as the US was actively involved in the OECD work regarding the attribution of profits to PE, it can eventually be concluded that they are aware that subsidiaries might also lead to the additional existence of a PE under certain circumstances. See Penn/Rinke (2014) United States, No. 59, p. 16.
140. See McCaffery (2011) p. 196, Tittle (2007a) pp. 53 ff.
141. The Technical Explanation of the US MC refers to the term of 'binding' the enterprise instead of acting 'in the name of' the enterprise. See US MC Technical Explanation (2006) p. 17.
142. See Penn/Rinke (2014) United States, p. 15.
143. See Arnold (2009) p. 683.

Foreign *service* providers have to derive business income from services that are effectively connected with a US trade or business in order to establish a US taxing right. Especially the performance of personal services qualifies as US trade or business according to section 864 (b) of the IRC.[144] Therefore, if a non-resident person such as a consultant, performs professional services in the US for a US person, basically just for one day, he earns income which is effectively connected with a US trade or business according to section 864 (b) IRC and is taxable in the US.[145] That can also hold for corporations if the corporate income is derived from the personal service performed by the professional.[146] This also holds for services provided in the US by non-independent employees of a foreign enterprise.[147] With regard to the secondment of employees, US case law indicates that the secondment of entertainers providing acting services at a US corporation does not establish a US PE for the non-resident workforce-lending company as the employees effectively work for the US company being present in the US.[148] In this case, the establishment of a PE of the workforce-lending company through secondment of employees depends on factors such as control over the business activities provided in the US and the bearing of risk and responsibility for the services performed by the seconded employees.[149]

Again similar to the OECD MC, a service PE is not included in the US MC and is usually not part of US *treaty policy* as well. Thus, for a non-resident, in order to constitute a PE by providing services on US ground to US persons, a fixed place of business, such as an own office, usually has to be established, thereby following Article 5 (1) of the US MC. In general, this is also confirmed by US case law. According to US revenue ruling 77-45, a Canadian corporation conducting planning and design services at the premises of a US customer was found not to have a PE since it did not have a fixed place of business under Article 5 (1) US MC.[150]

However, especially in US tax treaties with developing countries, deviations from the general US MC are possible which allow the creation of a service PE and thus a taxing right at source also without a fixed place of business, thereby only requiring a certain permanence of the relevant service-providing people in the source country.[151]

144. See Manolakas/Brown (2008) p. 34.
145. See Bischel/Levin (2005) pp. 715 ff.
146. See Vacovec/James/Hoiberg (2001) p. 405. In general, income from personal services rendered by a non-resident alien are not taxed in the US if three conditions are fulfilled according to section 864 (b) IRC: (1) The compensation is lower than USD 3000, (2) The US presence of the service provider is lower than ninety days, (3) The services are rendered for either a foreign party not 'engaged in US trade or business' or a foreign place of business of a US. See Bischel/Levin (2012) p. 723.
147. See West/Varma (2012) p. 188. There is also another opinion which states that the fixed physical presence test additionally has to be fulfilled in order for personal services provided by employees to be taxable in the US. See McCaffery (2011) p. 186.
148. See Arnold (2009) p. 678.
149. See Arnold (2009) p. 677.
150. See Arnold (2009) pp. 672 ff. In another outbound case, a US citizen who was performing services in Canada at his customer's office also did not establish a PE in Canada since he had a too small degree of control over the premises of his Canadian client. See Boidman (2000) pp. 339 f., Cockfield (2009) p. 378.
151. See Penn/Rinke (2014) United States, p. 11. See Appendix, Table A2 for US tax treaties including a service PE provision in the respective PE article.

One exceptional example involving a developed country is Article 5 (9) of the tax treaty between the US and Canada which includes a special rule with regard to the possible establishment of a service PE in the source country in case of services performed abroad.[152] According to this provision, a service PE is established at source either if a service-providing company performs services in the other state '*by an individual who is present in that state for a period (...) aggregating 183 days or more in any twelve-month period and, during that period (...), more than 50% of the gross active business revenues of the enterprise consists of income derived from*' that services or, second, if services are rendered for the same time period of 183 days '*with respect to the same or connected project*' for resident customers. However, this provision is only valid if other paragraphs of Article 5 of the US-Canadian Tax Treaty do not apply, such as the general paragraphs of Article 5 (1), Article 5 (3) or Article 5 (5).[153] Considering the significance of other articles of the US MC as fiscal nexus for the provision of cross-border services such as the royalty-article, US tax treaty policy is rather restricted and usually does not include the provision of services in there.[154] With regard to the secondment of employees, US treaty law obviously follows the OECD MC: As long as the seconded employees are under the direction, responsibility and control of the lessee of work, no PE is established for the workforce-lending company.[155]

In summary, the US fiscal nexus in domestic law uses the '*effectively connected income*' approach which is generally wider than the OECD PE concept (see Table 4.4). US treaty law is based on the US MC which is principally in line with the OECD MC with regard to the PE definition and interpretation.

Table 4.4 US PE Concept

	National Law	*Treaty Law*
Basic PE	- '*Effectively connected US income*' - approach - Case law based: considerable, continuous, regular activities	- Similar to OECD MC - Case law based: permanence requirement of twelve months
Construction site PE	No specific rules	- Similar to OECD MC - Reduced permanence threshold in some cases
Agency PE	Similar to OECD MC	Similar to OECD MC

152. This service PE provision is actually very similar to the OECD service PE proposal mentioned in section 3.2.3.1 above. See for an overview on differences i.a. Tittle (2007a) pp. 210 f., Arnold (2008a) pp. 191 f., Wilkie (2012) pp. 182 ff.
153. See Arnold (2008a) p. 191.
154. See US MC Technical Explanation (2006) p. 43. See Appendix, Table A2 for US tax treaties including services in the royalty-article.
155. See Bischel/Levin (2012) pp. 731 ff.

	National Law	*Treaty Law*
Service PE	- Specific *'personal services'* - rule indicates fiscal nexus	- Not included in US MC - Included in casual treaties mostly with developing countries

4.2.2.2 Attribution of Profits between Foreign Head Office and Domestic PE

US tax law does not include rules on the allocation of business profits between head office and PE similar to the OECD MC. Instead, it focuses on the fact whether income is qualified as US source or foreign income.[156] If income is US-based, a limited force of attraction principle holds for trade or business conducted in the US: All US source income independent of any factual connection is considered as being effectively connected to the US trade or business.[157] An exception to this force of attraction rule applies to passive investment income, such as interest, dividends, royalties, rents or leasing payments, so-called fixed or determinable, annual or periodical income (FDAP income) which generally stands on its own. Thus, basically two income categories exist under US national law: Business income effectively connected (ECI) to US trade or business, and business income not effectively connected to US trade or business which includes FDAP income.[158] Income which is neither ECI nor FDAP is not subject to US source taxation.[159] The major difference between ECI and FDAP income is related to the tax base and the tax rate applied. Whereas ECI is taxed at the regular US personal or corporate tax rate on a net basis including the deduction of certain expenses, FDAP income is taxed at a flat fixed rate of 30% on a gross basis.[160] Thus, under US domestic law, the major requirement of attribution of profits to a US PE is to identify income which is effectively connected to a US trade or business. According to section 864(c) (2) IRC, this is done by applying the two tests mentioned above in relation to the US PE definition, the asset-use and the business-activities test.[161] After having identified the effectively connected income, the next step is to determine deductible expenses as ECI is taxed on a net basis.[162] In general, expenses are allocated according to the direct method similar to the OECD approach.[163] In comparison to the OECD rules, an

156. See Ring (2012) p. 61.
157. See Djanani/Brähler/Lösel (2005) p. 70. See above section 4.2.2.1 for criteria of US 'effectively connected income'.
158. See for an overview Djanani/Brähler/Lösel (2005) p. 70.
159. See Ring (2012) p. 58.
160. See Ring (2012) p. 58.
161. See in detail above section 4.2.2.1.
162. See Ring (2012) p. 62.
163. Exceptions exist in the insurance and banking industry as well as for specific R&D companies which apply an indirect allocation mechanism following a formula apportionment. See Hannes (2006) p. 694, Penn/Rinke (2014) United States, p. 18.

allocation of functions, assets, risk and capital does not exist under US national law. In addition, internal dealings between foreign head office and US PE are generally not recognized for tax purposes.[164]

US *treaty policy* includes a business profits-article (Article 7 US MC) which is built up similar to the '*old*' view of the OECD MC.[165] According to Article 7 (2) US MC, those profits shall be attributed to a US PE under Article 7 (1) US MC it '*might be expected to make if it were a distinct and independent enterprise engaged in the same or similar activities under the same or similar conditions*'. In this sense, the allocation of profits has to be based on activities performed, assets used and risks assumed by the US PE which is basically consistent with the OECD theory of treating the PE as a fictitious separate legal entity for tax purposes.[166] It can also be argued that this provision is similar to the asset-use and business-activities test of US domestic law.[167] The regular US court view states that the PE book accounts are used as a starting point for the determination of US income. Still, if these book accounts are not in line with the functional analysis under treaty law, they will not be considered anymore.[168] According to the Technical Explanation of the US MC, the taxpayer is allowed to choose between the national allocation ECI concept and the US MC approach depending on which method generates the lowest tax burden for the taxpayer. The chosen method has to be applied consistently.[169] In fact, two US court decisions exist in the finance and insurance industry from which it can be derived to follow the respective tax treaty regulations and to consider the PE as separate legal entity instead of applying a complex formula approach given for the finance sector under US domestic law.[170] Therefore, US case law confirms the application of the arm's length principle in US domestic law by comparing PE book records with '*evidence from the marketplace*' which excludes '*extraneous data that do not reflect the real facts*'.[171]

In principle, it can be concluded that US treaty law accepts the AOA and the allocation of profits to the PE based on functions, assets and risk, especially as differentiation to the US domestic force of attraction principle under the ECI concept.[172] Still, the Technical Explanation of the US MC does not explicitly refer to '*significant people functions*' and does not include any detailed explanations on how to implement

164. See Ring (2012) p. 62.
165. In this work, only Para. (1) to (3) of Article 7 US MC is presented. Article 7 (4) US MC resembles Article 7 (5) of the 'old' OECD MC, Article 7 (5) resembles Article 7 (6) of the 'old' OECD MC, Article 7 (6) US MC resembles Article 7 (7) of the 'old' OECD MC, Article 7 (7) of the US MC includes a specific US national rule considering the deferred taxation of a US PE in case of termination of PE existence. See US MC Technical Explanation (2006) pp. 26 ff.
166. See Arthur/Herbert/Levey (2014) p. 794.
167. See Gustafson/Peroni/Pugh (2011) pp. 195 ff.
168. See Penn/Rinke (2014) United States, p. 18.
169. See US MC Technical Explanation (2006) p. 22.
170. These are the US court decisions NatWest I (1999) dealing with the question of allocation of interest expenses of a British bank to its US branches and North West Life Assurance (1996) dealing with the issue of allocating income from insurances to its US branches. See Hannes (2006) pp. 702 f., Gustafson/Peroni/Pugh (2011) pp. 197 ff.
171. See Hannes (2006) p. 707.
172. See US MC Technical Explanation (2006) p. 23.

the AOA.[173] According to Article 7 (3) US MC, a PE shall deduct all expenses '*incurred for the purposes of the permanent establishment, including executive and general administrative expenses so incurred, whether in the State in which the permanent establishment is situated or elsewhere*'. In fact, this provision is again similar to the '*old*' Article 7 (3) OECD MC and determines that expenses which occur for the purpose of the PE have to be deductible from PE profits independent of the enterprise's book accounts.[174] Here, it is questionable if those deductions are supposed to include a possible profit element under US treaty law and if internal dealings as under the AOA are considered.[175] The US MC Technical Explanation only mentions that internal dealings may be recognized for tax purposes if the risk of the assets included can be mirrored, especially for internal interest dealings.[176] It seems to be that the US strategy in this case is to implement the AOA with regard to the allocation of functions, assets and risk whereas under most treaties, restrictions with regard to the recognition of internal expenses and the overall implementation of the arm's length principle still exist.[177] Under current US treaty policy, i.a. the tax treaties with Canada, Poland and Belgium explicitly include the AOA in the treaties' explanations.[178]

With regard to the allocation of PE donation capital, the Technical Explanation of the US MC determines that the PE needs '*sufficient capital to carry on its activities as if it were a distinct and separate enterprise*'.[179] The allocation of capital shall be based on a certain risk allocation specified under national US Treasury Regulation section 1.882-5. However, as this regulation is rather complex and inflexible with regard to the degree of risk of the assets belonging to the PE and the head office, a more simplified approach of capital allocation based on a certain ratio of US liabilities is available as well.[180]

In contrast to Article 7 (3) of the OECD MC, US treaties generally refer to Article 23 of the US MC for the relief of double taxation. Thus, according to US treaty policy there is no '*automatic*' relief in case of possible double taxation situations in cross-border PE cases.[181]

173. See Kosters/Offermanns (2013) Chapter 11, p. 280. See for a sceptical view regarding the German-US tax treaty Klein (2009) No. 34, p. 199.
174. See US MC Technical Explanation (2006) pp. 24 ff.
175. See Penn/Rinke (2014) United States, pp. 20 ff.
176. See Kosters/Offermanns (2013) Chapter 11, p. 290.
177. This is also confirmed by a statement of the US Treasury Department from 7 June 2007. See Kosters/Offermanns (2013) Chapter 11, fn. 4, p. 274. US treaties in which the 'functionally separate entity approach' is principally adopted are the ones with the United Kingdom (2004), Japan (2005), Germany (2006), Canada (2007), Bulgaria (2009), Iceland (2009) and Hungary (2010/ not yet in force). However, the fiscal recognition of internal dealings between head office and PE is unclear. See Kosters/Offermanns (2013) Chapter 11, pp. 280 f., Huibregtse et al. (2015), pp. 372 ff. See Appendix, Table A13 for a general overview.
178. See Appendix, Table A13. See for the US treaty with Belgium Parillo (2013) p. 619, Ring (2015) p. 59.
179. See US MC Technical Explanation (2006) p. 24.
180. See Penn/Rinke (2014) United States, p. 21. According to the US Treasury Regulation section 1.882-5(c), the simplified capital allocation approach is based on the determination of US liabilities which is the result of the ratio of US assets divided by worldwide assets multiplied by the worldwide liabilities.
181. See Kosters/Offermanns (2013) Chapter 11, fn. 74, p. 302.

Due to the specific characteristics of the US system of effective connection, specific rules on the attribution of business profits for *special PE cases* such as the construction site, agency or the service PE are not considered under US domestic law.[182]

The allocation of income to special PE cases, such as the construction site, agency or service PE is also not mentioned explicitly in US treaty policy. Thus, it can be concluded that the general explanations under Article 7 US MC should also be relevant. The indirect method similar to Article 7 (4) of the '*old*' OECD MC is not included in the wording of the US MC but can eventually still be applied in accordance with Article 7 (2) US MC.[183]

In summary, similar to the US fiscal nexus, US domestic income allocation rules follow the ECI approach which actually implements a force of attraction principle under US law (see Table 4.5). US treaty policy basically approves the AOA but usually finds restrictions with regard to the recognition of internal dealings including a profit mark-up.

Table 4.5 US Approach of Allocation of Business Profits to PE

National Law	*Treaty Law*
- Allocation of profits according to ECI approach - Domestic force of attraction principle - Internal dealings between head office and PE usually not recognized	- US MC principally based on the '*old*' OECD MC in most treaties - Internal dealings between head office and PE usually not recognized

4.2.3 Brazil

4.2.3.1 Fiscal Nexus under National and Treaty Law

Under Brazilian *national law*, a PE definition similar to the OECD does not exist. According to Article 147 of the Brazilian Corporate Income Tax Regulation '*branches, agencies or representative offices of foreign companies*' as well as '*foreign principals to the extent of sales in Brazil done by their local commissionaire or nominee*' are supposed to be considered as legal entities under Brazilian tax law.[184] In general, non-resident investors need to register at the Brazilian Ministry of Commerce, Industry and Developments in order to conduct business activities in Brazil through a PE. However, the registration process involves high compliance costs as a separate registration is necessary for each single business activity performed including any change of the

182. A reason for this might be that in practice, US case law has not been confronted yet with issues of income allocation to such specific PE cases. See Penn/Rinke (2014) United States, p. 20.
183. See US MC Technical Explanation (2006) p. 23.
184. See De Souza Carvalho (2009) p. 154.

enterprises' by-laws which complicates the establishment of a PE in Brazil.[185] This is why PE cases are rather seldom in Brazilian tax jurisdiction and case law.[186] After the official authorization, the Brazilian branch is treated as resident taxpayer for tax purposes, similar to an independent entity.[187] As the registration rule can be considered as deemed provision, the fulfilment of certain PE criteria is principally not necessary under Brazilian national law.[188] Although it seems that the establishment of a basic PE is not possible under Brazilian national law without a formal registration, old-established Brazilian law provides for a corporate law regulation stating that any legal entity which can be considered as professional or business unit is liable to Brazilian taxation independent of its legal status.[189] A business unit can be defined according to Brazilian civil law as '*complex of assets aligned for conducting business activities*'.[190] However, this concept is not further interpreted and thus lacks concreteness.[191] Therefore, Brazilian business profits are usually taxed on a gross basis with Brazilian withholding taxes or allocated to another Brazilian subsidiary of the foreign investor.[192]

Brazilian *tax treaties* generally follow Article 5 of the OECD MC with specific deviations considering the non-concluding list of PE examples under Article 5 (2) OECD MC.[193] Thus, it can be concluded that tax treaty rules restrict the application of the vague national business unit requirement, especially with regard to the exclusion of auxiliary and preparatory activities according to Article 5 (4) OECD MC. Still, the criterion of registration is also necessary under Brazilian administrative law.

For the special PE case of *construction and installation sites*, Brazilian tax law does not provide for any specific regulations so that it can be concluded that the general registration clause described above is applied.[194]

Brazilian tax treaty policy follows the OECD MC with regard to the establishment of construction site PEs under Article 5 (3) OECD MC. However, the qualifying time threshold is reduced to six months in most treaties.[195] Due to the lack of Brazilian PE cases, no information is given with regard to further requirements of a construction site PE or the interpretation of special cases such as the delegation of work to subcontractors.[196]

185. See De Souza Carvalho (2009) p. 156
186. See Xavier (2006) p. 200.
187. See Zapata/Weiss/Ibarra/Martins (2012) p. 23, Bellaver/Wobeto (2015) p. 621.
188. See De Souza Carvalho (2009) p. 156.
189. See Zapata/Weiss/Ibarra/Martins (2012) p. 23.
190. See Zapata/Weiss/Ibarra/Martins (2012) p. 23.
191. In fact, one of the rare Brazilian national rules in which the PE term is explicitly included considers the World Cup 2014 in Brazil. Respective FIFA institutions located temporally in Brazil for the purpose of organization are not supposed to constitute a PE under Brazilian national law. See Rocha (2013) p. 444.
192. See De Carvalho/Bechara (2014) p. 160.
193. See Zapata/Weiss/Ibarra/Martins (2012) p. 24.
194. See Zapata/Weiss/Ibarra/Martins (2012) p. 24. There is only a definition of a construction site with regard to social security issues of involved which, however, does not include any details with regard to specific construction site PE requirements. See De Souza Carvalho (2009) pp. 159 ff.
195. See Zapata/Weiss/Ibarra/Martins (2012) pp. 24 ff.
196. See De Souza Carvalho (2009) p. 157.

With regard to the concept of an *agency PE*, two provisions exist which deal with the treatment of business income derived from activities performed by agents in Brazil: Article 398 in accordance with Article 147 of the Brazilian Corporate Tax Regulations which consider the activities of commissionaires (*commissários*), as well as Article 399 in accordance with Article 539 of the Brazilian Corporate Tax Regulations which especially consider sales activities conducted in Brazil by representatives including other agents (*mandatários*) working for foreign principals.[197]

According to Article 398 of the Brazilian Corporate Tax Regulations, *commissários* which are bound by instructions of the foreign principal but work in their own name and for the account of the principal constitute an agency PE in case they perform merchandise and sales activities in Brazil.[198] However, other business activities such as the provision of services are excluded from the establishment of an agency PE.[199] In contrast to OECD provisions, the PE requirement of habitually concluding contracts is irrelevant for the commissionaire agent.[200] Furthermore, there is no differentiation between PE-constituting dependent agents and PE-excluding independent agents for tax purposes.[201] Article 399 in accordance with Article 539 of the Brazilian Corporate Tax Regulations determine that sales activities conducted by representatives (*mandatários*) who have the power to regularly bind the principal, establish a Brazilian agency PE for the non-resident principal. In this case a certain degree of habitualness and regular practice is necessary in order to constitute a Brazilian agency PE based on sales activities by mere representatives.[202] In case the representative is used as intermediate entity forwarding orders of the principal, an agency PE is not established.[203] In general, both provisions of Brazilian national law focus on sales activities as PE-constituting activity whereas in contrast to a mere representative, a commissionaire is able to establish an agency PE even in case of only occasionally performed sales activities.[204] There is no further information with regard to the degree of authority to conclude contracts of the agent. Brazilian case law only states that the principal is not legally bound solely by being the 100% shareholder of the agent, i.e., a subsidiary. Instead, a certain level of selling activities by the agent has to exist in order to establish an agency PE.[205]

Brazilian *tax treaty policy* is in line with OECD practice following Article 5 (5) and Article 5 (6) of the OECD MC. Many Brazilian tax treaties explicitly exclude purchase or merchandise activities as preparatory activities from the establishment of an agency PE instead of referring in general to all auxiliary activities of Article 5 (4) OECD MC, as most treaties are based on the old version of the OECD MC of 1963.[206] In comparison

197. See Rocha (2013) p. 444.
198. See Zapata/Weiss/Ibarra/Martins (2012) p. 26.
199. See Rocha (2013) p. 445.
200. See De Carvalho/Bechara (2014) p. 164.
201. See Zapata/Weiss/Ibarra/Martins (2012) p. 26.
202. See Rocha (2013) p. 446.
203. See Zapata/Weiss/Ibarra/Martins (2012) p. 51.
204. See De Souza Carvalho (2009) p. 156.
205. See De Souza Carvalho (2009) p. 161.
206. See De Souza Carvalho (2009) p. 159.

to domestic law, Brazilian treaty policy narrows the domestic agency PE definition by the additional criterion of habitualness at least with respect to commissionaires (*commissários*) under Article 147 (3) of the Brazilian Corporate Tax Regulations and the differentiation between dependent and independent agents which is irrelevant for Brazilian domestic tax purposes.[207] Then again, the Brazilian tax treaty definition of the agency PE provides a wider scope as in contrast to national law, not only sales activities are able to establish an agency PE on tax treaty level.[208]

With regard to the establishment of a *service PE* under Brazilian national law, it can be concluded that the same registration requirements exist as for the basic PE case. In general, income earned from the provision of service activities in Brazil is related to the Brazilian beneficiary of services so that a withholding tax is levied on those service fees.[209] However, a PE might also be constituted in case of a non-registered service activity performed in Brazil if those service activities are considered as business unit.[210] Still, due to a lack of a clear interpretation of a business unit, the PE threshold under Brazilian national law is rather vague and unclear. In case the foreign service provider actively registers the service activity as a Brazilian branch under Article 147 of the Brazilian Corporate Tax Regulations, a PE is usually deemed to exist. If services are provided at third party premises, business profits are subject to Brazilian withholding taxes or allocated to the Brazilian entity and taxed as such if the place of service is a related entity of the foreign service provider.[211] Regulations considering the agency PE especially focus on the performance of sales activities and can thus be excluded from the service PE sphere. The treatment of service income derived from the secondment of employees to Brazil is not mentioned in Brazilian domestic law.

In Brazilian *treaty law*, the service PE is usually not included.[212] In general, Brazil disapproves the service PE alternative as described in the OECD MC Commentary.[213] Only the tax treaty with China includes a service PE provision similar to Article 5 (3b) of the UN MC stating that a service PE is established in case a foreign service provider renders services at source for a period of more than six months.[214] When it comes to the service PE issue, the Brazilian tax jurisdiction has its own interpretation of dealing with income from services earned by non-resident investors. According to a Brazilian ruling issued under the Normative Declaratory in the year 2000, income from technical services earned in Brazil '*without the transfer of technology*' is not supposed to be business income under Article 7 OECD MC but is deemed to be classified as '*other income*' similar to Article 21 of the UN MC.[215] Under Brazilian treaty law, in contrast to

207. See Rocha (2013) pp. 448 ff. Still, there is a differentiation between independent distributors and dependent agents under Article 710 of the Brazilian Civil Code.
208. See Rocha (2013) p. 448.
209. See Rocha (2012) p. 160.
210. See Zapata/Weiss/Ibarra/Martins (2012) p. 23.
211. See De Carvalho/Bechara (2014) p. 162.
212. See Appendix, Table A3.
213. See OECD MC Commentary (2014) Positions on Article 5 and its Commentary, No. 42, p. 463.
214. See Zapata/Weiss/Ibarra/Martins (2012) p. 25.
215. See Sheppard (2011) p. 13.

the OECD MC, the other income-article provides for a taxing right for both, source and residence state.[216] Income from services earned by a non-resident in Brazil is generally taxed on a gross basis with the respective Brazilian withholding tax. Thus, Brazilian treaty law finds another solution of taxing income from services provided by a non-resident without the establishment of a fixed place of business in Brazil.[217] However, considering a judgment of the Second Chamber of Brazil's Superior Court of Justice dated from May 2012, the special Brazilian way of allocating income from technical services to the other income-article is challenged and rejected. The Superior Court of Justice decided that income from services rendered to the Brazilian petroleum company *Companhia Petroquímica do Sul (COPESUL)* by foreign service providers being resident in Canada and Germany is qualified as business income under Article 7 of the respective Brazilian tax treaty.[218] This rejects the application of the Brazilian withholding tax regime for income from technical services as decided in 2000.[219] Still, the '*old*' guidance with regard to the Brazilian way of allocating income from services is in charge.[220] Business profits derived from services provided by seconded employees are generally considered as service income being taxable as other income on a gross basis similar to Article 21 UN MC.[221] A further statement of the Brazilian Federal Revenue Office in 2014 indicates that regardless of the criterion of '*transfer of technology*' all income from services have to be taxed under the royalty-article. Alternatively, the independent personal services-article which was deleted from the OECD MC but is still used in most Brazilian tax treaties can provide for a Brazilian source taxation right.[222] Thus, the PE concept is still less relevant for the taxation of services provided in Brazil.

In summary, the Brazilian PE concept lacks concreteness. This is probably due to the rare occurrence of the PE in tax practice. Only after an official registration process, the Brazilian PE is considered as separate legal entity for tax purposes (see Table 4.6). Brazilian treaty law is generally based on the OECD MC whereas a special interpretation exists with regard to the business income of services provided in Brazil.

216. See Rocha (2012) p. 163, Ferreira (2014) p. 427.
217. This view of the Brazilian tax authorities is actually criticized a lot and might be one of the reasons why e.g. Germany terminated the Brazilian-German Tax Treaty in 2005. See Dagnese (2006) pp. 195 ff.
218. See Schoueri/Barbosa (2013) p. 109.
219. See Soares da Silva (2012) p. 515.
220. In December 2013, the Brazilian National Treasury Attorney's General Office (*Procuradoria Geral da Fazenda Nacional* (PGFN)) published an opinion which confirms the COPESUL decision. Still, the tax authorities' established opinion is valid and guiding. See Kamath (2014a) p. 772, Ferreira (2014) pp. 430 ff.
221. See Rocha (2012) p. 166, De Carvalho/Bechara (2014) pp. 165 ff.
222. See Ferreira (2015) pp. 256 ff. Recent Brazilian case law related to the tax treaty between Brazil and the Netherlands indicates that services which were provided without additional transfer of know-how should be considered as business income. See Furtado/Verboom/Lütter (2015) p. 561. Still, it is not known if this policy will hold in general.

Table 4.6 Brazilian PE Concept

	National Law	*Treaty Law*
Basic PE	- PE considered as separate legal entity - Official registration process necessary	- Similar to OECD MC - Official registration process necessary
Construction site PE	No specific rules	- Similar to OECD MC - Reduced permanence threshold of six months
Agency PE	Two domestic concepts: *commissários* and *mandatários*	Similar to OECD MC
Service PE	- No specific rules - Official registration process necessary	- Usually not included - Article 21 UN MC as alternative fiscal nexus - Article 12 UN MC or Article 14 of the '*old*' OECD MC as further fiscal nexus

4.2.3.2 Attribution of Profits between Foreign Head Office and Domestic PE

Under Brazilian *domestic law*, an official registration is a basic requirement for a PE to be considered for tax purposes. In case of a successful registration, a PE is taxed similar to resident corporate entities.[223] Branches, agencies or representative offices under Article 147 (2) of the Brazilian Corporate Tax Regulations need to hold own accounts being in accordance with generally accepted accounting principles so that the income which is earned from business activities performed in Brazil can be determined.[224] Income of the foreign head office which is effectively connected to the Brazilian PE is not considered.[225] Only the profits earned from business activities which are performed directly by the PE in Brazil have to be allocated to it.[226] Still, Brazilian income attribution rules do not follow a force of attraction principle which means that not all income of Brazilian domestic source is attributed to the PE.[227] This is in line with the deduction of expenses from PE income: All expenses which are incurred by the Brazilian PE including depreciation of assets are deductible for tax purposes. This principle of territoriality excludes expenses of the foreign head office incurred on behalf of the domestic PE.[228] If adequate book accounts are not given, a sort of estimation procedure exists which determines the PE income based on fixed percentage amounts

223. See Xavier (2006) p. 201.
224. See Borges/Monguilod (2005) p. 96.
225. See Zapata/Weiss/Ibarra/Martins (2012) p. 52.
226. See De Carvalho/Bechara (2014) p. 168.
227. See Zapata/Weiss/Ibarra/Martins (2012) p. 34.
228. See Xavier (2006) p. 201.

of certain PE activities.[229] In theory, the same income allocation rules are valid for non-residents which provide business activities in Brazil in form of a non-registered business unit. However, it can be expected that due to missing registration this income will be treated as Brazilian source income taxed on a gross basis with Brazilian withholding taxes.[230]

Rules for the attribution of functions, assets, risk or capital to the basic PE similar to the AOA do not exist under Brazilian national law. The assets which are physically present in Brazil and used there are also allocated to the PE. As Brazilian tax law considers a PE as legal entity for tax purposes, intra-company dealings between PE and foreign head office should generally be recognized and valued according to the Brazilian transfer pricing rules.[231] An internal transfer of assets and the provision of services should thus be recognized at an arm's length price in accordance with the Brazilian transfer pricing rules for associated companies.[232] An exception applies to internal royalties which are only deductible from Brazilian income under conditions of registration and approval by the Brazilian Patent Office and the Brazilian Central Bank.[233] In addition, the deduction of internal royalties is limited to 5% of the net income earned from the sale of the product for which royalties are paid.[234] A similar limitation applies to technical, scientific and administrative services provided by the non-resident head office at the premises of the Brazilian PE. These service expenses are only deductible from PE income under conditions of approval by the Brazilian Patent Office and registration at the Brazilian Central Bank.[235] It is questionable if these rules also apply for deemed internal royalties as established by the AOA.[236]

Internal interest dealings between the Brazilian PE and the non-resident head office are recognized for tax purposes under Brazilian national law. Until 2012, the internal transfer of funds had to be registered at the Brazilian Central Bank being in charge of determining the amount of deductible interest. If the loan agreement was not registered the interest amount was limited respectively set to at least the six months-LIBOR rate plus an annual spread of 3%.[237] According to the new Brazilian Transfer Pricing Rules, the interest amount is equal to the interest of Brazilian government securities traded abroad or equal to the six months-LIBOR rate plus a spread determined by the Brazilian finance minister.[238]

229. See Zapata/Weiss/Ibarra/Martins (2012) p. 34.
230. See Xavier (2006) p. 201.
231. See Zapata/Weiss/Ibarra/Martins (2012) p. 37.
232. See Borges/Monguilod (2005) pp. 99 ff.
233. See Ernst & Young (2014) p. 102, Zapata/Weiss/Ibarra/Martins (2012) p. 38.
234. See Xavier (2006) p. 204. In addition, an old Brazilian tax ruling which is still in force determines that the deduction of internal royalty payments paid from the Brazilian PE to a foreign head office is even totally prohibited. See Zapata/Weiss/Ibarra/Martins (2012) p. 38.
235. See Xavier (2006) p. 204, Soares da Silva (2011) p. 121.
236. See for a negating view Gutiérrez (2013) Chapter 12, p. 322.
237. See Borges/Monguilod (2005) p. 105.
238. See Machado/Lagrasta/Dantas/Verboom/Dols (2013) p. 689.

In general, PE expenses resulting from the internal provision of intangible assets, services and funds provided by the foreign head office to the Brazilian PE are subject to Brazilian withholding tax ranging from 15% to 25%.[239]

The Brazilian transfer pricing rules which are supposed to hold for internal dealings between the PE and the foreign head office include specifications which are different from the OECD Transfer Pricing Guidelines 2010. Transactional profit methods such as the profit-split or the transactional net margin method, as well as any indirect formula apportionment (FA) methods, are denied. Furthermore, considering the use of the cost-plus or the resale price method, Brazilian transfer pricing rules determine fixed percentage amounts of mark-ups on profits instead of comparing the internal transactions to appropriate third party transactions.[240] The fixed margins under the resale price method which were changed in 2013 range from 15% to 40%, depending on certain industry sectors.[241]

Brazilian *tax treaty policy* continues to follow the '*old*' Article 7 of the OECD MC with regard to the allocation of income to a PE.[242] Similar to Brazilian domestic law, a PE is treated as a fictionally separate entity for tax purposes in accordance with Article 7 (2) of the '*old*' OECD MC. The AOA including the recognition of internal dealings is actually rejected in Brazilian treaty policy.[243] In contrast to Article 7 (3) of the '*old*' OECD MC which determines the deduction of '*expenses which are incurred for the purpose of the PE, including executive and general administrative expenses so incurred, whether in a state in which the PE is situated or elsewhere*', the part '*whether in a state in which the PE is situated or elsewhere*' is usually excluded in Brazilian tax treaties. This is in line with the prohibition under Brazilian domestic law of excluding expenses of the foreign head office incurred on behalf of the domestic PE.[244] Article 7 (4) and Article 7 (6) of the OECD MC which deal with the application of the indirect method of profit allocation to the PE are explicitly excluded in Brazilian tax treaties.[245] Article 7 (7) of the '*old*' OECD MC which allocates income to special articles considering i.a. dividends, interest and royalties (Article 10, 11 & 12 OECD MC), as well as the respective provisions of these articles reallocating income back to Article 7 in case of an effective connection to a PE, are also applied under Brazilian tax treaty policy. Article 7 (3) OECD MC allows the deduction of expenses incurred at PE level and is also usually part of Brazilian tax treaties. Thus, Brazilian treaty policy effectively contradicts with the Brazilian domestic restriction of deductibility of royalty payments from Brazilian PE income.[246]

For *construction site PEs*, special income allocation rules do not exist under Brazilian domestic or treaty law.[247] As Article 7 (4) of the OECD MC is generally not

239. See Borges/Monguilod (2005) pp. 102 ff.
240. See UN Transfer Pricing Practical Manual (2013) No. 10.2.1.2, p. 358.
241. See Dagnese (2013) p. 260.
242. See OECD MC Commentary (2014) Positions on Article 7 and its Commentary, No. 12, p. 467.
243. See Appendix, Table A14.
244. See Zapata/Weiss/Ibarra/Martins (2012) p. 36.
245. See OECD MC Commentary (2014) Positions on the Previous Version of Article 7 and its Commentary, No. 9 & 11, p. 469.
246. See Xavier (2006) pp. 208 ff.
247. See Zapata/Weiss/Ibarra/Martins (2012) p. 35.

included in Brazilian treaties, it can be concluded that the indirect method of profit allocation is rejected in Brazilian tax treaties. Obviously, a functional analysis following Article 7 (2) of the *'old'* OECD MC has to be applied.

As the income allocation to a Brazilian *agency PE* is limited to sales activities, the taxable PE income of the foreign principal for a Brazilian commissionaire (*commissário*) according to Article 398 of the Brazilian Corporate Tax Regulations amounts to the difference between the sales price of the goods sold in Brazil minus the expenses of the importation of the products to be sold including the remuneration paid to the agent.[248] Expenses of the principal before the importation, e.g., shipping expenses are not supposed to be deductible from the agency PE income.[249] With regard to representative agents according to Article 399 and Article 539 of the Brazilian Corporate Tax Regulations (*mandatários*), special income allocation rules exist which determine the taxable income of the local representative on the basis of fixed percentage amounts of the gross revenue earned, ranging from 1.92% to 38.40% plus a fixed profit amount of 20%, 30% or 40%, depending on the industry sector.[250]

Income allocation to an agency PE in Brazilian tax treaties generally follows the OECD approach. Still, it is questionable if sole sales activities of the agent (which according to Brazilian domestic view are the only activities being able to constitute an agency PE) generate an adequate degree of significant people functions in order to establish an economic ownership upon the assets sold and thus additional taxable agency PE income in accordance with the AOA.[251] In addition, the fixed percentage amounts of 20%-40% added to the deemed profit of an agency PE under Brazilian domestic law are not in line with OECD regulations.

With regard to the income allocation to *service PEs*, special rules under Brazilian national law do not exist. As the Brazilian *'way'* of recognizing income from services provided by non-residents in Brazil is based on regular source rules, the gross service income will generally be taxable without granting deductibility of any expenses.[252]

As service PEs are usually not included in Brazilian treaties, specific rules upon the allocation of income are neither. Due to the fact that the Brazilian tax authorities treat income from the provision of services as other income following Article 21 of the UN MC (or alternatively Article 12 (2) UN MC) which, in contrast to the OECD MC, grants a taxing right for the source country, Brazilian withholding taxes are levied on service income on a gross basis.

In summary, Brazilian domestic law is based on the separate legal entity approach with regard to the allocation of business profits to a Brazilian PE requiring adequate book accounts (see Table 4.7). Brazilian treaty law basically follows the *'old view'* of the OECD MC and rejects the AOA.

248. See Rocha (2013) p. 445, De Carvalho/Bechara (2014) p. 169.
249. See Zapata/Weiss/Ibarra/Martins (2012) p. 35.
250. See Zapata/Weiss/Ibarra/Martins (2012) p. 35, Machado et al. (2013) p. 690.
251. See e.g. OECD Report on the Attribution of Profits to PE (2008) Part I, No. 269, p. 67.
252. See Borges/Monguilod (2005) p. 94.

Table 4.7 Brazilian Approach of Allocation of Business Profits to PE

National Law	*Treaty Law*
- Allocation of profits similar to resident corporate entities - Adequate PE book accounts required - Internal dealings between head office and PE usually recognized - Still uncertainty about recognition of deemed internal dealings - Domestic limitation of deduction of PE royalty and service expense - Fixed deemed profit mark-ups	- Income allocation principally based on the '*old*' OECD MC - Rejection of the AOA - Internal dealings between head office and PE usually not recognized

4.2.4 Russia

4.2.4.1 Fiscal Nexus under National and Treaty Law

Russian *national law* contains an own PE concept which shows similarities to the OECD definition. The Russian Tax Code defines a PE as a '*branch, representative office, division, bureau, agency or any other separate subdivision or other place of activity of such foreign company through which the foreign company regularly conducts business activities in Russia*'.[253] Further, Russian national rules list PE-constituting examples which are wider than the OECD definition including the use of subsoil or other natural resources, construction, installation, montage or assembly, servicing and use of equipment, sales of inventory from Russian warehouses and performance of work, rendering of services or conducting any activity which is not preparatory or auxiliary.[254] Similar to Article 5 (2) OECD MC, this list is supposed to be non-exhaustive.[255] In contrast to the OECD MC, Russian tax law uses the wording of a separate subdivision which is existent if at least one working place is established in Russia.[256] A fixed place of business is actually not defined which offers room for interpretation with regard to the establishment of a Russian separate subdivision. What is defined, is a sort of duration criterion: Business activities which in total last more than thirty days are required to be officially registered in Russia implying the fulfilment of a duration requirement for a Russian PE.[257] Thus, the permanence threshold for Russian PEs is much shorter in comparison to the six months proposed by the OECD MC Commentary. In addition, the domestic Russian PE definition does not include explicit

253. See Konnov/Smirnov/Smith (2012) p. 19.
254. See Filinov et al. (2014) Russia, p. 18.
255. See Bruk/Konnov (2009) p. 541.
256. See Filinov et al. (2014) Russia, pp. 18 ff.
257. See Bruk/Konnov (2009) p. 541. See for details of the Russian registration process Wiesmann/Gerstner/Nast (2013) pp. 106 ff.

regulations considering the requirement of disposal over the place of business.[258] A pure legal right to use the place is not decisive for the existence of a place of business. The requirement of disposal is only mentioned in the context of private offices of employees which are supposed to be beyond the control of the foreign employer and thus do not constitute a Russian PE. However, a concrete interpretation of disposal is not given.[259] For PE-excluding preparatory and auxiliary activities, a non-exhaustive list similar to Article 5 (4) OECD MC exists under Russian national tax law. In comparison to the OECD MC, this list additionally designates marketing and advertising activities as being preparatory and thus not being able to establish a PE in Russia.[260] To qualify as being preparatory, the business activities have to support internal processes and should not be provided to third parties.[261] Still, a more concrete definition of preparatory activities is not included in Russian domestic law.[262]

The PE definition of the Russian tax *treaty policy* generally follows Article 5 of the OECD MC.[263] This is also approved in the Russian Government Resolution of 24 February 2010 in which Russia adopted an own Russian Model Tax Convention as a basis for future treaty negotiations.[264]

For a *construction site PE*, more detailed instructions are included in Russian national tax law. Business activities which can establish a construction site PE according to Russian rules especially involve working at sites where the focus is on constructing, expanding, repairing or installing real property or other constructions including equipment or machinery fixed on the basement.[265] Under Russian domestic rules, a construction site PE is established from the first day on so that the permanence requirement is, in fact, not existent unless there are different provisions under the construction site PE rule of a valid Russian tax treaty.[266] Working time spent in Russia by subcontractors or any affiliates of the general contractor, no matter whether the affiliate works under the direction and guidance of the general contractor or the customer demanding the construction, is considered as working time of the general contractor spent at the construction site.[267] In addition, there are diverging Russian court decisions with regard to the total delegation of work to subcontractors without any physical presence of the general contractor in Russia. In the *Stora Enso* case, Russian tax courts decided that Stora Enso had no PE in Russia in case it subcontracted all lumber service work to other non-resident companies with Russian PEs without itself establishing a fixed place of business in Russia.[268] However, in another Russian court decision, *Velmont Enterprises*, it was decided that a Cypriot company which

258. See Bruk/Konnov (2009) p. 544.
259. See Konnov/Smirnov/Smith (2012) p. 19.
260. See Bruk/Konnov (2009) p. 549.
261. See Filinov et al. (2014) Russia, pp. 20 ff.
262. See Bruk/Konnov (2009) p. 549.
263. See Konnov/Smirnov/Smith (2012) p. 20.
264. See Dzhalchinov/Popov (2012) p. 585.
265. See Konnov/Smirnov/Smith (2012) p. 21.
266. See Konnov/Smirnov/Smith (2012) p. 23.
267. See Bruk/Konnov (2009) pp. 547 ff.
268. See Konnov/Smirnov/Smith (2012) p. 24. A further question is if lumber services can be considered as construction site under Russian law.

subcontracted all construction work to a local agricultural company established a PE in Russia.[269] Another distinctive feature of the Russian construction site PE is the beginning and the end of the PE existence. Whereas the PE is deemed to exist from the earlier point in time of the actual start of the work or the formal act of the signature of the transferring contract of the construction site to the general contractor, the PE is supposed to end at the later dates of the two, either when the work is actually completed or the official acceptance protocol is formally signed.[270]

The similarity to the OECD MC is also resembled in the Russian treaty policy considering construction site PEs. In general, a time threshold varying from six to twenty-four months limits the possible establishment of a construction site PE from the first day as ruled under Russian domestic law.[271]

According to Russian national tax rules, an *agency PE* is defined as a person representing the interests of a foreign company, acting in the name of the foreign principal, having and regularly exercising the authority to negotiate important terms or to finally conclude contracts on behalf of the principal so that the foreign principal is legally bound in Russia.[272] An independent agent, such as a broker, commissionaire, or a professional securities market agent is not supposed to constitute a PE as long as he acts in the ordinary course of his business. A PE is also established if the agent fulfils the general PE criteria of the Russian domestic law.[273] Thus, the Russian national rules resemble Article 5 (5) and Article 5 (6) of the OECD MC with regard to the agency PE provision. What is different to the OECD MC, is the fact that a dependent agent is able to establish a PE for the foreign principal solely by activities of negotiating whereas the final contract does not have to be concluded in Russia.[274] Considering the degree of authority, Russian case law usually indicates a legal basis so that the Russian agent has to act legally in the name of the foreign principal.[275] This is in line with the *Grinsley Holdings Limited* case where a Cyprian resident negotiated and prepared contracts by a representative office located in Russia on behalf of a Cyprian and a German company. However, this agent did not have the official authority to legally bind the foreign principals. Although the activities of preparing and negotiating the contract eventually led to the existence of an agency PE in Russia, the Russian federal district court decided that the business activities conducted by the Cyprian agent did not establish an agency PE for the two represented foreign companies under Russian domestic law as the legal representation was missing.[276] Russian tax authorities changed this interpretation recently to be more in line with the OECD MC Commentary determining that the foreign principal can also be bound on an economic basis if the Russian agent acts in his own name but on behalf of the foreign principal.[277] This is shown in the recent case

269. See Williams (2014) p. 108. See also the PE Questionnaire in the Appendix, Table A20.
270. See Dölker (2013a) p. 2269, Filinov et al. (2014) Russia, p. 30.
271. See Konnov/Smirnov/Smith (2012) pp. 24 ff.
272. See Konnov/Smirnov/Smith (2012) p. 31.
273. See Konnov/Smirnov/Smith (2012) p. 31.
274. See Filinov et al. (2014) Russia, p. 27.
275. See Filinov et al. (2014) Russia, pp. 27 ff.
276. See Bruk/Konnov (2009) p. 554.
277. See Konnov/Smirnov/Smith (2012) p. 32. See for another, but older view Bruk/Konnov (2009) p. 554.

of *Fesco Lines Vladivostok* where a Russian limited-liability company provides container fleet management services in Russia for its Cypriot parent.[278] From the perspective of the Russian tax authorities, the Russian company established a dependent agent because it worked under detailed instructions of the parent and concluded contracts only under confirmation of the Cypriot principal although it did not act formally in the name of the Cypriot parent. Thus, the Russian company had the economic authority to conclude contracts for the non-resident principal and constituted an agency PE according to the Russian tax courts.

The definition of an agency PE in Russian *tax treaties* usually follows Article 5 (5) and Article 5 (6) of the OECD MC.[279] Russian tax treaty policy also includes a provision similar to Article 5 (7) OECD MC stating that the fact of a controlled affiliated company does not indicate a PE for the parent company in the country where the affiliate is located.[280]

A *service PE* is principally not existent under Russian national law. Income from services provided by a non-resident to a Russian customer is taxable in Russia if the services are conducted through a PE according to the general domestic definition which includes any kind of place of business located in Russia where the foreign entity performs its business activities.[281] Furthermore, according to the Russian Ministry of Finance, services which are provided on a regular basis at the premises of Russian clients can constitute a PE for the foreign service provider even if the place of business is not at his disposal.[282] Thus, a '*passive*' service PE is possible under Russian domestic tax law. Similar to the OECD MC, the secondment of employees only establishes a PE for the foreign entity if the seconded employees work for the benefit of the foreign workforce-lending company. For reasons of clarification, the Russian tax authorities determine certain characteristics from which it can be recognized if the seconded employee effectively works for the workforce-lending company or the Russian company where he is located. These include factors such as the degree of responsibility for the work of the employees, the method of calculation regarding the service fees (hourly or total) and a fixed mark-up on the employer's costs which may not exceed 10% of the secondment costs.[283] Independent of the fiscal PE requirements, Russian migration policy has to be considered: In fact, the strict Russian migration rules grant a work permit for the seconded employees performing services in Russia only in cases where foreign employees effectively work for the local Russian host entity.[284] This means that employees who are located in Russia but still have a legal working contract with the foreign home entity are not allowed to work in Russia at all.

In contrast to the OECD MC which offers a service PE option in the OECD MC Commentary, Article 5 (4) of the Russian MC especially includes a service PE provision in the text itself. With regard to content, this provision is identical to the service PE

278. See Konnov/Smirnova/Smith (2015) p. 31.
279. See Konnov/Smirnov/Smith (2012) p. 31.
280. See Filinov et al. (2014) Russia, p. 30.
281. See Dzhalchinov/Popov (2012) p. 583.
282. See Filinov et al. (2014) Russia, p. 26.
283. See Dzhalchinov/Popov (2012) p. 584.
284. See Vasutin (2013) p. 1.

alternative of the OECD MC: According to this rule, a service PE is established in Russia in case an individual provides services in Russia for more than 183 days in any 12-month period, and more than 50% of the gross income can be allocated to the service provided in Russia, or the services are rendered in Russia for more than 183 days within any 12-month period by several individuals as part of one or more connected projects.[285] Only the amended protocols of the tax treaties between Russia and Cyprus as well as between Russia and Luxembourg include this special service PE provision.[286] Otherwise, Russian tax treaties which follow the OECD MC generally do not include a service PE option in the respective PE article. In fact, Russian tax treaty policy also considers the provision of services under the independent personal services-article which relates to the outdated Article 14 of the OECD MC.[287] However, Russian tax treaties which follow the UN MC often include a service PE provision similar to Article 5 (3b) of the UN MC whereas the indicated time threshold varies from three to eighteen months.[288] Considering the secondment of employees, Russian treaty law does not provide for any regulations.[289]

In summary, the Russian domestic PE concept is similar to the OECD MC while the permanence threshold is wider in most cases (see Table 4.8). Russian treaty law and the Russian MC also follow the OECD with the exception of the service PE which is additionally included in the Russian MC.

Table 4.8 Russian PE Concept

	National Law	*Treaty Law*
Basic PE	- Similar to OECD MC - Lower permanence threshold of thirty days	Similar to OECD MC
Construction site PE	- Similar to OECD MC - Permanence requirement non-existent - Begin and end of PE determined by formal signature act	- Similar to OECD MC - Varying permanence threshold of six to twenty-four months
Agency PE	- Similar to OECD MC - Negotiation as indicator for PE status	Similar to OECD MC

285. See Dzhalchinov/Popov (2012) p. 588.
286. See Dzhalchinov/Popov (2012) p. 588.
287. See OECD MC Commentary (2014) Positions on Article 7 and its Commentary, No. 2.1, p. 465.
288. See Dzhalchinov/Popov (2012) p. 587. See Appendix, Table A4 for Russian tax treaties including a service PE.
289. See Dzhalchinov/Popov (2012) p. 589.

	National Law	*Treaty Law*
Service PE	- No specific rules - Passive service PE possible	- Seldom in treaty practice - Included in Russian MC - Identical to OECD MC Commentary

4.2.4.2 Attribution of Profits between Foreign Head Office and Domestic PE

In general, Russian *domestic law* prefers the direct method with regard to the attribution of profits to a PE. According to Article 307 of the Russian Tax Code, the profits shall be attributed to a Russian PE which are *'obtained by a foreign legal entity as a result of activities in Russia through the PE, less deduction of expenses incurred by the PE'*.[290] Similar to a corporation in Russia, a PE is required to adopt documentation records of tax accounting, especially with regard to the expenses deductible from Russian PE income for which special criteria apply such as the economic justification and the relation to an income-generating activity.[291] According to the Russian Methodological Recommendation of 2003, profits and expenses are supposed to be attributable to the PE if they are directly linked to the Russian PE activities, e.g., from the use of fixed assets by the PE, from the creation of intellectual property by the PE or from services performed by PE personnel.[292] Assets which are not acquired directly by the PE can be recognized at PE level if the asset is transferred from the foreign head office to the PE and the PE is the central user of the asset.[293] Similar to the AOA, new Russian Transfer Pricing Rules of 2012 determine that the income allocation to a Russian PE shall be based on the functionally separate entity approach including the consideration of significant people functions, the assets used and the corresponding risk borne.[294] Still, concrete rules with regard to the attribution of functions, assets, risk and capital do not exist under Russian tax law.[295] In addition, it is not clear if the recognition of internal dealings under the AOA also has to be implemented under Russian domestic income attribution rules.[296] Internal transfers of assets as well as the provision of internal services or loans generally have not been recognized for tax purposes due to

290. See Matchekhin/Vakhitov (2006) p. 547.
291. See Gutiérrez (2013) Chapter 12, p. 329. According to a Russian Guidance Letter published on 27 September 2013, Russian thin capitalization rules shall not apply for the deduction of interest expenses from Russian PE income. See Lungu (2013) p. 33.
292. See Matchekhin/Vakhitov (2006) p. 548. General expenses occurring at the level of the foreign head office for the benefit of the Russian PE are only deductible if explicitly provided by tax authority guidance. See Gutiérrez (2013) Chapter 12, p. 330.
293. See Gutiérrez (2013) Chapter 12, p. 330.
294. See Filinov et al. (2014) Russia, p. 33.
295. See Gotovtseva/Inozemtseva (2012) p. 458, Gutiérrez (2013) Chapter 12, p. 330.
296. See Matchekhin (2014) p. 618 who states that a clear guidance with respect to the taxation of attribution of income between PE and head office is not given in Russian domestic law.

the Russian consideration of the head office and PE as one legal entity.[297] However, it is questionable if this is still valid under the new Russian Transfer Pricing Rules of 2012.[298] If the Russian PE provides preparatory or auxiliary services to other companies except for the head office free of charge, the taxable PE income is deemed to be 20% of expenses allocated to the PE activity in order to avoid a minor Russian tax base in this case.[299]

The allocation of income under Russian *tax treaties* is generally in line with the OECD MC standard.[300] Most of the Russian tax treaties and the Russian MC include the '*old*' composition of Article 7 of the OECD MC.[301] Income is allocated to a Russian PE based on the amount it might be expected to earn given the fiction that it is a separate and independent enterprise. This also implies that the force of attraction principle with regard to the allocation of profits and expenses is usually not included in most Russian tax treaties. In accordance with the '*old*' Article 7 (3) OECD MC, expenses which occur at the level of the foreign head office for the benefit of the Russian PE, such as general administration or overhead costs, are deductible from the PE tax base if a permission is given in the relevant tax treaty.[302] It can be concluded that most Russian tax treaties currently follow the '*old*' view of income allocation and composition of the business profits-article including only certain aspects of the AOA. Therefore, the recognition of internal dealings as under the AOA is not mentioned in current Russian tax treaty policy. However, as the AOA obviously has been introduced in Russian tax law under the new Russian transfer pricing rules of 2012, it is not yet clear to what extent the Russian tax treaty policy will be amended.

For *special PE cases*, such as the construction site, agency or service PE, there are no special income allocation rules under Russian domestic law.[303]

Considering the allocation of income to special PE cases, Russian tax treaties do not include any specific provisions deviating from the '*old*' OECD MC approach. Similar to the '*old*' Article 7 (4) OECD MC, most Russian tax treaties provide for the usage of the indirect method of profit allocation with regard to construction site PEs. Again it is questionable if the provisions of the AOA introduced in the new Russian transfer pricing rules is applicable to special PE cases such as for the agency and service PE.

In summary, Russian future national and treaty law are supposed to follow the AOA according to the Russian Transfer Pricing Rules of 2012 (see Table 4.9). However, most details of the implementation of the AOA are unclear. Existing Russian tax treaties and the Russian MC are still based on the '*old*' version of Article 7 OECD MC.

297. See Matchekhin/Vakhitov (2006) p. 546.
298. See Filinov et al. (2014) Russia, p. 39.
299. See Filinov et al. (2014) Russia, p. 33.
300. See Matchekhin/Vakhitov (2006) p. 551.
301. Some also follow the UN MC. See Appendix, Table A15.
302. See Filinov et al. (2014) Russia, p. 36. See Lungu (2011) pp. 790 ff. which deals with a special provision dealing with the deduction of foreign expenses under the US-Russian tax treaty.
303. See Konnov/Smirnov/Smith (2012) p. 40.

Table 4.9 Russian Approach of Allocation of Business Profits to PE

National Law	*Treaty Law*
- Principle of direct economic connection - Documentation records necessary - Internal dealings between head office and PE usually not recognized - New Russian Transfer Pricing Rules 2012: Allocation of profits similar to the AOA - Further course of action unclear	- Income allocation principally based on the '*old*' OECD MC in most treaties and in the Russian MC - New Russian Transfer Pricing Rules 2012: Allocation of profits similar to the AOA - Further course of action unclear

4.2.5 India

4.2.5.1 Fiscal Nexus under National and Treaty Law

Indian *national tax law* follows its own approach of fiscal nexus, namely the concept of business connection. This concept is much broader than the OECD PE definition as it is based on the facts and circumstances of each specific case.[304] For Indian transfer pricing purposes, another PE definition similar to the OECD MC exists which is, however, rarely used for other domestic tax purposes.[305] Although Indian tax law includes a definition of the '*business connection*'-term under section 9 (1) (i) of the Indian Finance Act 2002, this definition is specific and resembles the agency PE provision of the OECD MC.[306] More general comments are included in case law of the Indian Supreme Court which states that a certain '*real and intimate*' relation is required between the non-resident investor and the business activity conducted which is decisive for profit-making in India.[307] In addition, a certain degree of continuity has to be fulfilled for the established business connection whereas a fixed time threshold is not mentioned.[308] In comparison to the OECD PE concept, a fixed place of business is not required for the Indian domestic business connection definition.[309] Thus, in practice, any form of business can constitute a PE under Indian domestic law as long as it is a '*real and intimate*' business connection of the non-resident on a continuous basis. With regard to the threshold of permanence, it can be concluded from Indian case law that also several consecutive dealings taking part in India for a short time can indicate the existence of a business connection if a certain '*element of continuity*' is included.[310]

304. See Goradia/Kapila (2009) p. 365.
305. See Rawal (2005) p. 225.
306. See Metha (2012) p. 23.
307. See Metha (2012) p. 24.
308. See Dalal/Shah/Sheth (2014) India, p. 15.
309. See Goradia/Kapila (2009) p. 348.
310. See Goradia/Kapila (2009) p. 350.

The PE definition under Indian tax *treaty policy* is generally based on Article 5 of the UN MC.[311] Similar to the OECD MC, Article 5 (1) of the UN MC also defines a PE as a '*fixed place of business through which the business of an enterprise is wholly or partly carried on*'. Therefore, similar to the OECD MC, the establishment of a PE in Indian tax treaties depends on the fulfilment of the general PE criteria, such as the fixed place of business, the functional carry-out of the business at that place, a permanence threshold and a disposal requirement. In this context, Indian case law considers a '*functional and factual analysis*' of each business activity on a case-by-case basis which indicates the existence of a PE.[312] With regard to the interpretation of the term '*fixed place of business*', India does not provide for official regulations. India explicitly made a reservation towards the geographical and commercial coherence examples of the OECD MC Commentary.[313] According to Indian view, in contrast to the OECD MC, the work of a painter under a series of unrelated contracts for a number of unrelated clients as well as the work of a consultant performing training activities to different employees located in several banks is both considered as one single project for the existence of a fixed place of business in Indian tax treaties.[314] In addition, the mere leasing activity of tangible or intangible assets provided by the non-resident in the source state shall be able to establish a PE according to Indian tax treaty policy.[315] Considering the permanence threshold, Indian case law indicates that obviously a short-time period of up to thirteen days can constitute a fixed place of business in India for the non-resident.[316] Indian tax treaty interpretation of the PE accepts the disposal criterion as decisive requirement and argues that the non-resident shall be able to accomplish a right of '*dominion or control*' over the place of business.[317] Indian case law obviously uses a wider interpretation of the disposal criterion.[318] This is exemplary shown in the *Renoir Consulting Ltd.* case where the Indian tax jurisdiction decided that the provision of services to an Indian customer by a foreign service provider carried out in hotel rooms located in India constitutes a PE for the foreign service provider since the criterion of disposal was supposed to be fulfilled by rendering business activities in third party premises.[319] Indian tax treaty policy has a special opinion with regard to the existence of a warehouse in the source state from where goods are delivered to Indian costumers. This is also indicated by reservations of India in the OECD MC Commentary stating that a warehouse shall be included in the non-exhaustive PE list of Article 5 (2) OECD MC and that the delivery of goods shall be explicitly excluded from the preparatory activities of Article 5 (4) OECD MC.[320] This view is consistent with Indian

311. See Dalal/Shah/Shet (2014) India, p. 16.
312. See Dalal/Shah/Sheth (2014) India, pp. 16 ff.
313. See OECD MC Commentary (2014) Article 5, No. 5.3 & 5.4, pp. 96 ff.
314. See Goradia/Kapila (2009) pp. 349 ff.
315. See OECD MC Commentary (2014) Positions on Article 5 and its Commentary, No. 26, p. 461.
316. See Dalal/Shah/Sheth (2014) India, p. 17.
317. See Goradia/Kapila (2009) p. 351.
318. See for another vague Indian case law decision with regard to the disposal requirement Kamath (2014b) pp. 778 ff.
319. See Padmakshan (2014) p. 247.
320. See OECD MC Commentary (2014) Positions on Article 5 and its Commentary, No. 4, p. 456 & No. 15, p. 459.

case law: In the case of *Seagate Singapore International Headquarters (P.) Ltd.*, the American hard drive manufacturer Seagate wanted to engage an independent service provider storing goods in a warehouse on behalf of Seagate and delivering them to original equipment manufacturers in India when needed.[321] Although the warehouse was not owned or operated by Seagate, a right to visit and check the inventory existed.[322] The Indian Authority for Advanced Rulings (AAR) decided that the warehouse was at the disposal of Seagate which thus constituted a PE for Seagate in India.[323]

Considering the special case of a *construction site PE*, Indian domestic law does not provide for specific rules.[324] With regard to the broad Indian concept of business connection, a construction site will probably establish a fiscal nexus in India under Indian domestic law.[325]

Indian *tax treaty policy* also follows the UN MC. In accordance with Article 5 (3a) UN MC, many of the Indian tax treaties explicitly mention supervisory activities in the wording of the construction site PE clause as PE-constituting activity.[326] While the provider of the supervisory activities does not have to be included in the construction or installation project, the supervisory service activities themselves have to be integrated and linked to the construction process.[327] In case the provisions of a service PE and the construction site PE are applicable with respect to the supervisory activities, the taxpayer has an option.[328] The required time threshold for construction site PEs in Indian tax treaties varies from 120 days to twelve months but is generally orientated towards the permanence requirement of six months as determined in the UN MC in contrast to the twelve months threshold of the OECD MC.[329] Similar to the basic PE case, Indian tax treaty policy brings forward the argument that a series of unrelated short-term consecutive construction site projects can be considered as one single project for the existence of a construction site PE.[330] With regard to the delegation of work to subcontractors, special provisions do not exist in Indian tax treaties. Indian case law indicates that a PE of the general contractor shall not be established in case the entire work is delegated to the subcontractor and only a few supervisory visits are conducted by the workers of the general contractor.[331]

The business connection term as defined in the Indian Finance Act of 2002 actually refers to the treaty concept of the *agency PE*: A person acting on behalf of a non-resident principal constitutes a PE in India if an authority to conclude contracts is exercised habitually in India, a stock of goods or merchandise is maintained in India for

321. See Metha (2012) p. 38.
322. See Shakow (2013) p. 378.
323. Following OECD rules, the use of the warehouse for the purpose of delivering goods is certainly determined as preparatory or auxiliary activity under Article 5 (4) OECD MC which will not lead to the establishment of a PE.
324. See Dalal/Shah/Sheth (2014) India, p. 25.
325. See Goradia/Kapila (2009) pp. 356 ff.
326. See Goradia/Kapila (2009) p. 356.
327. See Goradia/Kapila (2009) p. 358.
328. See Dalal/Shah/Sheth (2014) India, p. 24.
329. See Metha (2012) pp. 62 ff.
330. See Goradia/Kapila (2009) p. 358.
331. See Dalal/Shah/Sheth (2014) India, p. 25.

the foreign principal for the purpose of regular delivering of goods, or if orders are secured in India on a regular basis on behalf of the non-resident. In contrast to the OECD MC, Indian domestic law includes the maintenance of a stock of goods or merchandise as PE-establishing business operation and not as preparatory or auxiliary activity as under Article 5 (4) of the OECD MC. However, similar to the OECD MC, an exception applies for an independent agent who acts in the ordinary course of his business and does not work solely or almost solely for the non-resident principal.[332] Basically, this domestic rule is in accordance with Article 5 (5) of the UN MC.

India also follows the UN MC with regard to the agency PE in *tax treaties*. Similar to Indian domestic law, the agency PE definition is extended in Indian tax treaties in comparison to the OECD MC. An agency PE is not only defined by the habitual holding of an authority to negotiate and conclude contracts on behalf of the principal, but also in case of the maintenance of a stock of goods for the purpose of regular delivering and in case of securing orders for the principal or for other controlled enterprises.[333] The authority to conclude contracts in the name of the principal is given if a third independent party is convinced that the agent is authorized to act on behalf of the principal.[334] Facts and circumstances as well as common business practice are further external factors which play a role when determining the respective degree of authorization to conclude contracts.[335] Thus, the contractual authority is based on an economic obligation rather than on a legal one. In contrast to the OECD MC, Indian treaty policy regularly assumes that it is possible to constitute an agency PE by the mere participation in negotiations with a client at source, also for cases where not the complete contract, but only essential elements of it are part of the negotiations.[336] In addition, it is even questionable if the agent itself has to be physically present in India in order to constitute an agency PE.[337] Similar to Article 5 (6) OECD MC, an exception of the PE status applies for independent agents when acting in the ordinary course of their business. However, in accordance with Article 5 (7) UN MC, in case the independent agent works only or almost only on behalf of one single principal, the independence status of the agent is rejected.[338] This explicitly widens the fiscal nexus of the agency PE under Indian treaty law.[339] In order to avoid the automatic disqualification of the independent agency status in case of a single principal, the UN MC Commentary provides for an alternative formulation. This includes an additional condition stating that the agent is considered as being independent as long as commercial or financial relations between the principal and the agent are in line with the arm's length principle.[340]

332. See Metha (2012) p. 22.
333. See Dalal/Shah/Sheth (2014) India, pp. 20 f., Dölker (2013b) p. 2717.
334. See Dalal/Shah/Sheth (2014) India, p. 21.
335. See Goradia/Kapila (2009) p. 361.
336. See OECD MC Commentary (2014) Positions on Article 5 and its Commentary, No. 31, p. 461.
337. See Goradia/Kapila (2009) p. 363.
338. The Indian fiscal authorities determine the term 'acting almost wholly' for the foreign principal as acting more than 90%. See Gada/Sinha (2014) p. 374.
339. See Metha (2012) p. 80.
340. See UN MC Commentary (2011) Article 5, No. 32, p. 131. Some of the Indian tax treaties follow this alternative concept and include the arm's length condition in the 'independent agent' test.

Indian domestic law does not include special provisions with regard to a *service PE*. Apart from the general term of business connection, India follows the approach of considering service payments to non-residents as fees for technical services being taxable in India if the service fee arises or is received by the non-resident service provider in India.[341] Under Indian domestic law, fees for technical services are generally defined as '*any consideration for the rendering of any managerial, technical or consultancy services excluding considerations for construction work*'.[342] Thus, in case service payments are allocated to the category of cross-border technical service fees, a non-resident is liable to a withholding tax in India on a gross basis notwithstanding the fulfilment of the domestic business connection criteria. The Indian domestic business connection approach does not include special rules for the secondment of employees to India.

Considering the existence of a service PE in Indian *tax treaties*, India often follows the concept of the UN MC which includes a service PE provision in Article 5 (3b) UN MC.[343] Thus, the provision of services by a non-resident enterprise through employees or other personnel for the same or connected projects for a period of aggregating 183 days in a period of twelve months is supposed to constitute a PE in India despite the non-existence of a fixed place of business. In Indian tax treaty practice, the aggregated permanence requirement varies from 91 to 183 days.[344] However, in case services are rendered to a related enterprise the time threshold can be reduced to thirty days or is even non-existent. This exception is valid e.g., in the tax treaty between the US and India in which Article 5 (2l) (ii) determines that a PE is established by the provision of services to an associated enterprise without the reference to a permanence requirement. In addition, the inclusion of the '*same or connected project*'-criterion is also not given in the majority of Indian tax treaties. Thus, the provision of services at several short-term spots can be added as one project for the determination of a service PE in India.[345] India also rejects the OECD MC Commentary stating that the physical presence of the service-providing personnel is necessary for the existence of a service PE in India.[346]

With regard to the establishment of a PE for secondment arrangements, India also follows its own treaty policy: In contrast to paragraph 42 of the OECD MC Commentary regarding Article 5 of the OECD MC, India states that an associated company rendering services to another member of the group which is resident in another state can constitute a PE for the service beneficiary in case the other requirements of Article 5 OECD MC are fulfilled.[347] This basically indicates that a company located in India which provides services to its head office being resident in another state through '*hired*'

See Appendix, Table A9. In fact, this criterion is also mentioned in the OECD MC Commentary as possible indicator of independence but it is explicitly stated that this is not 'determinative'. See OECD MC Commentary (2014), Article 5, No. 38.6, p. 110.

341. See Bhattacharya/Sanghavi (2012) p. 359.
342. See Sanghvi/Shaktawat (2012) p. 453.
343. See Appendix, Table A5.
344. See Dalal/Shah/Sheth (2014) India, p. 19.
345. See Bhattacharya/Sanghavi (2012) p. 364.
346. See OECD MC Commentary (2014) Positions on Article 5 and its Commentary, No. 39, p. 462.
347. See OECD MC Commentary (2014) Positions on Article 5 and its Commentary, No. 32, p. 462.

personnel can still constitute a PE for the service provider.[348] This is also consistent with Indian case law: In the *Morgan Stanley* case, the US multinational investment bank Morgan Stanley had a subsidiary in India that provided several services to the US headquarters.[349] In addition, the US parent itself rendered monitoring services at the premises in India, so-called *stewardship activities* performed by US personnel in India, in each case for a certain short-time period.[350] Apart from that, Morgan Stanley sent additional own employees to the subsidiary in India for a longer time period to monitor and support the activities of the Indian subsidiary. These employees worked under the control and supervision of the Indian subsidiary. They were continued to be paid by the parent enterprise which was immediately reimbursed by its Indian unit so that a typical secondment arrangement existed.[351] Although the general services which were rendered by the US parent to the Indian entity were considered by the Indian tax authorities as '*stewardship activities*' similar to '*shareholder activities*' in an affiliated group (and thus were not regarded as PE-creating factor) the services provided by the seconded US employees to the Indian subsidiary constituted a service PE in India as a sufficient and inseparable link was supposed to exist between the US '*lessor*' of labour and the US employees according to the Indian tax courts.[352] The Indian tax court argued that the workers were still on the payroll of the US company. In addition, they had a '*lien*' on the job (a kind of right of retention) towards the foreign employer. As long as this claim on the job remained, Morgan Stanley could still control the terms of employment of the seconded workers and was supposed to be responsible for the service activities provided.[353] Thus, Indian case law determined that in such case a service PE was deemed to exist at the level of the Indian subsidiary.[354] Therefore, Indian treaty policy obviously demands for a more concrete checking of the working details, the carried-out functions and the influence of the parent company with regard to the question whether seconded employees working at an affiliated subsidiary eventually constitute a PE in India.[355] Occasionally, Indian tax treaties also apply the independent personal services-article in accordance with Article 14 of the former OECD MC as additional fiscal nexus for the provision of services in India.[356]

Under Indian tax treaty policy, another fiscal nexus exists for income from the provision of technical services. Managerial, technical or consultancy services which cannot be considered as service PE income still can be taxable in India as many Indian

348. See Palwe/Kulmar (2009) p. 239, Gada/Sinha (2014) p. 376.
349. See Jhabakh (2010) p. 159.
350. See Pijl (2008) p. 178.
351. See Sheppard (2006) p. 1456.
352. See Yang (2010) p. 249.
353. See Goradia/Kapila (2009) p. 365.
354. See Metha (2012) p. 92.
355. See Dalal/Shah/Sheth (2014) India, p. 23. The Indian tax courts decided in similar cases (*Centrica India Offshore Private Ltd* and *JC Bamford)* that a service PE was established for seconded employees working at Indian premises as the salaries were still paid by the foreign entity. See Gada/Sinha (2014) p. 376, Metha (2015) pp. 37 f., 70 f., 105 ff. In the case of Centrica, the Indian tax courts actually did not assume a service PE but still claimed a source taxing right by qualifying the income as income from technical services by considering the non-resident workforce-lending entity as economic employer. See Nitikman (2014) pp. 803 ff.
356. See OECD MC Commentary (2014) Positions on Article 7 and its Commentary, No. 2.1, p. 465.

tax treaties include these payments as fees for technical services in the wording of the royalty-article.[357] In accordance with Article 12 (2) UN MC, this article grants a taxation right for the source state in which the service was provided. Thus, according to Indian tax treaty policy, the royalty-article effectively works as *'collecting pond'* for income from services which cannot be allocated to a service PE.[358] Different to PE income, a withholding tax is levied on these fees for technical services on a gross basis.

In summary, the Indian domestic PE concept of business connection is generally wider than the OECD definition, following a *'facts and circumstances'*-approach (see Table 4.10). Indian treaty law is based on the UN MC which implies a wider fiscal nexus as proposed by the OECD, especially with regard to the special PE cases of agency and service PEs in Indian tax treaties.

Table 4.10 Indian PE Concept

	National Law	*Treaty Law*
Basic PE	- Wider concept of business connection - Case law based nexus	- Similar to UN MC - Reliance on case law - Wider fiscal nexus including the holding of warehouses for the delivery of goods
Construction site PE	No specific rules	- Similar to UN MC - Explicit mentioning of supervisory activities - Varying permanence threshold of 120 days to 12 months
Agency PE	- Similar to Article 5 (5) UN MC - Wider than OECD agency PE concept	- Similar to Article 5 (5) UN MC - Wider than OECD agency PE concept
Service PE	- No specific rules - Fiscal nexus possible as technical service fees under the royalty-article	- Similar to Article 5 (3b) UN MC - Generally included in tax treaties - Varying permanence threshold from 91 to 183 days - Inclusion of technical service fees in the royalty-article

357. See Sanghvi/Shaktawat (2012) p. 454. In fact, about 80% of Indian tax treaties include fees for technical services in the royalty-article. See Appendix Table A5. See e.g. with regard to the German-Indian Tax Treaty considering the application of the royalty-article, Strauß (1999) Article 12 Indien, pp. 87 ff.

358. See Bendlinger/Reinhold/Sennewald (2013) pp. 455 ff.

4.2.5.2 *Attribution of Profits between Foreign Head Office and Domestic PE*

Indian *domestic law* does not include any specific rules with regard to the attribution of business profits between head office and PE. In general, only profits which can be '*reasonably attributed*' to business activities carried out in India are considered as taxable PE income.[359] According to the Indian Income Tax Act of 1962, business profits of an Indian PE shall be determined by using specified presumptive methods. One of them is a computation method which estimates the PE revenue and deducts certain related expenses.[360] For specific business operations, a predetermined percentage of revenue is estimated as taxable PE income by the Indian tax authorities following a presumptive approach.[361] For certain industry sectors, such as R&D or IT-related services and car manufacturing which do not bear significant risks, predetermined safe harbour profit margins from 8.5% to 30% are set by Indian tax authorities.[362] Another modification is the consideration of labour costs upon which a certain mark-up is added as basis for attributed PE income.[363] A further income allocation method is based on proportions, such as the ratio of Indian PE revenue to global business revenue.[364] An example for which a presumptive method was allowed in Indian case law is the case of *Rolls Royce UK*. Rolls Royce Plc., a British car and engine producer, provided parts and equipment to Indian customers through its subsidiary, Rolls Royce Indian Limited (RRIL); both firms were resident in the UK. According to Indian tax authorities, the business activities operated in India by RRIL constituted an Indian agency PE as RRIL maintained a representative office in India. With regard to the taxable PE profit, the Delhi High Court came to the conclusion that 35% of sales revenue earned in India was estimated as Indian PE income.[365] The use of the '*outdated*' presumptive method was also based on the fact that Rolls Royce did not execute a concrete analysis of transfer prices.[366] The use of the estimated income allocation due to the incomplete application of the transfer pricing analysis is also shown in the case of *Convergys Customer Management Group Inc.* This US customer service provider had a PE in India due to its key position employees working frequently at the premises of the Indian subsidiary.[367] Indian tax courts decided that specific hardware and software assets provided free of charge to the Indian subsidiary were also included as taxable PE income. As the non-resident head office did not include these assets in the transfer pricing analysis, the Indian Income Tax Appellate Tribunal (ITAT) used a presumptive calculation approach estimating that 15% of the difference between the operating income of the Indian service operation and the profit before tax of the Indian subsidiary was supposed to represent a '*reasonable amount*' of attributable profits.

359. See Dalal/Shah/Sheth (2014) India, p. 26.
360. See Kapur/Rawal (2006) p. 388.
361. See Dalal/Shah/Sheth (2014) India, p. 26.
362. See Gada/Sinha (2014) p. 381.
363. See Dalal/Shah/Sheth (2014) India, p. 26.
364. See Kapur/Rawal (2006) p. 389.
365. See Metha (2012) p. 120.
366. See Mitra/Almoula/Pardiwala/Haldia (2012) p. 75.
367. See Chawla (2013) p. 449.

However, as these regulations seem to be outdated and no further concrete interpretation exists, the Indian Transfer Pricing Rules of 2001 are more present and thus are favoured from a practical point of view when determining PE income under Indian tax law.[368] Apart from a PE definition which is included in the Indian transfer pricing regulations, similar to the OECD MC, Indian transfer pricing rules state that a PE has to be considered as a separate legal entity for tax purposes.[369] Thus, the PE income is determined by considering PE book accounts which are in accordance with the Indian accounting standards under the premise of a '*reasonable attribution*' to the business operation in India.[370] Following the Indian transfer pricing regulations, external and internal dealings between the foreign head office and an Indian PE are recognized at arm's length which implies a functional analysis for which functions and risks of the PE have to be determined.[371] Thus, it can be concluded that the income allocation rules under Indian domestic law resemble the functionally separate entity approach of the OECD MC.[372] In principle, limitations with regard to the deductibility of PE expenses do not exist under Indian tax law except for general administrative head office expenses whose deduction is restricted to 5% of total PE income.[373] However, among several requirements of deductions under Indian domestic law, such as the exclusive incurrence of expenses for the business purpose, deduction is mostly only granted under the condition that withholding taxes were paid, partly even for the deduction of payments from an Indian PE.[374] In addition, for the allowance of deduction, the PE has to recognize the expenses in its accounts so that pure fictional payments are avoided.[375]

More than half of the Indian *tax treaties* follow the UN MC with regard to the PE income allocation.[376] In concurrence with Article 7 (2) UN MC, similar to the OECD MC, the profits are allocated to the PE which '*it might be expected to make if it were a distinct and separate enterprise engaged in the same or similar activities under the same or similar conditions and dealing wholly independently with the head office*'. In contrast to the OECD MC, some Indian tax treaties following the UN MC include a limited force of attraction rule with regard to PE income allocation.[377] Thus, not only income which can be effectively attributed to the PE is considered as taxable PE income but also

368. See Mitra/Almoula/Pardiwala/Haldia (2012) p. 74.
369. See Kapur/Rawal (2006) p. 390.
370. See Gutiérrez (2013) Chapter 12, p. 327.
371. See Gutiérrez (2013) Chapter 12, p. 328.
372. See Kapur/Rawal (2006) p. 407.
373. See Kapur/Rawal (2006) p. 390, Mitra/Almoula/Pardiwala/Haldia (2012) p. 75.
374. See Kapur/Rawal (2006) p. 393. See Metha (2012) pp. 157 ff. for an Indian case where the local Indian courts initially decided that withholding taxes shall also be levied on business profits paid by the Indian PE to the non-resident head office. However, the result of this case was finally re-decided in favour of the taxpayer.
375. See Gutiérrez (2013) Chapter 12, p. 328.
376. See Appendix, Table A16.
377. For Indian tax treaties which include the limited force of attraction principle in the wording of Article 7 see Appendix, Table A16.

income which is not related to the PE but still earned in the source state by the non-resident head office.[378] This is also included in the wording of Article 7 (1) UN MC. Not only these profits which can be directly attributed to the PE are taxed but also sales or other business activities '*of the same kind as those effected through the PE*' conducted in the source state.[379] With regard to the deduction of PE expenses, Indian tax treaties following the UN MC also include certain limitations. In accordance with Article 7 (3) UN MC, the deduction of royalty payments, service, management or similar fees are explicitly disallowed from PE income unless the payments are reimbursements for real expenses of the head office.[380] Deductions for internal interest expenses are only permitted for bank industry PEs. In addition, several Indian tax treaties indicate that the deduction of expenses from PE income depends on possible limitations in domestic law.[381] Indian tax treaties which are based on the OECD MC follow the '*old view*' of the OECD considering the attribution of business profits.[382] This means that for those treaties, internal dealings between head office and PE are generally not recognized for tax purposes.

With regard to the income allocation to a *construction site PE*, concrete rules do not exist under Indian domestic law. Indian tax treaty policy also does not contain any specifications. In contrast to the AOA, the indirect profit attribution to a PE, based on a certain formula or predetermined ratio, is generally applicable as alternative in Indian tax treaties. This policy is in line with the UN MC and the '*old*' OECD MC which both include the indirect profit allocation as alternative in Article 7 (4).[383]

For Indian *agency PEs*, it can be considered that the general domestic transfer pricing rules are applied.[384] Therefore, the allocation of business profits to an Indian agency PE is supposed to follow the arm's length principle which is also included in Indian case law: In the *SET Satellite* case, the Singaporean corporation Sony Entertainment Television (SET) Satellite, a buyer of television programs and sports events, provided marketing and advertisement activities in India through a dependent agent, SET India.[385] Apart from the question whether SET India constituted an agency PE for the principal SET Satellite (which it did) Indian Bombay High Court had to decide whether the remuneration payments made by the non-resident principal to its agent SET Satellite was determined as agency PE income thus being liable to tax in India. In this case, as the payment was considered as being at arm's length, the Indian High Court decided that no further profits are allocated to the agency PE.[386] For the allocation of income to agency PEs in Indian tax treaties, specific rules do not exist.

With regard to *service PEs*, Indian tax law does not include any specific regulations. Apart from the PE existence, the *Morgan Stanley* case described in section 4.2.5.1

378. See Dalal/Shah/Sheth (2014) India, p. 27.
379. See Rawal (2006) p. 35.
380. See Kapur/Rawal (2006) p. 402.
381. See Rawal (2006) p. 90.
382. See OECD MC Commentary (2014) Positions on Article 7 and its Commentary, No. 1.1, p. 464. See Appendix, Table A16.
383. See Rawal (2006) p. 131.
384. See Metha (2012) p. 122.
385. See Jhabakh (2010) p. 159.
386. See Mitra/Almoula/Pardiwala/Haldia (2012) p. 75.

also dealt with the question: which amount of income had to be allocated to the service PE constituted by seconded US employees. The Indian Supreme Court decided that the compensation payments incurred for the services provided to the Indian subsidiary of Morgan Stanley were in accordance with the arm's length principle and therefore, no further business profits had to be allocated to the service PE.[387] Thus, similar to the case of *SET Satellite*, it can be concluded that no further profits are allocated to a service PE if the remuneration paid by the non-resident to the service provider at source is at arm's length and thus based on a transfer pricing analysis of functions performed and risks assumed.[388]

For the allocation of income to an Indian service PE, the application of the limited force of attraction rule in Indian treaty policy was approved by Indian case law in the *Linklaters* case: The British law firm Linklaters provided services to Indian clients, partly at source in India, partly from the major office in London.[389] Apart from the issue that the services rendered in India constituted a PE according to Article 5 (2k) of the British-Indian Tax Treaty, the attributable PE income had to be determined. Article 7 (1) of the British-Indian Tax Treaty determines that only income which is '*directly or indirectly*' attributable to the PE is taxed as PE income. The ITAT decided that, in accordance with the limited force of attraction principle, the indirect attribution of business profits to the PE also included the profits derived from services provided by Linklaters to Indian customers from outside India.[390] Despite the fact that according to the limited force of attraction rules of the UN MC, only income which is connected to business activities provided in the source country is attributed to the PE, the Indian tax authorities decided that not only the Indian service income, but also the profits stemming from business activities conducted outside India were taxable PE income.[391] However, in a similar case decision of a UK law firm providing services in India, namely *Clifford Chance*, the Special Bench of the ITAT decided that the services rendered from outside India were not considered as indirectly attributable income under Article 7 (1) of the British-Indian Tax Treaty and thus could not be allocated to the Indian service PE.[392]

In summary, Indian domestic law is generally based on the Indian Transfer Pricing Rules of 2001 implying a functional analysis with regard to the income allocation to an Indian PE (see Table 4.11). Presumptive methods, however, also exist and are applied in Indian case law. Indian tax treaty policy partly follows the UN MC approach containing a limited force of attraction principle. Indian tax treaties with OECD countries are based on the '*old*' OECD MC and do not apply the AOA.

387. See Metha (2012) p. 148.
388. See Jhabakh (2010) p. 159.
389. See Metha (2012) p. 86.
390. See Chaturvedi (2011) p. 79.
391. See Arnold (2010) p. 607.
392. See Kamath (2013) p. 963, Gada/Sinha (2014) p. 379.

Table 4.11 Indian Approach of Allocation of Business Profits to PE

National Law	*Treaty Law*
- Principle of reasonable attribution - Predetermined presumptive methods in case of inadequate transfer pricing analysis - Otherwise functional analysis according to the Indian Transfer Pricing Rules 2001 based on the separate legal entity approach - External and internal dealings between head office and PE are recognized at arm's length	- Allocation of profits based on the UN MC in several Indian tax treaties - Limited force of attraction principle and disallowance of internal deduction of PE expenses - Income allocation based on the *'old'* OECD MC in Indian treaties with OECD countries - Internal dealings between head office and PE recognized at cost

4.2.6 China

4.2.6.1 Fiscal Nexus under National and Treaty Law

Chinese *domestic tax law* does not include a PE definition in accordance with the OECD approach. Instead, China uses the term of an *'establishment'* or *'place'*.[393] This concept includes several enumerated types of business activities a non-resident can conduct in China: These business activities include, among others, management and business organizations, representative offices as well as factories or workshops or other places of production.[394] A special characteristic of the Chinese establishment definition is the lack of a time requirement. Thus, in principle, every place of business activity falling under the domestic list of examples will constitute a fiscal nexus in China from the first day of the activity.[395] In addition, until 2010, the representative office has been a Chinese domestic fiscal nexus which was exempt from Chinese corporate income taxation in case only preparatory activities were conducted in relation to the sale of goods in China.[396] However, this rule has been abolished so that also a representative office generally constitutes an establishment under Chinese domestic tax law.[397] Apart from that, the Chinese establishment approach does not provide for a more concrete interpretation of the different PE requirements.

The PE definition in Chinese *tax treaties* partly complies with the OECD MC and partly with the UN MC depending on the respective treaty partner and the negotiated agreements. In accordance with the generally valid Circular *GuoShuiFa No. 75* issued by the State Administration of Taxation (SAT) dealing with the interpretation of the provisions of the Singaporean-Chinese Tax Treaty, similar to Article 5 (1) of the OECD

393. See Mui/Yam (2014) China, p. 10.
394. See Cheung/Jiang (2013) p. 40.
395. See Eichelberger/Liu/DeSouza (2012) p. 17.
396. See Cheung/Jiang (2013) p. 42.
397. See Cheung/Jiang (2013) p. 43.

MC and the UN MC, a Chinese PE is deemed to exist in case of a fixed place of business through which the business activity of the non-resident is carried on.[398] It can be indicated that similar to the OECD MC, the '*fixed*' place of business requires a certain geographical coherence whereas a reference to commercial coherence is not apparent.[399] In addition, a certain degree of permanence is mentioned whereas short project interruptions are disregarded.[400] Similar to the OECD MC, a concrete time requirement for the basic PE case is not specified. Another criterion is the disposal requirement over the location which can constitute a PE even if the place of business is not required or available for conducting the business activity in China.[401] However, no further explanation is given. With regard to the functional integration of the place of business, the SAT gives the example of a business deal of a non-resident with a Chinese client for which the place of business in China contributes to a considerable extent. Even if the business contract is concluded directly between the non-resident and the Chinese client, the business activity in this case is supposed to be conducted through the place of business in China.[402] Similar to the OECD MC, preparatory or auxiliary activities performed at the place of business do not constitute a PE in Chinese tax treaties. Most of Chinese tax treaties follow the OECD MC so that the maintenance of stock for the purpose of delivery is usually included as auxiliary activity.[403] The SAT lists further attributes of a preparatory business activity: The place of business shall not work independently or conduct an essential part of the overall enterprises' business. In addition, the activity shall be provided exclusively for the enterprise and routine actions shall be performed instead of activities directly linked to key profit-making.[404]

A Chinese domestic establishment can also be determined by business activities such as construction, installation or assembly work conducted by contractors. In Chinese tax treaties, the provision dealing with the *construction site PE* basically follows Article 5 (3a) of the UN MC. Thus, the definition of the construction site PE explicitly includes supervisory activities which are connected to the construction project.[405] The permanence threshold is generally set at six months, but can vary in practice up to twenty-four months.[406] Regardless of the time spent in China, foreign contract engineering projects in relation to construction sites are in any case obliged to be registered with the Chinese tax authorities.[407] Similar to the OECD and the UN MC, the SAT determines the geographical and commercial coherence of the different construction sites as additional requirement when calculating the time threshold.[408] The delegation of work to subcontractors is not mentioned in Chinese tax treaties.

398. See Mui/Yam (2014) China, p. 11.
399. See Li (2012) p. 458.
400. See Eichelberger/Liu/DeSouza (2012) p. 18.
401. See Eichelberger/Liu/DeSouza (2012) p. 18.
402. See Li (2012) p. 458.
403. See Li (2012) p. 459.
404. See Mui/Yam (2014) China, pp. 11 ff.
405. See Li (2012) p. 459.
406. See Eichelberger/Liu/DeSouza (2012) pp. 21 ff.
407. See Dölker (2014) p. 348.
408. See Mui/Yam (2014) China, p. 15.

Similar to the OECD and UN MC Commentary, the time that the subcontractor works at the Chinese construction site is considered as time of the general contractor in case of a partial delegation of work.[409]

Agents who undertake production or business activities for a non-resident principal in China also constitute an establishment under Chinese domestic tax law.[410] In accordance with the agency PE definition of the OECD MC, Chinese tax treaties generally assume an agency PE if the agent *'habitually exercises the authority to conclude contracts in the name of the non-resident enterprise'*.[411] Most Chinese tax treaties follow the wording of Article 5 (5) OECD MC with regard to the dependent agent as fiscal nexus.[412] An independent agent is not supposed to establish a PE in China if he acts in the ordinary course of his business. However, with regard to independent agents, China's tax treaties are more in line with Article 5 (6) of the UN MC: The status of independence is basically rejected or at least limited when the agent performs business activities solely or almost solely on behalf of a single principal enterprise.[413] According to the treaty interpretation of SAT, the authority to conclude contracts additionally includes the aspect of participating in negotiations and discussing contractual details.[414] Another requirement described by the SAT refers to the legal and economic independence of the agent. Considerable factors indicating independence include the missing supervision or control by the principal, the bearing of own business risk, the larger number of principals and the specific degree of knowledge and skill of the agent.[415] In this context, Chinese tax treaty law also regularly integrates Article 5 (7) OECD MC stating that the mere control over a subsidiary does not indicate a PE for the controlling enterprise. In case of an independent agent working for one non-resident enterprise, most Chinese tax treaties reject the status of independence as the agent works solely for one principal.[416] In this case, several Chinese tax treaties consider an additional requirement also proposed by the UN MC.[417] As long as the transactions between the agent and the non-resident principal follow the arm's length principle, the independence status will not be refused.[418]

The provision of *services* in China can also constitute a Chinese establishment and thus a fiscal nexus under Chinese domestic law.[419] A special Chinese rule, Circular 19, exists for the cross-border secondment of employees to a Chinese subsidiary performing business activities such as the provision of certain services in China. A non-resident entity which sends employees to China in order to perform service

409. See Li (2012) p. 459.
410. See Mui/Yam (2014) China, p. 11.
411. See Li (2012) p. 460. See for the rare case law Mui/Yam (2014) China, p. 14.
412. See Ecker/Tang (2010) p. 65.
413. See Wei (2008) p. 148, Li (2012) p. 460. Similar to Indian treaty policy, some Chinese treaties follow the alternative formulation as stated in the UN MC Commentary providing for the condition of being in line with the arm's length principle as counter-exception to the refusal of the independent agent status. See Appendix, Table A10.
414. See Pellone (2011) p. 144.
415. See Eichelberger/Liu/DeSouza (2012) p. 19.
416. See Appendix, Table A10.
417. See UN MC Commentary (2011) Article 5, No. 32, p. 131.
418. See Eichelberger/Liu/DeSouza (2012) p. 19.
419. See Mui/Yam (2014) China, pp. 10 ff.

activities there is supposed to constitute a Chinese establishment if the responsibilities assumed and risks taken by the seconded employees can be allocated to the non-resident '*hirer*' of the workers.[420] The SAT enumerates several factors which indicate if the seconded employees effectively work for the foreign service provider:

- there is a payment of service fees of the Chinese host subsidiary to the non-resident '*hirer*';
- the amount of these payments is higher than the regular compensation paid to the employees;
- the non-resident does not pay out all of the received payments to its employees;
- the seconded employee does not correctly or fully report and pay Chinese personal income tax;
- the non-resident can decide about the number of '*hired*' workers, exact locations and the amount of salaries.

If one of these factors is fulfilled it can already be deemed that the non-resident service provider constitutes a Chinese establishment.[421]

Chinese tax treaty policy generally includes the service PE as an alternative fiscal nexus without the establishment of a fixed place of business.[422] In accordance with Article 5 (3b) UN MC, a service PE is constituted in China in case of '*furnishing of services, including consultancy services, through employees or other personnel*' under the condition that the service activities are conducted for a period aggregating more than 183 days for the same or a connected project within China. Similar to the construction site PE, the permanence threshold of the service PE varies in Chinese tax treaties from six to twelve months.[423] A special feature of the Chinese service PE is the way of how the permanence requirement is determined, especially for tax treaties which are still based on the time unit of months. For the calculation of the total time period of a service project, each month in which the service activities are provided is counted as full month, independent of the real number of days the service provider is present in China.[424] On the other side, interceptions of the service activities are only subtracted from the time period if they are intercepted for the total comprehensive period of thirty days.[425] Although this rule has been effectively abolished in 2011, the method of calculation to be used in the tax treaties which still rely on the time unit of

420. See Wei (2013) p. 722.
421. See Liu/Eichelberger (2013) p. 552. There is also the opinion that, in addition to one of the mentioned practical factors, the question of who bears responsibility and risk for the actions of the seconded employees is decisive for determining the economic employer. See Ho/Zhao/Turley (2014) p. 637.
422. See Appendix, Table A6.
423. See for an overview Ecker/Tang (2010) pp. 59 ff.
424. See Eichelberger/Liu/DeSouza (2012) p. 20.
425. See Wang (2008) p. 243.

months is unclear.[426] The definition of services for the purposes of the tax treaty can basically include every form of professional service provision.[427]

With regard to the case of secondment of employees to a Chinese subsidiary, similar factors as laid down in the Circular 19, used by the older Circular 75 of the SAT, stating that a foreign hirer of workers can establish a service PE under Chinese tax treaties if the responsibilities and risk of the work performed in China is assumed to be carried by the non-resident.[428] The new Circular 19 states that also in Chinese tax treaties a service PE is established by the secondment of employees in case the Chinese establishment is '*relatively fixed and permanent*' whereas the time threshold as stated in the tax treaty has to hold in addition to the indicating factors enumerated.[429] Thus, it can be concluded that in accordance with the OECD MC, the concept of the '*economic employer*' is essential for the secondment of employees in Chinese domestic and treaty law.[430]

In summary, Chinese national law is based on the wider concept of the establishment and does not include specific regulations for domestic PE situations except for the secondment of employees (see Table 4.12). Chinese treaty law mostly follows the OECD MC with regard to the basic PE case. However, considering the special PE cases such as the construction site, agency or service PE, Chinese treaty policy is more in line with the UN MC.

Table 4.12 Chinese PE Concept

	National Law	*Treaty Law*
Basic PE	- Wider concept of 'establishment' - No permanence requirement	- Similar to OECD MC - Includes provisions of UN MC depending on the treaty
Construction site PE	No specific rules	- Similar to UN MC - Explicit mentioning of supervisory activities - Varying permanence threshold of six to twenty-four months
Agency PE	No specific rules	- Varies depending on MC followed - Generally wider fiscal nexus similar to UN MC as proposed by SAT

426. See Mui/Yam (2014) China, p. 13.
427. See Hasbargen/Preising (2012) p. 146.
428. See Wong (2013) p. 46.
429. See Wei (2013) p. 723.
430. See Wong/Mui/Yam (2012) China, p. 14.

	National Law	Treaty Law
Service PE	- No specific rules - Special rules for secondment of employees	- Similar to Article 5 (3b) UN MC - Generally included in tax treaties - Varying permanence threshold from six to twelve months - Special method of time calculation - Special rules for secondment of employees

4.2.6.2 Attribution of Profits between Foreign Head Office and Domestic PE

Chinese *domestic law* specifies that all effectively connected income has to be allocated to a Chinese establishment, including income arising in China and abroad.[431] Similar to a separate legal entity, the income has to be determined by own accounts maintained by the Chinese establishment additionally based on a functional and risk analysis.[432] If these accounting records are incomplete or inaccurate, three income allocation methods exist in Chinese domestic law which attribute the establishment income by using a deemed profit rate. If costs of the establishment cannot be determined, the actual gross revenue is multiplied by this deemed rate in order to identify the corporate tax burden of the Chinese establishment.[433] Vice versa, if the revenue cannot be reliably identified, the gross income is determined by considering the costs incurred and the deemed profit rate.[434] If the detailed costs are not available, but the total expenditures of the Chinese establishment are, the taxable profit of the establishment is calculated by using the total expenditures and again a deemed profit rate.[435] The level of this rate varies from 15% to 30% for construction projects and consulting services, to 30% and further up to 50% for management services with 15% as the general minimum threshold.[436] In practice, for the reasons of limited knowledge, capacity and revenue generation, Chinese tax authorities obviously prefer the use of the deemed profit methods also in cases where actual profits of the establishment are recognized in the accounts.[437] Considering the recognition and valuation of internal dealings between the Chinese establishment and the non-resident enterprise, transfer pricing rules apply, which means that, in general, all dealings have to comply with the arm's length standard.[438] Still, these dealings have to be recognized and certified in internal accounts held by the Chinese establishment. With regard to fictitious internal

431. See Mui/Yam (2014) China, p. 17.
432. See Gutiérrez (2013) Chapter 12, p. 324.
433. See Mui/Yam (2014) China, p. 18.
434. See Mui/Yam (2014) China, p. 18.
435. See Wong (2013) p. 47.
436. See Eichelberger/Liu/DeSouza (2012) p. 23.
437. See Gutiérrez (2013) Chapter 12, p. 324.
438. See Gutiérrez (2013) Chapter 12, p. 325.

payments such as royalty or interest payments as assumed by the AOA, a Chinese domestic rule prohibits the deduction of those payments between domestic entities.[439] It is questionable if this rule is also applied for international cases.

Chinese *treaty law* usually follows the '*old*' version of the OECD MC with regard to the allocation of business profits under Article 7 OECD MC.[440] Thus, in accordance with the separate legal entity fiction of Article 7 (2) of the '*old*' OECD MC, the profits are allocated to the Chinese PE which it earns as a '*distinct and separate enterprise*'. A limited force of attraction principle as under the UN MC, which enlarges the attributable PE income to profits additionally earned in the source country, is usually not adopted.[441] Still, the deduction of PE expenses in several Chinese treaties is in line with Article 7 (3) of the UN MC stating that the deduction of royalty, rental, service, or interest payments is not permitted unless it concerns reimbursements of real expenses of the head office.[442] Thus, in contrast to the AOA, internal dealings between head office and PE are usually not recognized in Chinese tax treaties. In addition, profit allocation methods based on a deemed profit rate as conducted in Chinese domestic law are regularly used in Chinese tax treaties as well.[443]

With regard to the cases of a *construction site, agency, or service PE,* special income allocation rules do not exist under Chinese domestic law. This means that the general domestic allocation rules including the deemed profit methods are applied for the special PE cases. Again, the level of the deemed profit rate depends on the activity conducted at the Chinese establishment. In general, a predetermined profit rate of 15%-30% is used for construction site PEs whereas this deemed rate increases to 50% for the provision of services. Considering services which are performed by a Chinese establishment partly inside and partly outside China, Chinese domestic rules allow the taxpayer to allocate the income depending on the location of the service provision whereas the burden of proof lies with the taxpayer.[444]

Chinese tax treaty policy also does not provide for specific regulations. With regard to income allocation to construction site PEs, the use of the indirect method in accordance with Article 7 (4) of the OECD and UN MC is usually possible in Chinese tax treaties. In addition, it can be indicated that the allocation of income to agency or service PEs in Chinese tax treaties also follows the domestic methods of profit estimation.

In summary, Chinese domestic law generally demands PE accounts based on a functional and risk analysis (see Table 4.13). However, deemed profit methods additionally exist for the allocation of income to Chinese PEs. Chinese treaty law is in

439. See Gutiérrez (2013) Chapter 12, p. 325.
440. See OECD MC Commentary (2014) Positions on Article 7 and its Commentary, No. 12, p. 467. See Appendix, Table A17.
441. In fact, the tax treaty of China with Pakistan is the only treaty which includes the limited force of attraction principle. See Eichelberger/Liu/DeSouza (2012) p. 24.
442. See Appendix, Table A17. This restriction is usually not included in Chinese treaties with developing countries. See Li (2012) p. 461.
443. See Mui/Yam (2014) China, p. 19.
444. See Mui/Yam (2014) China, pp. 19 ff.

principle in line with the '*old*' version of Article 7 of the OECD MC whereas the deemed profit methods are also applicable in Chinese tax treaties.

Table 4.13 Chinese Approach of Allocation of Business Profits to PE

National Law	*Treaty Law*
- Principle of effective connection - PE accounts based on functional and risk analysis - Otherwise deemed profit methods based on fixed rates regularly used by Chinese tax authorities - External and internal dealings between head office and PE recognized at arm's length under Chinese transfer pricing rules	- Income allocation principally based on the '*old*' OECD MC in most treaties - Disallowance of internal deduction of PE expenses similar to Article 7 (3) UN MC - Use of deemed profit methods possible in Chinese tax treaties

4.3 SYSTEMATIZATION OF THE COUNTRY-SPECIFIC PE CONCEPTS IN COMPARISON TO THE OECD VIEW

After the presentation of the different country-specific national and treaty concepts of the definition and the attribution of business profits to a PE, the domestic approaches of Germany, the US and the BRIC are briefly compared with the current OECD viewpoint. Against this background, it is elaborated if the prevailing trend of extended source taxation with regard to an enlargement of the PE concept at OECD level as presented in section 3.4 is also followed by the countries examined or if there are differences to the OECD policy. In addition, it is determined to what extent the PE income allocation is consistent with ongoing OECD tax policy and the development of the PE definition.[445]

4.3.1 Comparison of the National Regulations of the PE Definition with the OECD Approach

In order to evaluate the national PE concepts against the OECD approach, several indicators in relation to the PE definition and income allocation are determined which can indicate whether the PE concept and thus the fiscal nexus in the source country is widened or not. PE requirements which are discussable and provide for a certain scope of interpretation are used as indicators of a possible enlargement of the PE concept.

445. The following are conclusions derived from the results of the comparative analysis of the considered countries which try to determine a general statement about the countries' tax policy. They should not be generally valid for each tax treaty concluded by one of the countries.

Considering the basic PE case, there is one PE requirement which especially provides room for interpretation and should be compared with national and country-specific treaty PE statutes: the criterion of a necessary degree of disposal over the fixed place of business (see Table 4.14).

Table 4.14 Comparison of the Basic PE Case – OECD, DE, US, BRIC

	Disposal over Fixed Place of Business
OECD status quo and reform proposals	- Wide interpretation of functional integration (*in* or *at* place of business) - Painter example
German national & treaty law	Stricter principle of local connection (*Verwurzelung*) and exclusion
US national & treaty law	- *'Ultimate control'* over business asset - No reference in treaty law
Brazilian national & treaty law	No specific information
Russian national & treaty law	- Pure legal right not decisive - Disposal not required for services at foreign premises - No further interpretation in national and treaty law
Indian national & treaty law	- *'Dominion or control'* over the asset - Broad interpretation (*Seagate*)
Chinese national & treaty law	- Not given in national law - No concrete interpretation in treaty law

It has been elaborated in section 3.4 that the current OECD interpretation of certain PE requirements indicates an enlargement of the PE concept as fiscal nexus for cross-border business profits. This is derived from the OECD understanding of the PE criterion of disposal which offers a scope of interpretation and thus can lead to a higher number of PE cases in practice.[446]

Considering the criterion of disposal, Germany generally applies a stricter interpretation as it additionally demands a certain local connection (*Verwurzelung*) and an exclusive usage of the premises which indicates that the mere presence or the work at the business place does not constitute a fixed place of business as suggested by the painter example of the OECD MC.

446. Another PE requirement which is not considered here, is the permanence threshold. In fact, the six months mentioned by the OECD are only a guiding number, so that the duration period of the permanence threshold remains a matter of treaty negotiation. Therefore, the question of an enlargement of PE cases depends on the interpretation of the permanence threshold in the treaty.

The US demands '*ultimate control*' over the business asset but does not interpret the term in a more concrete way. US treaty law does not include any reference to the disposal term.[447]

Brazilian national and treaty law does not include any specific information considering the degree of disposal but generally refers to the criterion of official registration.

Russia mentions that a pure legal right shall not be decisive for the existence of a PE. In addition, a certain degree of disposal is obviously not required for services provided at foreign premises. More detailed explanations are not given.[448]

India refers to a certain degree of '*dominion or control*' over the asset. Indian case law though, especially the cases of *Seagate* and *Renoir Consulting Ltd*, for which a right to visit third party premises suffices to fulfil the necessary degree of disposal, indicates that India obviously applies a wide understanding of the disposal criterion similar to the OECD MC.[449]

Chinese national and treaty law does not include a concrete interpretation of the disposal term. At least, it is mentioned in the Chinese SAT treaty interpretation circular.[450]

In comparison to the regulations of the OECD MC which work as a benchmark for the allocation of taxing rights between residence and source country, only India is in line with the OECD approach (see Figure 4.2). For Russia, the requirement of disposal over the place of business is not decisive so that it can be assumed that services provided at third party premises create a PE in Russia given that all other PE criteria are fulfilled. Thus, the taxing right at source is widened from an inbound perspective. Germany, on the contrary, signals a stricter PE concept in comparison to the OECD MC so that the taxing rights in the source country are reduced. For the US, Brazil and China, no clear tendency can be derived from the national and country-specific treaty rulings or court decisions.

447. In fact, a US revenue ruling includes the 'separate bargaining for the consideration' of a room as indicator for a fixed place of business. In this context, the US view focuses more on the practical aspect of including the provision of the room in the service contract than on the question for disposal over the room. See for more details section 5.2.1.
448. See section 4.2.4.1.
449. See section 4.2.5.1.
450. See section 4.2.6.1.

*Figure 4.2 Comparison of the Basic PE Case – OECD, DE, US, BRIC**

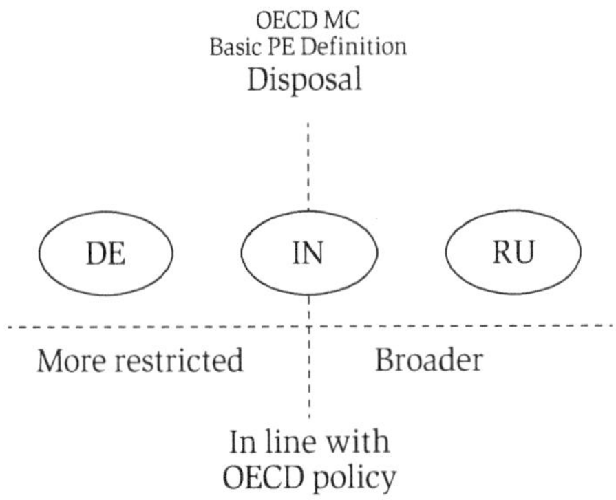

* No concrete statement possible for BR, CN, US

Considering the special PE case of the construction site PE, there is one aspect which can be an indicator of an increased fiscal nexus: the delegation of work to subcontractors.[451] As the OECD additionally involves the checking of the disposal criterion and even assumes a construction site PE for the general contractor in case of total delegation of work to the subcontractor according to the OECD Reform Proposal, room for interpretation exists especially with regard to the delegation of work to subcontractors (see Table 4.15).

Table 4.15 Comparison of the Construction Site PE Case – OECD, DE, US, BRIC

	Delegation of Work to Subcontractors
OECD status quo and reform proposals	– Involves additional checking of disposal over premises – Total delegation assumes PE for general contractor without physical presence (*Reform Proposal*)
German national & treaty law	– Working time of subcontractor is counted as time of general contractor – No PE for the general contractor in case of total delegation
US national & treaty law	– Working time of subcontractor is counted as time of general contractor – Not sufficient information with regard to total delegation of work to subcontractors
Brazilian national & treaty law	No specific information

451. Of course, the permanence requirement is the crucial criterion of the existence of a construction site PE which is set to twelve months by the OECD. The duration of the time threshold might also be interpreted as indicator of increased or decreased source taxation. However, as the permanence threshold is mostly a concrete matter of treaty negotiation, the focus of this work is on other aspects which provide for an increased room of interpretation.

	Delegation of Work to Subcontractors
Russian national & treaty law	- Working time of subcontractor and affiliate is counted as time of general contractor - Conflictive information with regard to total delegation of work to subcontractor
Indian national & treaty law	- Working time of subcontractor is counted as time of general contractor - No exclusion of PE in case of total delegation (if UN MC is followed)
Chinese national & treaty law	- Working time of subcontractor is counted as time of general contractor - No exclusion of PE in case of total delegation (if UN MC is followed)

The total delegation of work to subcontractors without the physical presence of the general contractor's employees does not constitute a construction site PE under German national and treaty law.[452]

US national and treaty law does not provide for much information with regard to the total delegation of work to subcontractors. The Technical Explanation of the US MC only mentions that the working time of the subcontractor is added to the time of the general contractor for the calculation of the permanence threshold.[453] This indicates that the US, similar to the OECD MC, effectively considers the time that the subcontractor worked at the construction site as working time of the general contractor. Still, it is not known if the general contractor should also be present in the source country in order to constitute a construction site PE.

Brazilian national and treaty law does not include concrete information considering the delegation of work to subcontractors.

Russian national law allocates the working time of the subcontractor and affiliates of the general contractor to the general contractor's time spent in the source country in case of a partial delegation of work. In addition, opposed information exists in Russian case law with regard to whether the total delegation of work to subcontractors is supposed to constitute a construction site PE for the general contractor.[454]

Indian national law does not provide for any specific rules with regard to the delegation of work to subcontractors. Similar to the OECD MC, the working time of the subcontractor is added to the time of the general contractor in case of partial delegation. Indian case law indicates a denial of a construction site PE in case the presence of the general contractor is minimal. Still, in accordance with the UN MC, it can also be assumed that Indian treaty law does not exclude the PE establishment in case of total delegation of work to subcontractors.[455]

452. See section 4.2.1.1.
453. See section 4.2.2.1.
454. See section 4.2.4.1.
455. See section 4.2.5.1.

China also does not include special rules considering the construction site PE in national law. Similar to India, Chinese treaty law follows the UN MC stating that the working time of a subcontractor is added to the time of the general contractor whereas in case of the total delegation of work to subcontractors, a PE can still be theoretically determined for the general contractor.[456]

In comparison to the rules of the OECD Reform Proposal, only Germany clearly contradicts with the OECD view and does not constitute a construction site PE in this case (see Figure 4.3). Thus, German tax policy again indicates a restricted PE concept and a limited taxing right at source. If Indian and Chinese tax treaties followed the understanding of the UN MC (what they actually do with regard to the construction site PE article in most treaties[457]), it can be derived that their tax treaty policy is in line with the OECD approach of assuming a PE through the total delegation of work to subcontractors. Still, this is a theoretical indication and cannot be settled clearly. For the other countries, due to a lack of information in the US and China or contradicting case law in Russia, it cannot be determined if the countries' policy is in line with or in opposition to the OECD approach.

Figure 4.3 Comparison of the Construction Site PE Case – OECD, DE, US, BRIC ***

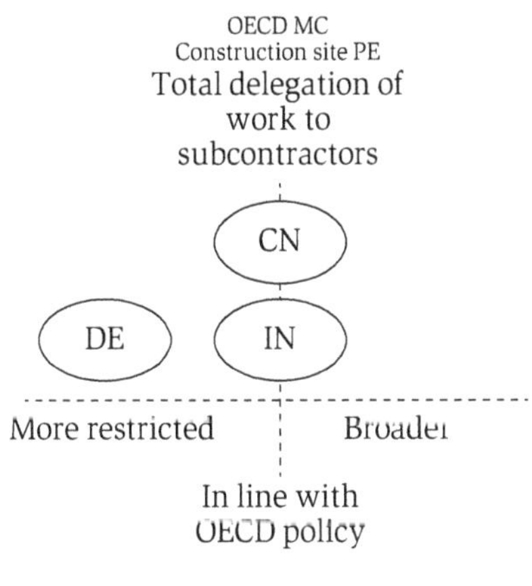

* No concrete statement possible for BR, RU, US

** CN and IN in line with OECD policy if UN MC is followed

With regard to the agency PE, there is one crucial criterion for which the OECD grants the possibility of interpreting it in a '*wide*' sense, namely the authority of the dependent agent to conclude contracts for the foreign principal.[458] According to the OECD MC Commentary and the OECD BEPS Action Plan 7, contracts which do not bind the

456. See section 4.2.6.1.
457. See Appendix, Tables A7 & A8. The inclusion of supervisory activities in the construction site-article is considered as indicator of similarity with the UN MC.
458. See section 3.2.2.

principal explicitly and legally '*in the name of*' the principal, can basically constitute an agency PE. Thus, the power to conclude contracts can be understood on an economic rather than on a legal basis. Another PE requirement to be considered is the existence of an independent agent as possible constraint to the determination of an agency PE (see Table 4.16).

Table 4.16 Comparison of the Agency PE Case – OECD, DE, US, BRIC

	Authority to Conclude Contracts in the Name of the Principal	*Existence of an Independent Agent Constraint for Tax Purposes*
OECD status quo and reform proposals	Legal and economic authorization	Given
German national & treaty law	- Not required in national law - Focus on economic authorization (but arguable)	Given for national and treaty law
US national & treaty law	- No specific rule in national law - No specific focus in treaty law - Common law	Given for national and treaty law
Brazilian national & treaty law	- Inclusion of commissionaire and agent performing sales activities under national law	- No differentiation in national tax law - Similar to OECD MC in treaty law
Russian national & treaty law	- Focus on legal authorization in domestic case law - Recent trend of focusing on economic authorization	Given for national and treaty law
Indian national & treaty law	- No specific focus in national law - Focus on economic authorization in treaty law	- Given for national and treaty law - Wider fiscal nexus of independent agent in treaty law
Chinese national & treaty law	- No specific rules in national law - No specific focus in treaty law	- Given for treaty law - Wider fiscal nexus of independent agent in treaty law

The German national permanent representative does not require that the authority to conclude contracts is conducted legally or economically in the name of the principal. German treaty law generally follows the concept of the OECD MC with regard to the agency PE.[459] Germany focuses on the economic authority to conclude contracts in the

459. See section 4.2.1.1.

name of the principal although the wording of the German tax authorities is questionable. The difference between dependent and independent agents is given for German national and treaty law.

US national and treaty law does not include any specific statement with regard to the degree of authority to conclude contracts but as a common law country, it can be assumed that the economic authorization is followed. Still, the US differentiates between dependent and independent agents.[460]

Brazilian national law generally includes sales activities of commissionaires (*commissários*) and representative agents (*mandatários*) as PE-constituting business activities.[461] The inclusion of commissionaires which act in their own name for the account of the principal and still establish an agency PE for the principal, basically implies that the authority to conclude contracts is interpreted on an economic basis according to Brazilian tax law. In addition, the differentiation between dependent and independent agents does not play a role in Brazilian domestic tax statutes. Brazilian treaty policy generally follows the OECD MC with regard to the existence of an independent agent constraint.

Russian domestic case law generally follows the legal obligation with regard to the authority to conclude contracts for the principal while pure negotiation activities are sufficient to constitute an agency PE. Still, a recent trend exists to focus more on the economic basis in national tax law under the new Russian transfer pricing rules.[462] An independent agent constraint similar to the OECD MC also exists in Russian domestic law. Russian treaty law and the Russian MC are basically in line with the OECD standard.

Indian national law mentions the authority to conclude contracts on behalf of the principal but does not specify if the principal is obliged legally or economically. Indian case law considering treaty policy indicates that the contractual authority has to be understood on a wider economic basis.[463] Both Indian national and treaty law include a differentiation between dependent and independent agents whereas the fiscal nexus of an independent agent is broader in accordance with the UN MC.

The Chinese national concept of establishment does not provide for any specific rules with regard to the authority to conclude contracts.[464] A differentiation between dependent and independent agents is not given. Chinese treaty law mentions the contractual authority as requirement of an agency PE but regulations towards the degree of interpretation are missing. Most Chinese treaties follow the OECD MC with regard to the dependent agent clause. Still, with regard to independent agents, a wider fiscal nexus is given as the independent agent provision in Chinese treaty policy is orientated towards the UN MC.

In comparison to the OECD approach, only the US is in line with the OECD policy considering the authority to conclude contracts and the independent agent constraint

460. See section 4.2.2.1.
461. See section 4.2.3.1.
462. See section 4.2.4.1.
463. See section 4.2.5.1.
464. See section 4.2.6.1.

of the agency PE provision (see Figure 4.4). This results from the '*common law*' concept of the US which determines a wide economic authorization of the agent as being decisive for the existence of an agency PE. Brazil is determined as following a broader agency PE definition mostly due to the independent agent constraint which is not existent in Brazilian domestic law. For India and China, the inclusion of an exclusionary criterion in most tax treaties which neglects the independence status of the agent by acting for one principal indicates a broader agency PE definition.[465] Thus, the agency PE concept is understood on a broader basis which leads to an increased source taxing right. In fact, the future OECD policy in terms of the current BEPS discussion will also adapt the exception of '*acting for one principal*' for an independent agent. Thus, the OECD approach basically aligns with the Chinese and Indian approach with regard to the understanding of the independent agent constraint.[466] In Germany and Russia, there are unclear official statements with regard to the understanding of the agent's necessary authority to conclude contracts so that concrete conclusions cannot be drawn.

*Figure 4.4 Comparison of the Agency PE Case – OECD, DE, US, BRIC**

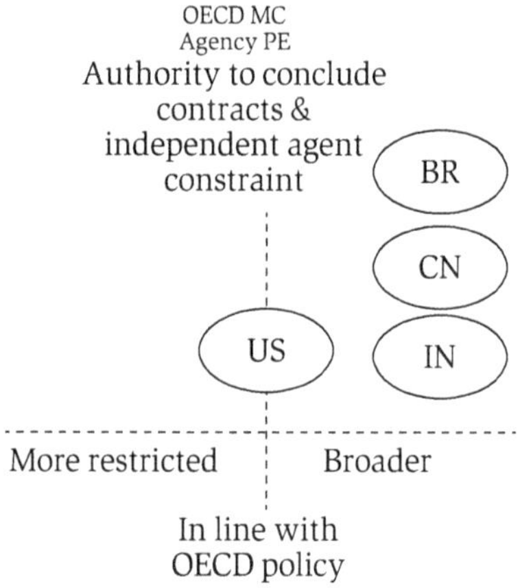

* No concrete statement possible for DE, RU

Considering the service PE, there are two debatable topics: One is whether a service PE and thus a fiscal nexus in the source country without the requirement of a fixed place of business exists in national and treaty law. The other topic which is related to the service PE provision is the treatment of employees which are seconded from a foreign workforce-lending company in order to provide services in the source country, in most

465. See Appendix, Table A9 & A10.
466. In contrast to Indian and Chinese treaty policy, the OECD additionally introduced an additional requirement of acting for 'closely-related' principals with a participation rate of over 50% in order to neglect the independence status of the agent. See OECD Final Report BEPS Action 7 (2015) p. 16.

cases at the premises of a client or at another subsidiary of the company group. The OECD includes the service PE as an alternative option in the OECD MC Commentary. The PE establishment by business activities performed by seconded employees depends on the concept of the economic employer including factors such as supervision, direction and control over the employees (see Table 4.17).

Table 4.17 Comparison of the Service PE Case – OECD, DE, US, BRIC

	Existence of a Service PE Provision	*Fiscal Treatment of Secondment of Employees*
OECD status quo and reform proposals	Given in the OECD MC Commentary as alternative option	- Supervision, direction and control as PE requirements - Concept of economic employer (*Reform Proposal*)
German national & treaty law	- Not given in national law - Seldom in treaty practice	Generally no PE for workforce-lending company under national and treaty law (except for 'active' activities)
US national & treaty law	- '*Personal services*'- rule in national law - Occasionally included in treaty law	- Control and risk as PE requirements under national law - Supervision, direction and control as PE requirements under treaty law
Brazilian national & treaty law	- Not given in national law - Focus on Article 21 UN MC or Article 12 UN MC as alternative fiscal nexus for services in treaty law	- No specific information in national law - Secondment treated as taxable service income in treaty law
Russian national & treaty law	- Not given in national law - Included in Russian MC - Seldom in treaty practice	- Practical factors of responsibility, calculation method, fixed level of margin as PE requirements under national law - Strict Russian migration law restricts PE issue - No specific information in treaty law
Indian national & treaty law	- Not given in national law - Generally included in treaty practice - Royalty-article as alternative fiscal nexus for technical service fees	- No specific information in national law - Responsibility, control and '*lien*' on employment as PE requirements under treaty law

	Existence of a Service PE Provision	*Fiscal Treatment of Secondment of Employees*
Chinese national & treaty law	- No specific rule in national law - Generally included in treaty practice	- Responsibility and risk as PE requirements under national and treaty law depending on several practical factors

German national law does not include a service PE provision but rather refers to the general domestic PE provision.[467] In German treaty law, the service PE provision is rare and is not included in the German basis for treaty negotiations of 2013. German national and treaty law are both restricted and usually do not consider the secondment of employees to a foreign host company as PE-constituting activity until the services performed by the seconded employees result in an active business operation of the workforce-lending company which is generally based on the economic employer approach.

US national law does not apply a special service PE provision. Still, profits derived from personal services provided in the US are explicitly taxed as US source income.[468] US treaty law occasionally includes the service PE clause in its tax treaties, mostly with developing countries. With regard to the secondment of employees, similar to the OECD approach, US national and treaty law includes factors such as control, responsibility and the bearing of risk when deciding about possible PE cases of the workforce-lending company.

Brazilian domestic law does not include a service PE.[469] Brazilian treaty law focuses on the other income-article, similar to Article 21 UN MC, or on Article 12 of the UN MC as fiscal nexus for business income derived from services. The secondment of employees is not considered in Brazilian national law. Under Brazilian treaty law, business income derived from services provided by seconded employees are probably considered as service income thus being taxable at source on a gross basis in accordance with the Brazilian specific '*way*' of taxing services.

Russian domestic law does not provide for a service PE provision. The Russian MC includes a service PE clause although Russian treaty practice only applies a service PE in rare cases.[470] With regard to the secondment of employees, Russian national law mentions practical factors such as the responsibility of work for the seconded employees, the calculation method or a fixed margin of the employer which indicate if a PE exists for the workforce-lending company. Still, Russian migration law has to be taken into account which effectively restricts the PE issue in case of secondment working relations. Russian treaty law does not provide for any guidance.

The Indian domestic business connection concept does not explicitly mention a service PE provision. Indian tax treaties usually include a service PE clause in the PE definition. In addition, the royalty-article is often used as alternative fiscal nexus for

467. See section 4.2.1.1.
468. See section 4.2.2.1.
469. See section 4.2.3.1.
470. See section 4.2.4.1.

technical service fees.[471] Considering the secondment of employees, Indian case law recommends the application of factors such as responsibility and control over the seconded employee's work and details of the legal employment contract in order to decide about the establishment of a PE for the foreign workforce-lending company. A '*lien*' on the employment with the foreign employer seems to be one of the most important indicators.

China mentions labour services in its domestic establishment definition but does not provide further information. Similar to India, Chinese tax treaties generally include the service PE clause.[472] Chinese domestic and treaty law contain detailed instructions considering the possible PE establishment of a foreign workforce-lending company in case of a secondment of employees. Specific factors of the working contract and payment instructions of the secondment deal indicate whether a service PE is established through the activities provided by the seconded employees. The fulfilment of just one criterion already seems to indicate the existence of a Chinese service PE.

In comparison to the OECD MC, the US is not completely in line with the OECD policy with regard to the existence of the service PE and the fiscal treatment of secondment of employees (see Figure 4.5). This results from the rarely used service PE provision in US tax treaties. Still, under US domestic law, a taxing right for personal services is generally given. In addition, the fiscal treatment of secondment of employees is similar. This is also true for Germany. Still, there is no domestic fiscal nexus for the provision of services in German domestic and treaty law so that the German approach is considered as being more restricted. On the other side, the specific Brazilian way of taxing services on a gross basis generally determines an increased taxing right at source. For Russia similar to the US, there are more indicators for a restricted service PE concept which mostly results from the fact that service PEs are only occasionally included in Russian tax treaties. With regard to the secondment of employees, Russia provides for detailed practical instructions which indicate a lower scope of interpretation and thus a possible reduction of PE cases. Despite the inclusion of the service PE term in the Russian MC, Russian migration law effectively restricts the PE issue with regard to secondment arrangements. For China, the inclusion of the service PE in treaty practice indicates an extension of the PE term. Considering the secondment of employees, China provides for detailed instructions. Still, this cannot imply a reduction of possible PE cases as the application of PE factors is strict. For India, the service PE is also generally included in treaty law. Considering the secondment of employees, the enlargement of the PE term depends on the specific Indian requirement of '*lien*' on the employment which has to be interpreted on a broad basis.

471. See section 4.2.5.1.
472. See section 4.2.6.1.

Figure 4.5 Comparison of the Service PE Case – OECD, DE, US, BRIC

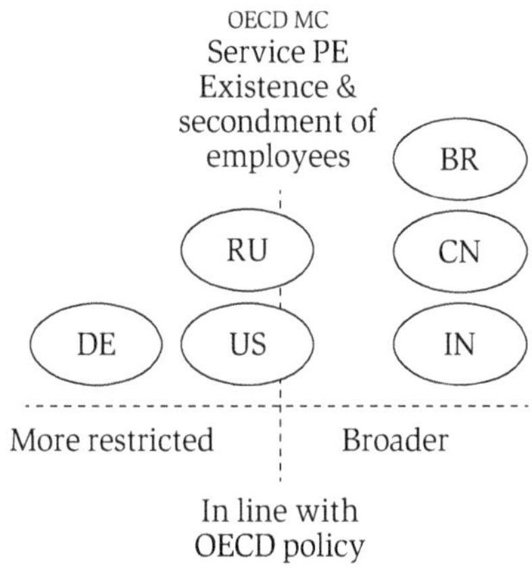

4.3.2 Comparison of the National Regulations on the Attribution of Business Profits to a PE with the OECD Approach

With regard to the allocation of business profits between head office and PE, the OECD follows the functionally separate entity approach, both for the basic PE case and the special PE cases such as construction, agency and service PEs (see Table 4.18). One of the crucial factors which is an indicator for the allocation of taxing rights between residence and source country is the fiscal treatment of internal dealings between the head office and the PE such as the internal transfer of assets, the internal provision of services, the inclusion of internal notional royalty or interest payments, e.g., due to the internal use of intangible assets or internal loans provided. By exclusively considering the proposed method of profit allocation of the OECD MC, a trend to strive for an increased residence or source taxation cannot be determined.[473] The increased taxable profit deductions with respect to profit-inducing internal dealings can affect the residence as well as the source countries' tax base. Still, also with respect to further investigations in this work, it can be questioned if national and country-specific treaty law of the considered countries are in line with the OECD approach or deviate to a considerable extent. In addition, it can be identified if a trend of allocation of the tax base might exist on a national basis (see Table 4.18).

473. See section 3.3.2.

Table 4.18 Comparison of Rules on the Attribution of Business Profits – OECD, DE, US, BRIC

	Basic PE	*Special PE*
OECD status quo	- AOA following functions performed, assets used, risk assumed, capital allocated - Internal dealings generally induce taxable profit	- No specific rules - Application of AOA - Rejection of '*single taxpayer approach*' for agency PE
German national & treaty law	- *National and treaty law*: Similar to AOA - Internal dealings generally induce taxable profit - *Treaty: 'Old'* OECD view more present: - Restriction with regard to taxable recognition of internal dealings	- Similar to AOA in current national and treaty law - Specific rules for construction site PE similar to AOA in national law - Application of '*single taxpayer approach*' for agency PE discussable
US national & treaty law	- *National*: ECI concept following force of attraction - Internal dealings generally not recognized for tax purposes - *Treaty*: Acceptance of AOA - However, '*old*' OECD view more present: Restriction with regard to taxable recognition of internal dealings	- No specific rules in national law and treaty law - Orientation towards '*old*' view in treaty law
Brazilian national & treaty law	- *National*: Similar to resident corporate entities - Internal dealings generally recognized for tax purposes - Restrictions with regard to internal royalties and services - *Treaty*: Rejection of AOA - Internal dealings generally not recognized for tax purposes - Fixed profit margins	- No specific rules in national law except for agency PE - Orientation towards '*old*' view in treaty law
Russian national & treaty law	- *National*: Principle of direct economic connection to PE - Internal dealings generally not recognized for tax purposes	- No specific rules in national law and treaty law

	Basic PE	*Special PE*
	- *Treaty*: '*Old*' OECD view more present:Restriction with regard to taxable recognition of internal dealings - However, new Transfer Pricing Rules 2012 prescribe AOA	
Indian national & treaty law	- *National*: Principle of reasonable attribution - Application of presumptive methods - Similar to resident corporate entities under Transfer Pricing Rules 2001 - Internal dealings generally recognized for tax purposes - *Treaty*: Limited force of attraction and disallowance of deduction of internal PE expenses in UN treaties - '*Old*' view more present in OECD treaties - Internal dealings generally recognized for tax purposes under transfer pricing rules	- No specific rules in national and treaty law - Case law indicates application of arm's length principle (*SET Satellite/ Morgan Stanley*) and limited force of attraction (*Linklaters*)
Chinese national & treaty law	- *National*: Principle of effective connection based on functional analysis - Application of deemed profit methods - Internal dealings generally recognized for tax purposes - *Treaty*: '*Old*' OECD view more present - Internal dealings generally not recognized for tax purposes - Application of deemed profit methods in treaty law	- No specific rules in national and treaty law

German national and treaty law generally follows the AOA which includes the allocation of business profits according to significant people functions performed and the general recognition of internal dealings for tax purposes.[474] However, most of the German tax treaties are still in line with the '*old*' view of the OECD MC and include

474. See section 4.2.1.2.

restrictions to the functionally separate entity approach, especially with regard to the inclusion of a profit mark-up for internal dealings and the deduction of PE expenses. In general, the AOA as implemented in German tax law also has to be applied for special PE cases despite the presence of the *'old'* view in most German tax treaties. Only with regard to construction site PEs, the new German PE Decree includes specific rules which, however, resemble the AOA in its basic direction. Especially for agency PEs, the *'single taxpayer approach'* or *'zero-sum'*-theory is present in German tax literature and it is discussable whether it should be implemented.

The US national law generally follows its own ECI concept which is based on a limited force of attraction approach. Internal dealings are generally not recognized for tax purposes.[475] US treaty law is open to the AOA but the current state of tax treaties indicates that the majority is more in line with the *'old'* view of the OECD MC. With regard to the attribution of business profits to special PEs, US national and treaty law do not include specific rules implying that, similar to the basic PE case, US treaty policy is orientated towards the *'old'* OECD view considering the attribution of PE business profits.

Brazil generally treats PEs similar to corporate resident entities in case of a successful registration. This means that according to national law, internal dealings are assumingly recognized for tax purposes although specific national restrictions exist.[476] In contrast to the OECD approach, fixed profit margins are additionally applied under Brazilian transfer pricing rules. Brazilian treaty policy rejects the AOA and thus basically limits the taxable recognition of internal dealings between head office and PE. Except for an agency PE, specific income attribution rules for special PE cases do not exist in Brazilian national and treaty law.

Russia usually applies a method of direct economic connection of PE income. Internal dealings are generally not recognized for tax purposes. However, the Russian Transfer Pricing Rules of 2012 effectively introduced the AOA in Russian national law.[477] Further consequences remain to be seen. Russian treaty practice and the Russian MC are more in line with the *'old'* view of the OECD MC. Specific rules with regard to the allocation of income to special PE cases do not exist in Russia.

Indian domestic law usually implements a functional analysis on the basis of the separate legal entity approach according to the Indian transfer pricing rules for the allocation of PE profits.[478] However, predetermined presumptive methods also exist in case law. Indian tax treaties which follow the UN MC occasionally include a limited force of attraction principle and a prohibition of deduction of certain internal PE expenses. The other OECD treaties are in line with the *'old'* OECD view. The AOA is not applied. For special PE cases, there are no specific rules. Indian case law confirms the application of the arm's length principle, especially for agency and service PEs. China generally applies a concept of economic connection based on a functional analysis in its

475. See section 4.2.2.2.
476. See section 4.2.3.2.
477. See section 4.2.4.2.
478. See section 4.2.5.2.

national law.[479] Chinese treaty policy is more in line with the '*old*' OECD concept whereas a prohibition of deduction exists for certain PE expenses. In addition, the use of deemed profit methods is ongoing and is also implemented in Chinese tax treaties. Specific rules for special PE cases do not exist in Chinese domestic and treaty law.

In general, *German* national and treaty policy is in line with the AOA (see Figure 4.6). Still, most of the current German tax treaties rely on the '*old*' OECD attribution including restrictions with regard to the taxable recognition of internal dealings. Similar to the OECD approach, a trend of increasing or decreasing source taxation due to profit attribution rules can hardly be considered under the German attribution rules as the arm's length recognition of internal dealings may have a positive or negative effect on the source or residence tax base of the involved head office and PE depending on the direction of flow of the income stream. In addition, especially for an agency PE, it remains to be seen if the single taxpayer approach is followed which decreases the tax base in the source country.

US domestic law generally provides for an increased source tax base as the ECI concept is based on a limited force of attraction principle. With regard to US treaty policy, a trend cannot be observed regardless of the US restriction on the recognition of internal dealings. Still, in principle, the US accepts the AOA as standard for the allocation of business profits.

Brazil treats a PE similar to resident corporate entities depending on an official registration but generally rejects the AOA in its treaties. Independent of the fiscal treatment of internal dealings, the use of fixed profit margins, the restrictions of deduction of certain PE royalty and service expenses, and the general classification of services as other income taxed on a gross basis, are indicators for an increased source tax base in Brazilian national and treaty law.

Russian attribution policy does not follow a trend. National and current treaty law apply a principle of effective connection for which restrictions exist with regard to the taxable recognition of internal dealings. Future Russian tax law indicates the application of the AOA under the new Russian Transfer Pricing Rules 2012 which can probably lead to a change considering the fiscal treatment of internal dealings. Still, as in Germany, this cannot be taken as indicator of an increased source taxation due to the possible reverse effect of taxable recognition of internal dealings including a profit mark-up which can affect the tax base of the source and the residence country.

India generally follows the trend of an increased PE tax base. Indicators are the application of fixed presumptive methods in Indian national law, a limited force of attraction principle occasionally applied in Indian tax treaties and approved by Indian case law, and the prohibition of deduction of internal PE expenses in accordance with the UN MC. However, this depends on the provisions included in the respective treaty. In addition, controversial Indian case law decisions which indicate the usage of the single taxpayer approach, e.g., for agency and service PEs, contradict the enlargement of the Indian PE tax base.

479. See section 4.2.6.2.

China also includes indicators of an increased source tax base. The application of deemed profits methods in Chinese national and treaty law and the prohibition of deduction of internal PE expenses similar to the UN MC imply an increased PE tax base independent of the fiscal treatment of internal dealings.

Figure 4.6 Comparison of Rules on the Attribution of Business Profits – OECD, DE, US, BRIC

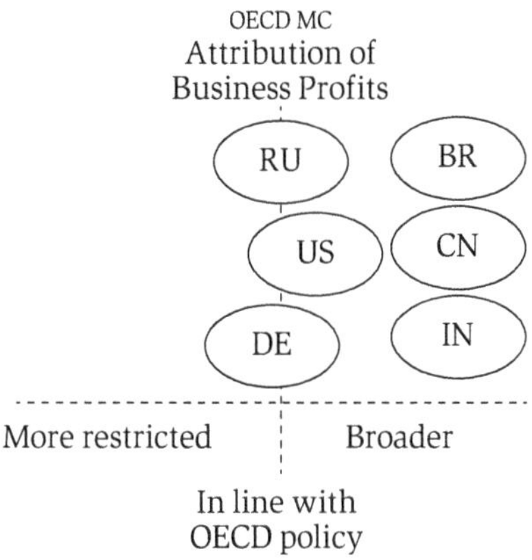

4.3.3 Summarized Conclusions

In summary two of the six countries considered, namely India and China, basically follow the recent OECD trend of an enlargement of the PE definition. In contrast to the OECD approach, both countries also show indicators of an increased PE tax base in their profit allocation rules. Especially with regard to the fiscal treatment of services, Brazil also shows preconditions for an enlargement of source taxation although the PE issue does not play a major role. In contrast, Brazil follows its '*own*' way of treaty interpretation which relies more on withholding taxes on a gross basis. Russia takes a middle position as most of the older tax treaties are not consistent with the current OECD policy. Still, recent guidance on Russian national and treaty regulations indicate the future application of the AOA in Russian tax law. It remains to be seen if the Russian approach on the PE definition will also follow the OECD policy. Germany is not in line with the OECD trend of an enlarged PE definition whereas it basically adopted the AOA in its future national and treaty law. Similar to Germany, the US generally accepts the AOA with practical restrictions in current treaty policy. Still, it tends to be not that restricted with regard to an enlargement of the PE definition in comparison to Germany.

In general, the current OECD policy with regard to the PE definition (status quo and reform proposals) has more in common with the country-specific approach of the non-OECD countries like India and China than with the concept of the '*traditional*' OECD states like Germany and the US. Still, with regard to the allocation of business profits, OECD policy is more in line with the profit allocation approach of the well-established OECD countries.

CHAPTER 5

Cross-Country Analysis of the OECD and National PE Concepts and the Rules on the Attribution of Business Income

5.1 GENERAL DESCRIPTION OF CONFLICTS AND ASSUMPTIONS OF THE SIMULATED CROSS-BORDER CASE

In general, double or non-taxation situations usually result from a qualification conflict, i.e., an inconsistent application of treaty law by the contracting states.[1] This can occur for the following situations.

A qualification conflict can arise from different classifications of the same taxable object by the residence and source country due to different provisions in the domestic tax law of the two countries involved. Following Article 3 (2) of the OECD MC, the stand-alone interpretation of each of the considered contracting states shall only be applicable if an own definition is not given in the treaty and an interpretation in treaty context is not possible.[2] As the PE is generally defined in the treaty, the treaty definition usually prevails in this case and Article 3 (2) of the OECD MC shall not be applied. Another qualification conflict occurs when different treaty provisions are used. A conflict in this context can arise with regard to the definition and extent of business profits which can be considered either as PE profits or other types of income such as dividend or interest income being taxed differently.[3] Other qualification conflicts can arise from the different interpretation of facts by the contracting states.[4] This can occur

1. See e.g. German Partnership Circular (2014) No. 4.1.3.1, p. 28. For an overview considering the different classifications of the term 'qualification conflict' see i.a. Wehrße (2011) pp. 77 ff.
2. See OECD MC Commentary (2014) Article 3, No. 12, p. 83.
3. See i.a. Jirousek (2005) p. 178.
4. See i.a. Lüdicke (2010) p. 617, Wehrße (2011) p. 81.

with regard to specific PE attributes not clearly defined in the treaty which can be interpreted differently by the considered states depending on the facts of the case.[5]

Irrespective of the type of qualification conflict, double or non-taxation situations generally occur if the residence and the source country do not agree on the existence of a PE at source. If the country of residence is of the opinion that there is no PE in the source country whereas the country of source determines a local PE, double taxation occurs regardless of the double taxation avoidance method used in the residence country. Both the source and residence country tax the PE income while the residence country of the head office neither exempt the PE income (if the exemption method applies) nor grant a tax credit (if the tax credit method applies) because from the viewpoint of the country of residence of the head office, no foreign income exists.[6] Vice versa, if the source country does not determine a PE at source whereas the country of residence believes a PE exists in the source country, non-taxation can occur if the residence country generally applies the exemption method and no subject-to-tax, switch-over or other anti-avoidance method exist in the residence country.

Double or non-taxation can also occur with regard to the attribution of PE profits. If the source country does not allow the deduction of expenses from PE income including a profit mark-up but the residence country recognizes this income for tax purposes, double taxation occurs. Vice versa, non-taxation occurs if the source country allows the deduction of an internal expense but the residence country does not recognize this income including a profit mark-up (given that the residence country applies the exemption method for foreign PE profits).[7] Furthermore, similar to the pricing of transfers between independent affiliated companies, double and non-taxation problems can occur if the residence and source country disagree about the adequate amount of profit mark-up for the allocation of income between head office and PE (transfer pricing problem).[8]

In order to reveal possible qualification conflicts for the presented countries, a simulated cross-border inbound case is considered where an investor from a residence country (country R) conducts business activities in a source country (country S). A valid tax treaty between country S and country R exists which is in line with the current OECD MC. Country R follows the regulations and interpretations of the OECD MC, the OECD MC Commentary and the ideas of the OECD Reform Proposal. Country S, the country of investment, is Germany, the United States, Brazil, Russia, India or China (see Figure 5.1).[9]

5. See already von Poser und Groß-Naedlitz (1972) p. 106, who considers the PE definition as most important example of a direct interpretation conflict.
6. See Blanluet/ Durand (2011) p. 31.
7. Similar effects can also arise due to differences regarding of income determination which occur due to country-specific tax accounting rules. See e.g. Bendlinger (2007a) p. 500. However, this is not considered here.
8. See e.g. Bennett/Dunahoo (2005) p. 55.
9. The PE interpretations of the respective countries are either taken from known common treaty policy or national case law.

Figure 5.1 Structure of the Cross-Border Case

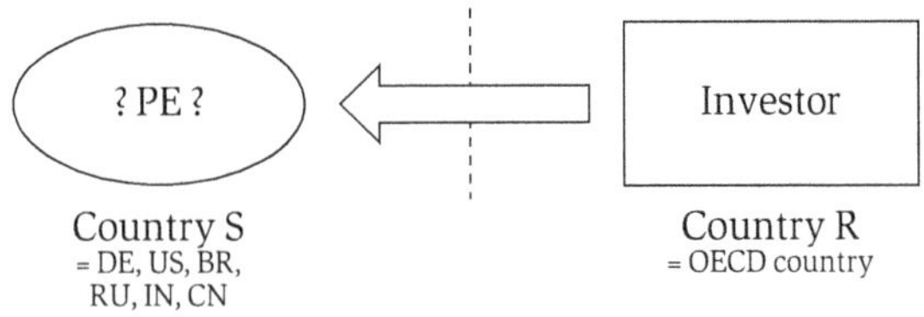

By constructing different cases, the analysis focuses on debatable PE requirements such as the disposal criterion (basic PE), the delegation of work to subcontractors (construction site PE), the degree of authority to conclude contracts (agency PE) and the secondment of employees (service PE). In addition, the recognition of internal dealings with regard to the attribution of business profits between head office and PE is examined. In all cases, it is assumed that the business activities do not have a preparatory or auxiliary character so that the PE exclusion of Article 5 (4) OECD MC is not considered.

The analysis takes into account qualification conflicts which arise due to vague PE attributes not clearly defined in the treaty and where a range of interpretation possibilities exist depending on the national viewpoints of the different countries involved.[10] Still, the following analysis focuses on cases which cannot be initially solved from the wording of the treaty and where differences in interpretation of PE requirements are in the details.

5.2 CONFLICTS WITH REGARD TO THE PE DEFINITION

5.2.1 Basic PE: 'Passive' Service PE

The first case to be considered is the '*passive*' service PE. By assumption, a worker of a corporation, resident in country R provides services at the premises of a client in the source country S.[11] The question is if the services provided at third party premises can constitute a PE for the resident corporation (see Figure 5.2).

10. See also van Raad (2000) p. 1096. In fact, further various qualification conflicts due to the different scopes of interpretation between contracting states are also possible, e.g. with regard to the permanence requirement for the existence of a PE or with regard to the definition and interpretation of PE-negating preparatory or auxiliary activities.
11. By assumption, for this case, a service PE is not included in the treaty between country R and country S.

Figure 5.2 Basic PE Case – 'Passive' Service PE

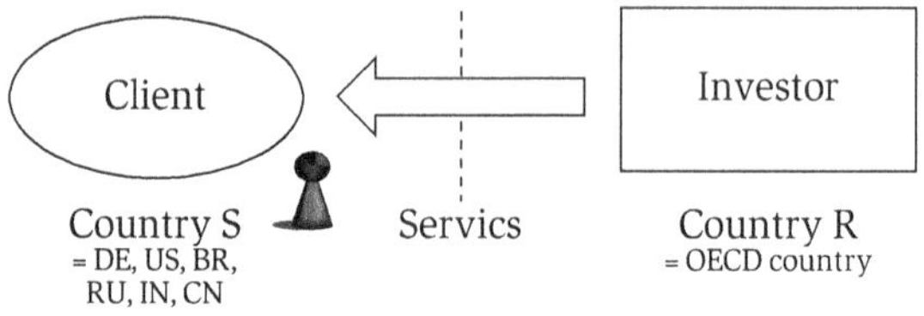

First, the necessary PE requirements of the basic PE definition (Article 5 (1) OECD MC) have to be checked. These requirements cover the existence of a fixed place of business and the conduct of the business in the source country.[12] By assumption, the worker provides major service activities which are main activities of the resident corporation. In addition, the work will be performed on a regular basis over a longer period of time (e.g., four days a week for eighteen months) and so the time threshold as basic PE requirement is considered to be fulfilled. Therefore, the crucial criterion in this case is whether the third party premises can establish a fixed place of business in country S for the corporation being resident in country R. One decisive point here is the disposal requirement meaning that a certain level of control is needed so that the service-providing company can use the place of business at its own choice at any time for its own business purposes.

According to the OECD MC, the presence and the working of a painter at the client's premises indicate a necessary degree of disposal and thus a fixed place of business.[13] This has not changed under the OECD Reform Proposal which considers the possession of an exclusive legal right and the fulfilment of a certain time threshold as additional indicators of disposal.[14] The service-providing company is not supposed to have an exclusive legal right to use the premises of the client for its own business activities as the client is generally authorized to enter his own premises. Still, a PE is established in country S from the perspective of residence country R because, in accordance with the current OECD view as expressed in the OECD MC Commentary, the presence and the service activities at the third party premises indicate a necessary degree of disposal. The permanence requirement is supposed to be fulfilled.

A qualification conflict occurs if the source country does not interpret the disposal criterion in the same '*wide*' way as the OECD MC. This is the case for *Germany*. Given the assumption that Germany is the source country S where the service activities are provided, German tax authorities will refuse the existence of a PE in such cases as the German understanding of the disposal criterion is stricter than the OECD viewpoint.[15] Especially Germany does not agree with the painter example of

12. For this example case, the existence of an agency PE which might probably be assumed by some countries is neglected.
13. See section 3.1.1.
14. See section 3.1.2.
15. See section 4.2.1.1.

the OECD MC Commentary.[16] According to the interpretation of the German tax jurisdiction, the disposal criterion usually requires a formal right to use the place of business which cannot be removed or amended without the agreement or assistance of the service provider. In addition, a certain local connection to the place of business has to exist (*Verwurzelung*). If services are provided at the client's premises the client usually has access to his own rooms so that the exclusive right to use the premises can be restricted. A certain strong local connection (*Verwurzelung*) is a vague criterion which is hard to identify in this case. Thus, German national law does not consider a PE in the case of services provided at third party premises in Germany whereas the residence country R recognizes a PE. Non-taxation of the resulting profits occurs if the residence country R applies the exemption method without any switch-over or subject-to-tax clause: Country R exempts the German PE income whereas Germany does not tax the income because a PE and thus a limited tax liability does not exist from a German viewpoint.[17]

If the *US* is the country of source in Figure 5.2, a concrete statement is hard to make. According to US national law, the performance of professional services is considered as being effectively connected to a US trade or business which also holds for service-providing employees of non-resident corporations (section 864 (b) IRC).[18] Although eventually a fixed physical presence in the context of a '*considerable, continuous and regular*' activity is necessary for such service providers, the establishment of a fixed place of business is not considered as single obligatory PE requirement but more as a signalling factor for generating a US taxing right.[19] Actually, the disposal criterion is not mentioned in this context. In the US asset-use test, in order to differentiate passive investment income from active US business income, the '*ultimate control*' over the investment of the asset is mentioned as comparable requirement.[20] However, in case of business income earned from the active provision of services, this requirement is supposed to be fulfilled. As the disposal requirement in the sense of an exclusive right to use is not elaborated in US domestic law, in a non-treaty case, a PE is thus probably recognized from a US point of view in case of regular services provided at the premises of a US client. In a treaty case, the PE definition of the US tax treaty prevails. In this context, US tax jurisdiction determined that planning services at the premises of a US client did not establish a PE since a fixed place of business according to the PE definition of the treaty was not given.[21] The reason i.a. was that the service provider did not '*separately bargain for the consideration*' of the room and the

16. See i.a. Eckl (2009) p. 325.
17. In fact, if the credit method is applied by the residence country, single taxation of profits is secured as the profits are taxed at least once following the worldwide principle of country R. In a comparable outbound case, double taxation occurs: The residence country R taxes the PE profits whereas the source country considers the foreign profits as income of the local service provider.
18. See section 4.2.2.1.
19. See section 4.2.2.1.
20. See section 4.2.2.1.
21. See section 4.2.2.1.

equipment used.[22] In relation to the '*passive*' service PE case above, the non-resident service provider probably constitutes a fixed place of business and thus a PE in the US if the provision of a room is a separate position in the service treaty negotiations between the foreign service provider and the US client. US treaty law thus focuses on a more practical requirement in this case: Instead of deciding on the degree of disposal over the third party premises, it can be assumed that the existence of a fixed place of business depends on the separate mentioning of the provision of the room in the service treaty. However, this qualification is case-driven so that it cannot be definitely concluded if an interpretation conflict occurs in this case. US domestic law is probably in line with the wide OECD view and assumes a US PE in case of services provided at the premises of a US client. US treaty policy focuses on the fact of separate bargaining for consideration of the third party premises as an indicator for a fixed place of business in the US. The US understanding of disposal thus focuses more on details of the service treaty and less on the question of the exclusive use of the rooms in the US.

A specific situation occurs in *Brazil*. Due to the rather vague and unclear PE definition, Brazilian national law does not include regulations with regard to the disposal requirement or the provision of services at third party premises at all.[23] As long as the complicated and expensive PE registration process is not carried out, income realized from services provided to a Brazilian client by a non-resident service provider is taxed on a gross basis in Brazil with the current Brazilian withholding tax rate.[24] Independent of the PE status, Brazilian treaty policy also treats the service income as other income following Article 21 of the UN MC, or alternatively, as royalty income similar to Article 12 (2) of the UN MC, so that both the residence country of the service provider and the source country are granted a taxing right.[25] In relation to the example in Figure 5.2, the OECD MC is applied between Brazil and country R so that the allocation of service income to the other income-article results in an exclusive taxing right for the residence country R. However, when considering the Brazilian tax treaty policy, the other income provision of all Brazilian tax treaties allocates a taxing right to both contracting states.[26] If this is assumed, Brazil levies a withholding tax on the gross service income whereas the residence country R either exempts the Brazilian income or credit the tax levied in Brazil against the worldwide income. Thus, at least an increased taxation in comparison to the PE case occurs as relevant PE expenses cannot be deducted from Brazilian PE income. If the limited tax credit method is used in country R, relevant PE expenses are recognized for the purpose of the calculation of the tax credit by the residence country so that the limit of the foreign tax credit increases. Therefore, the overall tax burden increases as well. In general, the concept of disposal is not brought up since the PE definition in this case does not play a role for Brazilian tax purposes.

22. See IRS revenue ruling 77-45 1977, CB 413. In fact, the term of disposal is not even mentioned in the US judgement.
23. See section 4.2.3.1. See the PE Questionnaire in the Appendix, Table A19.
24. See i.a. Rocha (2012) p. 160.
25. See section 4.2.3.1.
26. See Appendix, Table A11.

If the country of the service provision is *Russia*, a qualification conflict with the OECD country R will probably not occur. According to a statement of the Russian Ministry of Finance, services which are provided on a regular basis in the rooms of a client can establish a PE for the non-resident service provider even if the premises are not at the disposal of the service provider.[27] This obviously means that the disposal criterion does not play a major role when deciding about the fixed place of business in Russia.[28] In fact, this is in line with the '*wide*' OECD understanding of disposal implying that the mere presence and working at third party premises indicate a fixed place of business for the service provider. Also, according to the interpretation of both the OECD MC and the Russian tax authorities, a legal right to use the client's room is not necessary when questioning the degree of disposal.[29]

In *India*, similar to the OECD approach, the PE requirement of disposal is also interpreted in a broad way.[30] This is shown in two exemplary decisions of the Indian tax jurisdiction in the cases of *Seagate Singapore* and *Renoir Consulting Ltd* which approve that a fixed place of business and thus an Indian PE is established by regularly performing services at third party premises.[31] Independent of any legal requirement, the service provider is supposed to have disposal over the client's room in India if a certain right to visit and work at the premises is granted for a regular time period without considering any facts of exclusive usage and intensity of work in the source country. In fact, this is consistent with the OECD understanding of disposal as shown in the painter example of the OECD MC Commentary. Therefore, a qualification conflict with regard to the interpretation of the disposal criterion does not occur in Figure 5.2 as both countries assume a PE in the source country.

In case *China* is the source country in which the services are performed a concrete statement cannot be made due to the lack of information in national and treaty law. The term of disposal is only mentioned in an administrative tax notice of the Chinese SAT (Notice 75) stating that a certain degree of disposal over third party premises is sufficient to constitute a PE even if the place of business is not necessarily required or always available for conducting the business activity in China.[32] This can be interpreted in a sense that even if a place of business is not necessary in order to conduct business in the source country or this place is (temporally) not available for any reasons, a place of business still exists if this place is under the disposal of the taxpayer.[33] Still, no further information is given with regard to the range of the disposal term in Chinese tax law. Whether the interpretation resembles the wide understanding of the OECD MC or whether further criteria such as an exclusive use of the premises are required cannot be concluded. Therefore, a concrete statement with regard to a

27. See i.a. Filinov et al. (2014) Russia, p. 26.
28. See also the PE Questionnaire in the Appendix, Table A20 which states that the requirement of disposal is obviously considered as being subordinated in comparison to the other PE requirements.
29. See e.g. Bruk/Konnov (2009) p. 544.
30. See section 4.2.5.1.
31. See Metha (2012) p. 38 and Padmakshan (2014) p. 247.
32. See section 4.2.6.1.
33. See also the PE Questionnaire, Table A22.

possible qualification conflict between China and the residence country R in Figure 5.2 cannot be made. A reason for the missing details of interpretation of the disposal term in Chinese tax law might be that discussions about the existence of a '*passive*' service PE are usually avoided in Chinese treaty policy by implementing an '*active*' service PE provision in the tax treaty.[34] In fact, this is true for about 77% of Chinese tax treaties which all include a service PE provision in the relevant PE definition article.[35]

Table 5.1 summarizes the results for the basic PE in the inbound case ('*passive*' service PE).

Table 5.1 Basic PE – 'Passive' Service PE

Residence Country = OECD Country	*Non-taxation Risk*	*Single Taxation (Similar to OECD approach)*	*Double Taxation Risk*
Source country	DE	IN, RU	BR

No concrete statement possible: CN, US

As the Indian interpretation of the disposal term is similar to the OECD understanding, a qualification conflict with regard to service provisions at third party premises in one of the considered countries is improbable in this case. The same effect occurs for Russia where the requirement of disposal does not play a major role. Germany applies a more restricted concept with regard to the interpretation of the disposal requirement. Brazil, at the same time, applies an ever wider fiscal nexus as, independent of the creation of a PE, service income is taxed in Brazil on a gross basis. In these two country cases, qualification conflicts with regard to service provisions at local third party premises are probable if the residence country of the service provider follows the OECD regulations in the concluded tax treaty. Non-taxation occurs for the German case if the residence country of the foreign head office assumes a German PE whereas Germany does not. By contrast, in Brazil, the risk of double taxation or at least increased taxation rises due to the levy of withholding taxes on income from services. For the US and China, concrete conclusions cannot be drawn due to a lack of information.

5.2.2 Construction Site PE: Total Delegation of Work to Subcontractors

Another discussable case is related to the establishment of a construction site PE, i.a. the delegation of work from a general contractor to a subcontractor located in the source country. Figure 5.3 illustrates this case.

34. The establishment of a real service PE does not depend on the existence of fixed place of business so that the requirement of disposal over the place is irrelevant.
35. See Appendix, Table A6 for an overview of service PEs in Chinese tax treaties.

Figure 5.3 Construction Site PE – Delegation of Work to Subcontractors

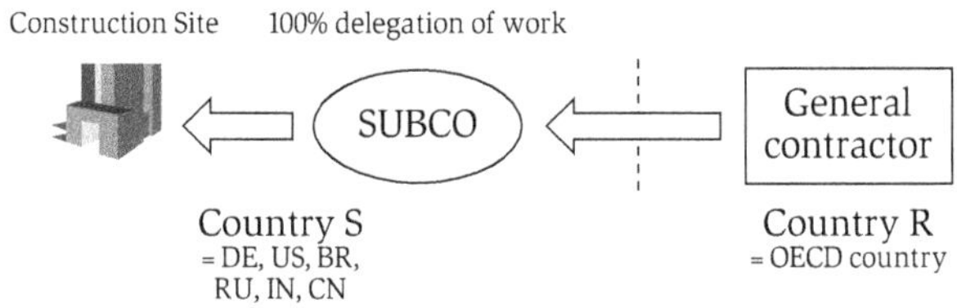

A general contractor located in country R delegates all work to a local subcontractor who performs the working activities at the construction site. Both, the local subcontractor and the construction site, are located in country S. The working time spent by the subcontractor at the construction site is supposed to last over twelve months. The general contractor legally possesses the construction site for the time of the construction project which means he is able to control the access and use of the site. However, workers of the general contractor are not present at all in country S. The question is whether a construction site PE is established for the general contractor by delegating all work to a subcontractor located in country S.[36]

According to the current OECD interpretation (including the OECD Reform Proposal), the general contractor establishes a construction site PE in the source country by delegating all work to subcontractors located in the source country without being physically present there.[37] In addition to the permanence threshold of twelve months under Article 5 (3) OECD MC, the requirement of disposal is an additional requirement to be checked in this case. Thus, the disposal criterion effectively replaces the physical presence of the general contractor's employees when checking the requirements of a construction site PE. According to the OECD interpretation, this criterion is fulfilled in the scenario laid down in Figure 5.3 so that country R assumes a construction site PE situated in country S.

If *Germany* is the country of source, a PE will not be established in case of the total delegation of work to the subcontractor.[38] In general, without any physical presence of employees of the general contractor in the source country, a construction site PE is not established for the general contractor in Germany.[39] Only if the general contractor is physically present in Germany, e.g., in order to supervise the construction process by its employees, a construction site PE is possible for the general contractor. In this case, the partial delegation of work to subcontractors does not harm the recognition of a construction site PE for the general contractor. For the total delegation of work, however, a qualification conflict occurs in the scenario laid down in Figure 5.3 as, in contrast to the OECD country R, Germany does not recognize a PE at source by the total delegation of work to a subcontractor, even if the general contractor

36. The subcontractor itself can also constitute a construction site PE in the source country. However, this is not asked here.
37. See section 3.2.1. See i.a. Bürkle/Ullmann (2013) p. 946.
38. See section 4.2.1.1.
39. See i.a. Wichmann (2005) p. 103, Eckl (2009) p. 329.

theoretically has access to the construction site. If the OECD country R applies the exemption method without any subject-to-tax or switch-over clause, non-taxation occurs as the taxing rights would be allocated to Germany whereas Germany does not tax the profits as a limited tax liability does not exist from a German viewpoint.

For the *US* as being the source country, the case is not that clear. US national law does not include specific regulations with regard to the construction site PE.[40] The Technical Explanation of the US MC considers the delegation of work to subcontractors by stating that the working time of the subcontractor is added to the time of the general contractor spent at the construction site.[41] However, this does not clearly imply that, from a US perspective, the general contractor is supposed to be at least partly physically present at the construction site. No information is given in relation to the period of presence of the general contractor, the conducted business activity or the degree of disposal over the construction site. Therefore, it cannot be clearly determined whether US treaties recognize a construction site PE for the general contractor if all work is delegated to the subcontractor and no employees of the general contractor are physically present in the US.[42] The Technical Explanation of the US MC emphasizes that the interpretation of the US MC is consistent with the interpretation of the current OECD MC Commentary.[43] Thus, it can be concluded that the US follows the OECD MC and recognizes a construction site PE by the total delegation of work to subcontractors. However, this is only a presumption. In fact, according to the US Council for International Business (USCIB), it shall be considered if the subcontractor performs the business activities of the general contractor in a fixed place of business in the source country under Article 5 (1) OECD MC.[44] From this perspective, only if the subcontractor performs the business activities of the general contractor, and not his own, a PE can be established for the general contractor. Still, it can only be presumed if US treaties follow this explanation.

If *Brazil* is the source country, a concrete statement is hard to find due to a lack of information. Neither Brazilian national law nor treaty law provide for any specific information with regard to the Brazilian treatment of the total delegation of work to a subcontractor.[45] Thus, it is hard to find out whether the Brazilian tax authorities assume the establishment of a construction site PE for the general contractor in case all work is delegated to a subcontractor located in Brazil.[46] Conclusions about qualification conflicts with regard to the possible establishment of a construction site PE in the scenario displayed in Figure 5.3 cannot be drawn.

If *Russia* is the country of source, the situation is not clear either. Russian treaty law indicates that the working time of the subcontractor or any affiliate working for the general contractor or customer is added to the time of the non-resident general

40. See section 4.2.2.1.
41. See Arnold (2009) p. 680.
42. See for a negating opinion, the PE Questionnaire in the Appendix, Table A18.
43. See US MC Technical Explanation (2006) p. 16.
44. See USCIB Response (2012) pp. 9 ff.
45. See section 4.2.3.1. See for negating view, the PE Questionnaire in the Appendix, Table A19.
46. In general, the OECD considerations are not involved in Brazilian tax jurisdiction issues. See Rocha (2009) p. 136.

contractor spent at the construction site in order to identify the time threshold of the construction PE provision in the treaty.[47] Again, this can imply that the general contractor has to be physically present in Russia to a certain extent. This interpretation is supported by Russian case law which determines that the total delegation of work to other subcontractors without the establishment of a fixed place of business in Russia does not lead to a construction site PE for the non-resident general contractor.[48] Therefore, a qualification conflict occurs in the scenario displayed in Figure 5.3 as, in contrast to the resident country of the general contractor, Russia does not assume the establishment of a construction site PE for the general contractor in case of a total delegation of work to a Russian subcontractor. However, there is also another court decision which establishes a PE for the general contractor without a physical presence at the construction site, similar to the OECD proposal.[49] Therefore, a concrete conclusion cannot be drawn.

In case *India* is the source country, the situation is unclear as well. On the one hand, Indian case law indicates that if the total work is delegated to the subcontractor and only a few supervisory visits are conducted by the workers of the general contractor, a PE of the general contractor is not established.[50] In relation to the case in Figure 5.3 this leads to a qualification conflict as India, in contrast to the OECD country R, would not assume a construction site PE in case of total delegation of work to subcontractors without physical presence of the general contractor in India.[51] On the other hand, as Indian tax treaties usually follow the UN MC with regard to the inclusion of supervisory activities in the construction PE clause, it is thinkable that the UN MC Commentary also plays a role for the interpretation of Indian tax treaties.[52] According to the UN MC Commentary, the working time spent by the subcontractor at the construction site is added to the general contractor's time for determining the permanence threshold.[53] Still, this does not automatically exclude the establishment of a construction site PE in case of the total delegation of work to a subcontractor.[54] In fact, if India follows the interpretation of the UN MC Commentary, the probability of a qualification conflict is diminished as in both cases a construction site PE exists for the general contractor in India (or at least is not neglected upfront) in case of total delegation of work to the subcontractor. However, a definite statement cannot be made.

If *China* is the country of source, the situation is similar to India. Chinese treaty law does not explicitly mention the case of the total delegation of work to subcontractors.[55] Similar to the OECD MC Commentary, Chinese treaty regulations, on the one

47. See section 4.2.4.1.
48. See for the *Stora Enso* case Konnov/Sminov/Smith (2012) p. 24.
49. See e.g. the PE Questionnaire in the Appendix, Table A20.
50. See section 4.2.5.1. See the Indian Ruling AAR, 11 September 2009, No. 790 of 2008, Ruling *Pintsch Bamag Antriebs- Und Verkehrstechnik GmbH*, pp. 16 ff.
51. See for a sceptical view Dalal/Shah/Sheth (2014) India, p. 25.
52. In fact, about 85% of Indian tax treaties include supervisory activities in the wording of the construction site PE provision. See Appendix, Table A7.
53. See UN MC Commentary (2011) Article 5, p. 109.
54. See UN MC Commentary (2011) Article 5, pp. 109 ff.
55. See section 4.2.6.1.

hand, mention that the time of the subcontractor working at the Chinese construction site is considered as time of the general contractor spent at the site.[56] This can indicate that the general contractor has to be physically present in China, so that a total delegation of work to a subcontractor does not lead to the establishment of a construction site PE in China.[57] On the other hand, Chinese treaty policy generally follows the UN MC with regard to the inclusion of supervisory activities in the construction PE provision.[58] One can argue that the UN MC Commentary thus can be used as guidance for Chinese tax treaties determining that the PE establishment for the general contractor in case of the total delegation of work to subcontractors is also possible.[59] Due to missing interpretation in Chinese treaty or case law, a definite statement cannot be made.

The comparison of the results shows that none of the countries considered clearly follows the interpretation of the OECD Reform Proposal with regard to the establishment of a construction site PE for the general contractor in case of the total delegation of work to subcontractors (see Table 5.2).

Table 5.2 Construction Site PE – Total Delegation of Work to Subcontractors

Residence Country = OECD Country	*Non-taxation Risk*	*Single Taxation (Similar to OECD Approach)*	*Double Taxation Risk*
Source country	DE	CN*, IN*	-

No concrete statement possible: BR, RU, US
* if UN MC is followed

Germany neglects the existence of a PE in this case and thus limits the source country's taxing right which leads to qualification conflicts and possible non-taxation situations for scenarios as displayed in Figure 5.3. China and India are in line with OECD policy if it is assumed that the UN MC is followed in the treaty policy. For the rest of the countries under consideration, a concrete statement with regard to the PE question is hard to make due to insufficient or contradicting information given in national and treaty regulations and case law. In summary, the interpretation of the OECD Reform Proposal is not consistent with the national tax policy of the considered countries, neither in the BRIC states nor in the industrial countries of Germany and the US.

56. See Li (2012) p. 459.
57. See for a negating view the PE Questionnaire in the Appendix, Table A22.
58. Almost all Chinese tax treaties, approx. 95%, include supervisory activities in the construction site PE provision. See Appendix, Table A8.
59. See UN MC Commentary (2011) Article 5, pp. 109 ff.

5.2.3 Agency PE: Authority to Conclude Contracts

Another critical agency PE case deals with the authority to conclude contracts for the principal company which can either be legally-based or economically-based. Figure 5.4 illustrates this case.[60]

Figure 5.4 Agency PE – Authority to Conclude Contracts

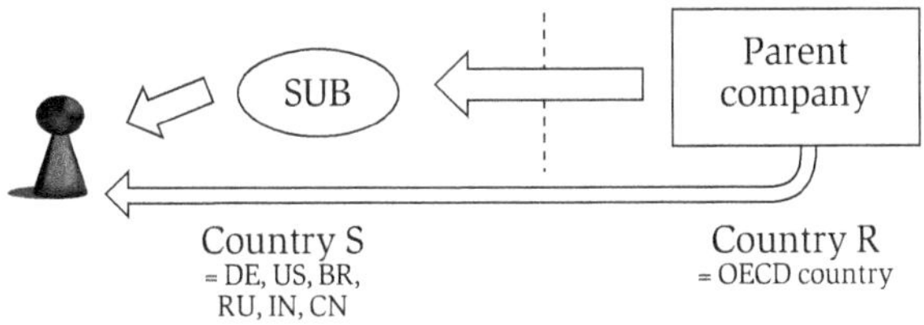

In this case, the resident investor of country R has a subsidiary located in country S. The resident investor sells most of his products to the customers located in country S under a standard contract. Some more important customers, however, require specific negotiations on-site. This is done by the subsidiary which acts in its own name on the account of the resident investor in country R and formally concludes legal contracts with the important customers. The subsidiary is paid a standard cost-based remuneration. In addition, the subsidiary is given detailed instructions by the resident parent company whereas some details of the contract such as price and warranty are directly negotiated by the subsidiary. The parent company further delivers the ordered products directly to the customer. Thus, it can be said that the parent company is economically bound in country S by the contract concluded in the name of the subsidiary which thus acts like a dependent commission agent.[61] The criterion of habitualness is supposed to be fulfilled. The question now is whether the activities of the subsidiary establish an agency PE for the parent company in country S.

According to the OECD MC, the existence of an independent agent under Article 5 (6) OECD MC shall be neglected as the subsidiary is bound by detailed instructions and is paid a cost-based remuneration from the parent company.[62] Still, a dependent agent can exist since contracts are concluded by the subsidiary which are binding for the parent company but are not actually concluded in the name of the latter. Considering the given facts, the wording of the OECD MC Commentary and the proposals by the OECD with regard to Article 5 of the OECD MC and Action 7 of the BEPS project, the residence country R can assumingly act like a '*common law*' country

60. The following case is based on discussions of the IFA-OECD Seminar (2012) 'The Elusive Concept of Permanent Establishment' which took place in Boston. See Vann (2012) pp. 1 ff.
61. See for the term Le Gall (2011) p. 88.
62. For this case, the independent agent exception is excluded. Further criteria which lead to an independent agent such as entrepreneurial risk or the number of principals are not considered here.

and determine an agency PE in this case since the parent company of country R is bound economically by the actions of its subsidiary in country S.[63]

In case *Germany* is the source country, it is not clear whether a qualification conflict occurs. There are views which approve a formalistic legal authority to conclude contracts literally '*in the name of*' the principal in order to constitute an agency PE in Germany.[64] In addition, there is the German civil law structure of '*Kommissionär*' who explicitly does not act in the name of the principal.[65] If Germany qualifies the subsidiary as an independent '*Kommissionär*' and thus demands a legal authority to conclude contracts in the name of the principal in the scenario laid down in Figure 5.4, a qualification conflict, and thus non-taxation occurs as the residence country of the parent company assumes a PE (and allocates the taxing right to Germany) whereas Germany does not establish a PE and thus does not tax the income.[66] Still, this conclusion is not sure, as, from another viewpoint, e.g., with regard to the wording of the German PE Circular, the economic authority to conclude contracts shall also be sufficient to establish an agency PE for the non-resident principal.[67]

The *US* as the country of source also does not provide for clear guidance with regard to the differentiation between legal and economic authority to conclude contracts. Decisive here is the differentiation between independent and dependent agent which is identified by certain characteristics such as the level of instructions or the number of principals.[68] The facts given, e.g., in Figure 5.4 indicate that the subsidiary is not an independent agent from an US point of view as the subsidiary is acting only for one principal, is paid on a cost-basis and has a certain scope of negotiation authority.[69] Thus, a dependent agent is given. The question is if the dependent agent also binds the principal. For the US as the source country, it can be assumed that in accordance with the general interpretation of '*common law*' countries, the agent has the authority to conclude contracts independent of the disclosure of the principal.[70] Thus, for the case described in Figure 5.4, no qualification conflict and thus no double or non-taxation situation occurs as the US and, by assumption, the OECD country R both assume an agency PE in the source country.

If *Brazil* is the source country where the subsidiary is located, no detailed information is given with regard to the interpretation of the authorization of the agent to conclude contracts for the principal. From Brazilian domestic law it can be concluded that the differentiation between independent and dependent agent does not play a role as both, *commissários* acting in their own name as well as *mandatários*

63. See section 3.2.2.2.
64. See section 4.2.1.1.
65. See Jones/Lüdicke (2014) p. 205.
66. Again, given that the residence country of the parent applies the exemption method for business profits and does not apply any subject-to-tax or switch-over clauses.
67. There is also the view that instead of considering the legal wording, Germany deals with the valuation of commissionaire structures in the context of business restructurings. See Sheppard (2010) p. 22. Thus, the focus is on the allocation of own entrepreneurial risk in order to identify whether the agent is independent or dependent.
68. See section 4.2.2.1.
69. See section 4.2.2.1.
70. See already Jones/Ward (1993) p. 158, Holland (2011) p. 37. See also Tittle (2007b) p. 610.

legally binding the principal, can constitute an agency PE.[71] Thus, without a tax treaty, Brazil probably assumes an agency PE in the case described in Figure 5.4 although it can be discussable if the negotiation activities of the subsidiary qualify as adequate sales activities. There is no further information with regard to the degree of legal authorization so that it cannot be said whether Brazil also recognizes an '*economic*' authority to conclude contracts in treaty law. Still, due to the wide domestic agent concept, it can be assumed that Brazilian tax authorities tend to constitute an agency PE in this case.[72]

If the subsidiary is located in *Russia*, the situation is again unclear. The former Russian view was that a legal authorization to conclude contracts in the name of the principal is necessary. Still, recent Russian case law indicates that the authority to conclude contracts is interpreted on a wider economic basis.[73] Thus, for the constructed case in Figure 5.4, no qualification conflict occurs as the Russian viewpoint is similar to the viewpoint of the residence country of the principal. In addition, the sole activities of negotiating without concluding a contract at source can indicate an agency PE under Russian domestic law.[74] Still, it is hard to say which terms of negotiation are sufficient to conclude that an agency PE is established for the foreign principal. Although an explicit determination by the Russian tax legislation is not given, recent developments indicate an alignment to OECD standards so one can consider a future tendency that qualification conflicts in this case are less probable.

For *India* as the residence country of the subsidiary of the case described in Figure 5.4, there are several indicators that an agency PE will be established in this case. First, Indian tax treaties usually include an independent agent provision which is wider than the current Article 5 (6) of the OECD MC to the extent that the independent agent status is declined if the agent works for one principal only.[75] This is the case here if the UN MC is followed. However, by assumption, the current OECD MC is valid for the tax treaty in the constructed case which does not include this additional criterion.[76] Still, as it is assumed that the subsidiary in the constructed case generally does not fulfil the requirements of the OECD independent agent provision, the Indian viewpoint with regard to independent agents does not play a role for this example. Even if it is assumed that the independent agent provision applies, India probably refuses it due to the fact that the subsidiary solely works for one principal. In addition, similar to Russia, substantial negotiations of the subsidiary without concluding final contracts with the customer at source are sufficient to assume an authority to conclude contracts and is

71. See section 4.2.3.1.
72. See for a negating view the PE Questionnaire in the Appendix, Table A19.
73. See section 4.2.4.1.
74. See also Appendix, Table A20.
75. This is given for 75% of Indian tax treaties. See Appendix, Table A9.
76. In fact, this criterion is also mentioned in the current OECD MC Commentary as possible indicator of independence but it is explicitly stated that this is not 'determinative'. See OECD MC Commentary (2014), Article 5, No. 38.6, p. 110. In the course of the ongoing BEPS discussion with regard to Action Plan 7, the OECD proposes to introduce this criterion in the wording of Article 5 (6) OECD MC under the additional condition that the principal shall hold at least 50% of beneficial interest in the agent. See OECD Revised Discussion Draft BEPS Action 7 (2015) p. 13.

thus regarded as indicator for the establishment of an agency PE in India.[77] With respect to the authority to conclude contracts, India follows an economic point of view based on facts and circumstances which neglects the question of whether the agent concludes contracts in the name of the principal. Rather, the focus is on the question of whether an independent third party considers the binding authorization of the agent as being adequate.[78] Thus, it can be considered that India as source country S is in line with the residence country R in the constructed case so that no qualification conflict and no double or non-taxation situation occurs. Still, with regard to independent agents, Indian treaty policy includes a broader basis of source taxation in comparison to the OECD MC. However, this depends on the specifications of the concluded treaty between India and the other contracting state.[79]

If the subsidiary is located in *China*, a concrete statement cannot be given as well since Chinese tax legislation does not explicitly deal with details of the requirement of the legal or economic authority to conclude contracts for the principal.[80] Chinese treaty policy only includes specific criteria with regard to the requirement of independence, such as the degree of control of the principal, the bearing of business risk, or the number of principals the agent works for. Thus, China obviously considers the independence criterion as a decisive requirement when deciding about the existence of an agency PE. In the constructed case of Figure 5.4 it is assumed that the subsidiary has one principal only (the parent company in the OECD country R) and bears a certain degree of risk, e.g., with regard to the price, but not all risk as the risk of delivery and loss is supposed to be with the delivering parent. In addition, similar to India, most of Chinese tax treaties include an exclusion rule stating that an independent agent will not be considered as being independent if he works solely for one principal.[81] Therefore, it is supposed that China also assumes a dependent agent in this case. Still, there is no further information on whether the fact that the agent does not act formally in the name of the parent company, but on his own name, plays a role in the decision process. What can be an indicator for the establishment of an agency PE is the fact that contracting authority according to Chinese understanding also includes major negotiation activities which will bind the principal, similar to India and Russia.[82] However, it is hard to say to what degree negotiations are substantial enough to establish an agency PE in China as in this case, the subsidiary does not negotiate every material element of the contract.

The comparison of results shows that there is mostly uncertainty among the countries under consideration with regard to the degree of authority to conclude contracts as requirement for the existence of an agency PE. Considering the position of the OECD in the constructed case, it is assumed that the country of residence of the

77. See section 4.2.5.1. See Sheppard (2010) p. 22.
78. See e.g. the description of Indian case law in Mehta (2011) pp. 563 ff.
79. In fact, some Indian treaties also include another condition which determines that the agent is considered as being independent as long as the relations between him and his principal follow the arm's length principle. See Appendix, Table A9.
80. See section 4.2.6.1. Other difficulties in understanding arise from Chinese civil law which obviously mixes elements of common and civil law with regard to the definition of an agency relationship. See Qiu (2014) p. 299.
81. This is given for about 75% of Chinese tax treaties. See Appendix, Table A10.
82. See the PE Questionnaire in the Appendix, Table A22.

parent company follows the literal wording of the OECD MC Commentary and the OECD BEPS Action 7 and applies an '*economic*' authorization of contract conclusion so that the agent can bind the principal without acting formally in the name of the latter.[83] Except for the US as common law country, no other country clearly follows the OECD viewpoint as determined in the example of Figure 5.4 (see Table 5.3).

Table 5.3 Agency PE – Authority to Conclude Contracts

Residence Country = OECD Country	*Non-taxation Risk*	*Single Taxation (Similar to OECD Approach)*	*Double Taxation Risk*
Source country	-	US, IN*	-

No concrete statement possible: BR, CN, DE, RU
* Still, double taxation risk given due to broad agency PE interpretation

Due to a lack of information in Brazil and China and different interpretation approaches in Germany and Russia, it cannot be determined if qualification conflicts will occur in these countries or if they follow the interpretation of the OECD MC. India applies the concept of a wide economic authority to conclude contracts for the principal similar to the OECD MC. Still, source taxation is extended in Indian treaty policy due to the wider agency PE threshold including the maintenance of warehouses in the PE article of Indian tax treaties and the restriction of the independent agent clause by the exclusionary criterion of working solely for one principal. In addition, Russia, India and China generally consider contracting authority to be fulfilled if the agent negotiates major elements of the contract regardless of any signature of the principal or disclosing of the principal's name. Still, if not all elements are negotiated by the local agent as it is the case displayed in Figure 5.4, it is hard to conclude which elements are sufficient to assume an agency PE in this case. In fact, the OECD BEPS report on Action 7 also states that the identification of material elements of a contract depends on the '*commercial realities*' of the situation.[84]

In summary, for this case, single taxation is provided only in the case of the US as source country. For India, despite the conformity in the model case, an increased double taxation risk can still occur due to the broad interpretation of the authority to conclude contracts and the strict exceptions for independent agents. For the other countries, the concrete consequences of this case cannot be drawn.

5.2.4 Service PE: Secondment of Employees

A discussable subject is the situation of the cross-border secondment of employees. Figure 5.5 illustrates a typical case.

83. See for an actual overview e.g. Obuoforibo (2013) pp. 66 ff.
84. See OECD Final Report BEPS Action 7 (2015), p. 22.

Figure 5.5 Service PE – Secondment of Employees

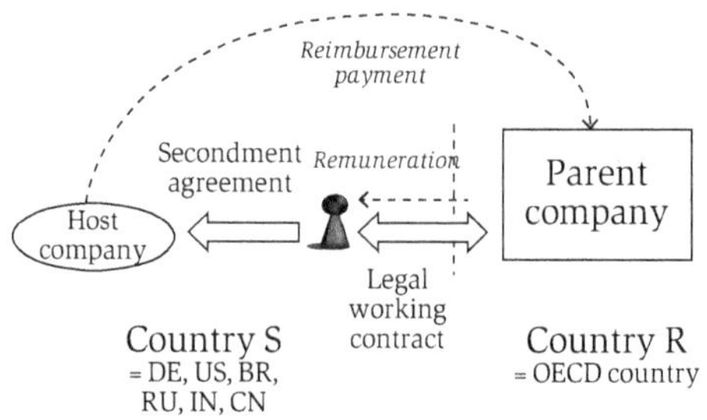

A parent company being resident in country R, has a secondment arrangement with the host company, subsidiary of the parent company and being resident in country S. The parent company sends qualified personnel to country S who perform management and personnel training services at the premises of the host company for a sufficient period of time. The legal working contract of the employees remains with the parent company. The seconded personnel receive their remuneration from the parent company which is immediately reimbursed by the host company at arm's length on a cost-plus basis. The parent company chooses the employees and determines all details of the working contract. They are also instructed by the parent company with regard to the work performed and have to report regularly. All the rules and regulations of the local employees of the host company also apply to the seconded personnel. The host company controls the work place; the parent company usually only has access on permission. The requirement of permanence is supposed to be fulfilled. It is further assumed that the service PE provision as formulated in the OECD MC Commentary is implemented in the treaty between country S and country R. The question is now: Can the reimbursement payment by the host company be considered as payment for the provision of services by the parent company? And can the activities of the seconded employees constitute a service PE for the parent company in country S?

From the viewpoint of the OECD MC, the case of secondment of employees is considered in the explanations of the OECD MC Commentary with regard to the service PE alternative.[85] Services can thus also be performed by other personnel than own employees also implying secondment arrangements. A crucial criterion is for whom the seconded employee effectively conducts service activities. For the determination of a possible service PE, the legal working contract of the employee does not play a role. Decisive factors are the supervision, direction and control which the employer has over the seconded employee. The employer can thus be considered as '*economic employer*', which can either be the host or the parent company. In this context, the OECD Reform Proposal suggests to take into account the criteria of the economic employer concept of the OECD MC Commentary on Article 15 OECD MC. This includes factors such as the authority of instruction, the control and responsibility over the workplace, the character of the remuneration payment, the responsibility for the employee's working tools

85. See section 3.2.3.

and the numbers of workers sent, the right of selection of the workers, configuration of details and termination of the working contract.[86] Thus, it can be concluded that the non-resident parent company does not constitute a service PE in the source country if the host company is considered as economic employer of the seconded employee.[87] If, however, the economic factors indicate that the parent company is the effective employer, a service PE of the non-resident parent company is created by the provision of services at the premises of the host company in the source country.[88] The character of the reimbursement payment from the host company to the workforce-lending parent company is relevant but not conclusive for determining whether the secondment is considered as employment service or business contract for services. Thus, an arm's length profit mark-up upon the reimbursement payment by the host company to the workforce-lending parent company is not a sufficient indicator for the qualification of the payment as business income from services instead of income from employment.[89]

With regard to the model case displayed in Figure 5.5, the fact that the workplace of the seconded personnel is controlled by the host company supports the assumption that the host company is the economic employer. In addition, the seconded workers have to work under the regulations of the host company. The fee charged by the workforce-lending parent company also includes the remuneration for the seconded employee. However, the seconded employees are chosen and instructed by the parent company and also have to report to the latter. Thus, it can be assumed that the parent company bears the responsibility and risk for the work performed. The profit mark-up obviously does not play a major role in decision-making here but, in combination with the other factors, the secondment arrangement can indeed be considered as contract for services provided by the parent company. Given the facts, it can be assumed that the resident country of the parent company which follows the OECD perspective creates a service PE established by the secondment of employees to country S.[90]

Even if the service PE is not part of the tax treaty between the considered countries, a basic PE can eventually be created by the services provided by the seconded employees at the premises of the host company, especially if the wide understanding of the disposal requirement is applied by the OECD country R.[91] Thus, a fixed place of business can be established from the OECD perspective if the parent company possesses a certain degree of control or disposal over the rooms of the host company in which the services are provided.

86. See OECD MC Commentary (2014) Article 15, No. 8.14, p. 268.
87. See Rosenberger/Vitali/Ziehr (2010) p. 7.
88. Although the requirements of the service PE indicate that the services have to be conducted to a third party, this is not relevant when the services are considered as business income under a contract for services. No matter whether the host company is a third party or an associated enterprise, the non-resident parent conducts services not for his own benefit, but for the benefit of another party. See Rautenstrauch/Binger (2009) p. 625, OECD MC Commentary (2014) Article 5, No. 42.30, pp. 119 ff.
89. See OECD MC Commentary (2014) Article 15, No. 8.15, pp. 268 ff. & No. 8.26, pp. 270 ff.
90. This result occurs, of course, given that the other requirements of the service PE alternative are fulfilled.
91. See section 5.2.1.

For the purposes of Article 15 OECD MC, the OECD determines that the domestic law of the source country where the service activities are provided is decisive for deciding whether the activities are treated as employment services or services from business income as long as objective criteria are applied.[92] Therefore, the interpretation of the source country is highly relevant (and also more relevant than the interpretation of the OECD country R).

In *Germany*, similar to the OECD MC, the economic employer concept is decisive for distinguishing between a business contract for services and a general secondment arrangement (employment services). In addition, German tax law also distinguishes between three kinds of cross-border secondment of employees: the (professional) supply of workers by manpower companies,[93] the occasional supply of workers[94] and the secondment of employees between associated companies.[95] For all three forms, the German tax legislation refers to the concept of the economic employer which applies similar criteria than those listed in the OECD MC Commentary.[96] In the model case displayed in Figure 5.5, only the rulings for the secondment of employees between associated companies are supposed to be relevant since the host company is deemed to be a subsidiary of the workforce-lending parent company. Similar to the OECD MC, the case of a business contract for services has to be distinguished from the general secondment agreement if the remuneration is part of the service or work performance provided by the seconded employees of the workforce-lending parent company.[97] According to German rules, a general secondment agreement between associated enterprises for which the host company either concludes a legal working contract with the employee or is considered as economic employer, usually cannot establish a PE for the lending parent company.[98] However, if the remuneration is part of the service or work performance provided by the seconded employees of the workforce-lending parent company and the reimbursement payment includes a profit mark-up, the income for the service provided is considered as business profit and the non-resident parent company is generally regarded as economic employer.[99] At the same time, the host company is considered as economic employer if the seconded employees are integrated in the working processes and the host company economically bears the remuneration.[100] The seconded employee is integrated if the host company has the responsibility and bears the risk for the working results and the seconded employees are bound by instructions of the host company.[101] In accordance with the economic

92. See OECD MC Commentary (2014) Article 15, No. 8.7, p. 266, No. 8.11, p. 267. Still, if the countries do not agree, a mutual agreement procedure shall apply. See OECD MC Commentary (2014) Article 15, No. 8.12, p. 267.
93. See BFH, 4 September 2002, IR 21/01, BStBl. II 2003, p. 306, German Wage Circular (2014) No. 4.3.4, pp. 38 ff.
94. See German Wage Circular (2014) No. 4.3.5, pp. 45 ff.
95. See German Administrative Principles – Staff Secondment (2001) No. 2.1, p. 3.
96. See German Wage Circular (2014) No. 4.3.4.1, p. 39 & No. 4.3.5, p. 45.
97. See German Administrative Principles – Staff Secondment (2001) No. 2.1, p. 3.
98. See Rautenstrauch/Binger (2009) pp. 624 ff.
99. See German Administrative Principles – Staff Secondment (2001) No. 2.1, p. 3.
100. See German Wage Circular (2014) No. 4.3.3.1, p. 30.
101. See German Wage Circular (2014) No. 4.3.3.1, p. 30.

employer concept, it has to be differentiated for whose interest the seconded employees effectively perform the service activities.[102] If the workforce-lending parent company conducts supervision, direction and control over the personnel's work which is not compensated separately, uses the experience of the employee after his return to the parent company or generally rotates the employees among its subsidiaries, the seconded employee works in the interest of the active workforce-lending company.

In the case displayed in Figure 5.5, the host company effectively bears the remuneration of the seconded employee. However, the inclusion of a profit mark-up in the reimbursement payment basically excludes the case from the German administrative rules on cross-border secondment as a profit element is not permitted for a cross-border secondment arrangement between associated enterprises according to the German rules for staff secondment.[103] In addition, the seconded employees obviously work under the responsibility of the parent company as they have to report to the latter although they also have to follow the regulations of the host company. Thus, it can be assumed that they are not fully integrated in the working process of the host company. With regard to those given facts and as the example in Figure 5.5 clearly includes a profit component, one can conclude that Germany as a source country will thus probably assume a contract for services which means that the non-resident parent company is considered as the economic employer. If a service PE is included in the tax treaty between Germany and country R, the taxing right will thus be allocated to Germany as a service PE of the non-resident parent company is created through the secondment of employees to Germany.[104] However, German domestic source taxation does not integrate the service PE as fiscal nexus.[105] Therefore, a German taxing right is only established under German domestic law if the general domestic PE requirements, such as a fixed place of business where the business activities are conducted habitually, are fulfilled. In this case, the seconded employees perform their working activities at the premises of the host company. A necessary criterion here is the requirement of disposal over the premises of the host company. As shown before, Germany interprets this requirement in a rather strict way and demands a certain degree of '*rootage*' (*Verwurzelung*) at the premises which cannot be restricted or removed without the permission of the service provider.[106] In this case, the host company controls the workplace whereas the parent company has to ask for permission. Thus, a necessary degree of disposal is not given and German legislation probably neglects the existence of a basic PE.

As a final result, both, the resident country of the workforce-lending parent company and Germany use the concept of economic employer and assume the

102. This is initially done in order to find out who bears the costs of the seconded employer. See German Administrative Principles - Staff Secondment (2001) No. 3.1, p. 5 & No. 3.3, pp. 8 ff.
103. See German Administrative Principles - Staff Secondment (2001) No. 2.3, pp. 4 ff., Portner (2014) p. 441.
104. Again, given that the other requirements of the service PE are fulfilled, such as the time threshold.
105. See section 4.2.1.1. In this case, it is also assumed that Germany does not consider the seconded employees as 'permanent representatives' according to section 13 of the German GTC.
106. See section 5.2.1.

establishment of a service PE in this case.[107] However, as German domestic law does not include a taxing right for service PEs, non-taxation occurs if the requirements of a basic PE are not fulfilled and country R exempts business profits without any switch-over or subject-to-tax clauses.

For the *US* as the source country of the service activities provided by the seconded employees, concrete information is rare.[108] US case law indicates that the existence of a PE also depends on the determination of the economic employer of the seconded employee with regard to so-called *single loan-out arrangements* conducted for the performance of services by non-resident seconded employees in the entertainment industry.[109] Thus, a facts and circumstances approach is followed. The most important factors for the determination of the effective employer are, among others, control and direction of the employer with regard to time, place and manner of performance of work of the seconded employees. Another factor mentioned which signals the non-resident workforce lender as economic employer is the profit-based salary of the seconded employee. However, more essential under US case law is the requirement of control and direction over the employee's work in order to determine the real employer. Since in the case displayed in Figure 5.5, the seconded employees are instructed by the parent company and have a duty to report, it can be assumed that the parent company exercises sufficient control over the seconded employees with regard to the performance and results of the work. Therefore, it can be concluded that the effective employer is the non-resident parent company from the viewpoint of the US as residence country of the host company. Given that all other conditions are fulfilled, this again leads to the establishment of a service PE in the US. In addition, also without a treaty, a taxing right for the provision of services is given under US domestic law.[110]

As a result, a qualification conflict does not occur between the US and the OECD country R as both assume a service PE in this case as provided in the tax treaty between the two contracting states.[111]

Brazil generally follows its own way with regard to the fiscal treatment of secondment of employees. Regardless of a service PE provision in the tax treaty, Brazil levies withholding taxes on the gross income achieved by the non-resident through the provision of services in Brazil.[112] Service income is generally treated as other income following Article 21 of the UN MC which also grants a taxing right to the source country.[113] In fact, this is implemented in almost all of Brazilian tax

107. What is not considered here, is the possibility of re-qualifying the secondment of the employees as transfer of know-how indicating a possible taxation of royalties. See Brunsbach (2012) p. 325, Pickering (2012) p. 52.
108. See section 4.2.2.1.
109. See IRS revenue ruling 74-330, 1974-2 CB 278.
110. See section 4.2.2.1.
111. Still, US case law concentrates on a specific subject in the referred judgment (cross-border secondment of entertainers) and it is not sure if the principles derived can be used for this specific case.
112. See e.g. De Carvalho/Bechara (2014) pp. 165 ff. See also Appendix, Table A19.
113. See for discussion section 4.2.3.1. An alternative is to treat the service income as 'royalty' income similar to Article 12 (2) OECD MC or even as income from 'independent personal services' according to the 'old' OECD MC which also provides a Brazilian source taxation right. See Ferreira (2015) pp. 256 ff.

treaties.[114] Therefore, service activities provided by seconded employees in Brazil will generally trigger source taxation in Brazil independent of questions of control and supervision or the characterization of the remuneration payment. Thus, a qualification conflict due to the use of different treaty provisions can occur if Brazil is the source country of the seconded employees. If the resident country of the parent company assumes a service PE in Brazil, the relevant service income is taxed once although Brazilian withholding taxes will be levied on a gross basis so that related expenses cannot be deducted from the source tax base. This does not result in a typical double taxation situation but can lead to higher taxation in comparison to a PE tax base due to the non-deductibility of related expenses.[115]

If the host company is located in *Russia*, the situation is different. Similar to the OECD MC, Russia also applies specific criteria in order to identify the economic employer of the seconded employees.[116] The economic employer has to be responsible and is supposed to control the work performed by the seconded personnel. In addition, the profit mark-up of the service fee has to be smaller than 10% of the secondment costs in order for the host company to become the economic employer. With regard to the model case displayed in Figure 5.5, no information is given on the amount of profit mark-up on the remuneration payment. Still, it can be assumed that from a Russian perspective, the economic employer is the non-resident workforce-lending parent company as it effectively bears risk and controls the working results of the seconded personnel. Thus, the Russian interpretation of facts is similar to the OECD understanding and a service PE is eventually established. However, due to Russian migration law, a seconded employee who still has a legal working contract with the non-resident parent company will not be granted a work permit in Russia.[117] This means that due to inconsistencies between Russian tax and legal law, Russia does not allow the seconded personnel to perform service activities in Russia as long as the legal working contract is concluded with the non-resident parent company and not with the Russian host company. For this case, a qualification conflict occurs as the residence country of the workforce-lending parent company assumes a service PE in Russia whereas Russia does not even let the people work without a legal employment contract. In fact, this reduces the possible PE cases to arrangements in which the employee legally works for the Russian host company but, for certain economic reasons, is still or also considered as employee of the non-resident parent company. In the case displayed in Figure 5.5, the risk of non-taxation is not given from a Russian perspective as the secondment arrangement as constructed in the case is not granted from the beginning.

India as the location of the host company has a wide understanding of the establishment of a service PE in the model case. In accordance with Indian case law,

114. See Appendix, Table A11.
115. Similar to the 'passive' service PE case, if the limited tax credit method is used in country R, relevant PE expenses are recognized for the purpose of the calculation of the tax credit in country R so that the limit of the foreign tax credit increases. This leads to an increased overall tax burden in comparison to the case where Brazilian PE expenses are deductible.
116. See e.g. Dzhalchinov/Popov (2012) p. 584. See also the PE Questionnaire in the Appendix, Table A20.
117. See section 4.2.4.1.

India also uses the economic employer concept as an indicator when deciding about possible PE cases for secondment arrangements.[118] However, this concept is interpreted on a wide basis. Thus, the fact that the remuneration is paid by the non-resident parent company to the seconded employees which are in '*lien*' on employment with the foreign employer is sufficient for the Indian jurisdiction to establish a service PE in India.[119] Obviously, this even overrides the fact that the host company may have control and supervision over the working activities of the seconded employee.[120] In the case displayed in Figure 5.5, the seconded employees work under regulations of the host company; still they have to report to the non-resident parent company that thus has the responsibility over the working results and bears the risk of failure. In addition, the remuneration is paid by the non-resident parent company. A profit mark-up or the fact that the host company reimburses the salary immediately, obviously does not play a major role in Indian case law. In addition, it can also be assumed that the seconded employees have a lien or '*claim*' on the employment with the foreign employer as they are supposed to retain their jobs at the workforce-lending parent company.[121] Therefore, the secondment of employees working for an Indian subsidiary creates a service PE from the perspective of Indian case law. As the residence country of the foreign parent company also assumes a service PE in this case, a qualification conflict does not occur and double or non-taxation situations are improbable. However, if facts change, e.g., due to a change in the assignment of tasks so that the seconded employee would not have to report to the parent company anymore, the residence country R can interpret the case in a way that the host company is considered as the economic employer and a service PE is neglected. In this case, a qualification conflict is probable as the Indian case law still assumes a service PE due to the fact that the seconded employees still have a '*lien*' on their (primary) foreign employment.[122] Even if the service PE is not established, most of Indian tax treaties include fees for technical services in the royalty-article which can provide at least for the levying of a withholding tax on the income from services provided by the seconded employees if the service income falls under this broad Indian definition.[123] In this context, a qualification conflict with regard to the application of different provisions by the contracting states can occur if it is not sure whether the income from services is considered as business profits or income from technical services. This can especially be the case for Indian tax treaties which mostly include technical services in the royalty-article and thus provide for another fiscal nexus at source apart from the service PE provision.[124] If the residence country R considers the payments as business income from services whereas India applies the royalty-article, a qualification conflict occurs. If the exemption

118. See section 4.2.5.1.
119. See e.g. Krishnamurthy (2015) p. 103.
120. See Butani/Jain (2014) pp. 249 ff.
121. See Metha (2012) p. 92.
122. See e.g. Gada/Sinha (2014) p. 376.
123. See Sanghvi/Shaktawat (2012) p. 453.
124. See Appendix, Table A5.

method is used in country R, non-taxation does not occur since the residence country exempts the business income from services but India still levies a withholding tax. However, the withholding tax is generally applied on a gross basis without the recognition of any expenses at source. This again leads to a higher tax burden in comparison to the case where both countries agree on the provision to be applied.[125] If the limited tax credit method is applied in country R, it can occur that the foreign tax credit's limit increases due to the recognition of relevant PE expenses by the residence country or that the respective foreign withholding tax is not credited at all in the country of residence as it falls under another income category.[126] Therefore, at least increased taxation occurs if India and the other contracting state do not agree on the provision to be applied for service income.

China as the location of the host company also applies the economic employer concept.[127] In national and treaty law, Chinese legislation mentions different practical factors which clarify the allocation of responsibilities and risks and indicate the economic employer of the seconded employees.[128] Relevant factors are, among others, the character and possible profit mark-up of the reimbursement payment paid by the host company to the non-resident workforce-lending parent company as well as the authority to choose the workers and to decide on details of their working contract. Obviously, Chinese local tax authorities also apply a strict interpretation and determine the parent company as economic employer if already one of the mentioned factors is fulfilled.[129] In the model case displayed in Figure 5.5, it is deemed that the workers are chosen and instructed by the non-resident parent company. Following Chinese law, this fact is sufficient to determine the workforce-lending parent company as economic employer. China therefore assumes a service PE by the secondment of employees in this case. A qualification conflict does not occur as, by assumption, both contracting states constitute a service PE in this example. Still, due to the rather strict interpretation of Chinese tax authorities who, in contrast to the OECD MC, obviously consider the fulfilment of just one criterion as sufficient for the establishment of a service PE, conflicts are still possible when evaluating all facts and circumstances.[130]

In summary, all countries under consideration know and apply the economic employer concept with regard to the possible establishment of a service PE for the cross-border secondment of employees (see Table 5.4). However, there are country-specific differences.

125. See UN Working Paper (2008) p. 27.
126. For example, one limitation of the US foreign tax credit can be the 'per-category' limitation whereby foreign income is separated into different 'baskets'. Although business and service income generally falls into one 'basket' the royalty income is allocated to another 'passive income-basket', such that the foreign tax credit of the royalty income cannot be offset against taxes resulting from business income from services. See Vacovec/James/Hoiberg (2001) pp. 402 ff.
127. See section 4.2.6.1. See also the PE Questionnaire in the Appendix, Table A22.
128. See Eichelberger/Liu/DeSouza (2015) pp. 39 ff.
129. See e.g. Wong (2013) p. 48.
130. This view is also supported by the fact that Chinese tax treaties include a service PE in most treaties signed. See Appendix, Table A6.

Table 5.4 *Service PE – Secondment of Employees*

Residence Country = OECD Country	*Non-taxation Risk*	*Single taxation (Similar to OECD Approach)*	*Double Taxation Risk*
Source country	DE*	CN***, IN**** US	BR

No concrete statement possible: RU**

* Despite similar concept, risk of qualification conflict still existent due to differences with regard to fiscal treatment of service PE

** Despite similar concept, no question of PE existence due to contrary Russian migration law

*** Despite similar concept, risk of qualification conflict still existent due to strict interpretation of factors

**** Despite similar concept, risk of qualification conflict still existent due to broad concept of *'lien'* on employment

The US and China follow the OECD interpretation of the economic employer. For both countries, the risk of qualification conflicts with regard to the case as displayed in Figure 5.5 is improbable as similar requirements are applied. However, it seems that China interprets the economic employer concept more strictly so that conflicts are still thinkable. A similar result is reached for India being the country of source in the model case. Due to a broader interpretation of the economic employer concept, an increased double taxation risk is still given for Indian inbound cases. Germany also follows the economic employer concept. However, differences with regard to the national recognition of a service PE might lead to qualification conflicts. For Russia, interference with Russian migration law might also lead to conflicts as work permits are actually not granted for a typical secondment arrangement. However, the question of the existence of a Russian PE through secondment arrangements is avoided from the beginning. Brazil usually treats income from the provision of services by seconded employees as service income taxed on a gross basis. Thus, qualification conflicts and double taxation situations are possible.

As a conclusion, if the service PE is integrated in the tax treaty, the risk of interpretation conflicts is existent for the case of cross-border secondment of employees. Still, similar to the OECD MC, most countries apply the economic employer concept. What is not considered here, is the fact that some countries might also interpret the service fee for the work provided by (highly-skilled) secondees as deemed royalty income, implying a transfer of know-how, or, if integrated in the respective tax treaty, as fee for technical services.[131] Apart from service PE questions, both interpretations indicate taxation at source on a gross basis.

5.2.5 Intermediate Result

With regard to the four model cases which deal which specific requirements of the PE definition, it can be determined that actually no country under consideration is

131. See e.g. Pickering (2012) pp. 51 ff.

completely in line with the OECD approach. For three model cases, except for the agency PE for which a concrete statement cannot be given, *Germany* generally neglects the establishment of a PE in contrast to the OECD interpretation. Qualification conflicts are thus possible and single taxation is not given for the simulated cases. For the *US* as a source country, a lack of information exists for the cases of a '*passive*' service PE and a construction site PE through subcontractors whereas for an agency PE and a service PE through secondment of employees, the US interpretation is consistent with the OECD view. Thus, for none of the four cases, it can be clearly determined that a qualification conflict exists from a US viewpoint. *Brazil* has a wider understanding of PE taxation than the OECD MC, especially for the cases of a '*passive*' service PE and a service PE through secondment of employees. Due to the taxation of services on a gross basis, increased taxation can occur if the Brazil case is the country of source. For a construction site and an agency PE, concrete conclusions cannot be drawn due to a lack of information. *Russia* agrees with the OECD interpretation of disposal in the '*passive*' service PE case. With regard to secondment of employees, Russia follows the OECD MC but does not establish a PE due to Russian contrary migration law. For a construction site and an agency PE, concrete conclusions cannot be drawn due to unclear and opposing information. *India* is in line with the OECD understanding of the '*passive*' service PE. A wider interpretation of the PE definition is given for an agency PE and a service PE through secondment of employees so that conflicts with the OECD interpretation are still possible for Indian inbound cases, despite the consistent result in the model cases. For the case of a construction site PE through subcontractors, India's position is only similar to the OECD approach if it is assumed that the UN MC is followed. The same is true for *China*. For the case of the establishment of a service PE through secondment of employees, China agrees with the OECD interpretation although it interprets the PE factors in a more strict way. For all other cases, a concrete statement is not possible due to a lack of or unclear information with regard to the Chinese interpretation of the given cases.

The countries of source for which the risk of double or non-taxation is minimal for most PE cases are the US and India. For India, however, there is a tendency of a broader PE definition so that conflicts with the OECD MC are generally possible. For Russia, but especially for China and Brazil, on the contrary, a lack of information exists for most cases, so that it is hard to draw concrete conclusions. For Germany, there is a tendency of a narrower interpretation of the PE requirements in comparison to the OECD view. Thus, conflicts are possible and a risk of non-taxation situations is given especially for most of the presented German inbound cases.

5.3 CONFLICTS WITH REGARD TO THE ATTRIBUTION OF BUSINESS PROFITS BETWEEN HEAD OFFICE AND PE

5.3.1 Recognition of Internal Dealings

Given that a PE exists in the country of source, it is necessary to allocate profits between head office and PE under the AOA. In this context, one of the major differences of the AOA as guidance for the allocation of business profits in comparison to the '*old view*' is the recognition of internal dealings between head office and PE.[132] In accordance with the arm's length principle, these internal dealings shall include a taxable profit mark-up following the OECD Transfer Pricing Guidelines.[133]

Figure 5.6 illustrates the case of an internal royalty payment as an example of an internal dealing which is considered here.

Figure 5.6 Recognition of Internal Dealings

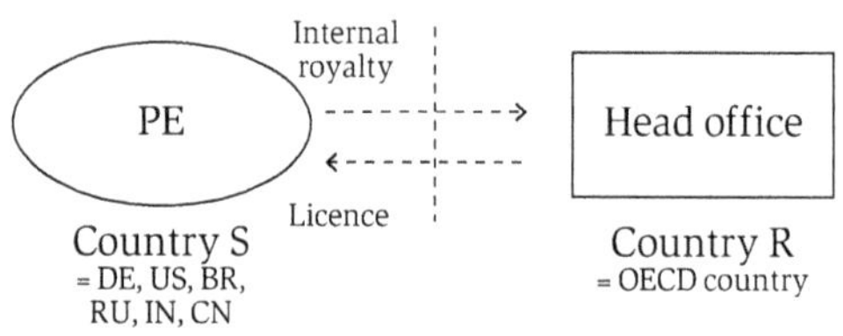

It is assumed that a PE exists in country S. The head office has its seat in country R which applies the AOA in its domestic tax law. The tax treaty concluded between country S and country R also follows the AOA as implemented in the current OECD MC. The head office grants a licence to its PE for which an independent separate legal enterprise would levy an arm's length royalty payment. Country R follows the OECD standard and thus recognizes an internal royalty payment including an adequate profit mark-up which becomes part of the head office's tax base. The question is now if the PE country S will agree with this regulation. Does the domestic tax law of country S accept the concept of internal dealings? Does it allow the deduction of the internal royalty payment from the PE tax base? Does it agree with the additional deduction of the profit element or does it only allow a deduction at cost? Otherwise, qualification conflicts and double or non-taxation situations can occur.[134]

The OECD MC states that the final decision on the deductibility of expenses remains at the level of domestic tax law of the contracting states.[135] Although the OECD MC does not intent to interfere with domestic deduction rules, the non-discrimination provision according to Article 24 (3) OECD MC has to be followed. This rule provides that PEs are treated equally for tax purposes in comparison to a company being resident in the same state conducting the same activities so that expenses are deductible under the same conditions.[136] In addition, the OECD MC determines that the non-deductibility of expenses resulting from the application of the AOA violates the OECD

132. See section 3.3.2.
133. See OECD MC Commentary (2014) Article 7, No. 22 f., pp. 138 ff.
134. What is not considered here, is the concrete amount of the profit mark-up which is additionally levied on the royalty payment. Of course, differences with regard to the adequate arm's length price can occur between the countries under consideration. Still, this is a transfer pricing problem and not an explicit problem of PE income allocation. See for the problematic of the arm's length principle as guiding principle for transfers between associated enterprises e.g. Luckhaupt/Overesch/Schreiber (2012b) pp. 359 ff.
135. See OECD MC Commentary (2014) Article 7, No. 30, p. 141.
136. See OECD MC Commentary (2014) Article 7, No. 33, p. 142.

principles.[137] In fact, the OECD rule of implying a deduction of expenses from internal dealings limits the taxation right of the source country S as the PE tax base is reduced. This is in line with the '*barrier effect*' of treaty law which cannot increase but only limit domestic taxing rights.[138] Therefore, country R in Figure 5.6 which follows the OECD view assumes that the internal royalty payment would be deductible from the PE tax base in country S.

In case *Germany* is country S in Figure 5.6, a conflict is improbable. Similar to the OECD MC, Germany introduced new business profit allocation rules which implemented the AOA in German national law.[139] However, being norms of correction in the German Foreign Tax Act, the German profit allocation rules only work '*one-sided*'. This means that only in cases where the German PE tax base of a non-resident is initially diminished through profit allocation (before the recognition of the internal dealing), the German domestic correction rules will be applied in order to re-increase the German tax base if the arm's length principle was not followed.[140] From the perspective of German domestic law, a legal basis for the application of the correction rules in the model case displayed in Figure 5.6 is thus not given, as the PE income was not reduced before, but is initially reduced by the internal royalty payment.[141] Still, it can be assumed that due to the '*barrier effect*' of the treaty which is allowed to limit the taxing rights of the source country, the German tax base can be diminished and the internal royalty payment is deductible.[142] In this case, a qualification conflict does not occur. However, if a treaty does not exist and the residence country of the recipient of the internal royalty payment applies the AOA, double taxation occurs as the deemed profit mark-up on the fictitious payment is non-deductible in Germany, but taxed in the country of the licenser.

If the *US* is the PE country, it is questionable whether it follows the OECD rules. US domestic law generally does not recognize internal dealings between head office and PE for income tax purposes.[143] This means that a domestic legal basis for the deduction of the internal royalty from the tax base of the US PE is not given from a US perspective. Although US treaty law generally supports the functionally separate entity approach as implemented in the AOA, it is questionable to which extent this includes the recognition of internal dealings. In a treasury statement, US tax authorities state that where the AOA is applied, '*it will apply in its entirety*'.[144] In the technical explanation of the tax treaty between Poland and the US for example, it is determined that for the purpose of the treaty, internal dealings can be used to allocate income

137. See OECD MC Commentary (2014) Article 7, No. 31, p. 141. See for discussion Nouel (2011) p. 10.
138. See e.g. Van Wanrooij (2009) p. 304.
139. See section 4.2.1.2.
140. See e.g. Schnitger (2012) p. 634.
141. See Baldamus (2012) p. 319.
142. See Schnorberger/Sassmann/Shekhovtsova (2014) p. 86. See for a similar example Paulitsch/Eckerstorfer (2014) p. 188. See for another example Barig (2013) pp. 809 ff. who takes into account a licensing agreement under a German tax treaty which does not apply the AOA.
143. See section 4.2.2.2.
144. See Kosters/Offermanns (2013) Chapter 11, fn. 4, p. 274.

despite the non-recognition of them in domestic law.[145] Thus, US treaty policy obviously overrides domestic law in this case. In the model case displayed in Figure 5.6, the '*barrier effect*' of the tax treaty thus leads to the deduction of an internal royalty including a profit mark-up although a legal basis is not given under US domestic law. Still, if the case is changed (e.g., due to a reallocation of significant people functions and risks) and the internal royalty is deemed to flow not from, but to the US PE as taxable income according to the treaty concluded, the US is not able to tax the deemed profit mark-up, as the treaty regulation alone cannot widen US taxing rights without a domestic legal base. Non-taxation occurs if the resident country of the head office applied the AOA and assumed a deductible royalty payment including a deduction of a profit element whereas the US does not tax this profit mark-up.

Brazil as country of source in the example taxes the PE similar to resident corporate entities.[146] Although Brazil does not follow the AOA in treaty policy, it treats PEs as separate legal entities for tax purposes under the condition that the PE is officially registered in Brazil. As a consequence, internal dealings should usually be recognized and valued according to the Brazilian transfer pricing regulations.[147] However, this is not sure for deemed internal payments between head office and PE which are not actually incurred.[148] If the deduction of an internal royalty was disregarded for tax purposes under Brazilian domestic law, it can only be assumed that the '*barrier effect*' of the tax treaty in charge still leads to a deduction of those payments in Brazil. Otherwise, double taxation occurs. If it is assumed that the internal dealing is recognized in Brazil similar to transactions between separate legal entities, another conflict can occur with regard to the valuation of the profit element as the specific Brazilian transfer pricing regulations generally use fixed profit margins.[149] An additional double taxation risk is given if the investing country which applies the AOA does not agree with the predetermined Brazilian profit mark-up. Furthermore, Brazil only allows the deduction of internal royalties if the licence is officially registered and approved by Brazilian legal authorities. In addition, the amount which can be deducted is limited up to 5% of the net sales income of the product for which royalties are paid.[150] If the deemed royalty payment is higher than this threshold, double taxation occurs for the residual royalty, as this amount is not deductible in Brazil but will be taxed in the country of the licenser. In addition, similar to cross-border payments between separate legal entities, it is thinkable that Brazilian tax authorities which do not know the concept of the AOA, eventually levy domestic withholding taxes on the deemed royalty payment although this is not in line with the treaty provisions and explicitly excluded from an OECD perspective.[151] Depending on whether the residence

145. See US-Poland Tax Treaty Explanation (2014) p. 32.
146. See section 4.2.3.2.
147. See e.g. Zapata/Weiss/Martins (2015) p. 32. See also the PE Questionnaire in the Appendix, Table A19.
148. See e.g. Gutiérrez (2013) Chapter 12, p. 322.
149. See UN Transfer Pricing Practical Manual (2013) Chapter 10.2, p. 358.
150. See e.g. Soares da Silva (2011) p. 121, Rigoni (2014) p. 734.
151. See Baker/Collier (2006) p. 60, Report on the Attribution of Profits to PE (2010) No. 203, pp. 53 ff.

country of the head office allows a tax credit for this withholding tax, double taxation or at least a higher administration and documentation effort might occur in this case.

The situation in *Russia* is also not clear. In general, Russian domestic law does not recognize internal dealings between head office and PE for tax purposes.[152] On the other side, the new Russian transfer pricing rules define the functionally separate entity approach as a future guiding principle for income allocation between head office and PE.[153] Due to lack of further clarifications or case law, it is unclear if the new transfer pricing rules also include the taxable recognition of internal dealings at arm's length. If the internal royalty is not recognized under Russian domestic law, only the '*barrier effect*' of the treaty applying the AOA leads to the deduction of the notional royalty from the Russian PE tax base. Otherwise, double taxation occurs.

For *India* as the PE country, a concrete statement is hard to make. In general, India applies its domestic transfer pricing rules also to the allocation of income between head office and PE.[154] Thus, it can be concluded that, similar to the AOA, internal dealings also follow the arm's length principle indicating a deduction from the Indian PE tax base and a recognition of a profit element for the internal royalty for the model case displayed in Figure 5.6.[155] However, it is questionable if Indian domestic law will also apply the transfer pricing rules to the deemed royalty as assumed under the AOA concept. In addition, as India refused to apply the AOA in its treaty policy, experience with regard to this topic simply does not exist. Most of the older Indian case law neglected the recognition of a profit element for internal dealings by following the argument that it is not possible to make profits from transactions with oneself.[156] Indian treaties which are based on the UN MC explicitly include a provision which disallows the deduction of such internal dealings from the PE tax base according to Article 7 (3) UN MC.[157] Due to these contradicting perspectives, a clear statement is not possible.

For *China* as the PE country, the situation is similar to India. In general, Chinese income allocation rules should also be applied for internal dealings between head office and PE.[158] However, it is not known if this also includes notional royalty payments.[159] In addition, there is a rule in Chinese national tax law which explicitly disregards the recognition of internal dealings between a domestic PE and a domestic head office. It is not known if this also applies in a cross-border case.[160] Chinese treaty policy refuses to use the AOA so that specific treaty practice is also missing.[161] About one-third of Chinese treaties follow Article 7 (3) of the UN MC and disallow the deduction of

152. See section 4.2.4.2. See also the PE Questionnaire in the Appendix, Table A20.
153. See e.g. Filinov et al. (2014) Russia, p. 35.
154. See section 4.2.5.2.
155. See also the PE Questionnaire in the Appendix, Table A21.
156. See Rawal (2004) pp. 85 ff.
157. See Appendix, Table A16.
158. See section 4.2.6.2.
159. See also the PE Questionnaire in the Appendix, Table A22.
160. See Gutiérrez (2013) p. 325.
161. See e.g. Hu/Li (2015) Chapter 7, p. 197.

internal royalties from the PE tax base.[162] In general, as the domestic treatment is unclear and the AOA is not applied by China, there is not enough information to draw concrete conclusions.

In summary, from the six countries under consideration, only Germany and the US follows the AOA with regard to the recognition of an internal royalty (see Table 5.5).

Table 5.5 Recognition of Internal Dealings

Residence Country = OECD Country	*Non-taxation Risk*	*Single taxation (Similar to OECD Approach)*	*Double Taxation Risk*
Source country	-	DE*, US*	BR

No concrete statement possible: CN, IN, RU
* Domestic legal basis for recognition not given

Still, the domestic legal basis of the deduction from the domestic PE tax base is not given for these countries so that only the '*barrier effect*' of the concluded treaty avoids qualification conflicts in this case. Brazilian domestic law includes specific restrictions on the deductibility of royalties whereas it is even questionable if internal deemed royalties are recognized at arm's length. As the deduction of royalties is thus restricted in Brazil, the source country's taxing right is widened in this case. Double taxation situations are possible. For India, Russia and China, the situation is similar. All three countries apply the respective national transfer pricing rules for the allocation of business profits between head office and PE but further regulations with regard to the application of these transfer pricing rules to the deemed royalty payment do not exist. Therefore, it is not possible to clearly determine whether double or non-taxation situations will occur for those countries.[163]

5.3.2 Allocation of Business Profits to Special PE Cases

The '*functionally separate entity approach*' as applied in the OECD MC describes a functional and factual analysis based on the allocation of assets, risks and PE capital determined by significant people functions performed by the personnel of the PE.[164] These significant people functions are the major allocation factor of the AOA. They determine the economic owners of the assets involved and the effective risk takers of the business activities, which have a direct influence on the amount of profit to be allocated due to the risks taken, the possible existence of internal dealings due to a separation of ownership and use of the assets, and the attribution of PE equity and debt

162. See Appendix, Table A17.
163. Still, it can also be possible to provide for a deduction of the notional payments from the PE tax base in these countries by applying the non-discrimination-article of Article 24 (3) OECD MC. If comparable expenses are deductible by comparable independent companies being resident in the PE state, a deduction of the deemed royalty payment is theoretically possible. See for an example Bobbett/Jones (2010) pp. 21 ff.
164. See section 3.3.2.

capital based on this allocation of assets and risk.[165] This concept should also be generally applied for all specific PE cases, such as the construction, agency and service PE. The question is now whether the AOA will work for those specific cases in the countries under consideration without offering a field for broad interpretation and possible conflicts. This is important as, independent of the existence of a PE as fiscal nexus, the allocation of income to the PE determines the amount of taxes to be paid in the source and residence country of the head office. What is not considered here, are tax accounting differences due to the country-specific rules to determine the PE tax base (e.g., different depreciation schemes of attributed assets, recognition of provisions, etc.). Again, this is not a specific PE problem but occurs in general for cross-border direct investments.[166]

5.3.2.1 Allocation of Business Profits to a Construction Site PE

With the abolishment of the indirect method of profit allocation according to the '*old*' Article 7 (4) OECD MC, the OECD introduced the AOA for the income allocation to construction site PEs.[167] The profit which has to be allocated between head office and construction site PE is determined from the construction order outcome which is the difference between the revenue earned through the construction and the net costs.[168] Relevant functions which occur in the construction or installation process are engineering activities, such as the modelling and drawing of construction plans and figures, procurement which involves the ordering, purchasing and manufacturing of the assets and components needed, also by subcontractors, and the construction itself which can also be delegated to subcontractors.[169] Further processes are the supervision and implementation of the installation, the instruction of personnel as well as technical and software assistance. Under the AOA, significant people functions have to be found for all of these processes which form the basis for the allocation of the economic ownership of assets and the allocation of business risks. However, all these processes, from planning and engineering to construction and supervision, are interleaved from a factual and temporal perspective and can change during the construction process.[170] A clear differentiation between different functions of the head office and the PE which all contribute to the overall outcome is hard to identify as single parts of the construction project have a subjective character based on individual requests of the client and liquidity aspects which are hard to be revalued at arm's length.[171] The direct method of

165. See Report on the Attribution of Profits to PE (2010) No. 44, p. 21.
166. For an European harmonization approach with regard to the problem of an unharmonized corporate tax base, see e.g. Spengel/Ortmann-Babel/Zinn/Matenaer (2012) pp. 185 ff.
167. See section 3.3.2.
168. See Bendlinger/Remberg/Kuckhoff (2002) p. 44. For so-called turn-key contracts, an overall price is determined which the client pays to the contractor when the construction is finished and approved. See Salzberger (2013) p. 139.
169. See e.g. Salzberger (2013) pp. 138 ff.
170. See Bendlinger/Remberg/Kuckhoff (2002) p. 41.
171. See Bendlinger (2005) p. 69. See Rehfeld/Goldner (2013) pp. 552 ff. for an illustrative example. See Seeleitner/Krinninger/Grimm (2013) pp. 224 ff. who suggest to consider the whole construction site PE as one 'dealing'.

profit allocation as proposed under the AOA is thus hard to be implemented. Although the indirect method is abolished, an alternative might be the cost apportionment method which allocates the income on the basis of the relation of overall costs between head office and PE.[172] Obviously, this *'mixture'* method is also accepted by the OECD MC as transactional profit-split method in the OECD Transfer Pricing Guidelines of 2010.[173]

Regardless of the general difficulties of allocating income to a construction site PE, the model case displayed in Figure 5.3 shall be considered in which the non-resident general contractor delegates all work to the local subcontractor. According to the OECD Reform Proposal, this leads to the establishment of a construction site PE for the general contractor in the country where the construction site is located given that the premises are under the disposal of the general contractor.[174] The question is now which significant people functions are allocated to this construction site PE when applying the AOA. On the one hand, there is the opinion that, similar to the agency PE, the profit allocation depends on the allocation of risks which the subcontractor eventually bears for the general contractor. This means that irrespective of an arm's length remuneration, an additional allocation of profit is still possible.[175] On the other hand, it can be argued that the functions which contributed to the profit of the general contractor, such as obtaining the order for constructing, ordering of components by suppliers or financing decisions, are generally conducted by people working at the premises of the general contractor in the foreign country.[176] Therefore, the profit to be allocated to the construction site PE of the general contractor following significant people functions remains to be minimal or zero.[177] In fact, this is a controversial topic for which the OECD MC does not provide clear statements.[178] *'Double taxation'* situations though for different taxpayers on the same income, are possible if both, the general contractor and the subcontractor, are deemed to establish a PE in the country where the construction site is located.[179]

Germany applies the general income allocation rules for a construction site PE which follows the AOA.[180] Thus, the income between the foreign contractor and the construction site PE shall be allocated on the basis of significant people functions involving the attribution of assets and risks. Similar to the OECD approach, despite the abolishment of the indirect method of profit allocation in German domestic law, a transactional profit-split method can also be applied for non-routine functions, so that methods like cost apportionment can be used in order to simplify the allocation of

172. See Salzberger (2013) pp. 145 ff.
173. See OECD Transfer Pricing Guidelines (2010) No. 2.109, pp. 93 ff. See Remberg (2006) p. 547.
174. See section 5.2.2.
175. See Wichman (2012) p. 713. See section 5.3.2.2. for the income allocation to agency PE.
176. See Bendlinger/Görl/Paaßen/Remberg (2004) p. 146.
177. See Wichmann (2012) p. 713.
178. This was also topic of the discussion in the case study conference 'Practical Problems of Tax Treaty Interpretation and Application' held in Vienna on 21 October 2013. See Somare/Turcan/Zeiler (2014) pp. 226 ff.
179. See Jirousek in Somare/Turcan/Zeiler (2014) p. 226.
180. See section 4.2.1.2.

otherwise interweaved structures and functions in the construction process.[181] With regard to the model case of the total delegation of work to subcontractors as shown in Figure 5.3, Germany does probably not assume a construction site PE for the general contractor.[182] Even if there is a German PE, it is possible that German tax practice follows the '*zero-sum*'-theory as developed for the allocation of income to an agency PE.[183] Similar to the agency PE, it can be argued that the arm's length provision paid to the subcontractor which performs all activities for the general contractor in the country of source equals the profits being allocated to the construction site PE, so that the residual PE income is zero.[184] This avoids the possible '*double taxation*' of income at the level of the subcontractor and the general contractor at any case. Similar to the OECD approach, it is also discussable which profits remain at the level of the construction site PE under the factual and functional analysis according to German income allocation rules if most of the profit-generating functions are usually performed by the general contractor abroad.

The *US* also does not provide specific rules with regard to the allocation of income to a construction site PE.[185] In general, one can assume that most of the essential activities performed at a US construction site fulfil the requirements of an effective connection with a US trade or business. Some US treaties, e.g., the one with the Netherlands, include a specific explanation which determines that not all profits from the construction contract are allocated to the PE, but only the profits from construction activities which are effectively carried out by the PE.[186] Still, it is questionable to what extent profits will be allocated to subcontractors similar to the model case displayed in Figure 5.3 under a functional analysis for US treaties which follow the AOA. According to the domestic ECI concept, the usage of a profit-split method is possible which leads to taxation of a part of the profit to the US PE given considerable functions and risks are allocated to the subcontractor. Thus, it can be at least assumed that the '*zero-sum*'-theory is not followed by US tax authorities.[187]

In *Brazil*, no specific regulations exist for the income allocation to a construction site PE.[188] As predetermined profit mark-ups are used and transactional profit-split methods are usually denied under Brazilian transfer pricing rules; conflicts can occur if the residence country of the general contractor insists on applying the AOA or another widely recognized method such as cost apportionment so that the determined PE tax bases differ. The same conflict can occur in the case of total delegation of work to a Brazilian subcontractor given that Brazilian tax authorities assume a PE from this activity. Still, there is no further information given.

181. See German PE Decree (2014) No. 33, p. 1391.
182. See section 5.2.3.
183. See section 5.3.2.2.
184. See e.g. Pijl (2006) p. 34.
185. See section 4.2.2.2.
186. See US-Netherlands Tax Treaty Memorandum of Understanding (2004) No. III, In Reference to Article 7 (Business Profits).
187. See the PE Questionnaire in the Appendix, Table A18.
188. See section 4.2.3.2.

In *Russia* it is not clear if a construction site PE is established for the non-resident general contractor if all work is delegated to Russian subcontractors.[189] If there is a PE, most Russian tax treaties explicitly offer the possibility to use indirect profit allocation methods in contrast to the AOA. Still, as for Germany, it can be interpreted that the use of transactional profit-split methods as '*mixture*' between the indirect and the direct method is still in line with the AOA so that conflicts are avoided. However, a clear guidance under Russian transfer pricing regulations for the application of the AOA to income allocation is still missing.[190]

India also does not apply any specific rules.[191] One topic in Indian case law examines whether offshore activities which were involved in the construction process, such as offshore supply of equipment and services can be considered as being taxable in India when starting a construction site.[192] In a recent case, the Indian High Court decided that such equipment and manufacturing activities which took part usually outside India are not considered as Indian income.[193] The same applies to related '*inextricable*' services which are performed in India unless income from these services is attributed to an Indian PE or is considered as fees for technical services and taxed according to Article 12 UN MC. Apart from start-up activities, the income allocation procedure is still questionable if e.g., a general contractor applies equipment and planning manufacturing functions while subcontracting the complete service and installation work on-site to a subcontractor working in India. Due to comparability reasons, it can be indicated that India eventually applies the same results derived from the *Morgan Stanley* or *SET Satellite* case.[194] If all work is delegated to an Indian subcontractor who is paid an arm's length remuneration for his work as it is assumed for the model case displayed in Figure 5.3, no further income shall be attributed in accordance with Indian case law. Therefore, it is thinkable that results similar to the '*zero-sum*'-theory also apply to the Indian construction site PE of the general contractor. The overall PE income resulting from the difference between the arm's length PE profit from the construction work performed by the subcontractor and the arm's length remuneration as PE expense eventually nets out. Thus, a PE profit would not occur for the general contractor. This also avoids '*double taxation*' of profits earned by the subcontracting enterprise being located in India and the non-resident general contractor. Still, this is a theoretical application of Indian case law to a similar topic where more concrete information is not given.

China uses deemed profit methods for the allocation of income to a construction site PE.[195] Thus, if revenue and costs cannot be clearly attributed, but the total local expenses are given, which is supposed to be the case for interrelated construction projects, a deemed profit rate of 15% to 30% is assumed from which the deemed gross

---

189. See section 4.2.4.1.
190. See e.g. Matchekhin (2014) p. 618 who states that the usual transfer pricing method in Russian tax practice is the direct method.
191. See section 4.2.5.2.
192. See e.g. Goradia/Kapila (2009) p. 357.
193. See Susarla/Krishnan (2014) p. 436.
194. See section 4.2.5.2.
195. See section 4.2.6.2.

revenue and the taxable income can be derived.[196] In fact, even if revenue and costs can be clearly attributed, this method often works as a common guidance for Chinese local tax authorities. In general, the usage of the deemed profit method is problematic if the residence country of the general contractor applies a functional and factual analysis following the AOA instead.[197] The double taxation effect increases for the total delegation of work to subcontractors as illustrated in Figure 5.3, if it is assumed that the functional analysis leads to the result that most of the profit-generating functions are performed at the premises of the general contractor outside China.

5.3.2.2 Allocation of Business Profits to an Agency PE

The OECD generally applies the AOA for the allocation of income to an agency PE.[198] Therefore, it has to be determined whether the employees of the dependent agent enterprise perform significant people functions being relevant for the attribution of the economic ownership of assets and the bearing of risks which indicate the allocation of taxable business profits at the level of the agency PE. In this context, the OECD MC differentiates between two different taxpayers: the dependent agent enterprise being resident in the source country and subject to an unlimited tax liability and the agency PE of the non-resident principal being subject to a limited tax liability.[199] This means that the OECD principally refuses the '*single taxpayer approach*' which treats the dependent agent enterprise as single taxpayer implying that the arm's length provision paid to the agent equals the profits allocated to the agency PE so that the net profit is zero.[200] However, similar to the single taxpayer approach, the OECD recognizes the arm's length remuneration paid to the agent as major element of the agency PE's profit respectively deductible expense. Additional profits shall only be allocated to the PE if the agent has active decision power with regard to the adoption or management of certain risks.[201] Considerable risks in this context might be, for instance, inventory risk (responsible for the amount of inventory and decisions on the economic ownership of the assets), credit risk (responsible for any losses from the non-payment of receivables by clients) or product liability and warranty risk for the assets sold.[202] Thus, from an OECD perspective, the allocation of additional income to the agency PE, apart from the arm's length provision, depends on the facts and circumstances of the case under consideration.

In the model case of the '*dependent commission agent PE*' displayed in Figure 5.4, for instance, the OECD country R might assume that the inventory and credit risk is borne by the non-resident principal who delivers the ordered assets whereas it is arguable to which degree warranty risks (or maybe also risks of currency losses) may

196. See e.g. Eichelberger/Liu/DeSouza (2015) p. 28.
197. See for an example Seeleitner/Krinninger/Grimm (2013) pp. 221 ff.
198. See Report on the Attribution of Profits to PE (2010) No. 232, pp. 59 ff.
199. See Ditz/Bärsch (2013) p. 412.
200. See Report on the Attribution of Profits to PE (2010) No. 236-No. 239, p. 61.
201. See e.g. Niehaves (2010) p. 149. See Rosalem (2010) pp. 15 ff. for a more concrete interpretation of the concept of 'active decision-making'.
202. See Report on the Attribution of Profits to PE (2010) No. 68, p. 21.

be allocated to the agency PE as the employees of the subsidiary are allowed to negotiate details of pricing and warranty.[203] Thus, in a broader sense, '*double taxation*' of the same income may occur at the level of the dependent agent enterprise although two different taxpayers are considered (the local agent enterprise and the non-resident principal). However, it is still questionable to what extent the adoption of those risks leads to an additional agency PE profit apart from the arm's length compensation which is generally netted out through the deduction of the compensation as PE expense.[204]

Germany is in line with the OECD approach.[205] Although German tax literature often favours the '*zero-sum*'-theory which is based on similar requirements as the single taxpayer approach and leads to the same consequences, the recent adoption of the AOA in national tax law implies to use a factual and functional analysis based on the allocation of significant people managing risks.[206] Still, German national law does not exclude that the relevant agency PE profit can also be zero.[207] With regard to German treaty policy, there is one treaty of Germany with Austria whose protocol includes a regulation similar to the single taxpayer approach. The protocol determines that as long as functions between associated enterprises are compensated with an arm's length remuneration, an agency PE shall not be established.[208] If applied to the model case as displayed in Figure 5.4, this excludes the existence of an agency PE from the beginning as the commission agent is a subsidiary of the non-resident principal. '*Double taxation*' in the sense of taxing agency profits at the level of the subsidiary and at the level of the agency PE does not occur. However, it is questionable if the '*zero-sum*'-theory is still applicable from a German perspective given that the income allocation to domestic permanent representatives follows the AOA.[209]

The *US* has no specific rules with regard to the allocation of income to an agency PE in place.[210] In general, similar to other business profits, income earned by a non-resident principal through the activities of a US agency PE has to be effectively connected to a US trade or business in order to be taxable in the US. With regard to

203. See section 5.2.3.
204. See e.g. Niehaves (2011) pp. 377 ff. who argues that the agency PE profit is zero or at least small if the allocation of profits is only based on additional risks borne by the agent without considering the main function of the agent to conclude contracts for income allocation. See critically to this opinion Ditz/Bärsch (2013) p. 413.
205. See section 4.2.1.2.
206. See i.a. Endres (1996) p. 4, Haiß (2000) p. 293 or Ditz/Bärsch (2013) p. 414 who favour the 'zero-sum' theory. In contrast to the single taxpayer approach, the 'zero-sum' theory differentiates between three cases. Only if the agent is an employee of the principal (and no independent agent or associated enterprise), the PE income is different from zero as it can be supposed that the provision paid to the agent as PE expense is smaller than the PE profit being allocated. See e.g. Niehaves (2011) p. 374.
207. See e.g. Rasch/Müller (2014) p. 422.
208. See Kroppen (2005) p. 704, Niehaves (2010) pp. 159 ff.
209. Also the German Administrative Principles with regard to Business Restructuring determine that the agency PE profit shall be determined independent of the dependent agent enterprise in accordance with the OECD Report on the Attribution of Profits to the PE of 2010. Still, there is no further explanation to this statement. See German Administrative Principles - Business Restructuring (2010) No. 215, p. 71.
210. See section 4.2.2.2.

income earned from assets sold in the US by a US agency PE, it can be assumed that the income is not US-based as the assets sold effectively belong to the non-resident principal. Thus, the foreign principal needs an office or another fixed place of business in the US in order to establish a US taxing right.[211] According to US Treasury Regulations, the office or a fixed place of business of a non-independent agent does not play a role with regard to US taxation of the sales income, unless that agent:

> has the authority to negotiate and conclude contracts in the name of the non-resident alien individual or foreign corporation, or has a stock of merchandise belonging to the non-resident alien individual or foreign corporation from which orders are regularly filled on behalf of such alien individual or foreign corporation.[212]

In conclusion, this means that the allocation of the sales profit of the non-resident principal to the US agent depends on the question whether the US agent also has the authority to conclude contracts in the name of the foreign principal.[213] However, if he has these authorities, he establishes a US agency PE in any case given that he is not an independent agent. In accordance with the results of the model case dealing with the '*dependent commission agent*' shown in Figure 5.4 for which the US accepts an agency PE, it can thus be concluded that also the sales income earned by the non-resident enterprise shall be allocated to the US agency PE and taxed there according to US domestic regulations.[214] '*Double taxation*' in the US in the sense of taxation of the US subsidiary and the US agency PE on the sales income occurs. Still, US treaty law can also override this domestic ruling.[215] However, in contrast to Germany, for instance, there are no further regulations in US treaty policy with regard to the income allocation to an agency PE. US treaties which follow the AOA obviously also follow the OECD approach of implying a factual and functional analysis based on significant people functions.[216]

Brazilian domestic law obviously takes into account the whole sales income (less related expenses) if earned through a Brazilian *commissário*.[217] There is no further information considering the allocation of functions and risks or the possible application of the single taxpayer approach. With regard to the agency PE example shown in Figure 5.4 it can be concluded that Brazil taxes a considerable amount given that an agency PE exists through the activities of the '*dependent commission agent*'. If this structure falls under the regulations of the Brazilian *mandatário*, the agency PE income is determined on the basis of deemed fixed revenue amounts. Conflicts with regard to the attributed PE income can occur if the residence country of the foreign principal applies the AOA and considers significant people functions whereas Brazilian law applies fixed percentage amounts of profit margins. It is questionable if the deemed profit method applies

211. See Ring (2015) p. 80.
212. See US Treasury Regulation 1.864-7(d)(1)(i).
213. The case of a stock of merchandise is neglected here.
214. See section 5.2.3.
215. See e.g. Hannes (2006) p. 302.
216. See for a supportive view, the PE Questionnaire in the Appendix, Table A18.
217. See section 4.2.3.2.

under Brazilian tax treaties.[218] Furthermore, there is no specific information on how the income allocation rules under Brazilian tax treaties which mostly follow the *'old view'* of the OECD MC differ from the AOA.

For *Russia*, there is no concrete information with regard to income allocation to an agency PE.[219] It is questionable if the Russian Transfer Pricing Rules of 2012 indicate the application of the AOA also for an agency PE and whether an arm's length commission paid to the agent shall be sufficient or whether further risks and resulting profits indicate additional PE profits.

Indian case law implies that as long as the commission payment from the principal to the Indian agency PE is in line with the arm's length standard, no additional profits shall be allocated to the agency PE.[220] In fact, this approach resembles the single taxpayer approach being refused by the OECD but often favoured, for instance, by German tax literature.[221] The *'dependent commission agent'* of the model case displayed in Figure 5.4 will therefore not be taxable in India as long as the remuneration paid by the non-resident principal is at arm's length.[222] Still, conflicts can occur if the residence country of the non-resident principal applies the AOA as implemented in the given treaty of the model case. If due to the functional analysis, the foreign country is of the opinion that additional risks (e.g., price or credit risks) can be allocated to India, the respective taxing right for this income will be shifted to India. However, when applying Indian case law, India will theoretically not tax this income derived from additional risks as the arm's length compensation already indicates an adequate allocation of functions and risks. Non-taxation occurs for this additional income if the residence country of the principal applies the exemption method for foreign business profits without any subject-to-tax or switch-over clauses.

China has no specific income allocation rules for agency PEs either.[223] In general, it applies its transfer pricing rules for associated enterprises in order to find out whether the commission fee paid by the foreign principal to the Chinese subsidiary is at arm's length.[224] If China assumed an agency PE in the model case shown in Figure 5.4, domestic deemed profit methods apply if direct accounts of the agency PE are inadequate or not existent.[225] Again, this leads to conflicts if the residence country of the foreign principal applies a functional and factual analysis based on the AOA and comes to different results. If, e.g., China determines a higher attributable agency PE income being subject to Chinese corporate income tax than being determined by the country of the principal, double taxation occurs. The relevant part of business income is effectively taxed twice, in China and in the residence state of the principal. As Chinese treaties do not apply the AOA, there is no information with regard to the details of a functional analysis or the position towards the single taxpayer approach.

218. See Rocha (2013) p. 449.
219. See section 4.2.4.2.
220. See section 4.2.5.2.
221. See e.g. Rosalem (2010) p. 28. See critically Pijl (2008) p. 182, Toro (2009) pp. 440 ff.
222. See also Metha (2015) p. 213.
223. See section 4.2.6.2.
224. See e.g. Eichelberger/Liu/DeSouza (2015) p. 36.
225. See Eichelberger/Liu/DeSouza (2015) p. 37.

5.3.2.3 Allocation of Business Profits to a Service PE

According to the OECD MC, the AOA shall apply in general which also includes the allocation of income to a service PE.[226] Detailed instructions are missing, except for a brief explanation in the OECD Report on the Attribution of Profits to PE of 2010.[227] This, however, focuses on the pricing of head office support functions which do not create a service PE under the OECD alternative since services have to be performed to third parties and not internally towards the own enterprise. The substantial income of the service PE, such as in the model cases displayed in Figure 5.2 or Figure 5.5, is the service fee which is paid by the clients as remuneration for the services provided.[228] Similar to the cases before, it is questionable if additional income can be allocated to the service PE in case the remuneration paid is at arm's length. There might be situations where the remuneration paid to the service providers by the parent company (PE expense) is equal or converges to the service fee received (PE income) so that the remaining taxable profit is minimal.[229] According to the OECD, this depends on the functional and factual analysis of significant people functions and the allocation of risk and the economic ownership of the assets involved which can be allocated to the PE. In addition, this might also depend on the status of the service-providing entity: If the service workers are considered as employees, and not as independent qualified personnel, the remuneration paid is usually lower than the income earned from the provision of services.[230] Thus, it can be concluded that the AOA can work for the allocation of income to a service PE. The question is if, similar to the agency PE, the whole process of the functional and factual analysis is necessary for the service PE or if it is sufficient to identify an adequate transfer price for the service fee. This thought, however, is a central part of the single taxpayer approach which is neglected by the OECD MC.[231] In addition, it is questionable if a functional analysis indeed leads to a significant taxable PE profit so that the specific identification of functions and risks is '*worth the effort*' or if the service PE profit is usually minimal after all.

In *Germany*, concrete rules with regard to the allocation of income to a service PE do not exist as service PEs are usually not regarded in German tax treaties.[232] In general, it can be concluded that Germany applies a functional and factual analysis similar to the AOA for the allocation of profits to a German service PE. It is questionable if the '*zero-sum*'-theory as mentioned in the German tax literature can also be applied in the case of the service PE as mentioned in the model cases in Figure 5.2 or Figure 5.5. Similar to the OECD MC, it is questionable if, apart from the service PE, additional profits are allocated to the service PE based on a functional analysis if the remuneration

226. See section 3.3.2.
227. See OECD MC Commentary (2014) No. 42.30, pp. 119 ff.
228. See Löwenstein (2011) No. 1533, p. 560.
229. See Report on the Attribution of Profits to PE (2010) No. 228, p. 59, No. 234, p. 60.
230. See e.g. Pijl (2006) fn. 36, p. 32.
231. See e.g. Baker/Collier (2009) p. 202.
232. See section 4.2.1.2.

received is at arm's length and no further functions, such as storage of goods or administration of receivables, are performed by the local service providers.[233]

The *US* and *Russia* do not provide specific rules with regard to the allocation of income to a service PE either. In US domestic law, the allocation of income depends on whether the income earned from the provision of services is considered as being effectively connected to a US trade or business and not as foreign-sourced or FDAP income.[234] US treaty policy, similar to Russia, is supposed to implement a functional analysis based on the AOA for PE income allocation.[235] Due to a lack of further explanations, it is again discussable if and how much income still can be allocated to the service PE if the remuneration paid to the service provider is considered to be at arm's length.

Brazilian tax law does not deal with the question of a service PE.[236] Fees earned from the provision of services in Brazil are taxed on a gross basis following Article 21 of the UN MC or at least Article 12 (2) of the UN MC depending on the qualification of services and the interpretation of the local tax courts.[237] The Brazilian special '*way*' of taxing services thus can generally lead to conflicts if the residence country of the foreign service provider determines a different Brazilian taxable profit including deductible expenses due to the application of the AOA in the national or treaty law.

In *India*, the allocation of income to service PEs obviously follows the same jurisdiction as for agency PEs. In accordance with the *Morgan Stanley* case, one can conclude that there shall not be any additional profits allocated to the PE if the compensation paid to the service provider is at arm's length.[238] The attribution of functions and risks is thus already supposed to be done in the transfer pricing analysis with regard to the identification of the adequate arm's length service compensation. Similar to the allocation of profits to an Indian agency PE, there might be situations where the service fee paid to the service provider is supposed to be at arm's length so that an additional functional analysis is not necessary. Further Indian case law also deals with the application of the limited force of attraction principle to Indian PE profits. The contradicting Indian decisions of *Linklaters* and *Clifford Chance* indicate that the limited force of attraction principle is at least possible for Indian service PEs given that the respective treaty also provides for its application.[239] In addition, services which are not considered as business profits can still be part of the Indian source tax base on a gross basis as '*technical service fees*' which are generally used in the Indian royalty-article.[240] A qualification conflict in this context is possible if the residence country of the non-resident service provider applies a different treaty provision than

233. See e.g. Ditz/Bärsch (2013) p. 414 who describe the agency PE as service PE which is 'deficient in functions'.
234. See section 4.2.2.2.
235. See section 4.2.2.2 & section 4.2.4.2.
236. See section 4.2.3.1.
237. See e.g. Ferreira (2014) p. 432.
238. See e.g. Sherchan/Rao (2010) p. 355, Jhabakh (2010) p. 159.
239. See section 4.2.5.2.
240. The introduction of technical service fees in the royalty-article is considered in ca. 80% of the Indian treaties. See Appendix, Table A5.

India due to an unclear definition of the service term.[241] Further conflicts can occur from the application of predetermined profit margins for certain IT and R&D services in India.[242] If the residence country of the foreign service provider comes to the conclusion that the profit margin to be allocated to the Indian service PE shall be lower than the given mark-up, double taxation upon the residual transfer price occurs.

Also in *China*, the usage of the presumptive profit methods can be problematic. Depending on the type of service provided, Chinese domestic law provides for different deemed profit rates, from 15% to 30% for designing or consultancy services to 50% for management services and not more than 15% for all other types of services performed.[243] According to another Chinese law regulation, supportive installation and guidance services related to the sale of machinery in China are deemed to be taxed at 10% of the contract price if the service fee is considered as being '*unreasonable*'.[244] As such deemed profit methods are commonly used by Chinese tax authorities, double or non-taxation situations can occur if the residence country of the foreign service provider applies a functional analysis under the AOA which comes to different results and determines a different PE tax base.

5.4 RECONSIDERATION

The following reconsiders the model cases of section 5.3 by additionally taking into account the allocation of profits between head office and PE. In order to evaluate possible sources of conflicts, the focus is on the allocation of profits to a PE. If the profits to be allocated to the PE are minimal or even zero, the double or non-taxation problem due to a differing interpretation of PE requirements by the considered countries eventually has to be re-evaluated.[245] In a double taxation case (i.e., the residence country of the investor does not assume a PE while the country of source does), double taxation of business profits effectively vanishes or is at least diminished if there are no (or very low) profits to be allocated to the PE. The same effect occurs for non-taxation in vice versa cases. Therefore, Tables 5.6-5.8 pick up the already presented specific PE model cases (first column) and determine whether there is a tendency that the respective PE profit to be allocated is significant (second column). Only in those cases where the PE tax base is significant, the risk of double or non-taxation is still existent (third column).

With regard to the total delegation of work to subcontractors, Germany contradicts with the OECD interpretation so that non-taxation can occur since, in contrast to the OECD MC, Germany does not assume a construction site PE if the general

241. Even if the foreign country applies the credit method for foreign taxes, it is not sure if the Indian withholding taxes due to the qualification of the service as 'technical service fee' can be credited, e.g. if the foreign country considers the service income as business profits.
242. See Gada/Sinha (2014) p. 381.
243. See Eichelberger/Liu/DeSouza (2015) pp. 28 ff.
244. See Mui/Yam (2014) China, p. 19.
245. For the following discussion, this implies that the countries under consideration agree on the income allocation to the PE. Double or non-taxation still occurs if the countries disagree about the adequate allocation of business profits and expenses between head office and PE.

contractor is not physically present in the source country (see Table 5.2). Still, this has to be reconsidered when taking into account the allocation of income to the subcontractor (see Table 5.6).

Table 5.6 Construction Site PE – Total Delegation of Work to Subcontractors – Reconsideration

	PE Definition Conflict with OECD MC?	*PE Profit to be Allocated Significant?*	*Double or Non-taxation Risk Still Existent?*
DE	Yes	No	No
US	Not enough information	Not enough information	Not enough information
BR	Not enough information	Not enough information	Not enough information
RU	Not enough information	Not enough information	Not enough information
IN	No conflict	Not enough information	No
CN	No conflict	Yes	Yes*

* No conflict with regard to PE definition, but still risk of double taxation due to usage of deemed profit methods by Chinese tax authorities

If, for instance, Germany follows the OECD interpretation and creates a construction site PE for the general contractor due to the total delegation of work to subcontractors, it is likely that, similar to the allocation of business profits to an agency PE, the '*single taxpayer approach*' can also be applied to the German subcontractor so that the PE profit to be allocated will be minimal or zero. Double or non-taxation situations are thus improbable as there are no profits to be allocated to the German PE. The same might apply for India when taking into account the relevant Indian court decisions of *Morgan Stanley* or *SET Satellite*. In Russia, due to a lack of information, it is hard to determine whether the PE profit to be allocated is significant. For China, the common usage of presumptive profit methods leads to the assumption that the PE profit is significant if China assumed a construction site PE. Thus, a double taxation risk is still given. For the US and Brazil, there is uncertainty with regard to the construction site PE definition in case of the total delegation of work to subcontractors and whether the PE profit to be allocated will be significant if such a PE was established. Therefore, it is hard to show concrete tendencies with respect to the risk of double or non-taxation in these countries.

In general, even if all countries under consideration apply the AOA and allocate the business profits based on a functional analysis, it is questionable if a PE profit can be allocated to the construction site PE anyway. Independent of the national or country-specific treaty perspective of the source country under consideration, there can be a minimal or zero allocation of business profits to the PE when applying the AOA if the profit-inducing functions are not performed by subcontractors at the PE site which is possible in this case.[246] Thus, even if a qualification conflict with regard to the necessary construction site PE requirement exists, the risk of double or non-taxation decreases if there are no or only minimal profits to be allocated to the construction site PE.

With regard to the '*dependent commission agent*' in the model case displayed in Figure 5.4, the analysis of the PE threshold of the authority to conclude contracts on behalf of the principal revealed a degree of uncertainty among most of the countries under consideration except for the US and India which follow the '*broad*' OECD view with regard to the authority to conclude contracts (see Table 5.3). In fact, only the US and India are in line with the OECD interpretation in the model case whereas a general double taxation risk is still given for India. Again, one can re-evaluate the risk of double or non-taxation when taking into account whether the PE profit to be allocated is significant (see Table 5.7).

Table 5.7 Agency PE – Authority to Conclude Contracts – Reconsideration

	PE Definition Conflict with OECD MC?	*PE Profit to be Allocated Significant?*	*Double or Non-taxation Risk Still Existent?*
DE	Not enough information	No	No
US	No	Not enough information	No
BR	Not enough information	Yes	Yes**
RU	Not enough information	Not enough information	Not enough information
IN	No*	No	No
CN	Not enough information	Yes	Yes**

* No conflict with regard to example in Figure 5.4, but still tendency of increased source taxation in India

** Conflicts with regard to attribution of business profits still possible due to usage of deemed profit methods by tax authorities

If it is assumed that Germany follows the single taxpayer approach as favoured by several tax literature, the taxable PE profits are zero. Furthermore, even if Germany follows the AOA as implemented in domestic law, it is questionable whether the PE profits which are allocated to the German agency PE are significant for a '*dependent commission agent*' who usually does not perform significant functions or bears considerable risk. Therefore, it can be determined that the risk of double or non-taxation is diminished for Germany when taking into account the allocation of profits to a PE. A similar situation occurs for India if it is assumed that the Indian approach towards the allocation of income to an agency PE is in line with the single taxpayer

246. See e.g. Bendlinger/Görl/Paaßen/Remberg (2004) p. 146.

approach. Still, the broad Indian PE understanding will probably lead to more PE cases. In Brazil and China, the PE profit to be allocated can be significant due to the broad domestic allocation rules and the usage of predetermined profit margins. Still, it is hard to draw conclusions on the risk of double or non-taxation caused by PE definition conflicts as there is no information with regard to the national PE definition rules for the agency PE and the interpretation of the authority to conclude contracts. In Russia, there is neither concrete information with regard to the national understanding of the authority to conclude contracts which leads to the establishment of an agency PE, nor whether there is a tendency that the agency PE profit to be allocated is significant. In the US, it is also hard to draw conclusions on the significant profit level of a US agency PE. Still, as the US is in line with the OECD MC with regard to the agency PE definition in this case, the risk of double or non-taxation cases is diminished.

Again, even if the AOA is applied by all countries, it is discussable if the resulting agency PE profit is significant due to the possible lack of functions performed and risks borne by the '*dependent commission agent*'. Even if there is an intangible at the level of the PE, e.g., by distributing goods with a valuable brand, it is questionable if additional profit arises at the level of the agency PE as the significant decision upon the development and protection of those brands is usually made by the head office.[247] In addition, an arm's length internal royalty similar to that in the model case shown in Figure 5.6 has to be paid so that the PE profit is additionally diminished.[248] Therefore, it is questionable if there is any considerable taxable PE profit at the level of the agency PE. If there is not, discussions about double or non-taxation situations due to differences with regard to the agency PE threshold become pointless.

Considering the establishment of a service PE through the secondment of employees (see Figure 5.5), implications about the significance of the PE profit can hardly be drawn for Germany, the US and Russia (see Table 5.8).[249]

Table 5.8 Service PE – Secondment of Employees – Reconsideration

	PE Definition Conflict with OECD MC?	*PE Profit to be Allocated Significant?*	*Double or Non-taxation Risk Still Existent?*
DE	Yes*	Not enough information	Yes
US	No	Not enough information	No
BR	Yes	Yes	Yes***
RU	No**	Not enough information	No

247. See Baldamus (2012) p. 318.
248. See Kropppen (2013) p. 274.
249. Figure 8 is not considered in this context as it deals with the establishment of a basic PE including a fixed place of business (also referred to as 'passive' service PE).

	PE Definition Conflict with OECD MC?	PE Profit to be Allocated Significant?	Double or Non-taxation Risk Still Existent?
IN	No	No	No****
CN	No	Yes	Yes***

* Conflict due to missing taxable nexus for service PE under German domestic law

** Conflict due to Russian migration law

*** Double taxation risk given due to usage of deemed profit methods

**** Double taxation risk still given for specific types of services due to usage of deemed profit methods

In Brazil and China, due to taxation at a gross basis respectively the usage of deemed profit methods, it can be determined that the service PE profit will be significant. Interpreting the *Morgan Stanley* case in India indicates that an arm's length service fee is sufficient as taxable PE profit so that it can be concluded that the PE profit will be minimal. Thus, despite the broad Indian interpretation of the economic employer concept, the probability of double or non-taxation situations is reduced as the respective Indian PE profit is most likely minimal. Still, conflicts through the usage of predetermined profit margins are possible for certain types of services in India. For Germany and Russia, the conflicts with regard to the necessary service PE threshold persist (see Table 5.4). In Germany, this is the case due to a lack of information with regard to the fact whether the service PE profit to be allocated is significant. In Russia, the migration law generally avoids a domestic taxing right in this case. For the US, it is also hard to draw further conclusions about the significance of PE profit. As the US is in line with the OECD interpretation of the secondment of employees, the risk of double or non-taxation is again reduced.

Due to a lack of information, one cannot draw conclusions on how the results are if all countries apply the OECD regulations. Similar to the agency PE case, it might happen that also under a functional and factual analysis, necessary functions and risks cannot be found at the level of the local service provider so that the taxable service PE profit will be minimal. Still, this always depends on the specific case under consideration and the concrete allocation of functions and risks between head office and PE.

In summary, it can be concluded that especially for the cases of the construction site PE established by subcontractors and the agency PE, double or non-taxation problems become less significant if the relevant PE profit is minimal. This can be especially given for Germany and India and can also occur even if all countries under consideration follow the AOA. With regard to the service PE, it is hard to draw conclusions on the influence of PE profit allocation to the risk of double or non-taxation as country-specific information is rare. From the perspective of a company investing into the analysed countries, the administrative difficulties of source taxation of business profits can therefore be more relevant than the occurrence of possible double or non-taxation situations for specific PE cases.[250]

250. In fact, this result also fits to the results of an empirical transfer pricing survey conducted by *Flick Gocke Schaumburg* and *Horváth & Partners* stating that of more than 300 international

What remains a general problem is the recognition of internal dealings including a profit mark-up if the AOA is applied in the countries under consideration. Table 5.5 shows that especially in relation to the BRIC countries which do not follow the AOA, conflicts with regard to the possible recognition of internal dealings as deductible PE expense exist.[251] But also for Germany and the US, a domestic legal basis is still not given for the specific case. Therefore, as long as the national law of the respective countries and the AOA are not in line, conflicts with regard to the deductibility of PE expenses still occur if a treaty with one of the considered countries applies the AOA. Therefore, a risk of double or non-taxation is still given.

5.5 FEASIBILITY OF SOURCE TAXATION OF BUSINESS PROFITS

In general, PE taxation has to be feasible, transparent and ideally simple meaning that the administration costs for the fiscal authorities and the compliance costs of the taxpayer have to be minimized.[252] In practice, apart from corporate and other business taxation liabilities, additional obligations can arise for the foreign head office which is subject to a limited liability to tax due to a PE in the country of source. It can be determined that conflicts of interpretation between the contracting states as shown in the previous chapters always lead to an increased amount of administration and compliance costs. The feasibility of source taxation of business profits is thus generally restricted if there is a lack of common interpretation of PE requirements and different country-specific opinions exists with regard to the allocation of business profits between head office and PE.

A difficulty which can occur in all countries under consideration is related to employment taxation. According to Article 15 (2c) of the OECD MC, if the foreign employer's PE bears the remuneration paid to the employee who is working at the premises of the PE at source, the foreign employer becomes liable to pay wage taxes in the country of source independent of the working time of the employees spent at the PE site.[253] If the PE is established ex post because from the beginning of the activity, the non-resident head office might not know exactly whether a PE will be created through the business activities provided in the country of source, he is suddenly liable to pay wage taxes in that country.[254] With regard to the model cases discussed in section 5.2, this might occur for instance for a German investor conducting business activities in an OECD country for the cases of the '*passive*' service PE, the total delegation of work to subcontractors and secondment of employees. In those cases, the PE definition is interpreted in a narrower way in comparison to the OECD MC and therefore Germany

companies, only 9 % of those consider the establishment of a PE as factor for the correction of business profits in audits by the fiscal authorities. See Ditz/Bärsch/Kluge (2015) p. 821.

251. See section 5.3.1.
252. See also section 6.1.3.
253. See Dziurdz (2013) pp. 126 ff. for a more detailed explanation of the meaning of 'borne by a PE'.
254. See e.g. Miller/Oats (2014) pp. 247 ff.

probably does not assume a PE. However, if the source country constitutes a PE and no records were kept during that time, and additionally no wage taxes were collected, it may be very difficult for the employer to recover those from his former employees, especially since he is generally liable, if no wage tax has been paid.[255] Compliance costs and administration costs will increase. In addition, double taxation of employment income can occur if the investor has to pay wage taxes twice, in the residence and in the source country, at least for a temporary period until the wage tax assessments are corrected.

Another aspect considers the specific understanding of the taxation of services, especially by countries like India or Brazil. The OECD MC clarifies that the relevant income from services at the level of a service PE shall be taxed on a net basis if considered as business profits.[256] However, the tax assessment in the countries mentioned often applies a system of withholding taxes for income from technical services which are treated as royalty income following Article 12 (2) of the UN MC or, as in Brazil, even as other income according to Article 21 UN MC.[257] If a service PE is implemented in a treaty with one of these countries and difficulties occur with regard to the definition of income from these services as business profit, other income or income from technical services, a qualification conflict might occur as Brazil and India and, in addition, the OECD residence country apply different treaty provisions. Apart from possible double or non-taxation situations, for practical reasons, it may often be the case in those countries that the service income is initially taxed on a gross basis which is eventually remunerated at the end of the fiscal year if the contracting states agree that the income is considered as service PE income.[258] Independent of the final decision on the provision to be applied to the service income, this situation always results in an interest and liquidity disadvantage for the taxpayer and leads to higher compliance and administration costs and at least to temporal double taxation until the time of tax refund.[259]

In addition, several other formal and organizational obligations can arise for the investor if a PE is established in the country of source, from further employee costs, like social security or unemployment taxes,[260] to several other expenses of registration and late or insufficient compliance due to misunderstandings with regard to the PE existence in the country of source.

Table 5.9 displays the compliance and administration costs which can arise due to the existence of a PE in the countries under consideration.

255. See Dehnen/Bacht (2005) p. 448.
256. See OECD MC Commentary (2014) No. 42.19, p. 117.
257. See section 4.2.3.1 and section 4.2.5.1. See Appendix, Table A5 for an overview on Indian treaties using the royalty-article for the taxation of services.
258. See BIAC Response (2007) No. 12, 13, pp. 5 ff. See for a description of increased taxation situations, section 5.2.4.
259. See Bendlinger (2007b) p. 158, BIAC Response (2007) No. 14, p. 6.
260. See Cohen et al. (2008) p. 1187.

Table 5.9 Formal Requirements with regard to the Establishment of a PE in Germany, the US and the BRIC States[261]

DE	- Registration at the competent trade and tax office - Eventually registration in a commercial register and certification by notary - Obligation to keep books and prepare annual financial statements for trade and tax purposes if German turnover above EUR 500,000 or German business profit above EUR 50,000 - Failure to comply leads to tax estimations by authorities and penalties of up to EUR 1 million
US	- Filing of tax return mandatory if 'engaged in US trade or business', even if no *'effectively connected'* income or US source income - Further mandatory information-based returns necessary - Possibility to file a protective return if US PE status unclear - Obligation to keep books and prepare annual financial statements - Failure to file tax return leads to various interest and penalties
BR	- Requirement of complex authorization petition submitted to the Ministry of Commerce, Industry and Development (including documents which prove the existence of the foreign investor and the consent of the local unit with Brazilian government terms) - Complex system of authorization for each single local business operation - Filing of tax and information returns mandatory - Failure to comply leads to interest and penalties of up to 20% of tax due
RU	- Requirement of registration as representative office, branch or subdivision - Requirement of accreditation with federal authorities (to be regularly renewed) - Filing of tax and information returns mandatory - Obligation to keep books and prepare annual financial statements - Failure to register or to file tax return leads to penalties of up to 10% of revenue or 30% of tax due - Exclusion from future public call for tenders in case of failure to comply
IN	- Requirement of registration and approval by Reserve Bank of India (except for certain predetermined project offices) - Obligation to keep books and prepare annual financial statements - Obtaining of an official tax number (Permanent Account Number (PAN)) - In case of missing PAN tax estimations at fixed tax rates possible - Failure to comply leads to various interest and penalties - Exclusion from future public call for tenders in case of failure to comply

261. See for Germany: Mattern/Zinny (2014) Germany, pp. 8 ff., Schnorberger (2015) pp. 53 ff., for the US: Arthur/Herbert/Levey (2014) p. 795, Penn/Rinke (2014) United States, p. 7, for Brazil: DeSouza/Carvalho (2009) p. 156, Zapata/Weiss/Martins (2015) p. 23, for Russia: Kromer/Pumpler/Henschel (2013) p. 794, Filinov et al. (2014) Russia, pp. 11 ff., Konnov/Smirnova/Smith (2015) pp. 35 f., for India: Ruh/Beyer (2010) pp. 642 f., Bhatia/Sharma (2011) p. 103, Kromer/Pumpler/Henschel (2013) p. 794, Dalal/Shah/Sheth (2014) India, pp. 10 f., Mehta (2015) pp. 144 f., for China: Mui/Yam (2014) China, pp. 7 f., Eichelberger/Liu/DeSouza (2015) pp. 25 ff.

CN	- Requirement of registration and approval by local authorities as representative office or foreign contractor - Representative offices need to commit a 'sponsor' company approved by authorities in order to submit application documents - Obligation to keep books and prepare annual financial statements - Deeming methods used by local tax authorities if filing tax revenue not adequate - Failure to comply leads to penalties of up to five times the tax due

It is difficult to make general statements on the concrete level of compliance costs the foreign investor has to bear in the country of source. The same is true for administration costs for the relevant tax authorities. If the aspect of tax planning is left out, meaning that the costs incurred are related to the additional compliance efforts which arise due to the late and unexpected existence of a PE in the source country, the following conclusions can be drawn: In all six countries considered, there is a requirement to register the business activity as a PE with the respective authorities. This process seems to be more costly and time-consuming in Brazil, Russia, India and China where a specific approval or accreditation by the relevant local authorities, or other special requirements, such as the application for a registration number in India (PAN) or the entrusting of a '*sponsor*' company in China, is additionally necessary. The requirement to comply with accounting standards and to prepare specific financial statements is also obligatory in all countries. Brazil's system of registering separately each change in contract for each single business operation increases the compliance and administration costs and hinders the feasibility of source taxation of business profits. Failure to comply due to late or missing tax payments resulting from the establishment of a PE at source leads to interest and penalties in every country. The penalties for non-compliance in China can sum up to five times the not-reported tax due and are extraordinarily high in comparison to the other countries under consideration. The exclusion from future public call for tenders as additional punishment in Russia and India in case of late or insufficient tax compliance also has to be noted.

In summary, one can conclude that the feasibility and simplicity of PE taxation is hindered when taking into account specific approval formalities and exaggerating penalties for late tax compliance. These occur especially in the BRIC states. General registration and accounting requirements, on the contrary, seem to be common for all countries under consideration in case of a PE establishment.

Another factor which influences the feasibility of PE taxation is the determination and attribution of business profits between head office and PE. If it is assumed that the countries under consideration follow the AOA according to national law and in their treaty policy (as Germany does), compliance and administration costs become relevant. On the one hand, there is the general concept of the AOA which is based on a functional analysis taking into account significant people functions and on the other hand, a risk allocation on which assets and capital is attributed.

The concept of significant people functions allocates the taxable profits to the PE being related to active decision-making with regard to the acceptance or management of risk.[262] Thus, the central connection of profits is geographically driven. It depends on the personnel, employees and agents of the company deployed worldwide on-site which can include tasks of sales and distribution to consultancy and technical services as well as administrative and management operations. As it was derived in the previous analysis, all of these activities can establish a construction site, agency or service PE. However, these activities also seem to have a mobile nature. Significant people being part of the analysis, such as technical, consultancy or management service providers, subcontractors, agents or seconded employees, usually have a continuously changing geographical place of work. In addition, the usage of modern communication technologies, such as mobile phones, e-mail or video conferences, makes the actual place of location of the significant people irrelevant for the realization of business activities.[263] Compliance and administration costs thus will increase if significant people who are actively involved in the decision-making process either move regularly from one country to another country or are hard to be identified due to modern communication technology. This general shortcoming of the AOA would also be a problem in the BRIC states if the AOA was implemented in respective national or treaty law.

With regard to the concretion of risk allocation rules, details of the OECD BEPS Final Report on the Actions 8, 9 and 10 can be taken into account. This report deals with possible changes of the transfer pricing analysis as proposed in the OECD Transfer Pricing Guidelines.[264] One segment also deals with risk management in the context of the functional analysis being inherent for the determination of the correct arm's length transfer price.[265] Risk management thus has to include the element of control over risk, i.e., the ability to make decisions with regard to taking over and administer risk which also includes the actual performance of such functions, and the ability to reduce risk as well as to check and monitor transferred risk.[266] It is possible that this procedure applies under the AOA for income allocation between head office and PE. Apart from the complexity of this process, it is questionable in particular if such a procedure is possible in the BRIC states and if necessary resources and requirements are given to see through the whole value-added process between head office and PE in order to identify significant people functions and risks. Although all countries under consideration apply a system of accounting and financial statements for a PE established at source, it is discussable if the identification of functions and the allocation of risk are realizable especially in the BRIC countries where experience and relevant capacities in order to identify such functions and risks are still missing. In addition, the determination of comparability values for risks of single transactions between head office and PE is barely possible as relevant data mostly only exists for the whole company or business sectors.[267] Still, relevant data established from the transfer pricing documentation between affiliated companies which is mostly established in the BRIC countries can

262. See OECD Report on the Attribution of Profits to PE (2010) No. 22, p. 17.
263. See e.g. for Germany Kroppen (2014) p. 2134, Roeder/Friedrich (2015) p. 1055.
264. See OECD Final Report BEPS Actions 8, 9 & 10 (2015) p. 13.
265. See OECD Final Report BEPS Actions 8, 9 & 10 (2015) No. 1.61, p. 22.
266. See Greinert/Metzner (2015) p. 65.
267. See Luckhaupt/Overesch/Schreiber (2012b) p. 360.

additionally be used for the analysis of PE functions and risks. Therefore, it cannot be concluded in detail to what extent compliance and administration costs will rise if the AOA was implemented. In general, the level of complexity will definitively increase so that the principles of feasibility, simplicity and transparency of taxation will not necessarily hold in this case.

This leads to the aspect of transfer pricing and valuation of dealings as another relevant factor. As the AOA implies the recognition of internal dealings between head office and PE at an arm's length price, detailed documentation of transfer pricing valuation also becomes more important for the PE sphere.[268] In fact, by applying the AOA, the well-known transfer pricing difficulties with regard to transactions between associated companies are inserted in the field of PE taxation, especially with regard to internal dealings between head office and PE. If tax authorities disagree on the profit mark-up resulting from the transfer price valuation method used by the head office and the PE, e.g., for an internal royalty, it is possible that not only the respective transfer price, but also the whole allocation process eventually has to be re-evaluated or repeated. With regard to the determination of an arm's length price, e.g., for notional internal royalties, this includes the application of comparability factors such as the calculation of expected benefits, the exclusivity, nature and duration of the patent, the respective R&D costs, the degree of protection needed under the respective patent law, the right of the patent-using PE to participate in developments and the valuation of the production component for which the patent is used.[269] All these steps are again based on a functional and risk analysis whose difficulties in implementation are mentioned above.

Therefore, it is probable that the relevant compliance and administration costs will increase due to additional documentation requirements if all countries under consideration follow the AOA. This can especially be true for the arm's length evaluation of internal dealings, such as the internal royalty payment of the model case displayed in Figure 5.6. In addition, if the AOA is applied unilaterally by the investing country, in countries such as Brazil and China, where predetermined domestic profit mark-ups and deemed profit methods are regularly used, compliance and administration costs increase even more due to conflicts arising from the implementation of the AOA by the residence country of the investor.[270]

5.6 RECAPITULATION

In summary, the following results can be concluded from the previous analysis:

The analysis in Chapter 5.2 focused on specific PE requirements of Germany, the US and the BRIC states, and identified conflicts in simulated cross-border business

268. See e.g. Luckhaupt/Overesch/Schreiber (2012b) p. 360.
269. See OECD Transfer Pricing Guidelines (2010) p. 198.
270. See e.g. for Brazil Falcão (2010) p. 505. See also Ditz/Bärsch/Kluge (2015) p. 821, who presented the results of an empirical transfer pricing survey of more than 300 international companies stating that the BRIC states belong to the countries with a specific critical examination of transfer prices.

cases with regard to the establishment of a PE in the mentioned countries under the condition that a fictitious OECD country conducts business activities in those states. The PE definition cases dealt with the requirement of disposal over the fixed place of business with regard to activities provided at third party premises, the total delegation of work to subcontractors with regard to the construction site PE, the interpretation of the authority to conclude contracts considering the agency PE, and the secondment of employees with regard to the service PE. It was identified that, of the six countries considered, the US and India have the highest conformity with OECD rules on the PE definition. For India, due to a broader PE concept, qualification conflicts are still probable. The same occurs for Germany due to a narrower interpretation of PE requirements. Russia, China and Brazil often do not provide necessary or opposing information so that it is hard to draw concrete conclusions.

In Chapter 5.3, the attribution of business profits between head office and PE was considered for specific cases. It was assumed that the risk of double or non-taxation of business profits is diminished if there are no or only limited profits to be allocated to the PE in question. From the analysis, it can be derived that especially for the construction site and the agency PE case, the PE profit to be allocated is often not significant according to country-specific practice of countries such as Germany or India. With regard to the service PE, conflicts still remain in most countries. In addition, the different fiscal treatment of internal dealings between head office and PE in accordance with the AOA might still lead to conflicts and double or non-taxation situations if it is assumed that the AOA is valid for all countries under consideration.

Chapter 5.5 focused on feasibility of source taxation of business profits in the considered countries. It became evident that from a company perspective, this tax criterion probably plays a more important role than the risk of double taxation of business profits when taking into account PE cases in the respective countries. Employment taxation and compliance with general registration and accounting standards are compliance and administration efforts which occur in all countries considered. Still, especially in the BRIC states, specific formal requirements of PE registration and approval as well as comparatively high late penalties increase compliance and administration costs which negatively influence feasibility, administrability and transparency of taxation. Another aspect is the practical implementation of the AOA which demands a functional analysis based on significant people functions and risk management structures. In general, this results in higher compliance and administration costs also for the BRIC states. Finally, the problem of the usage of the adequate transfer pricing method and the arm's length valuation of internal dealings under the AOA was addressed. This general transfer pricing problem is inserted into the PE sphere by the OECD and also increases compliance and administration costs in the BRIC states who often do not comply with OECD standards and the AOA.

CHAPTER 6

Reform Proposals with regard to the PE Definition and the Attribution of Business Profits

6.1 GUIDING TAX CRITERIA

After having determined and compared the OECD and national PE concepts and the rules on the attribution of PE income, the next step will be to develop reform proposals in order to overcome the mentioned problems. Therefore, adequate guiding tax principles have to be evaluated first which shall be valid for international PE taxation and which shall be used as standard for the formulated proposals. Although several generally accepted tax criteria exist,[1] the following considers three major fields to be emphasized in the context of cross-border taxation: efficiency and (international) tax neutrality, fairness considerations and inter-nation equity, as well as feasibility, simplicity and transparency.[2] In addition, these concepts are confronted with the principle of single taxation which additionally holds as major objective in international tax law. Two of the mentioned tax principles are then selected for the reform proposals.

6.1.1 Efficiency and (International) Neutrality

From a national context, the concept of tax neutrality respectively allocation efficiency is an approach based on public finance depending on the theory of utilization.[3] Starting point is a global distribution of economic resources which, in an ideal state, are allocated by market mechanisms so that the overall utility from the perspective of the

1. Other guiding tax criteria or generally formulated goals of taxation are the raising of revenue, the purpose of redistribution of income and the steering effect or effect of regulation. See i.a. Avi-Yonah (2006) p. 3, Hey (2013) pp. 64 f., Schön (2013) pp. 290 ff.
2. See i.a. Knirsch/Niemann (2008) pp. 103 f., Tresch (2002) pp. 332 ff.
3. See Spengel (2003) p. 224.

general welfare is maximized. In other words, a change in the welfare position in order to improve the status of an individual is not possible without downgrading the welfare position of another one.[4] This status is called pareto-optimal.[5] If taxes influence decisions on the market regarding the allocation of production factors, welfare losses occur and the pareto-optimal resource level is not achieved.[6] Therefore, decision neutrality has to hold which means that decisions have to be the same, no matter if one lives in a world with or without taxes.[7]

On the other side, tax neutrality can also be based on a microeconomic approach focusing on the effects of taxation on the single company and all related shareholders.[8] In this context, there are three forms of neutrality, which affect the allocation of resources and depend on the choice of the taxpayer: Neutrality of investment is existent if the order of precedence between a fixed asset and an alternative financial investment does not change due to taxation of the investment.[9] Financial neutrality holds if different ways of financing are treated equally for tax purposes so that taxation does not have an influence on the decision whether to finance investments via retained earnings, new equity issues or debt.[10] Another microeconomic tax neutrality is the neutrality of legal form, which demands an equal taxation of different legal entities of different legal form, such as incorporated companies and partnerships.[11]

Apart from the national sphere, the principle of efficiency and decision neutrality also has to hold for international cases.[12] This means that cross-border investment decisions must not be distorted by taxes imposed by the countries involved.[13] In this context, the mentioned national forms of neutrality with regard to the way of investment, financing, or choice of legal form effectively retreat in the background in favour of locational neutrality which should be valid worldwide.[14] Thus, locational or international decision neutrality demands for a neutral treatment of cross-border transactions of multinational investors, thereby involving at least two different tax systems. Given that those systems are in most cases non-identical, it has to be determined whether international decision neutrality can be fulfilled either from the viewpoint of the residence country of the investor or from the viewpoint of the foreign country of source where the investor generates income.[15] In this context, two neutrality concepts exist which provide international decision neutrality with regard to cross-border investments: capital export neutrality (CEN) based on the valuation in the residence state and capital import neutrality (CIN) based on the valuation in the source state.

4. See Kemmeren (2010) p. 289.
5. See i.a. Zuber (1991) p. 48.
6. See i.a. Wagner (1992) p. 4, Schön (2015) p. 272.
7. See Schneider (1992) p. 193.
8. See Zuber (1991) p. 49.
9. See Schreiber (2012) pp. 604 ff.
10. See i.a. Schwinger (1994) p. 48, Homburg (2010) p. 251.
11. See i.a. Hey (2001) p. 157, Wagner (2006) pp. 101 ff.
12. See Schindel/Atchabahian (2005) p. 35.
13. See Shay/Fleming/Peroni (2002) p. 107, Jacobs/Spengel/Schäfer (2003) p. 217.
14. See Musgrave (1987) p. 212, Spengel (2003) pp. 230 ff.
15. See Zuber (1991) p. 115.

The concept of CEN follows the residence or worldwide principle. Investors which either have their domicile or habitual place of abode (for individual taxpayers), their seat or their effective place of management (for corporate taxpayers) in the resident state are subject to tax on the worldwide income achieved in the country of residence. Thus, the resident market is decisive for taxation of investments, i.e., the country which exports the capital. From a domestic point of view, foreign and domestic investments are treated equally for tax purposes irrespective of the location of the investment.[16] Under the concept of CEN, there is no tax driven distortion between domestic and foreign investments of the resident investor as all investments are effectively taxed at the domestic level regardless of whether the income is earned in the residence state or abroad.[17] In general, CEN is achieved if the residence state grants an unlimited foreign tax credit including a refund of – otherwise unused – excess foreign tax credits in case the source country levies taxes on the cross-border investment.[18] As investors strive for the maximization of the after-tax return in the optimum and both, domestic and foreign investments are effectively taxed with the relevant domestic tax rate under the concept of CEN, the tax factor effectively cancels out which means that in the optimum, the domestic and foreign after-tax returns are identical.[19] Thus, investors will decide for the investment offering the highest pre-tax rate of return which equals the marginal productivity in each country, so that CEN leads to a *production efficient* allocation of capital.[20]

The principle of CIN follows the source principle. Irrespective from the location of the investor, from a tax perspective, domestic investments abroad are treated equally to investments of the competitors on the foreign market. This leads to the same tax level within a certain jurisdiction regardless of the residence of the investor.[21] Thus, from the viewpoint of the resident investor, the foreign market is decisive for taxation of income stemming from the resident investor's foreign business activities, i.e., the country which imports the capital.[22] In general, CIN is reached if the country of source exclusively taxes all income generated at source while the residence country correspondingly exempts foreign income from domestic taxation.[23] As investors strive for the maximization of net returns, domestic and foreign after-tax returns will become identical in the optimum under the concept of CIN.[24] However, as long as higher after-tax returns can be achieved due to tax rate differences between the residence and

16. See Griffith/Hines/Sörensen (2010) p. 926.
17. See Kemmeren (2010) p. 291.
18. See e.g. Roxan (2012) p. 4. In theory, another way to achieve CEN results from pure residence taxation, i.e., to tax the worldwide income of the investor in the country of residence at the domestic tax rate while the source country generally waives its taxing right. See Mason (2010) p. 130.
19. See Devereux/Pearson (1995) p. 1659, Homburg (2010) p. 304.
20. See Homburg (2005) p. 19, Schreiber (2012) p. 625. Or, from an economic perspective, the marginal rates of transformation of domestic and foreign companies are the same. See Homburg (2000) pp. 11 ff.
21. See Wissenschaftlicher Beirat (1999) p. 57.
22. See Kemmeren (2010) p. 292.
23. See Mason (2010) p. 130, Roxan (2012) p. 4.
24. See Schreiber (2012) pp. 627 ff.

the source state, investments will flow to the low-taxed state which will generally lead to diverging pre-tax returns for the resident investor.[25] Thus, CIN violates the principle of production efficiency: The higher the domestic tax rate (in comparison to the foreign rate), the higher has to be the domestic pre-tax rate of return and the lower is the amount of capital which stays in the country as the investor has the incentive to invest abroad.[26]

In general, the question of preference of one neutrality concept over another is hard to answer.[27] CEN secures production efficiency and thus theoretically has to be preferred.[28] However, apart from the pure economic view, other external current factors have to be considered. Eroding corporate residence principles, the limitation of the foreign tax credit in country practice, the complexity of administration and the possibility of tax deferral by foreign subsidiaries and the resulting lockout effect all determine possible limitations to the implementation of the CEN concept.[29]

CIN, on the contrary, only provides production efficiency in case of totally harmonized national tax systems.[30] The fact of different competitive relationships between domestic and foreign markets as major justification for the application of the exemption method in terms of CIN is modified when taking into account the business organizational structure of multinational companies which compete not only on foreign markets.[31] Still, the application of the exemption method is existent in international treaty practice, especially for foreign PE profits which implies CIN as '*preferential*' neutrality in practice apart from efficiency considerations.[32] Possible reasons are the higher costs of compliance and tax demand when applying the foreign tax credit method and competitive requirements of multinational investors who otherwise bear disadvantages compared to foreign competitors when including additional residence taxation under the concept of CEN.[33] From an economic viewpoint, there is also the argument that the exemption method and thus CIN is preferable if the assumptions are true that personal taxes of the resident provider of capital are irrelevant and domestic and foreign investments are considered as being complementary instead of being substitutes.[34] The assumption that domestic and foreign investments act like complementary goods implies that domestic investments do not react

25. See Homburg (2010) p. 305.
26. See Homburg (2010) p. 305. On the other side, the adjustment of net returns under CIN will lead to consumption efficiency as from an economic point of view, all participants can thus reach an optimal congruent marginal rate of substitution. See Homburg (2000) p. 11.
27. See for an overview of advantages and disadvantages of CEN and CIN Jacobs (2011) pp. 21 ff. See already critically Vogel (1993) p. 386 who argues that neither CEN nor CIN implies real neutrality as both concepts rely on certain viewpoints while negating other influences.
28. See i.a. Homburg (2000) p. 19.
29. See i.a. Griffith/Hines/Sörensen (2010) pp. 956 f., Schön (2009) pp. 68 f., Mason (2010) p. 132, Spengel (2013) p. 48.
30. See Homburg (2010) p. 307, Spengel (2013) p. 53.
31. See Schreiber (1994) p. 241, Jacobs (2011) pp. 29 ff.
32. See Endres/Spengel (2015) p. 244.
33. See i.a. Slemrod (1995) p. 486. See critically Spengel (2013) pp. 55 ff.
34. See Spengel (2013) pp. 50 ff.

negatively to an enlargement of foreign business activities as the modern capital market provides for an almost infinite availability of capital.[35] This means that the imposition of foreign taxes leads to decreasing foreign investments without increasing domestic investments. In this case, the domestic taxation of foreign profits under the concept of CEN leads to a reallocation of profits from the corporate to the governmental sector while corporations lose more than the governments gain as the corporate sector does not invest. Thus, the exemption method and CIN are to be preferred.[36] However, from an empirical perspective, the complementary theory of '*same signs*' is obviously only true for single companies, and not for an aggregated amount.[37] In summary, a clear preference for one of the neutrality concepts can hardly be given.[38]

Another form of international tax neutrality which especially plays a role in the field of merger and acquisitions (M&A) is capital ownership neutrality (CON). In contrast to regular direct investments which contain the allocation of capital and the build-up of new production entities as so-called *greenfield* investments, investments in M&A deal with the allocation of ownership rights considering the existing capital stock.[39] CON is achieved if taxation does not lead to a change in existing ownership patterns.[40] Under the condition of CON, international investors will acquire the assets which guarantee the highest pre-tax return and thus the highest after-tax return as taxes do not influence cross-border investment decisions under CON.[41] This leads to the fact that the investor who is willing to pay the highest pre-tax price is also the owner of the asset and thus the most productive owner.[42] CON can be established in two ways depending on whether personal taxes of the capital owner are considered as being relevant: Either a residence-based tax system is established based on the worldwide principle including an unlimited foreign tax credit (establishing CEN), or a source-based system applies including an exemption of foreign taxes in the residence state of the investor (determining CIN).[43] Thus, also the concept of CON does not clearly imply a preference for one of the double taxation avoidance methods and thus for one of the two mentioned international neutrality concepts. In general, irrespective whether CEN, CIN or CON holds, there is no additional value with regard to the concretization of the PE definition and the necessity for an allocation of business profits. Therefore, the focus on neutrality considerations does not lead to a constructive solution with regard to this work.

35. See Becker/Fuest (2011) p. 402.
36. See Spengel (2013) p. 51.
37. See i.a. Simpson (2008) pp. 699 f., Desai/Foley/Hines (2009) pp. 181 ff. for empirical studies demonstrating a non-negative relation between domestic and foreign investments. See i.a. Feldstein (1995) pp. 43 f., Desai/Foley/Hines (2005) pp. 33 ff. who show a negative effect for aggregated numbers.
38. See e.g. Lehner (1998) p. 165 who mentions that in comparison to CIN, CEN is just 'another' type of neutrality without trying to make a preference between the two types of neutralities.
39. See Spengel (2013) p. 52.
40. See Desai/Hines (2003) p. 494, Becker/Fuest (2010) pp. 171 ff.
41. See Griffith/Hines/Sörensen (2010) p. 953.
42. See Desai/Hines (2003) p. 494.
43. See i.a. Schön (2009) p. 81. See critically Fleming/Peroni/Shay (2008) pp. 50 ff.

6.1.2 Equity between Taxable Entities and Inter-Nation Equity

Another crucial criterion in international taxation is the principle of equity. Equity between taxable entities or inter-taxpayer entity demands an equal treatment of different taxpayers according to their '*contributive capacity*' in the sense of a fair allocation of the tax burden among taxable entities.[44] This is realized by the relative measure of the taxpayer's economic ability to pay resulting in the internationally accepted ability-to-pay principle.[45] More precisely, the ability-to-pay principle defines that taxpayers with the same ability to pay shall be taxed equally (horizontal equity) while taxpayers with a different ability to pay shall be taxed differently in relation to the existing difference (vertical equity).[46] The applied indicator in this case is the amount of earnings of the taxpayer.[47] If from an international point of view at least two different countries are involved, the ability-to-pay principle is either interpreted according to the valuation of the source or the residence state and thus can only hold in one tax jurisdiction.[48] However, the ability-to-pay principle is focused solely on the income of the taxpayer independent of whether the income flows from the residence or source state.[49] Thus, only the residence principle can represent the ability-to-pay principle as in contrast to the source principle both, domestic and foreign income, are taken into account.[50] Still, the source principle certainly continues to be implemented in taxation practice.[51] In conclusion, due to the '*one-dimensional perspective*' as *Schön* calls it, the ability-to-pay principle alone is obviously not appropriate when deciding about adequate tax criteria in order to evaluate the cross-border taxation rules and allocation of taxing rights.[52]

Therefore, from an international viewpoint, the equity principle does not only call for the equal treatment of the taxpayers but also for the appropriate allocation of tax revenues among the participating states in the sense of an inter-nation equity.[53] In the case of an investment by an investor realizing income in another country, inter-nation equity basically asks to which degree the respective source country is entitled to tax the income generated.[54] According to the benefit theory or principle of economic allegiance, the country which provides all the relevant public contributions

44. See Jacobs/Spengel/Schäfer (2003) p. 219, Homburg (2010) p. 287.
45. See i.a. Schindel/Atchabahian (2005) p. 31, Schaumburg/Schaumburg (2013) p. 62.
46. See i.a. Musgrave/Musgrave (1989) p. 223, Vogel (1994) p. 367, Tresch (2002) p. 334.
47. See i.a. Tipke (2000) p. 23.
48. See Jacobs/Spengel/Schäfer (2003) p. 219.
49. See i.a. Mössner (2000) p. 259, Fleming/Peroni/Shay (2001) p. 311.
50. See i.a. Mössner (2006) p. 505, Schön (2009) p. 71, Homburg (2010) pp. 287 ff. See critically Schaumburg (1995) pp. 131 ff.
51. See i.a. Avi-Yonah (2007a) p. 12 who descriptively mentions that the source state continues to have the '*first bite at the apple*' in case of cross-border business activities.
52. See Schön (2009) p. 73.
53. See Jacobs/Spengel/Schäfer (2003) p. 220, Schindel/Atchabahian (2005) pp. 33 ff.
54. See i.a. Musgrave/Musgrave (1972) p. 68, Kaufman (1998) p. 188, Musgrave (2000a) p. 54.

to support income realization of the company, such as infrastructure as well as the provision of a legal and economic system, is entitled to tax those profits in order to be compensated for the governmental services provided.[55] Still, from an economic point of view, a concrete method of equal allocation of tax revenue is necessary as an allocation based on obtained public goods and services following the concept of utilization under the benefit theory cannot be exactly measured.[56] Therefore, two economic concepts exist: the supply approach and the supply-demand approach. According to the supply approach, the profits have their source at the location of the production factors.[57] The supply-demand approach, as the name indicates, additionally considers the demand factor as possible source of business profits. Thus, the profits are allocated to the state in which the produced goods and provided services are demanded and thus can effectively be sold to customers.[58] As it is usually hard to exactly identify the place of demand, especially with regard to the upcoming interrelated communication and information technology where the place of demand can differ from the place of value production, the supply approach is usually preferred.[59] However, also against the background of the current BEPS discussion on OECD level, the increasing importance of two-sided transfer pricing methods such as the profit-split method, which is based on a value-contribution ratio, indicates a tendency towards the supply-demand approach.[60]

In summary, in accordance with the benefit theory and the supply approach, the country in which the income-generating production factors are located and which contributes to the realization of this income through its legal and business system, also has the taxing right upon this income.[61] Thus, in most cases of cross-border business activities, apart from taxation in the residence state, the source countries' taxing right cannot be neglected.[62] However, for the justification of source taxation, it is still necessary to have a certain adequate economic integration in the source country consisting of an effective and fixed connection within the source state's economy, society and policy.[63] Although this has to be determined on a case-by-case basis, one generally accepted threshold of source taxation is the PE.[64]

55. See i.a. Vogel (1988) p. 398, Zuber (1991) pp. 108 f., Graetz (2001) p. 298, Pinto (2006) p. 267. See for the differentiation between the benefit theory and the principle of economic allegiance Kaufman (1998) pp. 198 ff.
56. See Tipke (2000) pp. 25 f., Schön (2009) pp. 75 ff., Roxan (2012) p. 18.
57. See Musgrave (1984) p. 234.
58. See Oestreicher (2000) p. 179.
59. See Schreiber (1994) p. 243, Jacobs/Spengel/Schäfer (2003) p. 220. See in this context, especially in accordance with the OECD BEPS discussion Choudhary (2011) pp. 33 f., Sheppard (2013) pp. 297 f., Gaoua (2014) pp. 10 ff., Hongler/Pistone (2015) pp. 33 ff.
60. See e.g. Chand/Wagh (2014) pp. 405 f., DeWilde (2015) pp. 309 ff.
61. See i.a. Zuber (1991) p. 111.
62. See i.a. Vogel (1994) p. 376, Musgrave (2000a) p. 52. See See for critics, especially with regard to the allocation of profits following risk Schön (2009) pp. 76 ff.
63. See Vogel (1988) p. 401, Jacobs (2011) p. 28.
64. See Jacobs/Spengel/Schäfer (2003) p. 220, Pinto (2006) p. 270, Jacobs (2011) p. 29.

6.1.3 Feasibility, Simplicity and Transparency

Apart from neutrality and equity considerations, international taxation shall not only follow theoretical approaches but in addition, has to be feasible and enforceable.[65] Feasibility is interrelated to the equity principle mentioned above since only a tax system that can implement and guarantee a fair enforcement of tax laws can be recognized as being equal.[66] Moreover, feasibility or enforcement of taxation has to be valid in the context of cross-border business transactions with several participating countries which all have different national interests, requirements and fiscal nexuses.[67] Otherwise, as *Graetz* calls it, enacting tax rules is *'pointless'*.[68] Although an international feasible tax system cannot guarantee the implementation of neutrality or equity standards, even partial changes in tax compliance can contribute to approach the optimum and are able to improve efficiency in comparison to the status quo.[69]

Simplicity of taxation means that incurring costs for the operation of the tax system have to be minimized.[70] Thus, there are two cost factors which have to be reconsidered: administration costs of the fiscal authorities and compliance costs of the taxpayer.

Costs of administration incur at the level of the tax authorities which are obliged to establish and conduct a functioning and comprehensive tax system.[71] An optimal administration process indicates a simple and efficient tax collection whose costs are minimal in relation to the raised tax revenue.[72] An efficient administration process depends on several decisive factors:[73] One is the level of technology used in order to comprise a high amount of tax returns checked. Other factors are the level of penalty for illegal tax evasion and the degree of enforceability and control of tax collection in order to ensure a higher compliance. Further crucial criteria are the complexity of the tax structure depending on the type of tax (e.g., income or sales tax) or the permission of deductible expenses and the tax competence structure in the state (centralized or federal).

Tax compliance costs incur at the level of the taxpayer when actively complying with the tax obligations, filling out the tax returns, understanding the tax code, and involving third parties in the collection process such as employers or tax experts.[74] For a multinational corporation, tax compliance is part of the corporate strategy focusing on the aspects of minimizing tax and liability risks for the company and its employees

65. See i.a. Locher (1995) p. 190, Schön (2009) p. 87.
66. See Tipke (2000) p. 27, Jacobs/Spengel/Schäfer (2003) p. 221.
67. See i.a. Utescher (1999) p. 335 who refers to the 'principle of practicability' in this context.
68. See Graetz (2001) p. 312.
69. See Zuber (1991) pp. 70 f., Braunagel (2008) p. 19.
70. See European Commission (2001) p. 28.
71. See Shaw/Slemrod/Whiting (2010) p. 1106.
72. See Tresch (2002) p. 332.
73. See for the following Musgrave/Musgrave (1989) p. 278.
74. See Tresch (2002) p. 332. This can also include tax avoidance and even illegal tax evasion strategies of the taxpayer. See Shaw/Slemrod/Whiting (2010) p. 1106.

and providing planning reliability with regard to current and future tax burdens.[75] Empirical studies indicate that compliance costs increase especially with respect to cross-border business activities.[76]

Administration costs of the fiscal authorities and compliance costs of the taxpayer are interrelated as the level of administration costs also depends on the taxpayer's ability and will to participate in the tax collection process and to fill out tax returns honestly.[77] In this context, the level of tax compliance costs can either be influenced by actions of the taxpayer himself putting effort in hiring tax experts in order to implement tax planning and tax avoidance strategies, or by changes in tax law by fiscal authorities which also may have an influence on the compliance burden of the taxpayer.[78] Still, the interrelation is complex. Policy actions of the state in order to decrease administration costs can have a positive or negative influence on the amount of compliance costs of the taxpayer depending on the design and target group of the policy arrangement.[79] What tax authorities can do in order to minimize compliance costs for the taxpayer is implementing a risk management system including provisions such as easement of participation, provision of necessary information, issuing of binding statements and, especially in an international context, offering the conclusion of Advance Pricing Agreements (APAs) which limit certain scopes of interpretation in advance.[80] The level of enforcement also has an influence on compliance costs of the taxpayer. A complicated official tax calculation formula might not only have an impact on the compliance of the taxpayer which theoretically decreases as the compliance costs would reach an inadequate level, but also on the level of the tax base as the taxpayer might as well reduce the tax inducing economic activities.[81]

If the premise of simplicity of a tax system does not hold, both administration and compliance costs, are considered as excess use of resources or '*social waste*' which is not efficient from an economic point of view.[82] Thus, a reduction of administration and compliance costs through an increased level of simplicity is useful even if it leads to a reduction of tax revenue as from an economic point of view, the reduction of tax revenue only implies a diminished transfer of income from the taxpayer to the state and not an excess burden on the total welfare.[83] Especially in an international context, a generally valid simple tax system also avoids the development and usage of preferential tax regimes.[84] In this context, *Weisbach* figuratively refers to '*interaction costs*' which are the costs of avoiding and closing unintentional tax loopholes in the

75. See Greil/Kiesow (2013) p. 391.
76. See i.a. Blumenthal/Slemrod (1995) pp. 37 f., European Commission (2004) p. 5.
77. See Tresch (2002) p. 332.
78. See Guyton et al. (2003) p. 675.
79. See Sandford (1995) p. 94.
80. See Greil/Kiesow (2013) p. 392, Kerschner/Stiastny (2013) pp. 588 ff.
81. See James et al. (2001) p. 160.
82. See i.a. Graetz (2001) p. 310, Eichfelder/Schorn (2012) p. 192. These costs can also be considered as indirect costs of tax collection apart from the tax itself including distortions in the taxpayer's and tax collector's behaviour and with regard to the use of resources of operating the tax system itself. See Vaillancourt/Clemens (2008) p. 55.
83. See Wagner (2005a) p. 94.
84. See European Commission (2001) p. 28.

international structure of tax statutes.[85] Simplicity of tax rules thus can reduce these costs which effectively belong to administration costs of the tax authorities.

However, a certain level of administration and compliance costs is always inherent in national and international tax law.[86] In addition, a higher degree of simplicity also can have a negative impact on equity considerations if the level of collected tax revenue holds steady as complex tax statutes are usually created in order to forward thoughts of equity.[87] From a political perspective, the steering effect of taxation, the wilful passing of tax laws by the government in order to influence certain political actions or behaviour of the taxpayer, is a reason for the complexity of the tax system and counteracts the goal of simplicity.[88] This is especially true in an international context with highly integrated and mobile capital flows where countries enact international tax statutes not only to achieve a fair division of taxing rights but also to protect the national tax base.[89] Thus, also for cross-border investments, the implementation of simplicity of taxation which is achieved from an economic viewpoint can be negatively influenced by the politically motivated steering effect of certain tax rules. Still, at the same time, a too high degree of simplification of tax rules can promote international tax planning which then again increases planning and compliance costs for the taxpayer and administration costs for the tax authorities trying to identify the international tax avoidance structures.[90]

Furthermore, a tax system also has to be transparent meaning that taxable standards have to be certain, well-defined and easy to understand.[91] This avoids disputes over tax laws and can increase the enforcement of taxing rights especially from an international point of view.[92] Following the principle of determination, tax rules have to be clearly determined and defined, such that a legally binding and functioning interpretation is possible.[93] Under the principle of clarity, the relation and rank order of different tax statutes has to be clear especially if several tax norms can eventually be taken into account.[94] Otherwise, according to *Hey*, a '*lack of transparency of tax law*' can occur.[95] Still, the principle of flexibility must not be neglected which means that tax law is supposed to be responsive to changing business environments and also has to contribute to economic stability.[96]

With regard to the PE definition and the allocation of business profits, the described principles have to hold as well. Cross-border PE taxation thus has to be feasible and enforceable. PE requirements and allocation rules have to be applicable, comprehensible and clearly defined so that a homogenous interpretation by all

85. See Weisbach (1999) p. 871.
86. See European Commission (2001) p. 28.
87. See i.a. Slemrod (1996) p. 357, European Commission (2001) p. 28, Holtzman (2007) p. 421.
88. See Schön (2002) p. 29.
89. See i.a. Owens (2002) p. 127.
90. See Spengel/Malke (2008) pp. 68 ff.
91. See i.a. European Commission (2001) p. 28.
92. See Braunagel (2008) p. 21.
93. See Hey (2013) p. 118.
94. See i.a. Luttermann (2007) p. 20.
95. See Hey (2013) p. 119.
96. See Neumark (1970) pp. 54 f., p. 285, p. 298.

countries under consideration is reached. This also leads to a decreasing level of administration and compliance costs involved and contributes to a transparent tax system.

6.1.4 Principle of Single Taxation

The principle of single taxation determines that income which is earned by conducting cross-border activities is taxed once, '*not more nor less than once*'.[97] A taxpayer who earns foreign income is equated to a domestic taxpayer who establishes a fiscal nexus solely in one state and thus is liable to a single taxation upon income earned in the country of residence.[98] This means that both, international double taxation and non-taxation of cross-border income, shall be avoided.[99] If a taxing right is granted to the source country on the income earned, single taxation in a cross-border case can be achieved in two ways: First, the residence state of the investor applies the full tax credit method for foreign business income. Double taxation of income is thus completely avoided as the foreign taxes are credited against the domestic tax amount paid in the residence state. Even if the source country does not tax the income earned for any reason, one-time taxation is principally guaranteed as the residence country taxes the worldwide income independent of the amount of the foreign tax credit.[100] Second, the other double taxation avoidance method is the exemption method which implies the exclusion of foreign income from the resident tax base and thus the avoidance of double taxation. Non-taxation is generally possible if the source country does not tax the income earned as in this case, neither the residence nor the source country impose a taxing right. By including a subject-to-tax clause so that foreign income is only exempt from taxation in the resident state if a tax is effectively levied in the source country, non-taxation can be avoided and the principle of single taxation still holds.[101] Still, a major requirement for the principle of single taxation is a clarification of terms so that both countries involved agree upon the interpretation and understanding of specific definitions. If there is an interpretation conflict, the risk of double and non-taxation situations is higher regardless of the double taxation avoidance method used in the country of residence.[102]

97. See i.a. Avi-Yonah (1997) p. 517, Avi-Yonah (2013) p. 310.
98. See Zorn (2001) p. 459.
99. In the following, the term of international double taxation has to be understood as international jurisdictional double taxation referring to the identity of taxable subject, taxable object, time and type of tax. What is not considered is economic double taxation which does not imply the identity of one of the mentioned factors, e.g. for the double taxation of dividends in case of distributions from the subsidiary (taxation at corporate level) to its shareholder (taxation at shareholder level). See for the differentiation of the two terms, Krause (2003) pp. 8 f., Kemmeren (2010) pp. 239 ff. See in more detail Wassermeyer (2009) Vor Article 1, pp. 22 ff.
100. See Lang (2004a) p. 35.
101. See Kane (2004) p. 113.
102. See section 5.2 for various examples.

In a treaty context, the goal of avoidance of international double taxation is clearly determined.[103] The other way around, it is discussable if the avoidance of international non-taxation can be interpreted as official *'vice-versa goal'* of treaty law.[104] A practical reason why the prevention of international non-taxation has not been in the focus of international tax policy is that non-taxation in comparison to international double taxation does not have such an intense impact on international business relations. Whereas double taxation can result in a complete removal of international trade as in the worst case, the tax paid in the residence and source country can even be higher than the generated income, non-taxation actually does not initially eliminate cross-border business activities.[105] In addition, against the background of international tax competition over the years, national governments considered the effort to reduce the effective tax burden as support for multinational companies investing abroad.[106] However, under the OECD BEPS project caused by aggressive tax planning strategies of US multinational companies paying a drastically reduced effective tax rate on European profits, the avoidance of non-taxation has been put into focus of current OECD policy and is inserted as additional goal in the preamble of the OECD MC.[107]

From an economic viewpoint, the principle of single taxation clearly has to integrate the avoidance of international double taxation and the prevention of international non-taxation. Both double and non-taxation are not in line with international neutrality and efficiency concepts as both influences the cross-border investment decision of the taxpayer who either decreases foreign investment in case of double taxation or increases foreign investment in case of non-taxation opportunities.[108] Thus, neither from the viewpoint of the residence country of the taxpayer nor from the viewpoint of the source country in which the taxpayer competes, capital export respectively capital import neutrality holds. In addition, also the principle of inter-taxpayer equity does not hold if international double or non-taxation takes place as both, horizontal and vertical equity, is violated if a higher respectively lower tax is levied in case of cross-border business activities in comparison to domestic business.[109]

The principle of single taxation also has to hold for cross-border PE taxation. Decisive prerequisites are a homogeneous PE definition and harmonized rules for the allocation of business profits. If respective terms are unclear or a controversial scope of interpretation exists, e.g., with regard to the understanding of a specific PE requirement

103. See OECD MC Commentary (2014) Introduction, No. 1, p. 7.
104. See i.a. Lang (2002) pp. 609 ff. & (2004b) pp. 17 ff. who critically doubts the avoidance of international non-taxation being a goal of tax treaty policy. See i.a. Zorn (2001) pp. 459 ff. and Wolff (2004) p. 545 for a contrary view. See OECD Partnership Report (1999) No. 52, p. 20 which first mentions the prevention of international non-taxation as goal of the OECD.
105. See Ring (2002) p. 106.
106. See Ault (2013) p. 1195.
107. See OECD Report BEPS Action 6 (2014) pp. 98 ff. See for an advanced discussion about BEPS and profit shifting of multinational firms Fuest/Spengel/Finke/Heckemeyer/Nusser (2013) pp. 307 ff.
108. See Avi-Yonah (1997) p. 518. See i.a. for non-taxation effects Brauner (2003) fn. 21, p. 264.
109. See Li (2002) p. 827, Avi-Yonah (2007b) p. 134.

or the existence and valuation of an internal dealing between head office and PE, the risk for double or non-taxation situations will increase.

6.1.5 Prevailing Tax Criteria for the Reform Proposals

For the development of reform proposals which shall avoid the conflicts mentioned in Chapter 5, adequate general tax criteria have to be determined from which constructive conclusions can be derived. In this context, the principle of single taxation and the requirements of feasibility, simplicity and transparency shall prevail.[110]

The international neutrality concepts such as CEN and CIN both represent models promoting worldwide economic efficiency in case of cross-border business operations. Still, an optimal generally valid neutrality concept can hardly be given.[111] In this context, the fulfilment of CEN or CIN in case of cross-border investments depends more on the choice of the double taxation avoidance method by the country of residence and less on the PE definition and the allocation of business profits.[112] The focus of the analysis was on the identification of unclear PE requirements and possible conflicts with regard to the allocation of business profits between head office and PE. In this context, the analysis followed the principle of single taxation from the perspective of the source country and does not asked which double taxation avoidance method had to be used by the residence country of the investor. Therefore, the aim of the reform proposals is not to make a preference for one of the mentioned neutrality concepts. As *Kleinbard* names it, the focus is not on the '*battle of neutralities*'.[113] As described above, the principle of single taxation is a prerequisite for the implementation of at least one of the neutrality definitions and thus prevails. The same is true for the practical requirements of feasibility, simplicity and transparency which generally imply a higher degree of efficiency with regard to the resource allocation and decision-making process of the international investor.[114]

The PE definition as fiscal nexus established in the country of source is justified by the principle of inter-nation equity.[115] However, the previous analysis did not ask if the source country had a principle justification to tax foreign business profits or if a specific part of the business profits are allocated due to fairness reasons. Although the justification of the PE concept under the principle of inter-nation equity is accepted in principle, the focus is on the avoidance of double and non-taxation in case of

110. See for a similar orientation Bärsch (2012) pp. 74 ff. and with regard to international transfer pricing issues Luckhaupt/Overesch/Schreiber (2012a) p. 99.
111. See the discussion in section 6.1.2. International neutrality concepts also do not provide a clear answer of how to 'divide the tax cake' and how to adequately allocate the taxing rights between residence and source country in case of cross-border business activities. See i.a. Brown (2011) p. 600, Schön (2012a) p. 216. See from an US perspective Shay/Fleming/Peroni (2002) p. 110, Task Force (2006) p. 661.
112. See i.a. OECD Report E-Commerce (2003) No. 36, p. 13.
113. See Kleinbard (2007) p. 555.
114. See Holtzman (2007) p. 421. On the other side, under a valid concept of neutrality tax avoidance structures actively planned by investors are prevented which can also lead to a reduction of administration and compliance costs. See Wagner (2005b) p. 531.
115. See i.a. Daurer (2014) p. 22.

conflicting situations with regard to the PE issue.[116] The reason for neglecting the principle of equity in the reform proposals is that the PE concept is actually based on subjective and discussable equity considerations which are hard to be evaluated on a non-judgmental basis.[117] In general, the principle of equity alone does not provide answers with regard to interpretation of the PE requirements and the concrete amount of business profit to be allocated to the PE. As the issue of a fair distribution of the tax base between the residence and the source country is highly subjective, a constructive result cannot be derived from the principles of the benefit theory and tax fairness.[118] Single taxation at least leads to an adequate allocation of business profits so that the overall tax base is distributed on a consistent basis. Whether this basis is considered as being fair, shall not be answered in this work.

The other concepts which prevail for the reform proposals are feasibility, simplicity and transparency of taxation. In general, it was argued above that these principles support the fulfilment of single taxation and thus can form the basis for the fulfilment of neutrality considerations. In addition, while feasibility and enforcement of taxation also depend on the requirement of simple tax rules, a certain degree of complexity and diversification of tax provisions also benefits inter-taxpayer equity, e.g., by taking into account personal circumstances of the taxpayer.[119] Simple tax rules support transparency of tax law as well, which can also assist inter-taxpayer equity again by providing insights into tax administration and rule setting.[120] In addition, feasible and enforceable tax rules can prevent international tax avoidance which is also consistent with a fair allocation of the tax base under the concept of inter-nation equity.[121] Thus, apart from the principle of single taxation, the focus of the reform proposals shall be on the establishment and preservation of feasibility, simplicity and transparency with regard to international PE provisions. Questions of inter-nation equity and a fair allocation of taxing rights between residence and source country are of minor interest. Citing *Arnold*, the focus is on the '*practical enforcement of source-country taxation, not the theoretical justification for such taxation*'.[122]

6.2 RECOMMENDATIONS FROM A NATIONAL PERSPECTIVE

The previous analysis identified difficulties with regard to the interpretation of PE requirements and the attribution of business profits between head office and PE which lead to double or non-taxation situations and increased administration and compliance costs. In order to find an adequate solution, the following two preconditions have to be determined: First, the guiding tax criteria for reform proposals of the OECD and all

116. In case the principle of single taxation prevails for cross-border business activities, apart from inter-nation equity, inter-taxpayer equity is fulfilled anyway as the ability-to-pay principle holds in this case. See section 6.1.2.
117. See Rosenberger/Vitali/Ziehr (2010) p. 6.
118. See also Herzfeld (2015) pp. 104 ff.
119. See Holtzman (2007) p. 421.
120. See European Commission (2001) p. 28.
121. See section 6.1.3.
122. See Arnold (2003) p. 491.

countries under consideration shall be the principle of single taxation and feasibility of taxation.[123] It was derived that these criteria are the most constructive if the goal is to identify and solve interpretation conflicts of cross-border PE taxation. Second, the OECD MC has to be considered as international standard setter and guidance for the treaty policy and the respective understanding of PE attributes and allocation rules for all countries under consideration, including the BRIC states.[124] Irrespective from any political motivations and economic differences of the countries, the mentioned goals can only be reached if a common standard is found which is valid for all countries. In fact, this is given for the OECD MC which provides a basis for a homogenous application of international tax rules. The crucial and intuitive solution here is harmonization. Therefore, one approach is to align the respective PE understanding of the different countries under consideration to the current OECD approach.[125]

6.2.1 Harmonization of the PE Definition

In order to reach a harmonization with regard to the PE definition, all countries have to adapt their national and treaty law to the current OECD approach. Thus, discussions about the interpretation of PE requirements are avoided which is in line with the principle of single taxation and feasibility. Table 6.1 displays these necessary modifications.

Table 6.1 Recommendations of Alignment to the OECD Approach with regard to the PE Definition

	'Passive' Service PE	*Construction Site PE*	*Agency PE*	*Service PE*
DE	- Abolishment of principle of local connection (*Verwurzelung*) - Broadening the concept of exclusive usage of third party premises	- Existence of PE for general contractor in case of total delegation of work to subcontractors - Focus on disposal over construction site - Neglect of physical presence of general contractor	- Focus on economic authority to conclude contracts - Focus on independence criterion as decisive PE requirement	Introduction of service PE in national and treaty law

123. See section 6.1.5.
124. For reasons why to consider the BRIC states, see section 4.1.
125. In fact, the concept of harmonized interpretation is also mentioned in the OECD MC Commentary. See OECD MC Commentary (2014), Introduction No. 3, p. 7. See for a negating view Kahle/Kindich (2016) p. 48 who argue that the OECD claim for harmonization can never be reached completely.

	'Passive' Service PE	*Construction Site PE*	*Agency PE*	*Service PE*
US	Introduction of detailed explanations to disposal term (e.g., non-conclusive list of indicators)	- Existence of PE for general contractor in case of total delegation of work to subcontractors - Focus on disposal over construction site - Neglect of physical presence of general contractor	Focus on independence criterion as decisive PE requirement	- More detailed explanations with regard to the factors of control and direction in case of secondment arrangement
BR	- General application of the OECD PE concept - Abolishment of gross taxation for income from services - Introduction of detailed instructions with regard to the effective power to use a certain location	- General application of the OECD PE concept - Existence of PE for general contractor in case of total delegation of work to subcontractors - Focus on disposal over construction site - Neglect of physical presence of general contractor	- General application of the OECD PE concept - Focus on independence criterion as decisive PE requirement	- General application of the OECD PE concept - Abolishment of gross taxation for income from services
RU	Introduction of detailed instructions with regard to the effective power to use a certain location	- Existence of PE for general contractor in case of total delegation of work to subcontractors - Focus on disposal over construction site - Neglect of physical presence of general contractor	Focus on independence criterion as decisive PE requirement	Abolishment of conflict with migration law in case of secondment arrangement

	'Passive' Service PE	*Construction Site PE*	*Agency PE*	*Service PE*
IN	Broad interpretation of disposal in line with OECD approach	- Existence of PE for general contractor in case of total delegation of work to subcontractors - Focus on disposal over construction site - Neglect of physical presence of general contractor	Focus on independence criterion as decisive PE requirement	- Abolishment of broad concept of 'lien' on employment in case of secondment arrangements - Focus on concept of economic employer
CN	Introduction of detailed instructions with regard to the effective power to use a certain location	- Existence of PE for general contractor in case of total delegation of work to subcontractors - Focus on disposal over construction site - Neglect of physical presence of general contractor	Focus on independence criterion as decisive PE requirement	Abolishment of strict interpretation of PE factors in case of secondment arrangement

As derived from the previous analysis, *Germany* is one of the countries whose interpretation of decisive PE requirements is stricter in comparison to the current OECD status and reform proposals.[126] Therefore, misinterpretations and thus double or non-taxation situations can occur with regard to business relations to a country which is in line with the OECD policy. If it is accepted that the OECD serves as international guidance and standard setter, Germany has to adapt its policy with regard to its '*conservative*' PE approach. One PE requirement to be reformed is the criterion of disposal. To be in line with the current OECD agenda, Germany has to abolish the principle of local connection (*Verwurzelung*) and exclusion of other parties in order to establish a necessary degree of disposal when conducting business activities at third party premises.[127] Thus, although a mere presence at a certain location is not sufficient to determine a PE, a certain effective power to use that location (presumably e.g., a key to a customer's office where not only the service provider but also the customer has

126. See section 4.3.1.
127. See section 4.2.2.1.

access) leads to an affirmation of disposal.[128] In general, this implies that a certain presence in the country of source and permanence of the business activities is of higher importance than the question of the exclusive right to use the customer premises. This also means that in a German inbound case, more PEs are established. Still, the principle of single taxation holds if PE requirements are clear and a double taxation avoidance method, either the credit or exemption method, is applied in the residence country of the head office. The other PE requirement for which Germany's view is different from the current OECD approach is the case of the total delegation of work to subcontractors. In order to be in line with the OECD reform proposals, Germany has to indicate clearly that a construction site PE might also be established without the physical presence of the general contractor under the condition that the latter has a legal right to use the site, controls the access and possesses an '*overall responsibility*'.[129] In order to avoid misunderstandings with the OECD approach, Germany has to focus on the question whether the general contractor has disposal over the construction site and not whether personnel of the general contractor are present in the country of source. With regard to the question of qualification of the authority to conclude contracts for the principal as decisive PE requirement, Germany has to focus on the economic view and not on the formal legal authority to conclude contracts in the name of the enterprise.[130] This is also consistent with the OECD BEPS Final Report with regard to the artificial avoidance of the PE status.[131] In this report, the OECD proposes to circumvent the discussion between common law and civil law countries of whether legally acting in the name of the principal is necessary for the existence of a PE by widening the range of contract authorization in the wording of Article 5 (5) OECD MC. Therefore, the decisive requirement for German treaty policy shall be the independence status of the agent. With regard to the question of a possible service PE through the secondment of employees, both Germany and the OECD MC use the economic employer concept and thus would probably come to similar results. Still, the exclusion of a service PE in German treaty policy can lead to misunderstandings and thus to possible double or non-taxation situations.[132] Therefore, Germany should follow the OECD proposals and implement a service PE provision in its treaties. Thus, the existence of a PE by foreign service providers would depend on a certain time and quantitative revenue threshold. Actually, this is more intuitive and can prevent discussions about the '*passive*' service PE and the interpretation of the term of disposal over the fixed place of business. In general, source taxation is thus extended but as long as the rules are harmonized and the double taxation avoidance methods work, the principle of single taxation will hold.

The *US* does not include a separate explanation with regard to the disposal term in its treaty policy. From US case law it can be derived that a major factor is the separate bargain for a consideration of the place provided.[133] In order to prevent interpretation conflicts, the US needs to introduce more detailed explanations with regard to the

128. See OECD Reform Proposal (2012) p. 6.
129. See OECD Reform Proposal (2012) p. 18.
130. See section 4.3.1.
131. See OECD Final Report BEPS Action 7 (2015) p. 16.
132. See section 5.2.4.
133. See section 5.2.1.

disposal term in its explanations to the US MC which might include a non-conclusive list of indicators or at least some safe harbour exceptions, such as the existence of an exclusive legal right of the service provider to use the rooms provided. Considering the total delegation of work to subcontractors, the US also needs to introduce details with regard to the fact whether the general contractor is able to establish a construction site PE by delegating all work to a local subcontractor without being present in the country of source. In order to be in line with the OECD MC, the focus has to be on the question of disposal and control of the general contractor over the construction site and not on the physical presence of workers of the general contractor. Considering the agency PE, the US as a common law country is, in fact, in line with the current OECD approach. Similar to the OECD MC, the focus has to be on the differentiation between independent and dependent agents, and not on the question whether the agent has legal or economic authority to conclude contracts to bind the principal.[134] With regard to the secondment of employees, similar to the OECD MC, the US considers supervision, direction and control as decisive requirements for the question of the existence of a service PE.[135] Still, more detailed explanations with regard to the relevant factors of control and direction, such as the decision power on details of the working contract or the relevance of a profit mark-up upon the reimbursement payment, prevent misunderstandings in this complex area.

In *Brazil*, a general change in treaty policy is necessary so that the PE is accepted as a form of direct investment which is applicable for all kinds of business activities. If this is given, more details and information with regard to the interpretation of specific PE requirements can be implemented. The current analysis shows that the Brazilian '*way*' of source taxation obviously neglects the establishment of a PE in favour of an increased usage of withholding taxes on a gross basis.[136] With regard to the case of the '*passive*' service PE and the necessary degree of disposal, Brazil thus has to align to the OECD approach in order to avoid misunderstandings and resulting double or non-taxation situations. This also means that the gross taxation of services under the other income-article similar to Article 21 of the UN MC or the royalty-article under Article 12 (2) UN MC has to be abolished. Instead, the PE concept should be used which can either work by adapting a similar understanding of disposal or implementing a service PE which might even avoid discussions on the necessary right to use the fixed place of business. In addition, for the total delegation of work to subcontractors, the dependent commission agent and the secondment of employees, Brazil has to introduce detailed instructions, ideally similar to the OECD MC, in order to prevent misunderstandings with regard to cross-border PE cases. Still, in contrast to the other countries under consideration, Brazil has to adjust its treaty policy with regard to the PE in general before going into details of interpretation of specific PE requirements and special PE cases. As it was derived before, the current OECD trend strives for an increased source taxation with regard to the PE definition.[137] By following the OECD approach, Brazil

134. See section 5.2.3.
135. See section 5.2.4.
136. See e.g. section 5.2.1.
137. See section 3.4.

thus will not give up its source taxation right but instead aligning it in order to diminish conflicts of interpretation which eventually increases foreign investments and improve tax treaty negotiations.

In *Russia*, the requirement of disposal obviously does not play a major role when deciding about the existence of a Russian PE through services provided at third party premises.[138] In order to be in line with the current OECD approach, more detailed instructions with regard to the effective power to use a certain location have to be introduced. The solution to completely waive the concept of disposal can lead to a wider fiscal nexus in comparison to the OECD view and thus to further possible interpretation conflicts. In addition, Russia has to clarify whether a general contractor can establish a local construction site PE by delegating all work to a Russian subcontractor given that the construction site is at the disposal of the general contractor. If this is not the case, qualification conflicts are probable for treaty relations with a country that follows the OECD perspective. With regard to the qualification of the authority to conclude contracts, Russia shows tendencies to follow the current OECD approach. Still, it has to be clarified that the future focus shall be on the differentiation between a dependent and independent agent rather than on the question of importance of the legal or economic authority to conclude contracts for the principal. With regard to the secondment of employees, Russia also applies the economic employer concept similar to the OECD MC. However, Russian migration and tax law are in conflict in this case since seconded employees are not granted a work permit as long as a legal employment contract is existent with the non-resident head office.[139] First of all, this conflict of law has to be abolished, as it can limit business activities of non-residents in Russia. The Russian safe harbour limit of 10% of the secondment costs in order to determine the economic employer and thus the possible existence of a PE is a reasonable approach in order to provide legal certainty and transparency.

India applies an extensive understanding of the disposal criterion similar to the OECD MC. Given that the OECD approach has to be considered as international guidance, the current status quo in India prevents interpretation conflicts with regard to the case of the '*passive*' service PE. Considering the case of the total delegation of work to subcontractors, India's position has to be clarified.[140] In order to be in line with the OECD (and UN) approach, India shall assume a PE for the general contractor in case of total delegation of work to an Indian subcontractor given that the construction site is at the disposal of the general contractor. With regard to the differentiation between legal and economic authority to conclude contracts for the principal, India also follows the OECD approach and implements a wider economic approach based on an independent third party comparison.[141] Similar to the OECD MC, Indian treaty policy has to focus on the differentiation between independent and dependent agent under Article 5 (6) OECD MC as decisive criterion for the existence of an agency PE. Apart from factors

138. See section 5.2.1.
139. See section 5.2.4.
140. See section 5.2.2.
141. See section 5.2.3.

of legal independence, such as the entrepreneurial risk and control over the agent's actions, one of the main factors of economic independence is the number of represented principals.[142] In fact, Indian treaty policy often includes this additional wording in the agency PE provision determining that as long as an agent is acting for only one principal, he is not considered as being independent.[143] This is consistent with the OECD proposal with regard to the modification of Article 5 under the current OECD BEPS discussion. Some Indian treaties also apply the rule that acting for only one principal is not supposed to be a factor for dependence as long as the dealings between principal and agent follow the arm's length principle.[144] With regard to this exception, another option is to replace the concept of an arm's length comparison as additional criterion for the existence of an independent agent with the more quantitative approach of taking into account the share of beneficial interest in the agent's entity as recommended by the OECD BEPS report on Action 7.[145] Considering the case of secondment of employees, India shall focus on the economic employer concept and develop concrete criteria of supervision and control instead of relying on the wide and imprecise concept of '*lien*' on employment with the foreign employer.[146] In addition, the Indian approach of including the royalty-article as a fiscal nexus for the taxation of services at source has to be challenged. In order to prevent misunderstandings and qualification conflicts with regard to OECD countries, India shall instead favour the service PE as fiscal connecting factor for the taxation of secondment arrangements.

Chinese treaty policy does not include details with regard to the interpretation of disposal over a fixed place of business.[147] In order to be consistent with the OECD approach, detailed instructions with regard to the understanding of the effective power to use a third party location shall be introduced. At the same time, the Chinese focus on the service PE provision might also prevent further concentration on the disposal term in case of a '*passive*' service PE as the establishment of a fixed place of business is irrelevant according to an '*active*' service PE provision. With regard to the total delegation of work to subcontractors, China has to introduce clear instructions whether a construction site PE is established for the general contractor in this case. In order to be consistent with the OECD reform proposal, China shall decide to take over the OECD approach and assume a construction site PE for the general contractor given that the latter has a sufficient degree of disposal over the construction site. Considering the agency PE case, similar to the current OECD policy, China should focus on the independence criterion as decisive requirement when deciding about the establishment of an agency PE.[148] There is little information with regard to the differentiation between legal and economic authority to conclude contracts for the principal but as both, China and the OECD MC, are supposed to concentrate on other relevant agency PE factors, consistency is retained and thus the risk of interpretation conflicts is diminished. Still,

142. See e.g. Williams (2014) pp. 137 ff.
143. See Chapter 4.2.5.1.
144. See Appendix, Table A9.
145. See OECD Final Report BEPS Action 7 (2015) p. 16.
146. See section 5.2.4.
147. See section 5.2.1.
148. See section 5.2.3.

similar to India, China considers the number of principals bound by the agent as decisive criterion when deciding about the independence status of the agent. Again, an additional approach is to replace the concept of an arm's length comparison which is used by some Chinese tax treaties as additional test of independence, with the application of the beneficial interest or share ratio similar to Action 7 of the OECD BEPS report. Thus, it can be determined whether the principal and the agent are considered as related parties.[149] With regard to the possible service PE case for the secondment of employees, China applies specific factors signalling the economic employer who is decisive for the establishment of a service PE. Although Chinese treaty policy is thus consistent with the OECD approach, China shall avoid applying a too strict interpretation of single facts so that a service PE is already established by the fulfilment of one single factor.[150] Instead, all facts and circumstances of the secondment arrangement shall be considered so that no premature conclusions are drawn.

6.2.2 Harmonization of the Attribution of Business Profits

Apart from the PE definition, the countries under consideration also have to align with the rules of the attribution of business profits between head office and PE as proposed by the OECD MC. If it is accepted that the OECD MC is considered as international guidance, all countries have to apply the AOA in their national and treaty policy. In theory, if all countries follow the premise of harmonization, the probability of interpretation conflicts is diminished and the principle of single taxation and feasibility holds. In this context, this should also prevail over economic interests of the countries under consideration such as the BRIC states. The predominating goal is not to decide on an adequate and fair allocation of the tax base among the countries. Instead, striving for harmonization has to guarantee that interpretation conflicts and resulting double or non-taxation situations are avoided. Therefore, a common standard of income allocation is needed. Given that the OECD MC is accepted as this standard, the AOA has to be applied for all countries.[151]

Thus, PE income allocation has to be based on a functional analysis in which active decision-making of significant people is the major reference for the allocation of risks, assets and capital. In addition, internal dealings between head office and PE have to be accepted which also generally includes the valuation of a profit element through the usage of an adequate transfer pricing method. In general, the focus is on two aspects of profit allocation: the functional analysis and the recognition of internal dealings under national law of the countries under consideration (see Table 6.2). Two other aspects which are not considered in detail are the question of harmonization of national income determination rules and the choice of the adequate transfer pricing method in order to identify the arm's length price of the internal dealing. Of course, in

149. In fact, this is implemented in a new tax treaty of China with Chile, See Appendix, Table A10.
150. See section 5.2.4.
151. This does not mean that the AOA cannot be improved anymore with regard to the principle of single taxation and the additional application in the BRIC countries. See section 6.3.1.

order to reduce the probability of interpretation conflicts and possible double or non-taxation situations for cross-border PE cases, harmonization should also prevail in these areas.[152]

Table 6.2 Recommendations of Alignment to the OECD Approach with regard to the Allocation of Business Profits

	Attribution of Business Profits	*Recognition of Internal Dealings*
DE	Functional analysis based on significant people (AOA) given	- Given in national and treaty law - Introduction of 'two-sided' application necessary
US	- General acceptance of AOA given - Introduction of further explanations with regard to significant people and risk allocation	Introduction and clarification of recognition of internal dealings in national and treaty law
BR	- Introduction of functional analysis based on significant people and risk allocation - Abolishment of deemed profit allocation methods	- Introduction and acceptance of recognition of internal dealings in national and treaty law - Abolishment of limitations of deductions of expenses (e.g., for royalties) - Abolishment of withholding taxes on income from internal dealings
RU	- Introduction of further explanations with regard to significant people and risk allocation	Introduction and acceptance of recognition of internal dealings in national and treaty law
IN	- Introduction of further explanations with regard to significant people and risk allocation apart from transfer pricing rules - Abolishment of deemed profit allocation methods and the limited force of attraction principle	Introduction and acceptance of recognition of internal dealings in national and treaty law
CN	- Introduction of further explanations with regard to significant people and risk allocation - Abolishment of deemed profit allocation methods	Introduction and acceptance of recognition of internal dealings in national and treaty law also for cross-border cases

Germany has adopted the AOA in its national law and follows the AOA under future treaty law.[153] Apart from the need for a more concrete national interpretation of new legal terms, such as internal dealings or personal functions and questions of

152. In fact, the harmonization of national income determination rules and the finding of an adequate transfer price is not a specific PE problem and thus are not considered in this work in more detail.
153. See section 4.2.1.2.

interrelation with other German tax statutes, such as exit, trade tax or valuation rules, the '*core*' of the AOA, the recognition of fictitious internal dealings between head office and PE is generally provided in German national law.[154] Still, as a rule of correction, this rule only works '*one-sided*', i.e., at the expense of the German taxpayer.[155] Although the deduction of internal dealings from the German PE tax base is still possible under a given treaty which can limit domestic taxing rights, Germany is more in line with the principle of single taxation if it grants a full recognition of internal dealings. Formally, this can be done by shifting the regulations of the AOA from the national correction rules of the German Foreign Tax Act to the General Income Tax Act.[156]

The *US* accepts the functional analysis of the AOA in its treaty policy.[157] Still, further explanations with regard to the understanding of significant people functions and the allocation of risks shall be added. In addition, in order to completely implement the AOA in national policy, the US generally has to recognize internal dealings between head office and PE under national law. Otherwise, the application of the AOA in US treaties will lead to inconsistencies with US domestic law and thus to possible double or non-taxation situations.

Given that the AOA is regarded as international guidance, *Brazil* has to introduce detailed regulations with regard to a functional analysis based on significant people and risks as proposed by the OECD. In addition, deemed profit allocation methods used according to Brazilian domestic law have to be abolished in favour of a general functional analysis.[158] As Brazil usually treats a PE as separate legal entity for tax purposes, it can be assumed that internal dealings between head office and PE are eventually recognized if the AOA is introduced in Brazilian tax treaties. Still, problems can occur due to specific deduction limitations from the Brazilian PE tax base, e.g., for internal royalties.[159] These also have to be abolished. Additionally, it has to be clarified that, similar to the OECD approach, no withholding taxes are levied upon those fictitious internal dealings in order to prevent possible conflicts with regard to the application of the double taxation avoidance method in the country of residence of the investor.

As proposed in the Transfer Pricing Rules of 2012, *Russia* also intends to follow the AOA.[160] Still, concrete regulations with regard to the interpretation of significant people functions and the allocation of risks, assets and capital are necessary in order to minimize the risk of interpretation conflicts.[161] Furthermore, national law has to change so that internal dealings between head office and PE are recognized for tax purposes if the AOA is implemented.

154. See e.g. Ditz/Luckhaupt (2015) pp. 5 ff.
155. See section 5.3.1.
156. See also Schnitger (2012) pp. 634 f., Ditz (2013) pp. 262 ff.
157. See section 4.2.2.2.
158. See section 4.2.3.2.
159. See section 5.3.1.
160. See section 4.2.4.2.
161. See section 4.2.4.2.

If the AOA is implemented in *India*, the Indian transfer pricing rules can form a basis for the application of a functional risk analysis for the allocation of income between head office and PE.[162] An explicit focus on significant people functions with more detailed explanations is necessary in order to avoid interpretation conflicts. In addition, India has to refrain from the domestic usage of presumptive income determination methods and the limited force of attraction principle as both approaches can lead to misunderstandings, an increasing risk of double or non-taxation situations and higher compliance and administration costs in relation to countries which follow the OECD guidelines. Also, India should follow the separate legal entity approach as mentioned in the transfer pricing rules. This means recognizing fictitious internal dealings between head office and PE for tax purposes despite neglecting Indian case law and specific disallowances in Indian treaties which follow Article 7 (3) of the UN MC.[163]

In order to be in line with the AOA, *China* needs to abolish the regular usage of deemed profit methods with regard to PE income allocation.[164] Instead, it has to be clearly determined that a functional analysis based on significant people and risk allocation is implemented. Otherwise, the probability of conflicts with a country following the OECD approach will remain or even increase. In addition, it has to be clarified in national and treaty law that internal dealings between head office and PE are recognized for tax purposes. This implies a change in domestic law and a necessary shift in Chinese tax treaties from the limitation of deduction of PE expenses as stated in Article 7 (3) of the UN MC.[165]

6.2.3 Reduction of Complexity

In general, the number of conflicts will be reduced if the countries under consideration harmonize and find a common PE approach including a homogeneous understanding and interpretation of PE requirements and allocation of PE income. This initially leads to a reduction of complexity as double or non-taxation situations are diminished and less mutual agreement procedures are necessary in order to cope with the principle of single taxation. Compliance costs for the taxpayer and administration costs for the tax authorities are reduced. Feasibility, administrability and transparency of PE taxation increase if PE requirements are clear and the principle of harmonization is followed.

First of all, in order to be in line with the principle of feasibility of taxation, the countries under consideration need to simplify the registration and approval processes when establishing a PE at source. This is especially true for the BRIC states that usually require specific additional accreditation procedures with local authorities if a PE becomes existent in their country.[166] In order to decrease compliance and administration costs, those excessive authorization requirements, such as the requirement of

162. See section 4.2.5.2.
163. See section 5.3.1.
164. See section 4.2.6.2.
165. See section 5.3.1.
166. See section 5.5.

registration of every change of contract statutes of a business operation in Brazil, or the choice of a '*sponsor*' company for registration in China, need to be abolished. In addition, penalties which arise due to failures to comply because of an unexpected existence of a PE at source, such as the exclusion from future public calls for tenders in Russia and India, or the penalty payment of up to five times the tax due in China, have to be limited. On the other side, from a practical perspective, it has to be accepted that a certain level of compliance costs will remain, e.g., for general registration of the PE or the requirement to comply with country-specific accounting standards.

Another factor is the allocation of income to the existing PE. If it is accepted that the OECD MC is considered as general guidance, the implementation of the AOA can result in higher compliance and administration costs in all countries under consideration.[167] The reason is the fundamental characteristic of the PE as integrating part of the head office. As legal contractual relations between head office and PE are not possible, basic components of the AOA, namely the allocation of profits based on significant people and risk as well as the recognition and valuation of fictitious internal dealings between head office and PE, are based on notional assumptions. Therefore, the compliance effort is supposed to be higher than without a functional analysis and the recognition of internal dealings. One factor which inevitably leads to increased compliance and administration costs is the requirement for transfer pricing documentation which increases for the additional recognition of internal dealings between head office and PE. A supporting factor can be the experience of the countries with determining and identifying adequate transfer prices for associated enterprises. During this process, a functional analysis based on risk management and active decision-making of relevant parties is already an integrated part of the country-specific transfer pricing regulations.[168] Ideally, those transfer pricing regulations have to be harmonized as well in order to maximize initial agreement as well as minimizing compliance and administration costs for the parties involved. Still, especially for the BRIC states, the characteristics of the country-specific transfer pricing rules have to be considered, e.g., with regard to the usage of predetermined profit margins, the emphasis and choice of the transfer pricing method for the given types of transactions, the general finding of comparable independent third party information or the possible taxable recognition of location savings. In general, it has to be assured that, on the one hand, double or non-taxation situations with regard to transfer prices of internal dealings are avoided. At the same time, feasibility has to be guaranteed and complexity has to be reduced as far as possible.

Due to the complexity and variations of possible transactions and the existence and non-existence of different third party comparable figures and country-specific data as well as the resulting choice of one of several existing transfer pricing methods, there is no practical and realistic all-encompassing solution. One concept which helps

167. See section 5.5.
168. Brazil introduced transfer pricing rules in 1996, Russia in 2002, India in 2001, China in 2007, see IBFD (2015) Country Analyses.

reducing compliance and administration efforts is a safe harbour approach. In fact, the introduction of safe harbour profit margins, as already applied by Brazil, China and India, could also help assuring feasibility if negotiated a priori on a bilateral basis.[169] Especially for special PE cases under consideration for which a high level of substance and a full organizational structure can usually be neglected (e.g., for personal-based service or agency PEs), it can be assumed that internal dealings occur less frequently than for larger '*incorporated*' PEs. The usage of standardized profit margins for such internal dealings between a '*low-substance*' PE and its head office helps reducing complexity which leads to decreased administration and compliance costs.

At last, if the AOA is followed in a tax treaty with one of the BRIC states, BRIC domestic law might have the option of introducing a rule of adaption, similar to German national law (section 1 (5) sentence 8 German FTA). This regulation determines that the allocation rules of the tax treaty hold under the condition that the other state proves that it acts in accordance with the existing treaty and otherwise double or non-taxation occurs if the rules of the country of source are followed.[170] This secures, e.g., for the case of existing internal dealings between head office and PE, the deduction of those from the PE tax base as well as the congruent adequate pricing. The question of who carries the burden of proof is a matter of allocation of competences. In fact, if the residence country of the investor carries it, one might guarantee that, given the AOA was fixed on a bilateral basis, the country of source has to follow the treaty if, otherwise, double or non-taxation situations occur.

6.3 RECOMMENDATIONS FROM AN OECD PERSPECTIVE

The previous proposals were based on the assumption that OECD practice serves as international guidance and standard setter for all countries under consideration. Given that the premise of harmonization under OECD rules holds, further recommendations for the OECD regulations with regard to the PE definition and the allocation of business profits are necessary in order to be in line with the principle of single taxation and feasibility.

6.3.1 Basic Improvements

First of all, the OECD has to clarify basic PE requirements which are not included in the wording of the OECD MC but are only referred to in the OECD MC Commentary, if at all. Table 6.3 displays these recommendations.

169. See Luckhaupt/Overesch/Schreiber (2012b) pp. 366 ff. who support the usage of standards with regard to profit margins and the chosen transfer pricing method. See for OECD proposals which involve the introduction of a safe harbour approach especially for low-risk transactions OECD Report Safe Harbours (2013), OECD Discussion Draft Transfer Pricing Comparability (2014) and OECD Discussion Draft BEPS Action 10 (2015).

170. See section 4.2.1.2.

Table 6.3 Recommendations of Improvement considering the PE Tax Policy of the OECD MC

'Passive' Service PE	*Construction Site PE*	*Agency PE*	*Service PE*	*Attribution of Business Profits*
- Clarification of effective power to use a location (wide or narrow basis) in case of services provided at third party premises - Alternatively, fix introduction of service PE provision in the wording of Article 5 OECD MC	- Clarification of replacement of physical presence of general contractor through disposal over construction site - Additional explanations in case of more complex subcontractor structures - Clarification of profit allocation to a subcontractor PE	- Introduction of additional indicators with regard to the exclusion criterion for independent agents - Clarification of profit allocation to an agency PE	Concretion of factors of the economic employer concept	- Introduction of special income allocation rules for specific PE cases (construction site, agency, service PE) - Introduction of standardized profit margins for internal dealings (e.g., for low-substance PEs)

One of those terms refers to the interpretation of disposal over the fixed place of business in case of services provided at third party premises. In order to avoid interpretations on a wider or narrower basis as shown in the analysis, the OECD has to clarify to what extent the '*effective power to use a location*' shall be interpreted.[171] It can either be interpreted on a wider basis meaning that every usage of a third party location is considered as fixed place of business of the user, or it can be limited so that the criterion of exclusive usage of the room with the possibility to ban other parties from the premises is decisive. Either way, a clarification is necessary so that double or non-taxation situations due to diverging interpretations of terms are avoided. Another possible solution is to adopt US domestic law and emphasize the fact whether the usage of a room is part of a separate bargain process when negotiating the service contract details with the client.[172] Irrespective from any questions of exclusivity, if the room was separately mentioned in the service contract so that it is decisive for conducting the business activities in the country of source, a fixed place of business exists for the non-resident service provider. In fact, the whole discussion is avoided if the service PE alternative was implemented in Article 5 of the OECD MC since for the existence of a service PE, the decisive criteria are the fulfilment of a time and sales threshold which can be considered as measurable and quantifiable factors.

With regard to the existence of a PE through the total delegation of work to subcontractors, the OECD has to clarify that physical presence is exceptionally replaced

171. See section 3.1.2.
172. See section 5.2.1.

by the requirement of disposal over the construction site. If the OECD MC wants to keep this regulation as proposed in the OECD Reform Proposal of 2012, further explanations are necessary with regard to the fact to what extent this case is different from the case of local service-providing personnel which only establish a service PE for its non-present enterprise under supervision, direction and control of the latter.[173] Otherwise, it is possible that misunderstandings may occur amongst domestic tax authorities who can either focus on the requirement of control over the working site or control over the personnel working at the construction site. In addition, the OECD has to clarify what taxable consequences will occur in case of a more complex business structure where multiple subcontractors exist in the country of source subcontracting the work from level to level.[174] More importantly, the allocation of business profits to the construction site in this case has to be taken into account. As it was derived in the analysis, it is probable that no significant PE profits are allocated through the application of the AOA based on significant people of the general contractor which are not physically present in the source country.[175] Double or non-taxation situations with regard to business profits are thus improbable. Still, it has to be reconsidered whether the increasing compliance and administration costs for the parties involved through the existence of a construction site PE are worth the effort if the PE tax base is minimal or even zero.

Considering the agency PE, the current OECD BEPS report on Action 7 tends to focus on the independent agent criterion rather than taking into account the question whether the authority to conclude contracts for the principal is on a legal or economic basis.[176] Actually, this approach is in line with the principle of single taxation and feasibility as it avoids existing interpretation conflicts on treaty level between common and civil law understanding of the agency PE and the degree of authorization as shown in the previous analysis. Still, the OECD MC proposes to concentrate on the requirement of legal independence which indicates the number of connected principals as decisive criterion when deciding about the agency PE status.[177] At first sight, it seems straightforward to consider acting for one or more associated principals as a specific indicator for neglecting independence. Interpretation conflicts and thus double or non-taxation situations are avoided if contracting states can be sure that bounding exclusively one or more connected enterprises lead to the existence of an agency PE (given that the other factors of Article 5 (5) OECD MC are fulfilled as well). Otherwise, it can be assumed that a greater number of PEs will be created by mainly focusing on the legal relationship between agent and principal instead of considering the nature of the agent's activities. This again raises compliance and administration costs.[178] Therefore, the OECD has to introduce a more concrete catalogue of additional attributes which signal whether a dependent or independent agent exists so that the establishment of an agency PE in this case is based on fact and not only on the question of

173. See e.g. BIAC Response (2013) p. 9.
174. In fact, this is not unusual in practice. See ABB Response (2013) p. 3.
175. See section 5.4.
176. See section 3.2.2.2.
177. See OECD Revised Discussion Draft BEPS Action 7 (2015) p. 13 & pp. 19 ff.
178. See also critically Collier (2015) pp. 63 ff.

control. Indicators of independence are a variable profit-based remuneration, bearing loss risks and own business operating expenses, being responsible for its own organization of working time, or having its own equipment and premises.[179] Beyond this discussion, it is questionable to what extent considerable profits are allocated to an agency PE. Even if refusing the single taxpayer approach and the '*zero-sum*'-theory, the analysis showed that a regular dependent commission agent usually does not bear further significant risks so that the agency PE tax base can be minimal.[180] This means that a risk of double or non-taxation is probably not existent. Still, a higher number of PE cases lead to increased complexity for the companies involved which i.a. have to comply with country-specific registration and authorization rules as currently applied in the BRIC states. The OECD therefore has to align the profit attribution rules with its policy of a wider PE definition. The same argument arises for the other special personnel-based PE cases, such as the delegation of work to subcontractors or the introduction of a service PE. The question is: In order to derive a PE tax base for the mentioned cases, is it necessary to apply a complex investigation related to a transfer-pricing analysis of the whole value chain and allocate significant functions and risks? As specific profit allocation rules do not exist for the special cases of the construction site, agency and service PE, the OECD has to introduce additional regulations in order to provide more certainty which is more in line with the principle of single taxation and the rise of feasibility.[181]

Considering the possible service PE case with regard to the cross-border secondment of employees, the OECD relies on the economic employer concept as decisive PE criterion. Only if the non-resident active lender of workforce is considered as effective employer, a PE is possible in the country of source.[182] In order to concretize the factors of direction, supervision and control over the seconded employee, the OECD has to introduce more specific instructions. Similar to Russian or Chinese regulations, these can include factors such as a fixed profit margin threshold received by the employer or the question of decision power on the number of seconded employees, its locations and workplaces and the amount of salaries to be paid.[183] More concrete instructions help identifying the economic employer and avoid misunderstandings and interpretation conflicts so that the principle of single taxation and feasibility is preserved.

Apart from the changes in the PE definition, the OECD proposes to introduce the AOA as prevailing concept of profit allocation. As derived above, one major aspect deals with the introduction of specific income allocation rules for special PE cases. It has to be guaranteed that complexity with regard to the functional analysis and documentation requirements is reduced for PEs for which it is foreseeable that the compliance effort is larger than the profit to be taxed. Specific regulations with regard to the existence of an agency PE in the case of associated enterprises exist in certain treaties, e.g., between Germany and Austria. In the protocol of this treaty, it is

179. See Ott (2009) p. 69.
180. See section 5.4.
181. See section 6.3.2.
182. See section 3.2.3.
183. See e.g. section 4.2.4.1 & section 4.2.6.1.

determined that an agency PE is not given under the condition that the transfer pricing analysis conducted between the associated companies comes to the conclusion that the functions are appropriately compensated and a certain profit mark-up exists at the level of the associated enterprise.[184] Under this rule, discussions about the existence of an agency PE are avoided, at least if associated enterprises are involved. Instead, the focus is on the transfer pricing analysis following the arm's length principle under Article 9 of the OECD MC. In order to reduce the probability of interpretation conflicts and compliance costs, it is recommended to introduce such regulations as an option if an agent-principal relation exists between associated enterprises. This also resembles the exceptional allowance of the single taxpayer approach in the AOA as only the taxing sphere of the associated enterprise is considered in this case.

The other important topic is the increased risk of double or non-taxation due to the valuation of internal dealings between head office and PE (transfer pricing problem). As mentioned in section 6.2.3, the usage of standardized profit margins supports the concepts of feasibility and single taxation as interpretation conflicts with regard to the valuation of the internal dealing are minimized. Especially for PE cases with low substance and a minor organizational structure, safe harbour profit margins might be determined for internal dealings so that a disproportional effort is avoided. In this context, the OECD has to converge to the tax policy of the BRIC states in order to provide more convincing arguments with regard to an implementation of the AOA worldwide.

If conflicts occur with regard to the chosen transfer price, the OECD provides for different solutions:

One of them is described in Article 7 (3) of the OECD MC which provides for the application of a MAP according to Article 25 OECD MC for the prevention of double taxation, either indirectly through the arrangement of MAP by the taxpayer, or as alternative directly by the disagreeing contracting state.[185] Although double taxation effectively vanishes if an agreement is found under a MAP, taking into account the current OECD MAP statistics, one can doubt whether this is the appropriate solution in order to cope with the principle of feasibility. For 2013, the average completion time for the MAP procedure was about twenty-four months. In Germany, from 267 open requests in 2013 of which 106 concerned transfer pricing or PE income allocation, four cases were completed during the reporting period.[186] Despite limited data from other countries, it can be concluded that administration and compliance costs generally rise if a MAP is started. This effect can even increase in the BRIC states where there might be a lack of appropriately educated independently working personnel being responsible for the MAP process in the country of source.[187] An ultimate way of avoiding double or non-taxation situations from interpretation conflicts in the long term is a

184. See section 5.3.2.2.
185. See section 3.3.2.
186. See OECD MAP Statistics (2013).
187. See e.g. Protto (2014) pp. 176 ff.

mandatory arbitration clause as proposed by the OECD MC.[188] Given that on average the authorities under consideration do not agree on specific PE issues for at least two years, the taxpayer can request an arbitration procedure according to Article 25 (5) of the OECD MC. Still, several countries consider this process as abandonment of competences with regard to dispute resolution and thus do not include this provision in their tax treaties.[189] This is also conceivable for countries like the BRIC states which might argue that a costly mandatory arbitration process in the hands of private arbitrators is inappropriate also under the condition that a lack of experience might exist in those countries.[190] One example of a mandatory arbitration provision for specific treaty clauses, such as a common understanding of the PE term and the allocation of business profits, is included in the US-German Tax Treaty (Article 25 (5) US-GER TT).[191] Although the implementation of a mandatory arbitration procedure is in line with the principle of single taxation, it is literally the '*last step in the process*' which involves a large amount of compliance and administration during the multi-annual period of litigation.

Therefore, depending on the durance and intensity of negotiations, bilateral APAs between contracting states which try to avoid transfer pricing disputes a priori, can also be a solution for preventing conflicts with regard to PE issues.[192] Ideally, a multilateral agreement, e.g., between chosen industrialized countries and the BRIC states provides for even more certainty. Still, the effectiveness of an APA depends on the factors of costs involved, such as user fees, internal resource and external consulting costs, the duration of the proceedings and the determination and stability of critical assumptions.[193] Especially those critical assumptions are an important part of the APA as they have to be constant in the period of validity. Among others, these include requirements of constant participation ratios, constant functional, risk and capital structure and a stable business model.[194] As derived before, a PE is an integrating part of the head office and all internal dealings are fictitious without any legal contractual basis. It can be the case that a reorganization of certain internal processes or business structures in which a PE is involved leads to a change of critical assumptions for the APA which does not occur with legal stipulations between associated enterprises, e.g., with regard to the predetermined functional and risk structure. Therefore, an APA loses its protective effect and can be revoked. In addition, the negotiation period between the application of the APA by the taxpayer and the final implementation in EU countries with non-EU states can last to about thirty-two months

188. See also Kroppen/Dawid/Schmidtke (2012) p. 288. In fact, this is also part of Action Plan 14 of the OECD BEPS discussion which shall create a more effective dispute resolution process by ideally introducing such mandatory arbitration procedures. See OECD Discussion Draft BEPS Action 14 (2015) pp. 20 ff.
189. See OECD MC Commentary (2014) Article 25, No. 65, p. 389.
190. See Lennard (2014) pp. 180 ff.
191. See Monsenego (2014) p. 167.
192. See e.g. Kerschner/Stiastny (2013) pp. 588 ff.
193. See e.g. Vollert/Eikel/Sureth (2013) pp. 373 ff.
194. See Vollert/Eikel/Sureth (2013) p. 371.

which is even longer than the average completion time of a MAP.[195] In summary, an APA is beneficial under the following conditions:

- The costs incurred and the completion period are lower than the costs and the completion period of a regular transfer pricing process via a MAP.
- A regular revision of the APA is possible without any interruptions, also under the condition that the critical assumptions can be changed more easily for fictitious internal dealings between head office and PE.

From a political perspective, it is discussable if, apart from regular PE taxation under Article 7 of the OECD MC, a withholding tax shall be levied for internal dealings in order to adapt to the policy of countries like the BRIC states which can create an incentive to adopt the AOA worldwide.[196] On the one hand, this establishes the adjustment of PE taxation to taxation between independent associated enterprises for which the possibility of levying withholding taxes is given for certain legal transactions. On the other hand, it is questionable for which notional internal dealings between head office and PE a withholding tax can be levied at all. This can be the case for internal royalties given that Article 12 (2) of the UN MC is followed in the treaty. This cannot be the case for internal interest payments as those are generally not recognized, except for the case that the PE fulfils a significant treasury function.[197] Dividends also do not exist between head office and PE. Instead, there are several approaches given by the OECD MC Commentary such as the capital allocation or thin capitalization approach in order to allocate an adequate amount of equity capital to the PE.[198] On payments of internal leasing or renting arrangements, a withholding tax also generally does not exist. The same is true for income from the provision of internal services, except for the cases that those internal services are considered as part of a supply of know-how and taxed as royalties, or that technical services are separately mentioned in the royalty-article.[199] Therefore, a withholding tax can eventually only be levied on internal notional royalty payments. Still, it has to be assured that this withholding tax is creditable in the country of residence of the head office since otherwise this tax becomes final if PE profits are exempt. As the general introduction of the tax credit method is improbable in practice, the withholding tax thus represents an additional final tax burden for the investing enterprise. In addition, there is the question of enforceability. There has to be a system of adequate documentation requirements, quasi-contractual arrangements and ancillary PE accounts in order to

195. However, data was only available for eleven countries. See EU Joint Transfer Pricing Forum (2014) pp. 1 ff.
196. See e.g. Gutiérrez (2013) Chapter 12, p. 309. According to the OECD MC Commentary, a withholding tax for internal dealings is neglected. See OECD Report on the Attribution of Profits to PE (2010) Part I, No. 203, pp. 53 ff.
197. See section 3.3.2.
198. See section 3.3.2.
199. In fact, this is followed by most of Indian tax treaties instead of integrating services in the PE article. See Appendix, Table A5. In addition, the UN proposes to introduce a new article to the UN MC which grants the right to levy a withholding tax on technical services provided at source. See Herzfeld (2014) pp. 477 f., Kaeser (2014) pp. 709 ff.

provide a reliable tax base for the withholding tax levied on fictitious payments. In summary, due to reasons of lacking feasibility and a higher risk of an increased taxation, it cannot be recommended to introduce a withholding tax for internal dealings between head office and PE.[200]

6.3.2 Further Tax Policy Changes

With respect to all of the previous recommendations, it was assumed that the current OECD policy has to be followed in general. This implied the simultaneous implementation of the OECD reform proposals with regard to the PE definition of 2012 and 2015 and the AOA of 2010. If all approaches are followed, further recommendations were mentioned which align those ideas with the principle of single taxation and feasibility. Beyond those general improvements, additional basic tax policy changes could also be taken into account which were not considered by the OECD so far. Again, the overall premise is to decrease the risk of interpretation conflicts resulting in double and non-taxation situations and to increase feasibility of taxation. Nevertheless, it has to be considered how realistic and enforceable the practical implementation of those policy changes would be. So the question is: What are the options apart from the current OECD approach?

One intuitive approach which is practically not enforceable is the total abolishment of the PE concept in favour of an exclusive taxation of worldwide income in the country of residence (residence principle). In theory, as no taxation at source exists, the risk of double and non-taxation vanishes. From a macroeconomic point of view, a fewer number of PEs lead to a larger sum of the tax base in general as compliance costs with regard to registration, authorization and documentation decline.[201] Still, worldwide income has to be identified in all countries under consideration so that a certain level of compliance and administration costs continues to exist. In addition, the PE is a well-established form of direct investment and fiscal nexus in almost all tax treaties worldwide for over 100 years.[202] Therefore, from a political perspective, it is completely unrealistic to exclude taxation at source.

Another concept which deviates from the current corporate tax system and the co-existence of residence and source taxation is a destination-based corporate cash flow tax as proposed by *Devereux* and *de la Feria*.[203] This approach is based on the value-added tax with the differentiation that the destination as jurisdiction which possesses the taxing right is generally determined to be the location of the customer.[204] Thus, there is no need to establish a fiscal nexus in the form of a PE and to allocate

200. Still, it has to be considered as an option and incentive to convince the BRIC states of the introduction of the AOA under the concept of the approach of worldwide harmonization.
201. See Kroppen (2013) p. 272.
202. See e.g. Skaar (1991) p. 2, Kobetsky (2011) pp. 110 ff.
203. See Devereux/De la Feria (2014). Other studies which deal with the destination-based cash flow tax are i.a. McLure (1992), Grubert/Newlon (1995), Musgrave (2000b) or Barker (2012).
204. See Devereux/De la Feria (2014) p. 9.

profits between source and residence country.[205] Instead, the system works as follows: If a multinational conducts business activities in another state, selling goods or providing services to a customer, the taxing right is allocated to the residence country of the customer. The tax base is collected by the residence country of the multinational but taxed at the tax rate of the country where the customer is resident. Relevant expenses, such as labour costs, are deductible from the tax base. All the payments from the countries are supposed to be netted off and pooled in a clearing house, a sort of supranational institution, which guarantees for the adequate adjustments of the tax base payments between the countries.[206] Apart from questions of neutrality and equity which are not considered in this work, it has to be evaluated to what extent the principle of single taxation and feasibility is fulfilled. For this purpose, the model case displayed in Figure 5.3 is reconsidered where a foreign general contractor delegates all work to a local subcontractor which conducts business activities at the construction site in the country of source.[207] According to the destination-based tax, the country of destination has to be determined in order to allocate the taxing right upon the profits earned by the subcontractor working at the construction site. According to *Devereux* and *de la Feria*, this is the location of the customer.[208] In this case, it is supposed that the customer is the initiator of the construction site and hired the general contractor for the construction project. If it is assumed that the final customer is resident of a third country, according to the general theory of the destination-based tax by *Devereux* and *de la Feria*, the taxing right upon the profits is not allocated to the place of performance of the business activities, but to the residence country of the customer.[209] Thus, in theory, although the work order is given to the general contractor located in country A and delegated to the subcontractor which provided the services in country B at the construction site, the profits are taxed in country C, the residence country of the customer. In general, this would require a high level of cooperation and coordination among the states under consideration.[210] It is feasible that interpretation conflicts will occur with this approach as countries might argue that a fixed nexus is established in their country if a construction site is located there for an adequate period of time. Therefore, this example illustrates that all countries would have to agree to the destination-based tax in order to avoid such conflicts. Otherwise, there is still a risk of double or non-taxation of business profits. In addition, there is the question of feasibility. The establishment of a clearing house and the coordination of the whole tax levying process would lead to increased administration costs. Although compliance costs are reduced through the non-recognition of PE cases, it is questionable if this cost

205. See Auerbach/Devereux/Simpson (2010) p. 885. See Schreiber (2013) pp. 322 ff. who argues that the PE concept can alternatively be extended so that all trading activities and service provisions are taxable in the country of destination.
206. See Devereux/De la Feria (2014) p. 21.
207. See section 5.2.2.
208. See Devereux/De la Feria (2014) pp. 15 ff.
209. This is a specific assumption of the approach of *Devereux* and *de la Feria*. The place of performance is only supposed to be used as place of taxation in exceptional cases such as restaurant services or concerts or sporting events where the identification of the customer is too burdensome. See Devereux/De la Feria (2014) p. 17.
210. See Parillo (2015) p. 318.

reduction will in turn be absorbed by rising administration costs. In addition, the set-up costs would be tremendous as all tax treaties which are based on the residence and source principle have to be changed and the destination-based concept has to be implemented in domestic law as well.

Another approach which deviates from the current corporate tax system is the global FA. As the name indicates, according to the (global) FA, all worldwide income of a multinational company is consolidated and allocated to the countries where the business activities are conducted via a formula based on specific fractions such as sales, assets and payroll.[211] Actually, the introduction of a FA is a widely discussed topic and has been on the agenda for several years, lately by the European Commission (EC) proposing a Common Consolidated Corporate Tax Base (CCCTB) for European multinational companies.[212] Apart from fairness or neutrality considerations, the focus here is solely on the question whether the formulated general tax criteria, the principle of single taxation and feasibility of taxation, are still valid in the context of PE taxation if the concept of FA is followed. In fact, similar to the destination-based tax, a global FA disregards the concept of PE as fiscal nexus as the source principle is effectively replaced by allocation factors such as sales or payroll.[213] Still, under the consideration that FA is only applied for one or a certain group of countries, such as for the CCCTB, the PE term still remains as fiscal connecting factor for third party companies being non-members of the group.[214] This means that if a global FA is not implemented, the identification of PE requirements and the interpretation conflicts shown in the analysis still exists. What is replaced, is the process of attribution of business profits between head office and PE which follows a fraction of specific measurable business activities located in the respective state. However, also with regard to sales or services as decisive factor for profit allocation, it has to be clearly defined who the taxable subject is and to which country the taxing right is allocated. To illustrate the difficulties, one can again take into account the model case displayed in Figure 5.3 of section 5.2.2 which considered the total delegation of work to subcontractors conducting business activities at a construction site. First, it has to be determined whether the revenue from the work of the subcontractor at the construction site is allocated to the general contractor (and integrated in the formula of the general contractor's company) or whether only the subcontractor's sphere is considered. Then, the adequate fraction of the formula has to be determined. It can be assumed that the client who ordered the construction is a resident of country A, the general contractor is a resident of country B and the construction site where the subcontractor is working is located in country C. It can further be argued as the work is conducted at the construction site, that the place

211. See e.g. Auerbach/Devereux/Simpsons (2010) pp. 872 ff.
212. See European Commission (2011). See for more information Spengel/Ortmann-Babel/Zinn/Matenaer (2012) pp. 185 ff. In fact, the latest proposal by the EC picks up again the introduction of the CCCTB as solution of a more fair and efficient corporate tax system. See European Commission (2015). Supporters of the FA are, for instance, Avi-Yonah/Clausing (2008), Runkel (2012), Brauner (2014). Critics are Altshuler/Grubert (2010), Kroppen/Dawid/Schmidtke (2012), Fleming/Peroni/Shay (2014), Ditz (2015). See for an overview Rasch/Tillmann (2013) pp. 141 ff.
213. See McIntyre (1994) pp. 789 f., Morse (2010) p. 601, Spencer (2014) Part 3, p. 41.
214. See Staringer (2008) pp. 123 ff.

of performance is decisive so that all profit is allocated to country C. However, the case gets more difficult if it is assumed, for instance, that the subcontractor provides architectural services from another country D meaning he is not on-site in country C where the construction site is located. It could get even more difficult if it is assumed that the client ordered the construction of several objects in several countries and the architectural services of the subcontractor is used for more than one construction site. Which fraction is used and how is the profit allocated in this case? Are the profits to be allocated also to the residence country of the subcontractor where the services are performed or to the client who receives the invoice? And how can the profit from services be split if several construction sites in several countries benefit from it?[215] In general, this example shows that also the FA approach suffers from interpretation conflicts which can result in an increased risk of double and non-taxation as well as in a lack of feasibility and simplicity.[216] In fact, similar to the destination-based tax, a high level of cooperation and coordination among the states is necessary in order to avoid such effects.[217] In addition, the set-up costs of the introduction of a completely new tax system is probably high as well. It has to be evaluated whether these costs in addition to the ongoing compliance and administration costs of the FA are lower than the costs of the current system involving PE determination and the overall application of the arm's length principle. Therefore, from the perspective of the principle of single taxation and feasibility, it cannot be said whether FA leads to an improvement in comparison to the separate legal entity approach. Currently, the OECD rejects the FA approach for the reasons mentioned before.[218] This is exemplary shown in the introduction of the AOA for PE income determination which is based on the separate legal entity principle.

Apart from those system-changing reform proposals, another more realistic and straight-forward solution is to accept the current OECD policy as given and, apart from the basic improvements as described in section 6.3.1 (which can be described as '*fine-tuning*'), change further specific parameters of international tax policy in order to be consistent with the principles of single taxation and feasibility.

One concept which avoids interpretation conflicts with regard to cross-border PE cases is the so-called *new approach* proposed by the OECD Partnership Report.[219] In general, this approach suggests that in case of a qualification conflict, the country of residence is obliged to follow the qualification and judgment of the country of source which, in principle, guarantees single taxation either in the source or in the residence country.[220] However, this proposal is generally limited to qualification conflicts which are based on different provisions in domestic law when applying Article 3 (2) OECD

215. See for further discussion with regard to the US FA used to determine state tax liabilities Spencer (2014) Part 5, pp. 34 ff.
216. See Fleming/Peroni/Shay (2014) pp. 32 f., Spencer (2014) Part 2, p. 45 who argue that for both the separate legal entity approach and the FA, double and non-taxation situations are existent.
217. See Ditz (2015) p. 123.
218. See OECD Transfer Pricing Guidelines (2010) No. 1.19-1.31, pp. 37 ff., OECD BEPS Action Plan (2013) p. 14.
219. See OECD Partnership Report (1999) No. 103, p. 38.
220. See Reimer (2014) Fundaments, No. 85, p. 23. In fact, this is an interpretation of the wording of Article 23 OECD MC which states: 'Where a resident of a Contracting State derives income

MC so that different classifications of the same taxable object occur.[221] In order to serve as solution in the context of this work, the new approach has to be extended to conflicts resulting from different interpretations and understandings of specific PE requirements. Thus, if a specific PE requirement, which is not clearly determined in the respective treaty such as the criterion of disposal over the fixed place of business, is interpreted differently, the country of source has the primary right to decide. If a PE is established, the country of residence applies the double taxation avoidance method in accordance with Article 23 OECD MC. If a PE is not given, the country of residence taxes the worldwide income of the head office. Irrespective from any considerations of fairness, this is an effective instrument to guarantee the principle of single taxation for cross-border PE cases which can be implemented in a relatively straight-forward way, by re-interpreting the double taxation avoidance-article of the tax treaty and adding a further explanation to the respective protocol.[222] Still, questions of practical feasibility remain, since from a political perspective, the country of residence effectively gives up taxing rights and decision power.

Another approach is to introduce a quantitative PE threshold based on gross sales or services provided which indicates a fiscal nexus in the country of source.[223] In fact, there are two options how to implement this proposal:

One of them is to completely replace the PE definition of Article 5 of the OECD MC by a quantitative threshold so that a taxing right at source is established if a specific reference number is passed, e.g., gross sales in the country of source or revenue earned from the provision of services to customers being resident in the source country.[224] In addition, a specific time threshold can be explicitly determined, e.g., six months, so that business activities whose duration is smaller do not establish a PE at source. In the case of an existing PE, the determination of taxable income is based on the AOA as it can be assumed that the business activity conducted at source has the organizational structure and resources to implement a complex functional analysis and to identify internal dealings including a profit mark-up.[225] In general, a quantitative threshold based on revenue and time has the advantage that interpretation conflicts are diminished as the crucial PE requirements are relatively straightforward. Discussions about

---

or owns capital which, in accordance with the provisions of this Convention, may be taxed in the other Contracting State' where the emphasis is on whether the income may be taxed in the source country. See Vogel (2003) pp. 528 ff.

221. See Lang (2009) p. 205, Lüdicke (2010) p. 617. See section 5.1.
222. See also Haase (2015) p. 315.
223. This approach is based on the quantitative economic presence test as proposed by Cockfield (2003) pp. 650 ff. and on the 'sales and services' approach by Schön (2009) pp. 99 ff. It also considers aspects of the origin-based approach by Kemmeren (2006) p. 437.
224. A practical example for a quantitative threshold is the *maquiladora* regime applied by Mexico for inbound cross-border business activities. This business model provides tax incentives for the importation of machinery, raw materials and other equipment which are temporarily used for transformation and repair services in Mexico and then are sent back to the country of origin. One of those tax incentives is the avoidance of a Mexican PE in relation to the activities described. Under the *maquiladora* regime, a PE can thus be avoided if the yearly profit of the *maquiladora* is at least the greater of 6.9% of the total value of assets used in the Mexican entity or 6.5% of costs and expenses related. See Diaz de Leon Galarza (2014) pp. 205 ff.
225. See Schön (2012b) pp. 440 ff.

the degree of disposal over the fixed place of business, the fiscal treatment of agents and service providers are avoided since a quantitative number such as the revenue earned by the head office is decisive for the establishment of a fiscal nexus at source. Further details of the relevant PE criteria, such as the concrete level of revenue and the period of duration, can be arranged in a country-specific treaty on a bilateral basis. A connecting factor for the identification of the point of sales or the provision of services can be the invoice address of the business to which the assets are sold and the location where the services are provided.[226] In case of private customers, relevant data can be taken from the tax assessment of the VAT sphere. For specific cases such as the total delegation of work to subcontractors (Figure 5.3 in section 5.2.2), it can be argued that the revenue earned is allocated to the subcontractor if all work is shifted to the latter so that an economic presence is avoided for the general contractor. In case of secondment of employees (Figure 5.5 in section 5.2.4), it still has to be decided to which party the revenues earned by the seconded employees are allocated. If the seconded workers still effectively conduct business activities for the workforce-lending company and not for the host entity, the revenue earned has to be allocated to the former so that a fiscal nexus is established in the source country. Despite those detailed regulations for special cases, the risk of double or non-taxation situations due to misunderstandings with regard to the PE definition is reduced. In addition, administration and compliance costs are reduced as well since companies which do not fulfil the criteria of revenue earned and habitualness are not taxable in the country of source at all.[227] Those companies which do fulfil the criteria usually are deemed to have the substance to apply the AOA so that, by assumption, the compliance costs are not higher than the attributed PE tax base. In addition, set-up costs of introducing this approach are presumably not extensive as this approach is based on current international tax schemes. What has to be adapted is the PE definition of Article 5 of the OECD MC. Depending on the intensity and willingness of implementation of reform proposals, one could also take into consideration whether the preparatory and auxiliary business activity provision of Article 5 (4) OECD MC should maintain. Interpretation conflicts and thus double or non-taxation situations are still possible if the countries cannot agree on whether a specific business activity has a preparatory or auxiliary character and thus is not considered as PE-constituting activity.

A '*light version*' of this approach is to keep the PE definition as under the current OECD approach and introduce a safe harbour limit for the application of the AOA.[228] Only if a specific quantitative threshold is reached, such as gross sales or revenue from the provision of services, the AOA is applied for the allocation of business profits between head office and PE. If this threshold is not exceeded, a simpler profit allocation method has to be applied for which internal dealings do not have to be recognized.[229] This simpler profit allocation method would exclude a functional analysis based on

226. See Cockfield (2003) p. 653.
227. See Cockfield (2003) p. 651.
228. This variation is also based on the approach by Schön (2012b) pp. 241 ff. with the difference that the current PE term remains as it is.
229. See Schön (2012b) p. 442.

significant people and risk allocation. Instead, it determines the PE tax base as the gross revenue earned minus economically related expenses such as wage costs in case of services provided or costs of transportation and storage in case of selling goods. In fact, this approach at least reduces compliance and administration costs for enterprises with smaller cross-border business activities as they do not have to apply the AOA for every special PE case. A further requirement is an adequate PE accounting so that the total PE revenues and costs can be clearly determined. Still, relevant PE costs have to be identified and allocated to each entity. For those costs which cannot be clearly allocated, a further simplification method is the determination of a cost pool.[230] All relevant costs have to be pooled whereas the clearly attributable costs are removed. The residual costs are allocated between the head office and the PE according to the share of persons involved or the total revenue earned. The PE profit for business activities below the given threshold is thus the difference between the PE revenue and directly and indirectly allocated costs. Nevertheless, unless the concept of harmonization is not implemented and the OECD MC does not clarify specific PE requirements, the risk of double and non-taxation situations due to interpretation conflicts remains to be existent with this '*light*' approach. Therefore, it can also be argued to combine both approaches and abolish the current PE definition so that an '*AOA PE*' exists if a certain quantitative threshold is exceeded. If the threshold is not fulfilled, e.g., the gross sales in the country of source are below the given limit, a '*non-AOA PE*' exists with a simplified profit determination as described above. In fact, this resembles the approach proposed by *Schön*.[231]

What is important under the proposal of a quantitative PE threshold is the concept of geographical and commercial coherence. It has to be guaranteed that companies do not artificially split business activities and thereby avoid exceeding the given PE threshold. Whereas geographical coherence can be defined, orientation with regard to the interpretation of commercial coherence can be found in the OECD MC Commentary dealing with the connected projects-criterion in relation to the service PE alternative.[232] Relevant attributes of a commercial connection of different business projects can thus be derived from a single overall master contract, conclusion of the contract with the same client, the provision of work by the same persons, or the nature of the work involved.

6.4 AVOIDANCE OF PERMANENT ESTABLISHMENT RISK

Finally, the focus of the work is put on a tax planning perspective. It has been derived from the analysis that the establishment of specific PEs does not lead to significant PE profit in every case.[233] This minimizes the risk of double or non-taxation situations for

230. Orientation with regard to the allocation of business profits can be taken from the latest OECD BEPS Discussion Draft considering transfer pricing of low value-adding intra-group services. See OECD Discussion Draft BEPS Action 10 (2015).
231. See Schön (2012a) pp. 219 ff.
232. See OECD MC Commentary (2014) Article 5, No. 42.41, pp. 122 ff.
233. See section 5.4.

the head office as despite interpretation conflicts with regard to the PE definition, the PE tax base is minimal due to an insignificant allocation of functions and risks at PE level. Still, if the establishment of a PE at source is not planned or willingly accepted, intense discussions with the tax authorities on the interpretation of qualifying PE requirements occur. Further compliance efforts, such as costs for late registration including subsequent payment of taxes and penalties and the installation of an accounting system for tax and other social insurance issues will arise.[234] In addition, a functional analysis according to the AOA has to be carried out including the identification and arm's length valuation of internal dealings if included in the treaty. In this context, the PE risk can be briefly defined as the risk of unintentionally constituting a PE and thus bearing additional hardly assessable costs. Especially for border cases where a PE is probably not wanted from the beginning involving e.g., subcontractors, agents, service providers or seconded employees, it can thus make sense to take into account a company's view and analyse how to avoid the risk of establishing a PE in the countries under consideration. Thus, the following explanations can be considered as alternative solution from a company perspective if the status quo remains and no improvements occur.

Table 6.4 provides a general checklist for the evaluation of the PE risk in case of cross-border business activities between contracting states. On the basis of '*yes or no*'-answers, it can be determined if a PE risk exists for the inbound business operation under consideration. Similar to the analysis in section 5.2, the checklist refers to four different types of business activities: the provision of services at third party premises, the total delegation of work to subcontractors, the usage of an agent and the secondment of employees. The criteria of habitualness and the qualification of the activities as being of preparatory or auxiliary character are not considered. In fact, the aim of this checklist is not to provide for a complete evaluation of all possible PE risks a company could face. Instead, selective PE requirements are chosen for which the analysis already showed that there is room for interpretation which lead to a risk of unintentionally creating a taxing right in the country of source.[235]

Table 6.4 Checklist for Evaluation of PE Risk

	Evaluation of PE Risk	
(A) Basic PE: Requirement of Disposal	Yes	No
(1) Are services provided on-site at third party premises in another country?		
(2) Does the tax treaty with that country include a service PE provision?		

234. See section 5.5 for details with regard to the compliance and administration costs in the countries under consideration.
235. See Bendlinger (2009) pp. 293 ff. for a more general checklist on which Table 33 is also based on.

	Evaluation of PE Risk
(3) Does the service provider have a legal right to use the third party premises?	
(4) Does the service provider have a formal right to use the third party premises?	
(5) Can the right to use the place be restricted by the client or anybody else? *	
Score: Questions (1)-(4) answered with 'yes'? = PE risk ↑ Questions (5) answered with 'yes'? = PE risk ↓ for Germany	
(B) Construction Site PE: Total Delegation of Work to Subcontractors	
(6) In case of a construction site established in another country, is work delegated to a local subcontractor?	
(7) Is a part of work delegated to the subcontractor so that the general contractor is still present in the country of source?	
(8) Is all work delegated to the subcontractor so that the general contractor is not present in the country of source? **	
(9) Does the general contractor have a sufficient degree of disposal over the construction site so that it can effectively control access and use of the site?	
Score: Questions (6)-(7), (9) answered with 'yes'? = PE risk ↑ Question (8) answered with 'yes'? = PE risk ↑ except for Germany	
(C) Agency PE: Authority to Conclude Contracts	
(10) Does a person (individual or jurisdictional) who is present in the country of source conduct business activities for the principal although there is no fixed place of business at source?	
(11) Does the person conclude contracts for the principal legally in the name of the principal?	
(12) Does the person conclude contracts not legally in the name of the principal but still economically bounds the latter?	
(13) Is the person bound by detailed instructions or control?	
(14) Is the remuneration paid to the person standardized and mostly based on costs only?	
(15) Does the principal bear the complete loss risk with regard to the business activities conducted?	
(16) Is the person's business activities conducted at source related to solely or almost solely one principal?	
(17) Can the transactions between the person in the source country and the principal be considered as being at arm's length? ***	
(18) If the person is considered as being independent, does he only perform his own business activities (and not the business operations of the principal)?	

	Evaluation of PE Risk
Score: Questions (10)-(17) answered with 'yes'? = PE risk ↑ Question (18) answered with 'yes'? = PE risk ↓	
(D) Service PE: Secondment of Employees	
(19) Is personnel sent to another foreign company in order to perform specific business activities on-site?	
(20) Do the sent personnel still have a legal working contract with the workforce-lending company?	
(21) Is the remuneration of the sent personnel continued to be paid by the workforce-lending company?	
(22) Is the reimbursement payment paid by the host company where the sent personnel perform the business activities higher than the actual remuneration payment paid to the latter?	
(23) Does the reimbursement payment paid by the host company include a profit mark-up?	
(24) Can the workforce-lending company decide about the number of sent workers, the place of work, the nature of work or the amount of salary?	
(25) Do the sent personnel have to report their working results to the workforce-lending enterprise?	
(26) Does the workforce-lending company have a certain responsibility for the work performed by the sent personnel?	
(27) Are the domestic personal income taxes of the sent personnel (e.g., wage tax) correctly and fully reported to the tax authorities of the state in which the host company is located? ****	
Score: Questions (19)-(27) answered with 'yes'? = PE risk ↑	

* Among the countries under consideration, this exception is only relevant in Germany.

** Among the countries under consideration, a clear statement can only be given for Germany.

*** Among the countries under consideration, this counter-exception is mostly only relevant for India and China.

**** Among the countries under consideration, this requirement is mostly only relevant for China.

Considering the first five questions of part (A) of the checklist which deals with the PE requirement of disposal, the following conclusions can be drawn: If the first two questions are answered with '*yes*', the existence of a PE in the respective country is probable, given that the other PE requirements, such as habitualness and the exclusion of preparatory or auxiliary activities, are fulfilled. The reason is that the existence of a service PE provision in the respective tax treaty avoids the discussion about the disposal over a fixed place of business as this requirement is irrelevant for a service PE. Still, there also has to be a right to tax the services under domestic law. By considering the results of the analysis of the countries under consideration, only Germany does not grant a domestic taxing right for the inbound provision of services.[236] In case of a legal right to use the premises (question (3)), it is probable that the requirement of disposal over the fixed place of business is fulfilled for all countries under consideration.[237] In case there is only a formal right to use the third party premises (question (4)), countries like India, Russia and Brazil probably still determine a PE. Germany provides for a further requirement and considers the possibility of restriction of the service provider's activities at the third party premises as being decisive for the existence of a PE. So, how can the PE risk be avoided for foreign companies providing services at third party premises located in one of the countries under consideration? In fact, as the exception of question (5) is only relevant for Germany, a PE is probable in one of the other countries if the other four questions are answered with '*yes*'. In order to avoid insecurities, a company can follow a '*definitive*' approach and establish an own office in the country of source from which the services are provided. Given that the other PE requirements hold, a fixed place of business will thus be established for the foreign service provider without discussions about disposal over rooms of a third party. Otherwise, it is hard to avoid a PE in one of the countries under consideration solely based on the interpretation of the disposal requirement. Decisive PE factors are thus the time requirement or the qualification of the service activity as being preparatory. In Germany, it can be argued whether the right to use the place of business can be restricted by the client or anybody else. If this is the case, a PE will probably be neglected.[238] Therefore, in order to avoid the establishment of a PE in Germany, it has to be determined that the service provider has no exclusive right to use the premises. An example would be a '*neutral*' and changing workplace, such as a hotel room or premises for which the entry and usage is shared, embodied e.g., through a commonly shared key.

Part (B) of the checklist considers the case of delegation of work to subcontractors in case of a construction site established by the general contractor in a foreign country. If the first two questions (questions (6) and (7)) are answered with '*yes*' and the permanence threshold mentioned in the treaty under consideration is fulfilled, it can be concluded that a construction site PE is given for the general contractor in case of a partial delegation of work to subcontractors.[239] In general, most countries, except for Brazil, include a regulation that working time of the subcontractor shall be counted to the time of the general contractor for the identification of the time threshold. Thus, as long as the general contractor is physically present in the source country, the risk of establishing a construction site PE is given.[240] If all work is allocated to the subcontractor without being present at the construction site at all, the analysis showed that the establishment of a PE is not clear for all countries under consideration. Only in Germany, it can be concluded that a construction site PE is negated if the general contractor does not perform any business activities in the country of source on its own.

---

236. See section 4.2.1.1.
237. See section 5.2.1.
238. See section 4.2.1.1.
239. See section 5.2.2.
240. Of course, also for this PE case, the establishment of a PE is negated if the activities conducted at source have an auxiliary or preparatory character according to Article 5 (4) OECD MC.

For the other countries, it cannot be said whether the physical presence of the general contractor plays a role for the establishment of a construction site at source. Therefore, a certain PE risk still exists. In order to avoid a PE risk in the country of source in this case, a clear allocation and differentiation of tasks is recommendable. In this context, planning and design activities related to the construction can be exclusively conducted in the country of residence of the general contractor whereas active construction or further architectural work can be delegated to local subcontractors. Ideally, a presence of the general contractor in the country of source is avoided through this split of working activities. In addition, in order to circumvent the regulation of the OECD Reform Proposal, stating that a construction site PE might also be created in case of a total delegation of work to subcontractors if the general contractor has a necessary degree of disposal over the construction site, question (9) has to be answered with '*no*'.[241] Although this rule is not imposed by any country under consideration, companies bear no risk if access and use of the construction site cannot be effectively and exclusively controlled by the general contractor.

Part (C) of the checklist considers the risk of establishing an agency PE. Similar to the former cases, the PE requirement of habitualness and the PE-excluding qualification of the business activity as being preparatory are not considered here. Questions (10)-(12) consider the differentiation between legal and economic authority to conclude contracts as decisive PE criterion. In general, concluding contracts legally in the name of a foreign enterprise can be a PE indicator in all countries under consideration.[242] If the foreign enterprise is only economically bound, it can be derived from the analysis in section 5.2.3 that the establishment of an agency PE is nevertheless probable in the US and India. But also for the other countries, it is hard to draw a concrete conclusion with regard to the probability of the creation of an agency PE solely based on the evaluation of the authority to conclude contracts. Therefore, a PE risk cannot be excluded. More concrete indications are included in the questions (13)-(18) which deal with the independence criterion of the agent. Questions (13)-(16) ask for indicators of dependence with regard to the agent principal relationship, such as the extent of instructions and degree of control, the nature of the remuneration payment, the question of risk-bearing for losses and the number of principals. If these questions are all answered with '*yes*', there is a high probability that the agent is not considered as being independent which leads to the creation of an agency PE. This is the case for all countries under consideration. Question (17) includes a counter-exception which would re-qualify the dependent agent who acts solely for one or a few principals as still being independent if the transactions are at arm's length. However, this exception is only relevant for specific treaties of India and China.[243] In addition, the importance of the criterion of acting solely for one principal as being decisive for the question of independence is weakened in most treaties of the other countries under consideration which do not include this additional regulation. Still, according to the current OECD

241. See section 3.2.1.
242. See section 5.2.3.
243. See Appendix, Table A9 & Table A10.

BEPS report on Action 7, the importance of this requirement will increase.[244] Question (18) finally refers to a last independence test as formulated in Article 5 (6) of the OECD MC. If this question is answered with '*yes*', it can be concluded that the independent agent also conducts his own business and is not responsible for other operations of the principal.[245] The PE risk decreases. In order to avoid the risk of creating an agency PE through representations in foreign countries, companies have to focus on the aspect of independence of the agent. A profit-based variable salary, the allocation of business and loss risks to the agent, arm's length transactions and, ideally, a larger number of principals for whom the agent acts, are all indicators of independence so that a PE risk can be diminished.

Questions (19)-(27) of part (D) consider the PE risk in case of a secondment of employees by a workforce-lending company which work for a host company in the country of source. If the sent personnel provide services at or for the host company, question (2) which asks for the inclusion of a service PE provision in the respective tax treaty, becomes relevant again. If this question is answered with '*yes*', the probability of the creation of a PE is higher as a fixed place of business is not necessary to establish a fiscal nexus in the country of source. This also affects Germany which does not include a taxing right for the provision of services according to domestic law.[246] Therefore, it can be concluded that even if all questions of part (D) of the checklist are answered with '*yes*', the probability of a German PE is lower in comparison to the other countries where the provision of services is usually also taxable without the establishment of a fixed place of business.[247] Basically, all countries under consideration follow the economic employer concept so that a PE is established for the workforce-lending company if it is regarded as economic employer of the sent personnel.[248] The questions of part (D) thus cover detailed aspects of supervision, direction and control over the work of the seconded employees which signal the '*true*' economic employer, such as an inclusion of a profit mark-up upon the reimbursement payment to the workforce-lending company, the decision power upon the concrete working circumstances and regulations and the question of responsibility over the sent personnel's work. In fact, if all questions are answered with '*yes*', a PE risk exists as this implies that the workforce-lending company can be considered as economic employer. Question (27) is not relevant for all countries but refers to the specific secondment rules of China which apply a detailed but strict catalogue of factors which signal a PE at source.[249] In addition, India applies an indefinite concept of '*lien*' on employment which signals that the sent personnel keep the right to return to their former employment relationship with the workforce-lending company.[250] Therefore, it can be concluded that

244. See OECD Revised Discussion Draft BEPS Action 7 (2015) pp. 13 ff.
245. See OECD MC Commentary (2014) Article 5, No. 38.7, p. 110.
246. See section 4.2.1.1.
247. See section 5.3.1. In fact, the discussion in Germany is again related to the question of a necessary degree of disposal over the third party premises if PE questions come up.
248. See section 5.2.4. Only in Russia, the domestic migration law actually prevents the creation of a PE as seconded personnel without a legal working contract with the Russian host does not receive a working permit. See section 4.2.4.1.
249. See section 4.2.6.1.
250. See section 4.2.5.1.

irrespective from the answers of the checklist, an increased PE risk is given for secondments to Indian host companies. In order to reduce the PE risk for these cases, clear-cut working contracts are necessary so that the host company located in the country of source, and not the workforce-lending company, is considered as economic employer. Decisive indicators are a legal working contract between the sent personnel and the host, the exclusion of a profit mark-up upon the reimbursement payment (if the remuneration is continued to be paid by the workforce-lending company) as well as the allocation of decision power on working responsibilities, reporting requirements, supervision and control tasks to the sphere of the host company.

6.5 SUMMARIZED RECOMMENDATIONS

If it is accepted that the OECD regulations and proposals are considered as international guidance, the principle of single taxation and feasibility can be followed best by implementing an approach of harmonization. If all countries under consideration are in line with the OECD standards, the risk of interpretation conflicts with regard to the PE definition and the attribution of business profits is diminished. This demands harmonization and alignment to the OECD regulations on domestic and treaty level. In addition, this also means that countries such as the BRIC states have to implement the AOA including a recognition and valuation of internal dealings between head office and PE. Therefore, complexity will initially rise. In order to counteract and to make advances to the BRIC states, the AOA can be adapted by allowing the usage of safe harbour profit margins for the valuation of internal dealings. On the other hand, excessive domestic authorization and PE registration requirements of i.a. the BRIC states, have to be abolished as well.

In addition, also the OECD has to abolish rooms for interpretation with regard to specific PE requirements which are not included in the wording of the OECD MC. This includes a clarification and an inclusion of more detailed instructions considering the criterion of disposal over a fixed place of business, the delegation of work to subcontractors, the independence criterion of an agent and the economic employer concept relating to secondment of employees. With regard to the risk of double or non-taxation situations through the implementation of the AOA, it was derived that the MAP and the APA may be beneficial if compliance and administration efforts do not outweigh the costs of regular transfer pricing of internal dealings. Otherwise, those processes would rather be a costly reparation (MPA) or prevention (APA) and not a solution to the interpretation conflicts. A withholding tax on internal dealings as incentive for BRIC states to introduce the AOA cannot be recommended.

Instead, it has to be guaranteed that compliance and administration costs of the application of the AOA do not become larger than the tax base to be allocated. Against this background, a solution is to introduce a quantitative PE threshold or at least a quantitative threshold for the purposes of the application of the AOA. This ensures that non-substantial personal-based PEs as analysed in this work, such as service, subcontractor or agency PEs do not have to additionally implement a complex transfer pricing analysis as proposed by the AOA. In order to avoid double or non-taxation situations with regard to the PE definition, it can also be recommended to allocate the decision power upon the interpretation of specific PE requirements to the country of source in accordance with the OECD's '*new approach*'. Further fundamental changes of the tax system such as the introduction of a destination-based tax or a FA require a high degree of international cooperation and coordination and cannot be recommended. From a practical perspective, the problem of interpretation conflicts will remain and an increased amount of compliance and administration costs (including set-up costs) will occur.

If the reform proposals are not implemented and interpretation conflicts remain, a practical solution from the perspective of investing companies has to be found. Therefore, it is recommended to analyse planned business structures with the support of a checklist developed to avoid the risk of unintentionally constituting a PE in the country of investment.

CHAPTER 7
Final Conclusion in the Form of Theses

For cross-border business activities, the PE has two functions: the establishment of a taxing right in the country of source and the justification for the allocation of business profits between head office and PE. Both functions have to be considered simultaneously when analysing the PE concept.

With regard to the PE definition, the OECD MC follows a trend of enlargement. This can be concluded from the various proposals of the OECD Reform Proposal concerning the interpretation and application of Article 5 of the OECD MC from 2012 and the OECD BEPS report from 2014 to 2015 considering the prevention of the artificial avoidance of the PE status through commissionaire structures (Action Plan 7). Indicators of a widened OECD PE term are, in particular: the broad and discussable understanding of disposal over the fixed place of business, the proposal to establish a construction site PE for the total delegation of work to subcontractors, the vagueness with regard to the importance of the legal authority to conclude contracts and the introduction of an exception from the independent agent criterion in case of acting exclusively for connected enterprises, room for interpretation with regard to the understanding of the concept of economic employer as well as the introduction of an optional service PE alternative.

With regard to the attribution of business profits, there is no clear tendency to be concluded from the OECD proposals. The OECD MC favours the AOA as standard for the allocation of business profits which includes a functional analysis based on significant people and risk allocation as well as the recognition and arm's length valuation of internal dealings between head office and PE. As these internal dealings can flow in both directions, it cannot be concluded if source or residence taxing rights are diminished. Still, the AOA is mostly favoured by capital-exporting industrialized states which can be an indicator for a disposition towards increased taxing rights in the residence country of the head office.

The OECD thus strives for two different tax policies: an enlargement of source taxation rights considering the PE definition and at least an unclear direction considering the rules on attribution of business profits.

Due to the rising influence in OECD decision-making processes and the increasing economic importance, it is comprehensible to take into account the BRIC states besides the traditional industrialized OECD members of Germany and the US when comparing the national PE statutes with the OECD regulations.

The comparison of the national and country-specific treaty law with regard to basic and special PE cases, such as the construction site, the agency and the service PE indicates that there are considerable differences between the current OECD MC policy and the national PE standards. With regard to the PE definition, it was derived that the OECD MC standards and proposals have more in common with the treaty regulations of India and China which both show indicators of an increased source taxing right. In contrast, Germany follows a conservative approach. No clear trend-inducing indicators exist for the US and Russia. Brazil's source taxation provisions focus more on withholding taxation on a gross basis than on the PE concept as fiscal nexus.

With regard to the allocation of business profits, Brazil, China and India do not adopt the AOA and show indicators of an increased source tax base. Russia, the US and Germany, however, accept the AOA as basis for the allocation of business profits. Germany has already implemented the AOA in domestic law as well.

Based on the results of the country comparison, the subsequent analysis derives to what extent qualification conflicts can occur in the countries under consideration with regard to the PE definition and the attribution of business profits. The focus is on qualification conflicts which arise due to unclear and discussable PE requirements and differences with regard to the deduction of internal dealings from the PE tax base.

In the analysis, simulated cross-border inbound cases are taken into account in which an enterprise being resident in a fictitious OECD state conducts business activities in one of the countries under consideration (DE, US, BRIC). The focus is on special PE requirements which offer room for interpretation, such as the provision of services in third party premises, the delegation of work to subcontractors, the representation through dependent commission agents, the secondment of employees and the existence of an internal royalty payment from the PE to the foreign head office.

With regard to the cases considering the PE definition, it can be concluded that the lowest probability of conflicts with an OECD country would arise for the US and India as country of source. Still, for India, in most cases, there is a tendency towards a broader interpretation whereas for Germany, vice versa, the interpretation of the PE cases is stricter. Double or non-taxation situations due to conflicts and misunderstandings are thus still given for India and even more for Germany. For Brazil, Russia and China, concrete conclusions are hard to be drawn for many cases due to a lack of information in domestic tax statutes or treaty-related case law.

With regard to the deduction and valuation of internal dealings, the probability of conflicts is lowest for Germany and the US as both follow the AOA. For the BRIC states, insecurities and possible double or non-taxation situations are more probable.

When considering the rules on the allocation of business profits to special PE cases, such as the construction site, agency and service PE, the results above can eventually be modified. If it is assumed that the PE profit to be allocated for the non-substantial PE cases of the analysis is not significant, double or non-taxation situations are not existent. In fact, this can occur for the cases of a construction site PE through subcontractors and an agency PE. Therefore, from the viewpoint of an investing company, administrative and compliance efforts of a PE creation might be more problematic than double taxation risks.

Formal requirements of the establishment of a PE in the country of source can lead to an increased amount of administration and compliance costs, such as cost for registration, authorization and regular accounting. Especially the BRIC states require high compliance efforts and penalties for late registration which are not in line with the concept of feasibility and simplicity. In addition, if those countries implement the AOA, complexity will rise due to the application of a functional analysis and the recognition of internal dealings.

Formulated reform proposals shall be based on prevailing general tax criteria, namely the principle of single taxation and the requirement of feasibility, simplicity and transparency of taxation. One intuitive reform proposal is to follow the concept of harmonization. Therefore, the countries under consideration have to accept the OECD MC as international guidance and adapt their country-specific PE requirements and business profit allocation rules. This also means that the BRIC states have to follow the AOA so that administration and compliance costs will rise. A solution is to allow safe harbour profit margins for the valuation of specific internal dealings. Due to the complexity of the transfer pricing regulations, an all-encompassing solution does not exist for the problem of the arm's length valuation of internal dealings.

Fundamental reforms of the corporate tax systems, such as the destination-based tax or a FA are not recommended as it cannot be derived if the conflicts shown in the analysis will be solved. In addition, from a practical perspective, further factors of insecurity are the high degree of cooperation and the considerable set-up costs.

Instead, the reforms have to be based on the status quo. Therefore, the OECD MC has to improve its regulations and has to clarify the discussable PE requirements. In addition, it has to be ensured that the costs of applying the AOA do not outweigh the PE tax base. In this context, a solution is to introduce a quantitative PE threshold which functions as fiscal nexus or at least as limit for the application of the AOA. This is in line with the principle of single taxation and the concept of feasibility.

Appendices

APPENDIX I

Supplementary Tables

The treaties included in this chapter are all tax treaties with respect to taxes on income and capital. They are all effective or will enter into force by and by (Status: November 2015). The tables are based on own research taken from the International Bureau of Fiscal Documentation (IBFD) Tax Research Platform (2015) and the respective websites of the tax authorities of the countries under consideration.

See for Germany: http://www.bundesfinanzministerium.de/Content/DE/Downloads/BMF_Schreiben/Internationales_Steuerrecht/Allgemeine_Informationen/2015-01-19-stand-DBA-1-Januar-2015.html

For the US:
http://www.irs.gov/Businesses/International-Businesses/United-States-Income-Tax-Treaties---A-to-Z

For Brazil:
http://idg.receita.fazenda.gov.br/acesso-rapido/legislacao/acordos-internacionais/acordos-para-evitar-a-dupla-tributacao-1/acordos-para-evitar-a-dupla-tributacao

For Russia:
http://www.nalog.ru/eng/international_cooperation/dta/

For India:
http://www.incometaxindia.gov.in/Pages/international-taxation/treaty-comparison.aspx

For China:
http://www.chinatax.gov.cn/2013/n2925/n2955/index.html

(Access: 04.12.2015)

Table I.1 Fiscal Treatment of Services in German Tax Treaties

Tax Treaty of Germany With	*Existence of Service PE Provision*	*Inclusion of Services in the Royalty-Article*
Albania	No	No
Algeria	No	No
Argentina	No	No
Armenia	No	No
Australia	No	No
Austria	No	No
Azerbaijan	No	No
Bangladesh	No	No
Belarus	No	No
Belgium	No	No
Bolivia	No	No
Bosnia & Herzegovina	No	No
Bulgaria	No	No
Canada	No	No
China	Yes	No
Croatia	No	No
Cyprus	No	No
Czech Republic	No	No
Denmark	No	No
Ecuador	No	No
Egypt	No	No
Estonia	No	No
Finland	No	No
France	No	No
Georgia	No	No
Ghana	No	Yes
Greece	No	No
Hungary	No	No
Iceland	No	No
India	No	Yes
Indonesia	No	Yes
Iran	No	No
Ireland	No	No
Israel	No	No
Italy	No	No
Ivory Coast	No	No

Tax Treaty of Germany With	*Existence of Service PE Provision*	*Inclusion of Services in the Royalty-Article*
Jamaica	No	No
Japan	No	No
Kazakhstan	No	No
Kenya	No	Yes
Korea	No	No
Kuwait	No	No
Kyrgyzstan	No	No
Latvia	No	No
Liberia	Yes	No
Liechtenstein	No	No
Lithuania	No	No
Luxemburg	No	No
Macedonia	No	No
Malaysia	No	Yes
Malta	No	No
Mauritius	No	No
Mexico	No	No
Moldova	No	No
Mongolia	No	No
Morocco	No	No
Namibia	No	No
Netherlands	No	No
New Zealand	No	No
Norway	No	No
Pakistan	No	Yes
Philippines	Yes	No
Poland	No	No
Portugal	No	No
Romania	No	No
Russia	No	No
Serbia & Montenegro	No	No
Singapore	No	No
Slovak Republic	No	No
Slovenia	No	No
South Africa	No*	No
Spain	No	No
Sri Lanka	No	No
Sweden	No	No

Tax Treaty of Germany With	*Existence of Service PE Provision*	*Inclusion of Services in the Royalty-Article*
Switzerland	No	No
Syria	No	No
Taiwan	Yes	No
Tajikistan	No	No
Thailand	No	No
Trinidad & Tobago	No	No
Tunisia	No	No
Turkey	Yes	No
Turkmenistan	No	No
Ukraine	No	No
United Arab Emirates	No	No
United Kingdom	No	No
United States	No	No
Uruguay	No	No
Uzbekistan	No	No
Venezuela	No	No
Vietnam	No	Yes
Zambia	No	No
Zimbabwe	No	Yes
Sum	**94**	
Thereof 'Yes'	**5**	**8**
Percentage ('Yes')	***5.32%***	***8.51%***

Source: Own composition.

* The PE definition of the tax treaty from 2008 (not yet in force) also includes the performance of professional services.

Table I.2 Fiscal Treatment of Services in US Tax Treaties

Tax Treaty of the United States With	*Existence of Service PE Provision*	*Inclusion of Services in the Royalty-Article*
Armenia	No	Yes
Australia	No	No
Austria	No	No
Azerbaijan	No	No
Bangladesh	No	No
Barbados	No	No
Belarus	No	No
Belgium	No	No

Tax Treaty of the United States With	*Existence of Service PE Provision*	*Inclusion of Services in the Royalty-Article*
Bulgaria	No	No
Canada	No	No
China	Yes	No
Cyprus	No	No
Czech Republic	Yes	No
Denmark	No	No
Egypt	No	No
Estonia	No	No
Finland	No	No
France	No	No
Georgia	No	Yes
Germany	No	No
Greece	No	No
Hungary	No	No
Iceland	No	No
India	Yes	Yes
Indonesia	Yes	No
Ireland	No	No
Israel	No	No
Italy	No	No
Jamaica	Yes	No
Japan	No	No
Kazakhstan	Yes	No
Korea	No	No
Kyrgyzstan	No	Yes
Latvia	No	No
Lithuania	No	No
Luxembourg	No	No
Malta	No	No
Mexico	No	No
Moldova	No	No
Morocco	No	No
Netherlands	No	No
New Zealand	No	No
Norway	No	No
Pakistan	No	No
Philippines	Yes	No
Poland	No	No

Tax Treaty of the United States With	*Existence of Service PE Provision*	*Inclusion of Services in the Royalty-Article*
Portugal	No	Yes
Romania	No	No
Russia	No	No
Slovak Republic	Yes	No
Slovenia	No	No
South Africa	Yes	No
Spain	No	No
Sri Lanka	Yes	No
Sweden	No	No
Switzerland	No	No
Tajikistan	No	No
Thailand	Yes	No
Trinidad & Tobago	No	No
Tunisia	No	No
Turkey	No	No
Turkmenistan	No	No
Ukraine	No	No
United Kingdom	No	No
Uzbekistan	No	No
Venezuela	Yes	No
Sum	**66**	
Thereof ('Yes')	**12**	**5**
Percentage ('Yes')	***18.18%***	***7.58%***

Source: Own composition.

Table I.3 Fiscal Treatment of Services in Brazilian Tax Treaties

Tax Treaty of Brazil With	*Existence of Service PE Provision*	*Inclusion of Services in the Royalty-Article*
Argentina	No	No
Austria	No	No
Belgium	No	No
Canada	No	No
Chile	No	No
China	Yes	No
Czech Republic	No	No
Denmark	No	No

Tax Treaty of Brazil With	*Existence of Service PE Provision*	*Inclusion of Services in the Royalty-Article*
Ecuador	No	No
Finland	No	No
France	No	No
Hungary	No	No
India	No	No
Israel	No	No
Italy	No	No
Japan	No	No
Korea	No	No
Luxembourg	No	No
Mexico	No	No
Netherlands	No	No
Norway	No	No
Peru	No	No
Philippines	No	No
Portugal	No	No
Slovak Republic	No	No
South Africa	No	No
Spain	No	No
Sweden	No	No
Trinidad & Tobago	No	No
Turkey	No	No
Ukraine	No	No
Venezuela	No	No
Sum	**32**	
Thereof 'Yes'	**1**	**0**
Percentage ('Yes')	***3.13%***	***0.00%***

Source: Own composition.

Table I.4 Fiscal Treatment of Services in Russian Tax Treaties

Tax Treaty of Russia With	*Existence of Service PE Provision*	*Inclusion of Services in the Royalty-Article*
Albania	No	No
Algeria	Yes	No
Argentina	Yes	No
Armenia	Yes	No

Tax Treaty of Russia With	*Existence of Service PE Provision*	*Inclusion of Services in the Royalty-Article*
Australia	No	No
Austria	No	No
Azerbaijan	No	No
Belarus	No	No
Belgium	No	No
Botswana	Yes	No
Bulgaria	No	Yes
Canada	No	No
Chile	Yes	No
China	Yes	No
Croatia	Yes	No
Cuba	Yes	No
Cyprus	No	No
Czech Republic	Yes	No
Denmark	No	No
Egypt	Yes	No
Finland	No	No
France	No	No
Germany	No	No
Greece	No	No
Hungary	No	No
Iceland	No	No
India	No	Yes
Indonesia	Yes	No
Iran	No	No
Ireland	No	No
Israel	No	No
Italy	No	No
Japan	No	No
Kazakhstan	Yes	No
Korea (Dem. People's Rep.)	Yes	No
Korea (Rep.)	No	No
Kuwait	Yes	No
Kyrgyzstan	Yes	No
Latvia	No	No
Lebanon	No	No
Lithuania	No	No

Tax Treaty of Russia With	*Existence of Service PE Provision*	*Inclusion of Services in the Royalty-Article*
Luxembourg	No	No
Macedonia	No	No
Malaysia	No	No
Mali	No	No
Malta	Yes	No
Mexico	No	No
Moldova	No	No
Mongolia	No	No
Morocco	No	No
Namibia	Yes	No
Netherlands	No	No
New Zealand	No	No
Norway	No	No
Philippines	Yes	No
Poland	No	No
Portugal	No	No
Qatar	No	No
Romania	No	No
Saudi Arabia	Yes	No
Serbia & Montenegro	No	No
Singapore	Yes	No
Slovak Republic	No	No
Slovenia	No	No
South Africa	No	No
Spain	No	No
Sri Lanka	Yes	No
Sweden	No	No
Switzerland	No	No
Syria	No	No
Tajikistan	No	No
Thailand	Yes	No
Turkey	No	No
Turkmenistan	No	No
Ukraine	No	No
United Kingdom	No	No
United States	No	No
Uzbekistan	No	No
Venezuela	No	Yes

Tax Treaty of Russia With	*Existence of Service PE Provision*	*Inclusion of Services in the Royalty-Article*
Vietnam	Yes	No
Sum	**80**	
Thereof 'Yes'	**21**	**3**
Percentage ('Yes')	***26.25%***	***3.75%***

Source: Own composition.

Table I.5 Fiscal Treatment of Services in Indian Tax Treaties

Tax Treaty of India With	*Existence of Service PE Provision*	*Inclusion of Services in the Royalty-Article*
Albania	Yes	Yes
Armenia	No	Yes
Australia	Yes	Yes
Austria	No	Yes
Azerbaijan	No	Yes
Bangladesh	No	No
Belarus	No	Yes
Belgium	No	Yes
Botswana	Yes	Yes
Bhutan	Yes	Yes
Brazil	No	No
Bulgaria	No	Yes
Canada	Yes	Yes
China	Yes	Yes
Colombia	Yes	Yes
Croatia	No	Yes
Cyprus	No	Yes
Czech Republic	No	Yes
Denmark	No	Yes
Egypt	No	No
Estonia	Yes	Yes
Ethiopia	Yes	Yes
Faroe Islands	No	Yes
Fiji	Yes	Yes
Finland	Yes	Yes
France	No	Yes
Georgia	Yes	Yes

Tax Treaty of India With	*Existence of Service PE Provision*	*Inclusion of Services in the Royalty-Article*
Germany	No	Yes
Greece	No	No
Hungary	No	Yes
Iceland	Yes	Yes
Indonesia	No	No
Ireland	No	Yes
Israel	No	Yes
Italy	No	Yes
Japan	No	Yes
Jordan	No	Yes
Kazakhstan	No	Yes
Kenya	No	Yes
Korea	No	Yes
Kuwait	Yes	Yes
Kyrgyzstan	No	Yes
Latvia	Yes	Yes
Libya	No	No
Lithuania	Yes	Yes
Luxembourg	Yes	Yes
Malaysia	Yes	Yes
Malta	Yes	Yes
Mauritius	No	No
Mexico	Yes	Yes
Moldova	No	Yes
Mongolia	No	Yes
Morocco	No	Yes
Mozambique	Yes	No
Myanmar	No	No
Namibia	Yes	Yes
Nepal	Yes	No
Netherlands	No	Yes
New Zealand	No	Yes
Norway	Yes	Yes
Oman	No	Yes
Philippines	No	No
Poland	No	Yes
Portugal	No	Yes
Qatar	No	Yes

Tax Treaty of India With	*Existence of Service PE Provision*	*Inclusion of Services in the Royalty-Article*
Romania	No	Yes
Russia	No	Yes
Saudi Arabia	Yes	No
Serbia & Montenegro	No	Yes
Singapore	Yes	Yes
Slovak Republic	No	Yes
Slovenia	No	Yes
South Africa	No	Yes
Spain	No	Yes
Sri Lanka	Yes	No
Sudan	No	Yes
Sweden	No	Yes
Switzerland	Yes	Yes
Syria	Yes	No
Taiwan	Yes	Yes
Tajikistan	No	No
Tanzania	Yes	No
Thailand	Yes	No
Trinidad & Tobago	No	Yes
Turkey	No	Yes
Turkmenistan	No	Yes
Uganda	No	Yes
Ukraine	No	Yes
United Arab Emirates	Yes	No
United Kingdom	Yes	Yes
United States	Yes	Yes
Uruguay	Yes	Yes
Uzbekistan	No	Yes
Vietnam	No	Yes
Zambia	No	Yes
Sum	**95**	
Thereof 'Yes'	**36**	**77**
Percentage ('Yes')	***37.89%***	***81.05%***

Source: Own composition.

Table I.6 Fiscal Treatment of Services in Chinese Tax Treaties

Tax Treaty of China With	*Existence of Service PE Provision*	*Inclusion of Services in the Royalty-Article*
Albania	Yes	No
Algeria	No	No
Armenia	Yes	No
Australia	Yes	No
Austria	Yes	No
Azerbaijan	Yes	No
Bahrain	No	No
Bangladesh	Yes	No
Barbados	Yes	No
Belarus	Yes	No
Belgium	Yes	No
Bosnia & Herzegovina	Yes	No
Botswana	Yes	Yes
Brazil	Yes	No
Brunei	Yes	No
Bulgaria	Yes	No
Canada	Yes	No
Chile	Yes	No
Croatia	Yes	No
Cuba	Yes	No
Cyprus	Yes	No
Czech Republic	Yes	No
Denmark	Yes	No
Ecuador	Yes	No
Egypt	Yes	No
Estonia	No	No
Ethiopia	No	No
Finland	Yes	No
France	Yes	No
Georgia	No	No
Germany	Yes	No
Greece	No	No
Hong Kong	Yes	No
Hungary	Yes	No
Iceland	Yes	No

Tax Treaty of China With	*Existence of Service PE Provision*	*Inclusion of Services in the Royalty-Article*
India	Yes	Yes
Indonesia	Yes	No
Iran	No	No
Ireland	No	No
Israel	Yes	No
Italy	Yes	No
Jamaica	Yes	No
Japan	No	No
Kazakhstan	Yes	No
Korea	Yes	No
Kuwait	Yes	No
Kyrgyzstan	Yes	No
Laos	No	No
Latvia	No	No
Lithuania	No	No
Luxembourg	Yes	No
Macau	Yes	No
Macedonia	No	No
Malaysia	Yes	No
Malta	Yes	No
Mauritius	Yes	No
Mexico	No	No
Moldova	No	No
Mongolia	Yes	No
Morocco	Yes	No
Nepal	Yes	No
Netherlands	Yes	No
New Zealand	Yes	No
Nigeria	No	No
Norway	Yes	No
Oman	Yes	No
Pakistan	No	No
Papua New Guinea	Yes	No
Philippines	Yes	No
Poland	Yes	No
Portugal	Yes	No
Qatar	No	No
Romania	Yes	No

Tax Treaty of China With	*Existence of Service PE Provision*	*Inclusion of Services in the Royalty-Article*
Russia	Yes	No
Saudi Arabia	Yes	No
Serbia & Montenegro	No	No
Seychelles	Yes	No
Singapore	Yes	No
Slovak Republic	Yes	No
Slovenia	Yes	No
South Africa	Yes	No
Spain	Yes	No
Sri Lanka	Yes	No
Sudan	Yes	No
Sweden	Yes	No
Switzerland	Yes	No
Syria	No	No
Tajikistan	Yes	No
Thailand	Yes	No
Trinidad & Tobago	Yes	No
Tunisia	No	No
Turkey	Yes	No
Turkmenistan	Yes	No
Uganda	Yes	No
Ukraine	Yes	No
United Arab Emirates	Yes	No
United Kingdom	Yes	No
United States	Yes	No
Uzbekistan	No	No
Venezuela	No	No
Vietnam	Yes	No
Zambia	Yes	No
Sum	**102**	
Thereof 'Yes'	**79**	**2**
Percentage ('Yes')	***77.45%***	***1.96%***

Source: Own composition.

Table I.7 Inclusion of Supervisory Activities in the Construction Site PE Provision of Indian Tax Treaties

Tax Treaty of India With	*Supervisory Activity Included in the Construction Site PE Provision*
Albania	Yes
Armenia	Yes
Australia	Yes
Austria	Yes
Azerbaijan	Yes
Bangladesh	No
Belarus	Yes
Belgium	Yes
Bhutan	Yes
Botswana	Yes
Brazil	No
Bulgaria	Yes
Canada	Yes
China	Yes
Colombia	Yes
Croatia	Yes
Cyprus	Yes
Czech Republic	Yes
Denmark	Yes
Egypt	No
Estonia	Yes
Ethiopia	Yes
Faroe Islands	Yes
Fiji	Yes
Finland	Yes
France	No
Georgia	Yes
Germany	Yes
Greece	No
Hungary	Yes
Iceland	Yes
Indonesia	Yes
Ireland	Yes
Israel	Yes
Italy	Yes

Tax Treaty of India With	*Supervisory Activity Included in the Construction Site PE Provision*
Japan	No
Jordan	Yes
Kazakhstan	Yes
Kenya	No
Korea	Yes
Kuwait	Yes
Kyrgyzstan	Yes
Latvia	Yes
Libya	No
Lithuania	Yes
Luxembourg	Yes
Malaysia	Yes
Malta	Yes
Mauritius	Yes
Mexico	Yes
Moldova	Yes
Mongolia	Yes
Morocco	Yes
Mozambique	Yes
Myanmar	Yes
Namibia	Yes
Nepal	Yes
Netherlands	No
New Zealand	Yes
Norway	Yes
Oman	Yes
Philippines	Yes
Poland	Yes
Portugal	Yes
Qatar	Yes
Romania	Yes
Russia	Yes
Saudi Arabia	Yes
Serbia & Montenegro	Yes
Singapore	No
Slovak Republic	Yes
Slovenia	No
South Africa	No

Tax Treaty of India With	*Supervisory Activity Included in the Construction Site PE Provision*
Spain	Yes
Sri Lanka	No
Sudan	Yes
Sweden	Yes
Switzerland	Yes
Syria	Yes
Taiwan	Yes
Tajikistan	Yes
Tanzania	Yes
Thailand	Yes
Trinidad & Tobago	Yes
Turkey	Yes
Turkmenistan	Yes
Uganda	Yes
Ukraine	Yes
United Arab Emirates	Yes
United Kingdom	Yes
United States	Yes
Uruguay	Yes
Uzbekistan	Yes
Vietnam	Yes
Zambia	Yes
Sum	**95**
Thereof 'Yes'	**81**
Percentage ('Yes')	***85.26%***

Source: Own composition.

Table I.8 Inclusion of Supervisory Activities in the Construction Site PE Provision of Chinese Tax Treaties

Tax Treaty of China With	*Supervisory Activity Included in the Construction Site PE Provision*
Albania	Yes
Algeria	No
Armenia	Yes
Australia	Yes
Austria	Yes

Tax Treaty of China With	*Supervisory Activity Included in the Construction Site PE Provision*
Azerbaijan	Yes
Bahrain	Yes
Bangladesh	Yes
Barbados	Yes
Belarus	Yes
Belgium	Yes
Bosnia & Herzegovina	No
Botswana	Yes
Brazil	Yes
Brunei	Yes
Bulgaria	Yes
Canada	Yes
Chile	Yes
Croatia	Yes
Cuba	Yes
Cyprus	Yes
Czech Republic	Yes
Denmark	Yes
Ecuador	Yes
Egypt	Yes
Estonia	Yes
Ethiopia	No
Finland	Yes
France	Yes
Georgia	No
Germany	Yes
Greece	Yes
Hong Kong	Yes
Hungary	Yes
Iceland	Yes
India	Yes
Indonesia	Yes
Iran	Yes
Ireland	No
Israel	Yes
Italy	Yes
Jamaica	Yes
Japan	Yes

Tax Treaty of China With	*Supervisory Activity Included in the Construction Site PE Provision*
Kazakhstan	Yes
Korea	Yes
Kuwait	Yes
Kyrgyzstan	Yes
Laos	Yes
Latvia	Yes
Lithuania	Yes
Luxembourg	Yes
Macau	Yes
Macedonia	Yes
Malaysia	Yes
Malta	Yes
Mauritius	Yes
Mexico	Yes
Moldova	Yes
Mongolia	Yes
Morocco	Yes
Nepal	Yes
Netherlands	Yes
New Zealand	Yes
Nigeria	Yes
Norway	Yes
Oman	Yes
Pakistan	Yes
Papua New Guinea	Yes
Philippines	Yes
Poland	Yes
Portugal	Yes
Qatar	Yes
Romania	Yes
Russia	Yes
Saudi Arabia	Yes
Serbia & Montenegro	Yes
Seychelles	Yes
Singapore	Yes
Slovak Republic	Yes
Slovenia	Yes
South Africa	Yes

Tax Treaty of China With	*Supervisory Activity Included in the Construction Site PE Provision*
Spain	Yes
Sri Lanka	Yes
Sudan	Yes
Sweden	Yes
Switzerland	Yes
Syria	Yes
Tajikistan	Yes
Thailand	Yes
Trinidad & Tobago	Yes
Tunisia	Yes
Turkey	Yes
Turkmenistan	Yes
Uganda	Yes
Ukraine	Yes
United Arab Emirates	Yes
United Kingdom	Yes
United States	Yes
Uzbekistan	Yes
Venezuela	Yes
Vietnam	Yes
Zambia	Yes
Sum	**102**
Thereof 'Yes'	**97**
Percentage ('Yes')	***95.10%***

Source: Own composition.

Table I.9 Fiscal Treatment of the Independent Agent Provision in Indian Tax Treaties

Tax Treaty of India With	*Wording of Independent Agent Provision Resembles OECD MC*	*Wording of Independent Agent Provision Resembles UN MC (Including Independent Agent Exception of Acting Solely for One Principal)*	*Inclusion of Counter-Exception to Independent Agent Criterion (Transactions Follow Arm's Length Principle)*
Albania		x	No
Armenia		x	No

Tax Treaty of India With	*Wording of Independent Agent Provision Resembles OECD MC*	*Wording of Independent Agent Provision Resembles UN MC (Including Independent Agent Exception of Acting Solely for One Principal)*	*Inclusion of Counter-Exception to Independent Agent Criterion (Transactions Follow Arm's Length Principle)*
Australia		x	No
Austria		x	No
Azerbaijan	x		
Bangladesh		x	No
Belarus		x	No
Belgium		x	No
Bhutan		x	No
Botswana		x	No
Brazil		x	No
Bulgaria	x		
Canada		x	Yes
China		x	No
Colombia		x	No
Croatia		x	No
Cyprus		x	No
Czech Republic		x	No
Denmark		x	No
Egypt	x		No
Estonia		x	No
Ethiopia		x	No
Faroe Islands		x	No
Fiji		x	No
Finland		x	No
France		x	Yes
Georgia		x	No
Germany		x	Yes
Greece		x	No
Hungary		x	No
Iceland		x	No
Indonesia		x	No
Ireland		x	Yes
Israel		x	Yes
Italy		x	No
Japan	x		

Tax Treaty of India With	*Wording of Independent Agent Provision Resembles OECD MC*	*Wording of Independent Agent Provision Resembles UN MC (Including Independent Agent Exception of Acting Solely for One Principal)*	*Inclusion of Counter-Exception to Independent Agent Criterion (Transactions Follow Arm's Length Principle)*
Jordan		x	No
Kazakhstan		x	No
Kenya		x	No
Korea	x		
Kuwait		x	No
Kyrgyzstan		x	No
Latvia		x	Yes
Libya	x		
Lithuania		x	No
Luxembourg		x	No
Malaysia		x	Yes
Malta		x	No
Mauritius		x	No
Mexico		x	Yes
Moldova	x		
Mongolia		x	No
Morocco		x	No
Mozambique		x	No
Myanmar		x	No
Namibia		x	No
Nepal		x	No
Netherlands		x	Yes
New Zealand	x		
Norway		x	Yes
Oman	x		
Philippines		x	Yes
Poland		x	No
Portugal	x		
Qatar		x	No
Romania		x	No
Russia		x	No
Saudi Arabia		x	No
Serbia & Montenegro		x	No

Tax Treaty of India With	*Wording of Independent Agent Provision Resembles OECD MC*	*Wording of Independent Agent Provision Resembles UN MC (Including Independent Agent Exception of Acting Solely for One Principal)*	*Inclusion of Counter-Exception to Independent Agent Criterion (Transactions Follow Arm's Length Principle)*
Singapore		x	No
Slovak Republic	x		
Slovenia		x	Yes
South Africa	x		
Spain		x	No
Sri Lanka		x	No
Sudan		x	No
Sweden		x	No
Switzerland		x	No
Syria		x	No
Taiwan		x	No
Tajikistan		x	No
Tanzania		x	No
Thailand		x	No
Trinidad & Tobago		x	No
Turkey	x		
Turkmenistan		x	No
Uganda		x	No
Ukraine		x	No
United Arab Emirates		x	No
United Kingdom		x	No
United States		x	Yes
Uruguay		x	No
Uzbekistan		x	No
Vietnam		x	No
Zambia		x	No
Sum	**95**		
Thereof	**13**	**81**	**13**
Percentage	***13.68%***	***85.26%***	***13.68%***

Source: Own composition.

Table I.10 Fiscal Treatment of the Independent Agent Provision in Chinese Tax Treaties

Tax Treaty of China With	*Wording of Independent Agent Provision Resembles OECD MC*	*Wording of Independent Agent Provision Resembles UN MC (Including Independent Agent Exception of Acting Solely for One Principal)*	*Inclusion of Counter-Exception to Independent Agent Criterion (Transactions Follow Arm's Length Principle)*
Albania		x	No
Algeria	x		
Armenia		x	No
Australia		x	No
Austria		x	No
Azerbaijan		x	Yes
Bahrain		x	No
Bangladesh		x	No
Barbados		x	No
Belarus	x		
Belgium		x	No
Bosnia & Herzegovina		x	No
Botswana	x		
Brazil		x	No
Brunei		x	No
Bulgaria	x		
Canada		x	No
Chile*		x	No
Croatia		x	No
Cuba		x	No
Cyprus	x		
Czech Republic	x		
Denmark		x	Yes
Ecuador	x		
Egypt		x	No
Estonia		x	No
Ethiopia		x	No
Finland		x	No
France		x	Yes
Georgia	x		
Germany	x		

Tax Treaty of China With	*Wording of Independent Agent Provision Resembles OECD MC*	*Wording of Independent Agent Provision Resembles UN MC (Including Independent Agent Exception of Acting Solely for One Principal)*	*Inclusion of Counter-Exception to Independent Agent Criterion (Transactions Follow Arm's Length Principle)*
Greece		x	No
Hong Kong		x	No
Hungary		x	No
Iceland		x	No
India		x	No
Indonesia		x	No
Iran		x	No
Ireland		x	Yes
Israel		x	No
Italy		x	No
Jamaica		x	No
Japan	x		
Kazakhstan		x	No
Korea		x	No
Kuwait		x	No
Kyrgyzstan		x	No
Laos		x	No
Latvia		x	No
Lithuania		x	No
Luxembourg		x	No
Macau		x	No
Macedonia		x	No
Malaysia		x	No
Malta		x	Yes
Mauritius		x	No
Mexico	x		
Moldova		x	No
Mongolia		x	No
Morocco		x	Yes
Nepal		x	No
Netherlands		x	Yes
New Zealand		x	No
Nigeria		x	Yes
Norway	x		

Tax Treaty of China With	*Wording of Independent Agent Provision Resembles OECD MC*	*Wording of Independent Agent Provision Resembles UN MC (Including Independent Agent Exception of Acting Solely for One Principal)*	*Inclusion of Counter-Exception to Independent Agent Criterion (Transactions Follow Arm's Length Principle)*
Oman		x	No
Pakistan		x	No
Papua New Guinea	x		
Philippines	x		
Poland		x	No
Portugal	x		
Qatar	x		
Romania	x		
Russia		x	No
Saudi Arabia		x	No
Serbia & Montenegro	x		
Seychelles		x	No
Singapore		x	Yes
Slovak Republic		x	No
Slovenia	x		
South Africa	x		
Spain		x	Yes
Sri Lanka		x	No
Sudan		x	No
Sweden		x	No
Switzerland		x	No
Syria		x	No
Tajikistan	x		
Thailand		x	No
Trinidad & Tobago		x	No
Tunisia		x	No
Turkey	x		
Turkmenistan		x	No
Uganda		x	No
Ukraine	x		
United Arab Emirates		x	No

Tax Treaty of China With	Wording of Independent Agent Provision Resembles OECD MC	Wording of Independent Agent Provision Resembles UN MC (Including Independent Agent Exception of Acting Solely for One Principal)	Inclusion of Counter-Exception to Independent Agent Criterion (Transactions Follow Arm's Length Principle)
United Kingdom		x	Yes
United States		x	Yes
Uzbekistan		x	No
Venezuela		x	No
Vietnam		x	No
Zambia	x		
Sum	**102**		
Thereof	**24**	**78**	**12**
Percentage	***23.53%***	***76.47%***	***11.76%***

Source: Own composition.

* The tax treaty between China and Chile (conclusion date 25 May 2015; not yet in force) resembles the wording of the OECD proposal with regard to changes to Article 5 (6). See OECD BEPS Final Report Action 7 (2015) pp. 16 f.

Table I.11 Fiscal Treatment of the Other Income Provision in Brazilian Tax Treaties

Tax Treaty of Brazil With	Other Income Provision Resembles OECD MC (Taxing Right Allocated to Residence Country)	Other Income Provision Resembles UN MC (Taxing Right Allocated to Both Countries)
Argentina		x
Austria		x
Belgium		x
Canada		x
Chile		x
China		x
Czech Republic		x
Denmark		x
Ecuador		x
Finland		x
France*		
Hungary		x
India		x

Tax Treaty of Brazil With	*Other Income Provision Resembles OECD MC (Taxing Right Allocated to Residence Country)*	*Other Income Provision Resembles UN MC (Taxing Right Allocated to Both Countries)*
Israel		x
Italy		x
Japan		x
Korea		x
Luxembourg		x
Mexico		x
Netherlands		x
Norway		x
Peru		x
Philippines		x
Portugal		x
Slovak Republic		x
South Africa		x
Spain		x
Sweden		x
Trinidad & Tobago		x
Turkey		x
Ukraine		x
Venezuela		x
Sum	**32**	
Thereof	**0**	**31**
Percentage	***0.00%***	***96.88%***

Source: Own composition.

* There is no other income-article in the tax treaty between Brazil and France.

Table I.12 Attribution of Business Profits in German Tax Treaties

Tax Treaty of Germany With	*Attribution of Business Profits Resembles OECD MC from 2010 (AOA)*	*Attribution of Business Profits Resembles OECD MC before 2010*	*Attribution of Business Profits Resembles UN MC 2011*
Albania		x	
Algeria		x	
Argentina		x	
Armenia		x	

Tax Treaty of Germany With	*Attribution of Business Profits Resembles OECD MC from 2010 (AOA)*	*Attribution of Business Profits Resembles OECD MC before 2010*	*Attribution of Business Profits Resembles UN MC 2011*
Australia		x	
Austria		x	
Azerbaijan		x	
Bangladesh		x	
Belarus		x	
Belgium		x	
Bolivia		x	
Bosnia & Herzegovina		x	
Bulgaria		x	
Canada		x	
China		x	
Costa Rica		x	
Croatia		x	
Cyprus		x	
Czech Republic		x	
Denmark		x	
Ecuador		x	
Egypt		x	
Estonia		x	
Finland		x	
France		x	
Georgia		x	
Ghana		x	
Greece		x	
Hungary		x	
Iceland		x	
India			x
Indonesia		x	
Iran		x	
Ireland*	x		
Israel		x	
Italy		x	
Ivory Coast		x	

Tax Treaty of Germany With	*Attribution of Business Profits Resembles OECD MC from 2010 (AOA)*	*Attribution of Business Profits Resembles OECD MC before 2010*	*Attribution of Business Profits Resembles UN MC 2011*
Jamaica		x	
Japan		x	
Kazakhstan		x	
Kenya		x	
Korea		x	
Kuwait		x	
Kyrgyzstan		x	
Latvia		x	
Liberia		x	
Liechtenstein	x		
Lithuania		x	
Luxembourg	x		
Macedonia		x	
Malaysia		x	
Malta		x	
Mauritius		x	
Mexico		x	
Moldova		x	
Mongolia		x	
Morocco		x	
Namibia		x	
Netherlands	x		
New Zealand		x	
Norway*	x		
Pakistan		x	
Philippines		x	
Poland		x	
Portugal		x	
Romania		x	
Russia		x	
Serbia & Montenegro		x	
Singapore		x	
Slovak Republic		x	

Tax Treaty of Germany With	*Attribution of Business Profits Resembles OECD MC from 2010 (AOA)*	*Attribution of Business Profits Resembles OECD MC before 2010*	*Attribution of Business Profits Resembles UN MC 2011*
Slovenia		x	
South Africa		x	
Spain		x	
Sri Lanka		x	
Sweden		x	
Switzerland		x	
Syria		x	
Taiwan		x	
Tajikistan		x	
Thailand		x	
Trinidad & Tobago		x	
Tunisia		x	
Turkey		x	
Turkmenistan		x	
Ukraine		x	
United Arab Emirates		x	
United Kingdom*	x		
United States**	x		
Uruguay		x	
Uzbekistan		x	
Venezuela		x	
Vietnam		x	
Zambia		x	
Zimbabwe		x	
Sum		**94**	
Thereof	**7**	**86**	**1**
Percentage	***7.45%***	***91.49%***	***1.06%***

Source: Own composition.

* The AOA is not implemented in the wording but in the tax treaties' protocol.

** The treaty with the United States is based on the '*functionally separate entity approach*'. The fiscal recognition of internal dealings is, however, unclear.

Table I.13 Attribution of Business Profits in US Tax Treaties

Tax Treaty of the United States With	*Attribution of Business Profits Resembles OECD MC from 2010 (AOA)*	*Attribution of Business Profits Resembles OECD MC before 2010*	*Attribution of Business Profits Resembles UN MC 2011*
Armenia		x	
Australia		x	
Austria		x	
Azerbaijan		x	
Bangladesh		x	
Barbados		x	
Belarus		x	
Belgium*	x		
Bulgaria**	x		
Canada**	x		
China			x
Cyprus		x	
Czech Republic		x	
Denmark		x	
Egypt		x	
Estonia		x	
Finland		x	
France		x	
Georgia		x	
Germany**	x		
Greece		x	
Hungary**	x		
Iceland**	x		
India			x
Indonesia			x
Ireland		x	
Israel		x	
Italy		x	
Jamaica		x	
Japan**	x		
Kazakhstan			x
Korea		x	

Tax Treaty of the United States With	*Attribution of Business Profits Resembles OECD MC from 2010 (AOA)*	*Attribution of Business Profits Resembles OECD MC before 2010*	*Attribution of Business Profits Resembles UN MC 2011*
Kyrgyzstan		x	
Latvia		x	
Lithuania		x	
Luxembourg		x	
Malta		x	
Mexico			x
Moldova		x	
Morocco		x	
Netherlands		x	
New Zealand		x	
Norway		x	
Pakistan		x	
Philippines			x
Poland*	x		
Portugal		x	
Romania		x	
Russia		x	
Slovak Republic		x	
Slovenia		x	
South Africa			x
Spain		x	
Sri Lanka			x
Sweden		x	
Switzerland		x	
Tajikistan		x	
Thailand			x
Trinidad & Tobago		x	
Tunisia			x
Turkey		x	
Turkmenistan		x	
Ukraine			x
United Kingdom**	x		
Uzbekistan		x	

Tax Treaty of the United States With	*Attribution of Business Profits Resembles OECD MC from 2010 (AOA)*	*Attribution of Business Profits Resembles OECD MC before 2010*	*Attribution of Business Profits Resembles UN MC 2011*
Venezuela			x
Sum		**66**	
Thereof	**9**	**45**	**12**
Percentage	***13.64%***	***68.18%***	***18.18%***

Source: Own composition.

* The application of the AOA is determined in the competent authority agreement (Belgium and Canada) respectively technical explanation (Poland) of the tax treaty.

** The tax treaties principally follow the '*functionally separate entity approach*' as stated in the AOA. Still, the fiscal recognition of internal dealings between head office and PE is not clearly determined.

Table I.14 Attribution of Business Profits in Brazilian Tax Treaties

Tax Treaty of Brazil With	*Attribution of Business Profits Resembles OECD MC from 2010 (AOA)*	*Attribution of Business Profits Resembles OECD MC before 2010*	*Attribution of Business Profits Resembles UN MC 2011*
Argentina		x	
Austria		x	
Belgium		x	
Canada		x	
Chile		x	
China		x	
Czech Republic		x	
Denmark		x	
Ecuador		x	
Finland		x	
France		x	
Hungary		x	
India		x	
Israel		x	
Italy		x	
Japan		x	
Korea		x	
Luxembourg		x	
Mexico			x
Netherlands		x	
Norway		x	

Tax Treaty of Brazil With	*Attribution of Business Profits Resembles OECD MC from 2010 (AOA)*	*Attribution of Business Profits Resembles OECD MC before 2010*	*Attribution of Business Profits Resembles UN MC 2011*
Peru		x	
Philippines		x	
Portugal		x	
Slovak Republic		x	
South Africa		x	
Spain		x	
Sweden		x	
Trinidad & Tobago		x	
Turkey		x	
Ukraine			x
Venezuela			x
Sum		**32**	
Thereof	**0**	**29**	**3**
Percentage	**0.00%**	**90.63%**	**9.38%**

Source: Own composition.

Table I.15 Attribution of Business Profits in Russian Tax Treaties

Tax Treaty of Russia With	*Attribution of Business Profits Resembles OECD MC from 2010 (AOA)*	*Attribution of Business Profits Resembles OECD MC before 2010*	*Attribution of Business Profits Resembles UN MC 2011*
Albania		x	
Algeria			x
Argentina		x	
Armenia			x
Australia		x	
Austria		x	
Azerbaijan		x	
Belarus		x	
Belgium		x	
Botswana			x
Bulgaria		x	

Tax Treaty of Russia With	*Attribution of Business Profits Resembles OECD MC from 2010 (AOA)*	*Attribution of Business Profits Resembles OECD MC before 2010*	*Attribution of Business Profits Resembles UN MC 2011*
Canada		x	
Chile		x	
China		x	
Croatia		x	
Cuba		x	
Cyprus		x	
Czech Republic		x	
Denmark		x	
Egypt		x	
Finland		x	
France		x	
Germany		x	
Greece		x	
Hungary		x	
Iceland		x	
India		x	
Indonesia			x
Iran		x	
Ireland		x	
Israel		x	
Italy		x	
Japan		x	
Kazakhstan			x
Korea (Dem. Rep)		x	
Korea (Rep.)		x	
Kuwait		x	
Kyrgyzstan			x
Latvia		x	
Lebanon		x	
Lithuania		x	
Luxembourg		x	
Macedonia		x	
Malaysia		x	
Mali		x	

Tax Treaty of Russia With	*Attribution of Business Profits Resembles OECD MC from 2010 (AOA)*	*Attribution of Business Profits Resembles OECD MC before 2010*	*Attribution of Business Profits Resembles UN MC 2011*
Malta		x	
Mexico			x
Moldova		x	
Mongolia		x	
Morocco		x	
Namibia			x
Netherlands		x	
New Zealand		x	
Norway		x	
Philippines		x	
Poland		x	
Portugal		x	
Qatar		x	
Romania		x	
Saudi Arabia			x
Serbia & Montenegro		x	
Singapore		x	
Slovak Republic		x	
Slovenia		x	
South Africa		x	
Spain		x	
Sri Lanka		x	
Sweden		x	
Switzerland		x	
Syria		x	
Tajikistan		x	
Thailand			x
Turkey		x	
Turkmenistan		x	
Ukraine			x
United Kingdom		x	
United States		x	
Uzbekistan		x	
Venezuela			x

Tax Treaty of Russia With	*Attribution of Business Profits Resembles OECD MC from 2010 (AOA)*	*Attribution of Business Profits Resembles OECD MC before 2010*	*Attribution of Business Profits Resembles UN MC 2011*
Vietnam			x
Sum	**80**		
Thereof	**0**	**67**	**13**
Percentage	***0.00%***	***83.75%***	***16.25%***

Source: Own composition.

Table I.16 Attribution of Business Profits in Indian Tax Treaties

Tax Treaty of India With	*Attribution of Business Profits Resembles OECD MC from 2010 (AOA)*	*Attribution of Business Profits Resembles OECD MC before 2010*	*Attribution of Business Profits Resembles UN MC 2011*	*Inclusion of Limited Force of Attraction Principle**
Albania			x	No
Armenia			x	No
Australia		x		No
Austria			x	No
Azerbaijan		x		No
Bangladesh		x		No
Belarus			x	Yes
Belgium			x	Yes
Bhutan			x	No
Botswana			x	No
Brazil		x		No
Bulgaria			x	No
Canada			x	Yes
China		x		No
Colombia		x		No
Croatia		x		No
Cyprus			x	Yes
Czech Republic		x		No
Denmark			x	Yes
Egypt		x		No
Estonia			x	No
Ethiopia			x	No

Tax Treaty of India With	*Attribution of Business Profits Resembles OECD MC from 2010 (AOA)*	*Attribution of Business Profits Resembles OECD MC before 2010*	*Attribution of Business Profits Resembles UN MC 2011*	*Inclusion of Limited Force of Attraction Principle**
Faroe Islands			x	Yes
Fiji		x		No
Finland			x	No
France			x	No
Georgia			x	No
Germany			x	No
Greece		x		No
Hungary		x		No
Iceland			x	No
Indonesia			x	Yes
Ireland		x		No
Israel		x		No
Italy			x	Yes
Japan		x		No
Jordan		x		No
Kazakhstan			x	No
Kenya			x	Yes
Korea		x		No
Kuwait			x	No
Kyrgyzstan		x		No
Latvia			x	No
Libya		x		No
Lithuania		x		No
Luxembourg			x	No
Malaysia			x	No
Malta			x	No
Mauritius		x		No
Mexico			x	No
Moldova		x		No
Mongolia			x	Yes
Morocco		x		No
Mozambique			x	No
Myanmar			x	No
Namibia			x	No
Nepal			x	No

Tax Treaty of India With	*Attribution of Business Profits Resembles OECD MC from 2010 (AOA)*	*Attribution of Business Profits Resembles OECD MC before 2010*	*Attribution of Business Profits Resembles UN MC 2011*	*Inclusion of Limited Force of Attraction Principle**
Netherlands			x	No
New Zealand			x	Yes
Norway			x	No
Oman		x		No
Philippines		x		No
Poland			x	Yes
Portugal			x	Yes
Qatar		x		No
Romania			x	Yes
Russia		x		No
Saudi Arabia			x	No
Serbia & Montenegro			x	No
Singapore		x		No
Slovak Republic			x	Yes
Slovenia		x		No
South Africa		x		No
Spain			x	Yes
Sri Lanka			x	Yes
Sudan		x		No
Sweden		x		No
Switzerland		x		No
Syria		x		No
Taiwan			x	No
Tajikistan		x		No
Tanzania			x	No
Thailand			x	Yes
Trinidad & Tobago		x		No
Turkey		x		No
Turkmenistan		x		No
Uganda		x		No
Ukraine		x		No
United Arab Emirates		x		No

Tax Treaty of India With	*Attribution of Business Profits Resembles OECD MC from 2010 (AOA)*	*Attribution of Business Profits Resembles OECD MC before 2010*	*Attribution of Business Profits Resembles UN MC 2011*	*Inclusion of Limited Force of Attraction Principle**
United Kingdom			x	No
United States			x	Yes
Uruguay		x		No
Uzbekistan		x		No
Vietnam		x		No
Zambia		x		No
Sum	95			
Thereof ('Yes')	**0**	**45**	**50**	**19**
Percentage	***0.00%***	***47.37%***	***52.63%***	***20.00%***

Source: Own composition.

* The limited force of attraction principle is considered here for the allocation of business profits to show for which countries it frequently occurs in Indian treaty policy. Due to rare usage, it is not considered for the other countries under consideration.

Table I.17 Attribution of Business Profits in Chinese Tax Treaties

Tax Treaty of China With	*Attribution of Business Profits Resembles OECD MC from 2010 (AOA)*	*Attribution of Business Profits Resembles OECD MC before 2010*	*Attribution of Business Profits Resembles UN MC 2011*
Albania		x	
Algeria			x
Armenia			x
Australia			x
Austria		x	
Azerbaijan		x	
Bahrain			x
Bangladesh		x	
Barbados		x	
Belarus		x	
Belgium		x	
Bosnia & Herzegovina		x	
Botswana		x	

Tax Treaty of China With	*Attribution of Business Profits Resembles OECD MC from 2010 (AOA)*	*Attribution of Business Profits Resembles OECD MC before 2010*	*Attribution of Business Profits Resembles UN MC 2011*
Brazil		x	
Brunei		x	
Bulgaria		x	
Canada			x
Chile		x	
Croatia		x	
Cuba		x	
Cyprus			x
Czech Republic		x	
Denmark		x	
Ecuador		x	
Egypt		x	
Estonia		x	
Ethiopia		x	
Finland		x	
France			x
Georgia		x	
Germany		x	
Greece		x	
Hong Kong			x
Hungary			x
Iceland		x	
India		x	
Indonesia		x	
Iran		x	
Ireland		x	
Israel		x	
Italy		x	
Jamaica			x
Japan		x	
Kazakhstan			x
Korea			x
Kuwait		x	
Kyrgyzstan			x
Laos		x	
Latvia		x	

Tax Treaty of China With	*Attribution of Business Profits Resembles OECD MC from 2010 (AOA)*	*Attribution of Business Profits Resembles OECD MC before 2010*	*Attribution of Business Profits Resembles UN MC 2011*
Lithuania		x	
Luxembourg		x	
Macau			x
Macedonia		x	
Malaysia			x
Malta		x	
Mauritius		x	
Mexico			x
Moldova		x	
Mongolia		x	
Morocco			x
Nepal			x
Netherlands			x
New Zealand		x	
Nigeria			x
Norway		x	
Oman		x	
Pakistan			x
Papua New Guinea		x	
Philippines		x	
Poland			x
Portugal		x	
Qatar		x	
Romania			x
Russia		x	
Saudi Arabia			x
Serbia & Montenegro		x	
Seychelles		x	
Singapore		x	
Slovak Republic			x
Slovenia		x	
South Africa		x	
Spain			x
Sri Lanka			x
Sudan		x	

Tax Treaty of China With	*Attribution of Business Profits Resembles OECD MC from 2010 (AOA)*	*Attribution of Business Profits Resembles OECD MC before 2010*	*Attribution of Business Profits Resembles UN MC 2011*
Sweden			x
Switzerland		x	
Syria		x	
Tajikistan		x	
Thailand		x	
Trinidad & Tobago		x	
Tunisia			x
Turkey		x	
Turkmenistan		x	
Uganda		x	
Ukraine			x
United Arab Emirates		x	
United Kingdom		x	
United States			x
Uzbekistan			x
Venezuela			x
Vietnam			x
Zambia		x	
Sum	**102**		
Thereof	**0**	**68**	**34**
Percentage	***0.00%***	***66.67%***	***33.33%***

Source: Own composition.

Appendix II

PE Questionnaire

The following self-developed questionnaire takes into account further detailed questions with regard to the PE definition and the allocation of business profits in the countries under consideration. The results of the work were thus supported by structured and reliable answers of country-specific tax experts of the global auditing and tax advisory company *PricewaterhouseCoopers* (PwC) so that more concrete conclusions about possible conflicting situations can be drawn. The questionnaire consists of eight questions in total and addresses five countries (one questionnaire per country; the United States, Brazil, Russia, India and China).

Table II.1 PE Questionnaire – United States

PE Definition
Q1: Does the requirement of disposal play a decisive role for the existence of a PE under **US** national and country-specific treaty law? How important is it?
A1: *The following answers to the questions basically refer to the taxation at the national level (Federal Tax). A fiscal nexus for a tax liability ('tax nexus') can also occur independently of this result depending on the activity at the level of states. These states each have independent arrangements for adoption of a tax liability. The US tax treaties do not include the 'state tax' and do not apply on state level. The United States put its treaties a special US model treaty which differs from the OECD. With regard to PE taxation (i.a. definition and income allocation) the US MC follows the provisions and interpretations of the OECD.* *The feature of the power of disposition (disposal) for determining the existence of a fixed place of business does not play a role in the context of limited tax liability for non-resident taxpayers (by way of determination of US source income) under US national law. The US tax law does not link domestic taxation to the PE definition but on income relating to the pursuit of commercial activities in the United States*

PE Definition
('income effectively connected to a US trade or business'). The term of the US trade or business is broader and is limited by the concept of the PE. However, the US model treaty and the interpretation of the PE follow the principles of the OECD Model. This means that in the context of determining the existence of a PE for tax treaty purposes, the requirement of disposal for non-resident taxpayers becomes more important. Despite the lack of a formal tenancy or ownership, a place of business can be attributed to or is existent (e.g., home office, premises in a subsidiary, etc.).
Q2: Does the total delegation of work to a subcontractor located in the **United States** lead to the existence of a construction site PE for a foreign general contractor (even if the foreign general contractor is not physically present in the source country)?
A2: *The total delegation of construction to a subcontractor in the US does not lead to a US PE for the general contractor unless the general contractor deployed further activities with its own staff on-site in the US (e.g., supervisory activities).*
Q3: Can there be an agency PE in the **United States** if the agent located there only has an *'economic' authority to conclude contracts* for the foreign principal (i.e., the agent does not formally act *'in the name'* of the foreign principal)?
A3: *Yes. According to the OECD interpretation, the substantial involvement in the negotiation of contracts, is sufficient in order to justify an agency PE.*
Q4: Can there be a service PE in the **United States** through the performance of services by employees of a non-resident service provider who seconds these employees to the **US** host company (secondment of employees)?
A4: *Not fundamentally. Here, it is crucial that the seconded staff act in the interests of the company of the United States and the authority to give directives to the employees lies with the US company.*
Attribution of Business Profits
Q5: Is the concept of internal dealings as proposed by the AOA known by **US** domestic law? Does the national law allow the deduction of such internal payments from the PE tax base? Does it also agree with an additional deduction of a profit element or does it only allow deduction at cost?
A5: *The United States has not yet implemented the AOA into national law. The 'effectively connected income (ECI)' is determined based on an 'asset-use test' and a 'business activities test'. Internal transactions between PEs are not recognized ('single entity' approach). In practice, the United States, however, approximates the 'separate entity approach' which is applied based on the respective tax treaty.*
Q6: If there was a construction site PE in the **United States** for a foreign general contractor due to the total delegation of work to a **US** subcontractor, what amount of profit will be allocated to this construction site PE in the **United States**? Is it thinkable that the construction site PE profit derived by the work of the subcontractor can be minimal in accordance with the *'zero-sum'*-theory?
A6: *If a US PE exists for the general contractor in spite of a complete delegation due to other activities, the PE income is determined after arm's length principles (section 482 IRC). In this context, it should be noted that under domestic US tax law all income from*

PE Definition
US sources with the exception of certain passive income may be assigned as ECI to the PE income (force of attraction, section 864 (c) (3) IRC). Thus, the Internal Revenue Service (IRS) is put in a position by using a profit split (regularly recognized Transfer Pricing (TP) method in the United States on the basis of function and risk distribution) to submit further profits of the general contractors' agreement to US taxation. The application of the zero-sum-theory to a US PE is regularly not followed by the IRS.
Q7: If there was an agency PE in the **United States,** what amount of profit will be allocated to that agency PE given the agent's remuneration paid by the foreign principal is at arm's length? Is it thinkable that the agency PE profit can be minimal in accordance with the *'zero-sum'*-theory?
A7: *See A6.*
Q8: If there was a service PE in the **United States,** what amount of profit will be allocated to that service PE? Is it thinkable that the service PE profit can be minimal in accordance with the *'zero-sum'*-theory?
A8: *See A6.*

Table II.2 PE Questionnaire – Brazil

PE Definition
Q1: Does the requirement of disposal play a decisive role for the existence of a PE under **Brazilian** national and country-specific treaty law? How important is it?
A1: *Brazilian legislation has very few rules on the concept of a PE. In general terms, in line with internal civil and tax law, a non-resident company may be treated as having a taxable presence if it operates in Brazil either through: (i) a fixed place of business (which is normally understood as a legal entity, branch or representative office), (ii) or an agent who has the power to enter into contracts in Brazil in the name or on behalf of a non-resident. The definition of a PE is not further defined in Brazilian national law. The right to actually dispose over the fixed place of business is not a criterion / not defined by Brazilian law.*
Q2: Does the total delegation of work to a subcontractor located in **Brazil** lead to the existence of a construction site PE for a foreign general contractor (even if the foreign general contractor is not physically present in the source country)?
A2: *No. As previously outlined, the Brazilian legislation foresees only two specific situations in which a non-resident could have a PE in Brazil (i.e., a fixed place of business or an agent with binding powers). In this sense, assuming that only the delegation of work to a subcontractor takes place and that no branch/agent exists, there would not be a PE of the non-resident in Brazil.*
Q3: Can there be an agency PE in **Brazil** if the agent located there only has an *'economic' authority to conclude contracts* for the foreign principal (i.e., the agent does not formally act *'in the name'* of the foreign principal)?

PE Definition
A3: *The decisive criteria from a Brazilian tax perspective are the power to contractually bind the non-resident, which would require a formal authorization of the agent. The facultative right to conclude such contracts is however not sufficient (form over substance) and contracts have to be actually signed by him in the name of the German enterprise.*
Q4: Can there be a service PE in **Brazil** through the performance of services by employees of a non-resident service provider who seconds these employees to the **Brazilian** host company (secondment of employees)?
A4: *An operating, fixed place of business is sufficient to establish a PE in Brazil. Thus, there is a risk that the Brazilian tax authorities would qualify such activities as a PE in case those are performed within a fixed place depending on the extend of such service provision, although being performed within the premises of the Brazilian host company. Please note that services being performed in Brazil by a non-resident are usually regarded as an import of services rather than a PE of the non-resident.*
Attribution of Business Profits
Q5: Is the concept of internal dealings as proposed by the Authorised OECD Approach (AOA) known by **Brazilian** domestic law? Does the national law allow the deduction of such internal payments from the PE tax base? Does it also agree with an additional deduction of a profit element or does it only allow deduction at cost?
A5: *Brazil is not an OECD member and does not adopt its guidelines with respect to PE. Therefore, the concept of 'internal dealings' is not recognized. Deductions of the income attributed to the PE are allowed, however, and must correspond to the expenses incurred by the PE to maintain itself.*
Q6: If there was a construction site PE in **Brazil** for a foreign general contractor due to the total delegation of work to a **Brazilian** subcontractor, what amount of profit will be allocated to this construction site PE in **Brazil**? Is it thinkable that the construction site PE profit derived by the work of the subcontractor can be minimal in accordance with the '*zero-sum*'-theory?
A6: *With respect to the allocation of profits to any independent company, Brazilian tax legislation does not provide detailed guidelines. It only states that, for the purpose of assessing the amount of tax payable in Brazil, the agent or representative of the principal domiciled abroad must write up its commercial books in such a way that they reflect, in addition to its own income, the profits from operations in lieu of an alien account in each year.*
Q7: If there was an agency PE in **Brazil,** what amount of profit will be allocated to that agency PE given the agent's remuneration paid by the foreign principal is at arm's length? Is it thinkable that the agency PE profit can be minimal in accordance with the '*zero-sum*'-theory?
A7: *There are no special rules dealing specifically with the attribution of income to agency PEs.*
Q8: If there was a service PE in **Brazil,** what amount of profit will be allocated to that service PE? Is it thinkable that the service PE profit can be minimal in accordance with the '*zero-sum*'-theory?
A8: *There are no special rules dealing specifically with the attribution of income to service PEs.*

Table II.3 PE Questionnaire – Russia

PE Definition
Q1: Does the requirement of disposal play a decisive role for the existence of a PE under **Russian** national and country-specific treaty law? How important is it?
A1: *Based on Article 306.2 of the Russian Tax Code, a foreign company may have a PE in the territory of Russia if it conducts business activities in the territory of Russia through a representative office, branch, other subdivision or a place of business on a regular basis. The Russian Tax Code contains a definition of a separate subdivision: a separate subdivision is a separate location equipped with permanent (for a period of more than one month) working places. However, a PE may be theoretically created even if no permanent working places are organized (since the definition 'place of business' does not necessarily mean conduction of activities for a long period). No further explicit description of a 'place of business' is provided in the Russian tax law. Given the above, the main criteria for identification of a PE under Russian law are conduction of business activities on a regular basis. Requirement of disposal may be considered only as a next step.*
Q2: Does the total delegation of work to a subcontractor located in **Russia** lead to the existence of a construction site PE for a foreign general contractor (even if the foreign general contractor is not physically present in the source country)?
A2: *Based on Article 308.2 of the Russian Tax Code, delegation of a portion of construction works in the territory of Russia by a foreign company (general contractor) to a subcontractor should be included into the term of the Russian construction site of the foreign general contractor. Due to the above provision, it is likely that entering into arrangement on construction works in Russia (even in case of total delegation of work to a subcontractor) will lead to creation of a construction PE. There is also court practice which confirms the above position (e.g., Resolution of the Federal arbitration court of the Moscow district N KA-A40/4739-10 of 20.05.2010). Special conditions in relation to construction site PEs may be determined in the Double Tax Treaties between Russia and other countries (e.g., particular period of exemption for creation of a PE for construction sites). Such special conditions should override domestic tax rules and should be taken into account while considering the question on the date of creation of a construction PE.*
Q3: Can there be an agency PE in **Russia** if the agent located there only has an *'economic' authority to conclude contracts* for the foreign principal (i.e., the agent does not formally act '*in the name*' of the foreign principal)?
A3: *The Russian Tax Code establishes the 'dependent agent' concept. Based on Article 306.9 of the Russian Tax Code a foreign company is considered to have a PE in the territory of Russia in case it inter alia conducts business activities in Russia through an entity which is entitled to conclude agreements or negotiate sufficient terms of the agreements in the name of this foreign company and actually uses this right in practice on a regular basis and, therefore, determines legal implications for such foreign company in Russia. Therefore, even in case such local entity (a representative office of the foreign company in question or other company) is not authorized to formally sign contracts in the name of the foreign company, but still negotiates its sufficient terms with the counter parties, the foreign entity in question will very likely be considered as having a PE in Russia.*

PE Definition
Q4: Can there be a service PE in **Russia** through the performance of services by employees of a non-resident service provider who seconds these employees to the **Russian** host company (secondment of employees)?
A4: *Article 306.7 of the Russian Tax Code provides for an exemption from creation of a PE in the territory of Russia in case of provision of personnel for the purposes of conduction of their employment duties in the territory of Russia (i.e., secondment) by a foreign company to a host company acting in the territory of Russia if such personnel will conduct its duties only in the name and in the interest of the host company.*
Attribution of Business Profits
Q5: Is the concept of internal dealings as proposed by the Authorised OECD Approach (AOA) known by **Russian** domestic law? Does the national law allow the deduction of such internal payments from the PE tax base? Does it also agree with an additional deduction of a profit element or does it only allow deduction at cost?
A5: *The 'internal dealings' concept as such is not known by the Russian domestic law. The main principles of the Russian rules on determination of a PE taxable profit may be summarized as follows: Profit of a Russian PE of a foreign company should be determined as the amount of income generated as a result of the respective activities in the territory of Russia (given the functions, risks and assets attributable to the Russian PE) less expenses incurred by the respective PE (Article 307.1 and 307.9 of the Russian Tax Code).* *Allocation of additional costs incurred at the level of the foreign head office rather than the Russian PE (including management and administrative expenses) to the Russian PE's taxable base may be allowed under certain Double Tax Treaties between Russia and other countries which override the domestic tax rules.*
Q6: If there was a construction site PE in **Russia** for a foreign general contractor due to the total delegation of work to a **Russian** subcontractor, what amount of profit will be allocated to this construction site PE in **Russia**? Is it thinkable that the construction site PE profit derived by the work of the subcontractor can be minimal in accordance with the '*zero-sum*'-theory?
A6: *General principles of allocation of income and expenses between the foreign head office and the Russian PE are summarized under question (5) above and are not fully compliant with the 'zero-sum' theory. However, there may be strong arguments to claim that the cost of subcontractors' services should be recognized as tax deductible expenses of the Russian PE given that such costs directly relate to activities in Russia and provided that the costs meet the general deductibility criteria and are not viewed as non-deductible per se under the Russian Tax Code. In addition, it is important that total income derived from activities in Russia is included in the taxable base of the PE.*
Q7: If there is an agency PE in **Russia,** what amount of profit will be allocated to that agency PE given the agent's remuneration paid by the foreign principal is at arm's length? Is it thinkable that the agency PE profit can be minimal in accordance with the '*zero-sum*'-theory?
A7: *Since the Russian regulations on determination of the amount of profit of the Russian PE are rather broad, it is difficult to develop a common approach for determination of an agency PE's profit. Generally, the methodology on allocation of income and expenses between the foreign head office and its Russian PE should be in any case in line with the rules outlined under question (5) above. As already discussed above, 'zero-sum' theory as*

PE Definition
such is not known in Russian law. There may be arguments to allocate expenses which have been actually incurred within the activities in Russia (e.g., payroll costs, expenses on involvement of third parties in negotiation of contractual terms, etc.) to the local PE. However, tax treatment of such costs still depends on particular circumstances. In any case, the expenses to be allocated to the Russian PE should be clearly related to the business activities in Russia and meet general deductibility criteria, as well as should not be viewed as non-deductible per se.
Q8: If there is a service PE in **Russia,** what amount of profit will be allocated to that service PE? Is it thinkable that the service PE profit can be minimal in accordance with the '*zero-sum*'-theory?
A8: *See comments to question (7) above.*

Table II.4 PE Questionnaire – India

PE Definition
Q1: Does the requirement of disposal play a decisive role for the existence of a PE under **Indian** national and country-specific treaty law? How important is it?
A1: *Yes. The disposal test plays a decisive role in the determination of a fixed place PE under national and country-specific treaty law of India. India generally follows the OECD position in this regard and accordingly disposal test assumes significance importance.*
Q2: Does the total delegation of work to a subcontractor located in **India** lead to the existence of a construction site PE for a foreign general contractor (even if the foreign general contractor is not physically present in the source country)?
A2: *This would depend upon the language used in the tax treaty under consideration. It is also largely dependent upon the terms of the agreement between the contractor and the subcontractor. Generally, subcontracting of work on a principal to principal basis may not constitute a construction PE in India. However, one needs to be mindful since it is not necessary that an entity is required to be present in India through its employees only. Even a presence through a subcontractor in certain situations could lead to constituting a PE in India.*
Q3: Can there be an agency PE in **India** if the agent located there only has an '*economic*' *authority to conclude contracts* for the foreign principal (i.e., the agent does not formally act '*in the name*' of the foreign principal)?
A3: *This depends upon the tax treaty under consideration and underlying facts. Generally, a dependent agent who has the authority to conclude contracts on behalf of the foreign principal would constitute an agency PE for such foreign principal. India generally looks at 'substance over form', and hence it should not make a difference if the agent does not formally act 'in the name' of foreign principal.*
Q4: Can there be a service PE in **India** through the performance of services by employees of a non-resident service provider who seconds these employees to the **Indian** host company (secondment of employees)?

PE Definition
A4: *This depends upon the tax treaty under consideration and underlying facts. Generally, secondment agreements principally should not constitute a service PE in India. However, recently there has been a negative Court ruling on this aspect by and hence the issue has become more litigated.*
Attribution of Business Profits
Q5: Is the concept of internal dealings as proposed by the Authorised OECD Approach (AOA) known by **Indian** domestic law? Does the national law allow the deduction of such internal payments from the PE tax base? Does it also agree with an additional deduction of a profit element or does it only allow deduction at cost?
A5: *Attribution of profits is a fact specific exercise. Most of the Indian tax treaties provide for the PE being treated as a separate and independent enterprise. Thus, the concept of 'internal dealings' is recognized in such treaties. There is a restriction under the Indian domestic law to the extent of payment made to the head office which is allowable as deduction. Further, the tax treaties also provide for limitation on deduction of interest and royalties being paid to the head office. Considering the base erosion principle, the Indian authorities may not allow inclusion of profit element on such payments.*
Q6: If there is a construction site PE in **India** for a foreign general contractor due to the total delegation of work to an **Indian** subcontractor, what amount of profit will be allocated to this construction site PE in **India**? Is it thinkable that the construction site PE profit derived by the work of the subcontractor can be minimal in accordance with the '*zero-sum*'-theory?
A6: *Generally, if the subcontractor is remunerated at arm's length then there will not be any additional profit attribution to such PE. While determining the profit attributable to the PE, it is important to take into consideration the functional profile of the foreign entity which is attributable to such PE. Merely considering the functions performed in India may not be sufficient.*
Q7: If there is an agency PE in **India,** what amount of profit will be allocated to that agency PE given the agent's remuneration paid by the foreign principal is at arm's length? Is it thinkable that the agency PE profit can be minimal in accordance with the '*zero-sum*'-theory?
A7: *Generally, if the Indian agent is remunerated at arm's length then there will not be any additional profit attribution to such PE.*
Q8: If there is a service PE in **India,** what amount of profit will be allocated to that service PE? Is it thinkable that the service PE profit can be minimal in accordance with the '*zero-sum*'-theory?
A8: *Generally, the profits attributable to the Indian service PE will be based on the functions performed, assets employed and risks assumed by such PE taking into consideration the functional profile of the affiliated entity related to such PE.*

Table II.5 PE Questionnaire – China

PE Definition
Q1: Does the requirement of disposal play a decisive role for the existence of a PE under **Chinese** national and country-specific treaty law? How important is it?
A1: *In 2010, China's State Administration of Taxation ('SAT') released GuoShuifa [2010] No. 75 ('Circular 75') to spell out the article-by-article interpretation of the China-Singapore Double Taxation Agreement ('DTA'). Circular 75 provides a master guide of China's positions on most of the treaty issues and it highlighted that the interpretation therein shall be applicable to other DTAs concluded by China if the Provisions of the relevant articles in those DTAs are the same as those in the China-Singapore DTA. In this regard, most of the answers to this questionnaire in relation to China SAT's position on the PE are cited from Circular 75, unless otherwise specified. On question (1), the requirement of 'disposal' plays an important role for the existence of a PE in China. Circular 75 provides three considerations for the existence of a PE, namely, (a) it should usually have a physical place at the disposal, (b) it is relatively fixed and has a certain degree of permanency in time, and (c) business activities are wholly or partly carried on through it. When considering the physical place at the disposal, no matter the place is owned or leased from others and regardless of its size or scale, a place of this kind will be regarded as physical. A place which may only occupy a small part of a market or a portion of a warehouse leased on a long-term basis or be situated inside another enterprise shall be deemed as a place of business if it has certain available space at its disposal.*
Q2: Does the total delegation of work to a subcontractor located in **China** lead to the existence of a construction site PE for a foreign general contractor (even if the foreign general contractor is not physically present in the source country)?
A2: *Yes, the situation you mentioned constitutes a construction PE in China. Circular 75 stipulates that if the enterprise subcontracts any part of the contracted construction projects to any other enterprise, the time spent by the subcontractor should be counted as time spent by the main contractor.*
Q3: Can there be an agency PE in **China** if the agent located there only has an *'economic' authority to conclude contracts* for the foreign principal (i.e., the agent does not formally act *'in the name'* of the foreign principal)?
A3: *If the agent has the prescribed 'economic' authority an agency PE could be deemed in China. According to Circular 75, the phrase of 'conclude contracts in the name of the enterprise' has an extensive meaning. It also applies to an agent who concludes contracts which are binding on the enterprise even if these contracts are not in the name of the enterprise. In addition, the term 'conclude' does not only refer to the signing activity, but it also includes the negotiation of all the elements and details of a contract which is in a way binding to the enterprise. Moreover, the principle of 'substance over form' should also be adopted for the purpose of determining an agency PE. For example, if an agent in China is authorized by a foreign enterprise to negotiate all the elements and details of a contract which is binding on the foreign enterprise, the agent should be deemed as 'exercising' authority in China, even if the contract is finally signed by another person outside China.*
Q4: Can there be a service PE in **China** through the performance of services by employees of a non-resident service provider who seconds these employees to the **Chinese** host company (secondment of employees)?

PE Definition

A4: *It depends on who is the economic employer of the secondee. In 2013, SAT issued SAT Public Notice [2013] No. 19 (Notice 19) to address the issue on Non-Tax Resident Enterprises ('Non-TRE') providing services by secondees to work in China. The overriding principle laid down in Notice 19 is that where a Non-TRE partially or fully bears the responsibilities and risks associated with the secondees' work and normally assess the secondees' work performance, the Non-TRE shall be deemed as providing service in China (instead of real secondment). Based on the overriding principle, Notice 19 also sets out five supplementary factors for consideration, including (a) Whether the Chinese Host Entity pays management fees or service fees to the Non-TRE Home Entity for the secondee; (b) Whether the Host Entity over-reimburses the Home Entity for the salaries, social security and other expenses of the secondees; (c) Whether the Home Entity does not pay the full amount received from the Host Entity to the secondees and retains certain amount; (d) Whether the China Individual Income Tax has not been fully paid on the income of the secondees that is borne by the Home Entity; (e) Whether the Home Entity determines the number, qualifications, pay standards and the working locations of the secondees.*

Attribution of Business Profits

Q5: Is the concept of internal dealings as proposed by the Authorised OECD Approach (AOA) known by **Chinese** domestic law? Does the national law allow the deduction of such internal payments from the PE tax base? Does it also agree with an additional deduction of a profit element or does it only allow deduction at cost?

A5: *China recognizes the 'internal dealings' concept when calculating how much profit should be attributed to the PE. Circular 75 stipulates that expenses which are incurred for the purposes of the business of the PE, including executive and general administrative expenses allocated to the PE by the head office, shall be allowed for deduction. So far, there is no specific rule on whether the deduction of a profit element is allowed. Circular 75 only mentions that the allocation method should be reasonable. The enterprise should provide relevant documents to justify the deduction.*

Q6: If there is a construction site PE in **China** for a foreign general contractor due to the total delegation of work to a **Chinese** subcontractor, what amount of profit will be allocated to this construction site PE in **China**? Is it thinkable that the construction site PE profit derived by the work of the subcontractor can be minimal in accordance with the '*zero-sum*'-theory?

A6: *There is no specific rule on the attribution of business profits of a PE in China. Therefore, the answer to question (6), (7) and (8) will be the same. Usually, the profit allocated to a PE in China is restricted to the profit belonging to the PE, which includes not only the profit obtained by such PE from China but also various income that have connections with such PE, including dividend, interest, rent, royalty and other incomes. In addition, Circular 75 sets forth the 'independent enterprise principle'. That is, the PE shall be treated as an independent tax-paying entity. The profit attributed to the PE, whether from the business transaction with its head office or other PEs of the head office, shall be calculated in the fair trade rule based on the fair market value. In China, since the primary rule is to calculate the profit of a PE on actual account book basis, the profit attributed to PE could be minimal in accordance with the zero-sum theory, given that most profit has been earned by the subcontractor and subject to China tax. However, please note that tax authorities may also incline to assess the PE profit on a deemed basis in practice, which might result in the breach of zero-sum theory.*

PE Definition
Q7: If there is an agency PE in **China,** what amount of profit will be allocated to that agency PE given the agent's remuneration paid by the foreign principal is at arm's length? Is it thinkable that the agency PE profit can be minimal in accordance with the '*zero-sum*'-theory?
A7: *Please refer to the answer to Question (6).*
Q8: If there is a service PE in **China,** what amount of profit will be allocated to that service PE? Is it thinkable that the service PE profit can be minimal in accordance with the '*zero-sum*'-theory?
A8: *Please refer to the answer to Question (6).*

Bibliography

Journals, Books, Working Papers, Series, Online Sources

ABB Response (2013), *Comment on the Revised Public Discussion Draft 'Interpretation and Application of Article 5 (Permanent Establishments) of the OECD Model Tax Convention'*, pp. 1-4.

Altshuler, R./Grubert, H. (2010), Formula Apportionment: Is it Better Than the Current System and Are There Better Alternatives?, *National Tax Journal* 63, No. 4, Part 2, pp. 1145-1184.

Amann, R. (1998), *Dienstleistungen im Internationalen Steuerrecht*, 1st Edition, Munich.

Amendment of the German PE Circular (2009), *Grundsätze der Verwaltung für die Prüfung der Aufteilung der Einkünfte bei Betriebsstätten international tätiger Unternehmen (Betriebsstätten-Verwaltungsgrundsätze); Änderung auf Grund des Gesetzes über steuerliche Begleitmaßnahmen zur Einführung der Europaischen Gesellschaft und zur Änderung weiterer steuerrechtlicher Vorschriften - SEStEG*, IV B 5 - S 1341/07/10004, 25 August 2009.

Andresen, U. (2010), Tarifabsenkung - Renaissance der Betriebsstätten -, in: Schaumburg, H./Piltz, D. (Eds.), *Grenzüberschreitende Gesellschaftsstrukturen im Internationalen Steuerrecht*, Cologne, pp. 1-31.

Andresen, U. (2013), Einkünfteabgrenzung für das Einlagengeschäft inländischer Bankbetriebsstätten unter Berücksichtigung des AOA, *Internationale Steuer-Rundschau* 9, pp. 320-328.

Andresen, U./Busch, O. (2012), Betriebsstatten-Einkünfteabgrenzung: steuerliche Untiefen bei der Transformierung des Authorised OECD Approaches in nationales Recht, *Die Unternehmensbesteuerung* 7, pp. 451-458.

Arnold, B. J. (2003), Threshold Requirements for Taxing Business Profits under Tax Treaties, *Bulletin for International Fiscal Documentation* 57, No. 10, pp. 476-492.

Arnold, B. J. (2008a), The New Services PE Rule in the Canada-U.S. Tax Treaty, *Tax Notes International* 51, No. 2, pp. 189-200.

Arnold, B. J. (2010), Tax Treaty News, *Bulletin for International Taxation* 64, No. 10, pp. 602-608.

Arnold, J. C. (2009), United States Report, in: IFA Cahiers Vol. 94a, *Is There a Permanent Establishment?*, Rotterdam, pp. 667-687.

Arthur, B. P./Herbert, A. E./Levey, M. M. (2014), United States Report, in: IFA Cahiers Vol. 99a, *Cross-Border Outsourcing*, Rotterdam, pp. 781-804.

Auerbach, A./Devereux, M. P./Simpson, H. (2010), Taxing Corporate Income, in: Mirrlees, J./Adam, S./Besley, T./Blundell, R./Bond, S./Chote, R./Gammie, M./ Johnson, P./Myles, G./Poterba, J. (Eds.), *Dimensions of Tax Design: The Mirrlees Review*, Oxford, pp. 837-913.

Ault, H. J. (2013), Some Reflections on the OECD and the Sources of International Tax Principles, *Tax Notes International* 70, No. 12, pp. 1195-1201.

Avi-Yonah. R. S. (1997), International Taxation of Electronic Commerce, *Tax Law Review* 52, No. 1, pp. 507-555.

Avi-Yonah, R. S. (2006), The Three Goals of Taxation, *Tax Law Review* 60, No. 1, pp. 1-28.

Avi-Yonah, R. S. (2007a), *International Tax as International Law*, 1st Edition, Cambridge.

Avi-Yonah, R. S. (2007b), Tax Competition, Tax Arbitrage and the International Tax Regime, *Bulletin for International Taxation* 61, No. 4, pp. 130-138.

Avi-Yonah, R. S. (2013), Who Invented the Single Tax Principle? An Essay on the History of US Treaty Policy, *School Law Review* 59, pp. 309-319.

Avi-Yonah, R. S./Clausing, K. A. (2008), Business Profits (Article 7 OECD Model Convention), in: Lang, M./Pistone, P./Schuch, J./Staringer, C. (Eds.), *Source versus Residence – Problems Arising from the Allocation of Taxing Rights in Tax Treaty Law and Possible Alternatives*, Alphen aan den Rijn, pp. 9-20.

Baistrocchi, E. A. (2013), The International Tax Regime and the BRIC World: Elements for a Theory, *Oxford Journal of Legal Studies* 33, No. 4, pp. 733-766.

Baker, P./Collier, R. (2006), General Report, in: IFA Cahiers Vol. 91b, *The Attribution of Profits to Permanent Establishments*, Rotterdam, pp. 21-67.

Baker, P./Collier, R. (2009), 2008 OECD Model: Changes to the Commentary on Article 7 and the Attribution of Profits to Permanent Establishments, *Bulletin for International Taxation* 63, No. 5, pp. 199-203.

Bal, A. (2012), Tax Implications of Cloud Computing – How Real Taxes Fit into Virtual Clouds, *Bulletin for International Taxation* 66, No. 6, pp. 335-339.

Baldamus, E. A. (2012), Neues zur Betriebsstättengewinnermittlung, *Internationales Steuerrecht* 9, pp. 317-324.

Barig, R. (2013), Abgrenzung der Betriebsstätteneinkünfte nach dem AOA - Die wesentlichen Änderungen durch den Authorised OECD Approach anhand eines Praxisfalls, *Internationale Wirtschafts-Briefe* 22, pp. 801-812.

Barker, W. B. (2012), A Common Sense Corporate Tax: The Case for a Destination-Based, Cash Flow Tax on Corporations, *Catholic University Law Review* 61, No. 4, pp. 955-1012.

Bärsch, S.-E. (2012), *Taxation of Hybrid Financial Instruments and the Remuneration Derived Therefrom in an International and Cross-Border Context – Issues and Options for Reform*, 1st Edition, Berlin Heidelberg.

Becker, J./Fuest, C. (2010), Taxing Foreign Profits with International Mergers and Acquisitions, *International Economic Review* 51, No. 1, pp. 171-186.

Becker, J./Fuest, C. (2011), Steuerliche Freistellung oder Anrechnungsverfahren für ausländische Einkommen?, *Wirtschaftsdienst* 6, pp. 401-405.

Bellaver, R./Wobeto, J. (2015), Brazilian Withholding Tax on Cross-Border Remittances: A New Understanding, *Tax Notes International* 79, No. 7, pp. 619-624.

Bendlinger, S. (2005), Die ertragsteuerliche Ergebnisaufteilung zwischen inländischem Stammhaus und ausländischer Betriebsstätte - Besonderheiten bei internationalen Anlagenerrichtungen, in: Lang, M./Jirousek, H. (Eds.), *Praxis des Internationalen Steuerrechts - Festschrift für Helmut Loukota zum 65. Geburtstag*, Vienna, pp. 45-79.

Bendlinger, S. (2007a), Gewinnabgrenzung und Gewinnermittlung im DBA-Recht, *Steuer und Wirtschaft International* 11, pp. 496-503.

Bendlinger, S. (2007b), Die Dienstleistungsbetriebsstätte im DBA-Recht, *Steuer und Wirtschaft* 4, pp. 151-158.

Bendlinger, S. (2008), Gewinnermittlung und Gewinnabgrenzung bei Auslandsbetriebsstätten im Steuerrecht, in: Renner, B./Schlager, J./Schwarz, R. (Eds.), *Praxis der steuerlichen Gewinnermittlung - Gedenkschrift für Walter Kögelberger*, Vienna, pp. 495-529.

Bendlinger, S. (2009), *Die Betriebsstätte in der Praxis des Internationalen Steuerrechts*, 1st Edition, Wien.

Bendlinger, S./Görl, M./Paaßen, K. H./Remberg, M. (2004), Neue Tendenzen der OECD zur Ausweitung des Betriebsstättenbegriffs und deren Beurteilung aus Sicht des Maschinen- und Anlagenbaus, *Internationales Steuerrecht* 4, pp. 145-149.

Bendlinger, S./Reinhold, M./Sennewald, D. (2013), Das deutsch-indische DBA und dessen Anwendung auf den deutschen Maschinen- und Anlagenbau, *Internationales Steuerrecht* 12, pp. 453-459.

Bendlinger, S./Remberg, M./Kuckhoff, H. (2002), Betriebsstättenbesteuerung im Großanlagenbau - Ein Unternehmen und steuerlich doch mehrere?, *Internationales Steuerrecht* 2, pp. 40-46.

Bennett, M. C./Dunahoo, C. A. (2005), The Attribution of Profits to a Permanent Establishment: Issues and Recommendations, *Intertax* 33, No. 2, pp. 51-67.

Bernales, R. (2013), The Authorised OECD Approach: An Overview, in: Gutiérrez, C./Perdelwitz, A. (Eds.), *Taxation of Business Profits in the 21st Century – Selected Issues under Tax Treaties*, Amsterdam, pp. 135-181.

Bhatia, P./Sharma, A. (2011), Taxation of Foreign Service Providers, *Asia-Pacific Tax Bulletin* 17, No. 2, pp. 101-104.

Bhattacharya, S./Sanghavi, D. (2012), India Report, in: IFA Cahiers Vol. 97a, *Enterprise Services*, Rotterdam, pp. 351-371.

BIAC Response (2007), *BIAC Comments on the OECD Public Discussion Draft: The Tax Treaty Treatment of Services: Proposed Commentary Changes*, 16 February 2007, pp. 1-6.

BIAC Response (2013), *BIAC response to the OECD Model Tax Convention: Revised Proposals Concerning the Interpretation and Application of Article 5 (Permanent Establishment)*, 31 January 2013, pp. 1-14.

Bischel, J. E./Levin, L. D. (2005), United States Report, in: IFA Cahiers Vol. 90a, *Source and Residence: New Configuration of Their Principles*, Rotterdam, pp. 707-724.

Bischel, J. E./Levin, L. D. (2012), United States Report, in: IFA Cahiers Vol. 97a, *Enterprise Services*, Rotterdam, pp. 721-732.

Blanluet G./Durand, P. J. (2011), General Report, in: IFA Cahiers 97a, *Key Practical Issues to Eliminate Double Taxation of Business Income,* Rotterdam, pp. 17-57.

Blumenthal, M./Slemrod, J. B. (1995), The Compliance Cost of Taxing Foreign-Source Income: Its Magnitude, Determinants, and Policy Implications, *International Tax and Public Finance* 2, No. 1, pp. 37-53.

Bobbett, C./Jones, F. A. J. (2010), The Proposed Redraft of Article 7 of the OECD Model, *Bulletin for International Taxation* 64, No. 1, pp. 20-27.

Boidman, N. (2000), Does Time Alone Create a Permanent Establishment? The Courts and Revenue Canada Go Their Separate Ways, *Bulletin for International Fiscal Documentation* 54, No. 7, pp. 339-342.

Böing, C./Prang, I. (2012), Das neue DBA-Niederlande 2012 - Die wesentlichen Änderungen, *Betriebs-Berater* 36, pp. 2211-2220.

Borges, A. S./Monguilod, A. C. (2005), Comparative Survey - Brazil, in: Russo, R. (Ed.), *The Attribution of Profits to Permanent Establishments – The Taxation of Intra-company Dealings*, Amsterdam, pp. 93-108.

Braunagel, R. U. (2008), *Gemeinsame Körperschaftsteuer-Bemessungsgrundlage in der EU*, 1st Edition, Cologne.

Brauner, Y. (2003), An International Tax Regime in Crystallization, *Tax Law Review* 56, pp. 259-328.

Brauner, Y. (2014), Formula Based Transfer Pricing, *Intertax* 42, No. 10, pp. 615-631.

Brown, F. B. (2011), An Equity-Based, Multilateral Approach for Sourcing Income Among Nations, *Florida Tax Review* 11, No. 7, pp. 555-642.

Bruk, B./Konnov, O. (2009), Russia Report, in: IFA Cahiers Vol. 94a, *Is There a Permanent Establishment?*, Rotterdam, pp. 541-558.

Brüninghaus, D. (2011), Kapitel K: Einkunftsabgrenzung bei Betriebsstätten und Personengesellschaften, I. Betriebsstätten, in: Vögele, A./Borstell, T./Engler, G. (Eds.), *Verrechnungspreise: Betriebswirtschaft, Steuerrecht*, Munich, pp. 811-901.

Brunsbach, S. (2003), *Electronic Commerce und Internationale Unternehmensbesteuerung*, 1st Edition, Cologne.

Brunsbach, S. (2012), Germany Report, in: IFA Cahiers Vol. 97a, *Enterprise Services*, Rotterdam, pp. 319-337.

Brunsbach, S./Endres, D./Lüdicke, J./Schnitger, A. (2012), *Deutsche Abkommenspolitik – Trends und Entwicklungen 2011/2012*, ifst-Schrift No. 480, Berlin.

Buchner, M. (2013), Die Ansicht der OECD zur Zurechnung von Kapital und Zinsaufwendungen zu einer Betriebsstatte: Vergleichende Gegenüberstellung vor und nach lnkrafttreten des AOA und steuerliche Gestaltungsmöglichkeiten, *Internationales Steuerrecht* 6, pp. 228-235.

Buciek, K. (2011), AO §12, in: Beermann, A./Gosch, D. (Eds.), *Abgabenordnung, Finanzgerichtsordnung Kommentar,* loose leaf (88th Suppl. Delivery 2011), Munich, pp. 1-34.

Bürkle, F./Ullmann, R. (2013), Die Betriebsstättendefinition des Art. 5 OECD-Musterabkommen: Aktuelle Änderungen bei Bau- und Montage- sowie Dienstleistungsbetriebsstätten, *Deutsches Steuerrecht* 19, pp. 944-949.

Butani M./Jain, P. (2014), Permanent Establishment Concept – An Indian Perspective, *Asia-Pacific Tax Bulletin* 20, No. 4, pp. 247-254.

Chand, V./Wagh, S. (2014), The Profit Split Method: Status Quo and Outlook in Light of the BEPS Action Plan, *International Transfer Pricing Journal* 21, No. 6, pp. 402-408.

Chaturvedi, A. (2011), Permanent Establishments and Force of Attraction: Some Implications of TD Securities, in General and from an Indian Perspective, *Bulletin for International Taxation* 65, No. 2, pp. 75-79.

Chawla, A. (2013), Does the Convergys Judgment Demystify Profit Attribution?, *Tax Notes International* 71, No. 5, pp. 449-450.

Cheung, D./Jiang, Z. (2013), Contemporary Issues of Taxation of Representative Offices in China, *International Tax Journal* 39, No. 4, pp. 39-54.

Choudhary, V. (2011), Electronic Commerce and Principle of Permanent Establishment Under the International Taxation Law, *International Tax Journal* 37, No. 4, pp. 33-57.

Cicconi, L. (2012), U.S. Tax Issues for Foreign Mobile Application Companies, *Tax Notes* 134, pp. 715-723.

Cockfield, A. J. (2003), Reforming the Permanent Establishment Principle Through a Quantitative Economic Presence Test, *Tax Notes International* 33, No. 7, pp. 643-654.

Cockfield, A. J. (2009), The Taxation of Permanent Establishments in Canada, *Bulletin for International Taxation* 63, No. 8, pp. 374-380.

Cohen, H./Morrison, P./Sina, J./Sinclair, L./Slaats, S./Tuerff, T./Wanek, M. (2008), Technical Explanation Provides Guidance on Canada-U.S. Protocol, *Tax Notes* 120 No. 12, pp. 1183-1190.

Collier, R. (2013), BEPS Action Plan, Action 7: Preventing the Artificial Avoidance of PE Status, *British Tax Review* 5, pp. 638-645.

Collier, R. (2015), Revised BEPS PE Proposals: Indeterminate Agents, Principals, and Principles, *Tax Notes International* 79, No. 1, pp. 61-64.

Dagan, T. (2015), BRICS: Theoretical Framework and the Potential of Cooperation, in: Brauner, Y./Pistone, P. (Eds.), *BRICS and the Emergence of International Tax Coordination*, Amsterdam, pp. 15-32.

Dagnese, N. (2006), Is Brazil 'Developed'? Termination of the Brazil-Germany Tax Treaty, *Intertax* 34, No. 4, pp. 195-198.

Dagnese, N. (2013), Neue Verrechnungspreisregeln in Brasilien - Wird das Enfant terrible erwachsen?, *Internationale Wirtschafts-Briefe* 7, pp. 257-264.

Dalal, K./Shah, V. J./Sheth, S. (2014), India, in: Reimer, E./Schmid, S./Orell, M. (Eds.), *Permanent Establishments – A Domestic Taxation, Bilateral Tax Treaty and OECD Perspective*, Alphen aan den Rijn, pp. 1-32.

Daurer, V. (2014), *Tax Treaties and Developing Countries*, 1st Edition, Alphen aan den Rijn.

De Carvalho, J. R./Bechara, C. H. T. (2014), Brazil Report, in: IFA Cahiers Vol. 99a, *Cross-Border Outsourcing*, Rotterdam, pp. 155-177.

De Souza Carvalho (2009), Brazil Report, in: IFA Cahiers Vol. 94a, *Is There a Permanent Establishment?*, Rotterdam, pp. 151-167.

Debatin, H. (1989), Das Betriebsstättenprinzip der deutschen Doppelbesteuerungsabkommen, Teil I & Teil II, *Der Betrieb* 34, pp. 1692-1697, 1739-1744.

Dehnen, P. H./Bacht, S. (2005), Recent Problems of Definition and Taxation of German Permanent Establishments, *Bulletin for International Fiscal Documentation* 59, No. 10, pp. 445-452.

Demme, U. H. (2013), Betriebsstättenbegründung durch Aufsichtstätigkeiten über eine Bauausführung oder Montage?, *Internationales Steuerrecht* 15, pp. 559-564.

Desai, M. A./Foley, F./Hines, J. R. (2005), Foreign Direct Investment and the Domestic Capital Stock, *American Economic Review* 95, No. 2, pp. 33-38.

Desai, M. A./Foley, F./Hines, J. R. (2009), Domestic Effects of the Foreign Activities of US Multinationals, *American Economic Journal: Economic Policy* 1, No. 1, pp. 181-203.

Desai, M. A./Hines, J. R. (2003), Evaluating International Tax Reform, *National Tax Journal* 56, No. 3, pp. 487-502.

Devereux, M. P./Pearson, M. (1995), European Tax Harmonisation and Production Efficiency, *European Economic Review* 39, pp. 1657-1681.

Devereux, M./De la Feria (2014), *Designing and Implementing a Destination Based Corporate Tax*, Working paper 14/07, May 2014, Oxford.

DeWilde, M. F. (2015), *'Sharing the Pie'; Taxing Multinationals in a Global Market*, 1st Edition, Rotterdam.

Diaz de Leon Galarza (2014), Tax Reforms to the Maquiladora Regime, *International Transfer Pricing Journal* 21, No. 3, pp. 205-208.

Ditz, X. (2004), *Internationale Gewinnabgrenzung bei Betriebsstätten - Ableitung einer rechtsformneutralen Auslegung des Fremdvergleichsgrundsatzes im internationalen Steuerrecht*, 1st Edition, Berlin.

Ditz, X. (2009), Aufgabe der finalen Entnahmetheorie - Analyse des BFH Urteils vom 17. 7. 2008 und seiner Konsequenzen, *Internationales Steuerrecht* 4, pp. 115-121.

Ditz, X. (2013), Der 'Authorised OECD Approach' wird Wirklichkeit - Kritische Analyse des § 1 Abs. 5 AStG i.d.F.d. AmtshilfeRLUmsG, *Internationale Steuer-Rundschau* 8, pp. 261-267.

Ditz, X. (2015), Die Grenzen des Fremdvergleichs - Zugleich Plädoyer für ein Festhalten am Fremdvergleichsgrundsatz, *Finanz-Rundschau* 4, pp. 119-125.

Ditz, X./Bärsch, S.-E. (2013), Gewinnabgrenzung bei Vertreterbetriebsstatten nach dem AOA - ein Plädoyer für die Nullsummentheorie, *Internationales Steuerrecht* 11, pp. 411-417.

Ditz, X./Bärsch, S.-E./Kluge, S. (2015), Verrechnungspreise in der Unternehmenspraxis - Ergebnisse einer empirischen Studie, *Internationales Steuerrecht* 21, pp. 819-823.

Ditz, X./Bärsch, S.-E./Quilitzsch, C. (2013), Betriebsstätteneinkünfte und Gewinnabgrenzung zwischen verbundenen Unternehmen nach der deutschen Verhandlungsgrundlage für Doppelbesteuerungsabkommen, *Internationale Steuer-Rundschau* 5, pp. 156-164.

Ditz, X./Bärsch, S.-E./Schneider, M. (2013), Internationale Rechtsprechung zur Begründung von Vertreterbetriebsstätten - Implikationen für Kommissionärsstrukturen in Deutschland?, *Die Unternehmensbesteuerung* 8, pp. 493-500.

Ditz, X./Luckhaupt, H. (2015), Betriebsstättengewinnaufteilungsverordnung - Neues Gewinnermittlungsrecht für Betriebsstätten, *Internationale Steuer-Rundschau* 1, pp. 1-10.

Ditz, X./Quilitzsch, C. (2012), Aktuelle Entwicklungen im Hinblick auf die Definition der Betriebsstätte, *Finanz-Rundschau* 11, pp. 493-501.

Ditz, X./Schneider, M. (2010), Änderungen des Betriebsstättenerlasses durch das BMF-Schreiben vom 25. 8.2009, *Deutsches Steuerrecht* 3, pp. 81-87.

Djanani, C./Brähler, G./Lösel, C. (2005), *Investitionen und Steuern in den USA – Doing Business in USA*, 1st Edition, Herne/Berlin.

Dölker, A. (2013a), Investitionen in den BRICS-Staaten aus steuerlicher Sicht - Teil 2: Russland, *Betriebs-Berater* 38, pp. 2269-2272.

Dölker, A. (2013b), Investitionen in den BRICS-Staaten aus steuerlicher Sicht - Teil 3: Indien, *Betriebs-Berater* 45, pp. 2717-2721.

Dölker, A. (2014), Investitionen in den BRICS-Staaten aus steuerlicher Sicht - Teil 4: China, *Betriebs-Berater* 7, pp. 347-350.

Dzhalchinov, D./Popov, P. (2012), Russia Report, in: IFA Cahiers Vol. 97a, *Enterprise Services*, Rotterdam, pp. 579-591.

Dziurdz, K. (2013), Article 15 of the OECD Model: The 183-Day Rule and the Meaning of 'Borne by a Permanent Establishment', *Bulletin for International Taxation* 67, No. 3, pp. 1-6.

Ecker, T./Tang, J. (2010), Chapter 2: Business Profits (Articles 5, 6, 7, 8, 9, and 14 OECD Model), in: Lang, M./Liu, J./Tang, G. (Eds.), *Europe-China Tax Treaties*, Alphen aan den Rijn, pp. 33-78.

Eckl, P. (2009), Germany Branch Report, in: IFA Cahiers Vol. 94a, *Is There a Permanent Establishment?*, Rotterdam, pp. 317-335.

Eichelberger, J./Liu, J./DeSouza, G. (2012), China – Permanent Establishments, in: *IBFD Tax Research Platform, Topical Analyses: Permanent Establishments*, Access: September 2012.

Eichelberger, J./Liu, J./DeSouza, G. (2015), China - Permanent Establishments, in: *IBFD Tax Research Platform, Topical Analyses: Permanent Establishments*, Access: January 2015.

Eichfelder, S./Schorn, M. (2012), Tax Compliance Costs: A Business-Administration Perspective, *FinanzArchiv* 68, No. 2, pp. 191-230.

Endres, D. (1996), Die Vertreterbetriebsstätte im Konzern, *Internationales Steuerrecht* 1, pp. 1-5.

Endres, D./Freiling, C. (2012), Musterfälle zu aktuellen Tendenzen in der deutschen Abkommenspolitik - Teil 2, *Praxis Internationale Steuerberatung* 7, pp. 189-196.

Endres, D./Spengel, C. (2012), *Unternehmensbesteuerung in Deutschland – Corporate Taxation in Germany*, 3rd Edition, Düsseldorf.

Endres, D./Spengel, C. (2015), *International Company Taxation and Tax Planning*, 1st Edition, Alphen aan den Rijn.

Ernst & Young (2014), *Doing Business in Rio – Brazil in the Path of a Sustainable Future*, 2nd Edition.

EU Joint Transfer Pricing Forum (JTPF) (2014), *Statistics on APAs at the End of 2013*, JTPF/007/2014/EN, October 2014, Brussels.

European Commission (2001), *Company Taxation in the Internal Market*, Working Paper, US Securities and Exchange Commission (SEC) 2001, 1681, 23 October 2001.

European Commission (2004), *European Tax Survey*, Taxation Papers, Working Paper No. 3, 2004.

European Commission (2011), *Proposal for a Council Directive on a Common Consolidated Corporate Tax Base (CCCTB)*, COM (2011) 121/4, Brussels.

European Commission (2015), *Communication from the Commission to the European Parliament and the Council – A Fair and Efficient Corporate Tax System in the European Union: 5 Key Areas for Action*, COM (2015) 302 final, 17 June 2015, Brussels.

Falcão, T. (2010), Contributing a Developing Country's Perspective to International Taxation: United Nations Tender for Development of a Transfer Pricing Manual, *Intertax* 38, No. 10, pp. 502-508.

Feldstein, M. S. (1995), The Effects of Outbound Foreign Direct Investment on the Domestic Capital Stock, in: Feldstein, M. S./Hines, J. R./Hubbard, G. R. (Eds.), *The Effects of Taxation on Multinational Corporations,* Chicago, pp. 43-66.

Fernández, N.C. (2013), The Concept of Permanent Establishment in the Courts: Operating Structures Utilizing Commission Subsidiaries, *Bulletin for International Taxation* 67, No. 6, pp. 1-12.

Ferreira, V. A. (2014), Service Income under Brazilian Tax Treaties: The Possible End of the Article 7 v. Article 21 Battle, but the Start of a New Old One?, *Intertax* 42, Nos 6/7, pp. 427-432.

Ferreira, V. A. (2015), The New Brazilian Position on Service Income under Tax Treaties: If You Can't Beat 'em, Join 'em, *Intertax* 43, No. 3, pp. 255-262.

Filinov, M./Kuznetsova, N./Lukina, V./Ostrovskiy, B. (2014), Russia, in: Reimer, E./Schmid, S./Orell, M. (Eds.), *Permanent Establishments – A Domestic Taxation, Bilateral Tax Treaty and OECD Perspective*, Alphen aan den Rijn, pp. 1-44.

Fleming, J. C./Peroni, R. J./Shay, S. E. (2001), Fairness in International Taxation: The Ability-to-Pay Case for Taxing Worldwide Income, *Florida Tax Review* 5, No. 4, pp. 299-354.

Fleming, J. C./Peroni, R. J./Shay, S. E. (2008), Some Perspectives from the United States on the Worldwide Taxation vs. Territorial Taxation Debate, *Journal of the Australasian Tax Teachers Association* 3, No. 35, pp. 35-86.

Fleming, J. C./Peroni, R. J./Shay, S. E. (2014), Formulary Apportionment in the U.S. International Income Tax System: Putting Lipstick on a Pig?, *Michigan Journal of International Law* 36, No. 1, pp. 1-57.

Förster, H. (2008), Der OECD-Bericht zur Gewinnermittlung bei Versicherungsbetriebsstätten, *Internationales Steuerrecht* 22, pp. 800-805.

Fresch/Strunk, G. (2012), OECD-MA Art. 5, in: Strunk, G./Kaminski, B./Köhler, S. (Eds.), *Außensteuergesetz-Doppelbesteuerungsabkommen-Kommentar*, loose leaf (28th Suppl. Delivery 2012), Bonn, pp. 1-96.

Friedrichsen, K.-U. (2013), Internationale Verständigung über die Erfolgsabgrenzung bei Betriebsstätten mithilfe multilateraler Advance Pricing Agreements, in: Oestreicher, A. (Ed.), *Modernisierung des Unternehmenssteuerrechts*, Herne, pp. 163-194.

Fuest, C./Spengel, C./Finke, K./Heckemeyer, J./Nusser, H. (2013) Profit Shifting and 'Aggressive' Tax Planning by Multinational Firms: Issues and Options for Reform, *World Tax Journal* 5, No. 3, pp. 307-324.

Furtado, M.F./Verboom, H./Lütter, C. (2015), No Brazilian Withholding Tax on Payments for Technical Services?, *Bulletin for International Taxation* 69, No. 10, pp. 558-562.

Gada, V./Sinha, H. S. (2014), India Report, in: IFA Cahiers Vol. 99a, *Cross-Border Outsourcing*, Rotterdam, pp. 365-384.

Gaoua, N. (2014), Taxation of the Digital Economy: French Reflections, *European Taxation* 54, pp. 10-14.

Gassner, W./Lang, M./Lechner, E. (1998), *Die Betriebsstätte im Recht der Doppelbesteuerungsabkommen - Voraussetzungen der Besteuerung von Unternehmensgewinnen im Quellenstaat*, 1st Edition, Vienna.

German Wage Circular (2014), *Steuerliche Behandlung des Arbeitslohns nach dem Doppelbesteuerungsabkommen*, IV B 2-S 1300/08/10027, 12 November 2014.

German Administrative Principles – Business Restructuring (2010), *Grundsätze für die Prüfung der Einkunftsabgrenzung zwischen nahestehende Personen in Fällen von grenzüberschreitenden Funktionsverlagerungen (Verwaltungsgrundsätze Funktionsverlagerung)*, IV B 5-S 1341/08/10003, 13 October 2010.

German Administrative Principles – Staff Secondment (2001), *Grundsätze für die Prüfung der Einkunftsabgrenzung zwischen international verbundenen Unternehmen in Fällen der Arbeitnehmerentsendung (Verwaltungsgrundsätze - Arbeitnehmerentsendung)*, IV B 4-S 1341/20/01, 9 November 2001.

German Bundesrat (2014), *Verordnung zur Anwendung des Fremdvergleichsgrundsatzes auf Betriebsstätten nach §1 Absatz 5 des Außensteuergesetzes (Betriebsstättengewinnaufteilungsverordnung-BsGaV)*, Printed Matter, 401/41, 28 August 2014.

German Income Tax Guidelines (2012), *Einkommensteuer-Richtlinien 2012 - Allgemeine Verwaltungsvorschrift zur Anwendung des Einkommensteuerrechts*, 16. 12. 2005, as amended by EStÄR 2012 on 25 March 2013.

German Law on the Implementation of the Directive on Mutual Assistance (2013), *Gesetz zur Umsetzung der Amtshilferichtlinie sowie zur Änderung steuerlicher Vorschriften (Amtshilferichtlinie-Umsetzungsgesetz - AmtshilfeRLUmsG)*, Bundesrat Drucksache 477/13, 6 June 2013.

German Partnership Circular (2014), *Anwendung der Doppelbesteuerungsabkommen (DBA) auf Personengesellschaften*, BMF Circular, IV B 5-S 1300/09/10003, 26 September 2014.

German PE Circular (1999), *Grundsätze der Verwaltung für die Prüfung der Aufteilung der Einkünfte bei Betriebsstätten international tätiger Unternehmen (Betriebsstätten-Verwaltungsgrundsätze)*, IV B 4-S 1300/111/99, 24 December 1999.

Goradia, S./Kapila, S. (2009), India Report, in: IFA Cahiers Vol. 94a, *Is There a Permanent Establishment?*, Rotterdam, pp. 345-366.

Graetz, M. J. (2001), Taxing International Income – Inadequate Principles, Outdated Concepts, and Unsatisfactory Policy, *Tax Law Review* 54, pp. 261-336.

Greier, M./Persch, A. (2012), Auswirkungen der Änderung des Art. 7 OECD-MA auf die Gewinnabgrenzung bei Bankbetriebsstätten, *Betriebs-Berater* 21, pp. 1318-1326.

Greil, S./Kiesow, S. (2013), Tax Compliant Transfer Pricing, *Deutsche Steuer-Zeitung* No. 11, pp. 389-397.

Greinert, M./Metzner, S. (2015), Die Bedeutung von Risiken bei der Ermittlung fremdüblicher Verrechnungspreise - Diskussionsentwurf der OECD zu den Maßnahmen 8, 9 und 10 des BEPS-Aktionsplans, *Die Unternehmensbesteuerung* 2, pp. 60-68.

Griffith, R./Hines, J./Sörensen, P. B. (2010), International Capital Taxation, in: Mirrlees, J./Adam, S./Besley, T./Blundell, R./Bond, S./Chote, R./Gammie, M./ Johnson, P./Myles, G./Poterba, J. (Eds.), *Dimensions of Tax Design: the Mirrlees Review*, Oxford, pp. 914-1027.

Grotherr, S. (2001), Internationale Steuerplanung: Betriebsstätte oder Tochtergesellschaft?, *Steuer und Studium* 4, pp. 182-196.

Grubert, H./Newlon, T. S. (1995), The International Implications of Consumption Tax Proposals, *National Tax Journal* 48, No. 4, pp. 619-647.

Gustafson, C. H./Peroni, R. J./Richard, C. P. (2011), *Taxation of International Transactions – Materials, Text and Problems*, 4th Edition, St. Paul.

Gutiérrez, C (2013), The UN Model and the BRICS Countries - Another View, in: Gutiérrez, C./Perdelwitz, A. (Eds.), *Taxation of Business Profits in the 21st Century – Selected Issues under Tax Treaties*, Amsterdam, pp. 307-339.

Gutiérrez, C./Perdelwitz, A. (2013), *Taxation of Business Profits in the 21st Century – Selected Issues under Tax Treaties*, 1st Edition, Amsterdam.

Guyton, J. L./O'Hare, J. F./Stavrianos, M. P./Toder, E. J. (2003), Estimating the Compliance Cost of the U.S. Individual Income Tax, *National Tax Journal* 56, No. 3, pp. 673-688.

Haase, F. (2015), Forderungen an die künftige Steuerpolitik im deutschen internationalen Steuerrecht, *Internationales Steuerrecht* 9, pp. 313-319.

Haiß, U. (2000), *Gewinnabgrenzung bei Betriebsstätten im Internationalen Steuerrecht*, 1st Edition, Neuwied, Kriftel.

Haiß, U. (2011), Steuerliche Abgrenzungsfragen bei der Begründung einer Betriebsstätte im Ausland, in: Grotherr, S. (Ed.), *Handbuch der internationalen Steuerplanung*, Herne, pp. 31-49.

Hannes, S. P. (2006), United States Report, in: IFA Cahiers Vol. 91b, *The Attribution of Profits to Permanent Establishments*, Rotterdam, pp. 691-710.

Hasbargen, U./Preising, T. (2012), Grundsätze der Besteuerung von Arbeitnehmern und Betriebsstätten bei Mitarbeiterentsendungen nach China, *Internationales Steuerrecht* 4, pp. 143-148.

Heinsen, O. (2011), Einführung, Betriebsstättenbegriff, in: Löwenstein, U.W./Looks, C./Heinsen, O. (2011), *Betriebsstättenbesteuerung- Inboundinvestitionen, Outboundinvestitionen, Steuergestaltungen, Branchenbesonderheiten*, Munich, pp. 1-40, 41-90.

Heinsen, O./Voss, O. (2012) Cloud Computing under Double Tax Treaties: A German Perspective, *Intertax* 40, No. 11, pp. 584-592.

Hellerstein, W. (2014), Jurisdiction to Tax in the Digital Economy: Permanent and Other Establishments, *Bulletin for International Taxation* 68, No. 6/7, pp. 346-351.

Hemmelrath, A./Kepper, P. (2013), Die Bedeutung des 'Authorised OECD Approach' (AOA) für die deutsche Abkommenspraxis, *Internationales Steuerrecht* 2, pp. 37-42.

Henkes-Wabro, R. C. (2009), *Gewinnabgrenzungen bei Bankbetriebsstätten im Internationalen Steuerrecht*, 1st Edition, Frankfurt a.M.

Hensel, C. (2012), Das neue Doppelbesteuerungsabkommen mit Südafrika, *Internationale Wirtschafts-Briefe* 6, pp. 227-232.

Herzfeld, M. (2014), The U.N. Rewrites International Tax Rules, *Tax Notes International* 76, No. 6, pp. 477-479.

Herzfeld, M. (2015), Tax Planning and Fairness in International Tax, *Tax Notes International* 79, No. 2, pp. 103-105.

Heußner, J. (2014), Vertreterbetriebsstätte einer ausländischen Kapitalgesellschaft - die Praxis wartet auf eine höchstrichterliche Entscheidung, *Internationales Steuerrecht* 5, pp. 161-166.

Hey, J. (2001), Besteuerung von Unternehmensgewinnen und Rechtsformneutralität, in: Ebling, I. (Ed.), *Besteuerung von Einkommen*, Herausgegeben im Auftrag der Deutschen Steuerjuristischen Gesellschaft e.V., (DStJG 24), Cologne, pp. 155-223.

Hey, J. (2013), § 3 A. System des Steuerrechts, B. Das Leistungsfähigkeitsprinzip als allgemein anerkanntes Fundamentalprinzip gerechter Besteuerung, in: Tipke, K./Lang J. (Eds.), *Steuerrecht*, 21th Edition, Cologne, pp. 59-129.

Hilbert, L./Engel, B. (2012), OECD Discussion around the Definition of Permanent Establishments: A German view on Proposed Amendments to the Model Commentary and Their Effect on Business Profit Allocation and International Assignments, *Intertax* 40, No. 8/9, pp. 462-476.

Ho, K./Zhao, A./Turley, C. (2014), How Does Tax Affect International Secondments in China?, *Tax Notes International* 73, No. 7, pp. 635-638.

Holland, D. (2010), United States - Commissionaire Agency Permanent Establishments, *International Transfer Pricing Journal* 18, No. 1, pp. 33-38.

Holtzman, J. (2007), Challenges in Achieving Transparency, Simplicity and Administering of the United States Tax Code, *Journal of Management Development* 26, No. 5, pp. 418-427.

Homburg, S. (2000), Perspektiven der internationalen Unternehmensbesteuerung, in: Andel, N. (Ed.), *Probleme der Besteuerung III*, Berlin, pp. 9-61.

Homburg, S. (2005), B. Wohnsitzprinzip, in: Endres, D./Oestreicher, A./Scheffler, W./Schreiber, U./Spengel, C. (Eds.), *Die internationale Unternehmensbesteuerung im Wandel - Symposium für Otto H. Jacobs zum 65. Geburtstag*, Munich, pp. 14-27.

Homburg, S. (2010), *Allgemeine Steuerlehre*, 6th Edition, Munich.

Hongler, P./Pistone, P. (2015), *Blueprints for a New PE Nexus to Tax Business Income in the Era of the Digital Economy*, IBFD Working Paper, 20 January 2015.

Hoogterp, P (2009), Internal Interest Dealings for Financial and Non-Financial Enterprises and Art. 7 of the OECD Model Tax Convention, *International Transfer Pricing Journal* 6, pp. 396-400.

Höreth, U./Zimmermann, C. (2014), Verordnung zur Anwendung des Fremdvergleichsgrundsatzes auf Betriebsstätten nach § 1 Abs. 5 AStG - Betriebsstättengewinnaufteilungsverordnung - BsGaV, *Deutsche Steuer-Zeitschrift* 21, pp. 743-752.

Hu, T./Li, N. (2015), China Tax Treaty and Policy: Development and Updates, in: Brauner, Y./Pistone, P. (Eds.), *BRICS and the Emergence of International Tax Coordination*, Amsterdam, pp. 181-230.

Huibregtse, S./Verdoner, L./Valutyte, I./Offermanns, R. (2015), Status of Implementation of the Authorised OECD Approach into Domestic Tax Law and Tax Treaties - Part 1, *European Taxation* 55, No. 8, pp. 363-373.

IBFD (2015), *Tax Research Platform*, http://online.ibfd.org/kbase/, 04 December 2015.

IFA (2006), *The Attribution of Profits to Permanent Establishments*, IFA Cahiers Vol. 91b, Rotterdam.

IFA (2009), *Is There a Permanent Establishment?*, IFA Cahiers Vol. 94a, Rotterdam.

IFA-OECD Seminar (2012), *The Elusive Concept of Permanent Establishment*, Seminar F, Boston, 30 September-4 October 2012.

IMF World Economic Outlook (April 2015), *World Economic Outlook Database*, https://www.imf.org/external/pubs/ft/weo/2015/01/weodata/index.aspx, 04 December 2015.

IMF World Economic Outlook (October 2013), *World Economic Outlook, October 2013 – Transitions and Tensions*, Washington.

Jacobs, O. H./Endres, D./Spengel, C. (2007), *Internationale Unternehmensbesteuerung-Deutsche Investitionen im Ausland- Ausländische Investitionen im Inland*, 6th Edition, Munich.

Jacobs, O. H./Endres, D./Spengel, C. (2011), *Internationale Unternehmensbesteuerung-Deutsche Investitionen im Ausland- Ausländische Investitionen im Inland*, 7th Edition, Munich.

Jacobs, O. H./Spengel, C./Schäfer, A. (2003), ICT and International Corporate Taxation: Tax Attributes and Scope of Taxation, *Intertax* 31, No. 6/7, pp. 214-231.

James, S./Hasseldine, J./Hite, P./Toumi, M. (2001), Developing a Tax Compliance Strategy for Revenue Services, *Bulletin for Fiscal Documentation* 55, No. 4, pp. 158-164.

Jhabakh, P. R. (2010), Withdrawal of Circular 23: Will It Lead to Taxing Times for Non-residents?, *International Transfer Pricing Journal* 72, No. 2, pp. 156-161.

Jirousek, H. (2005), Methodische Ansatze zur Konfliktvermeidung bei der Anwendung von Doppelbesteuerungsabkommen, in: Lang, M./Jirousek, H. (Eds.), *Praxis des Internationalen Steuerrechts - Festschrift für Helmut Loukota zum 65. Geburtstag*, Vienna, pp. 175-194.

Jones, A. F. J./Lüdicke, J. (2014), The Origins of Article 5(5) and 5(6) of the OECD Model, *World Tax Journal* 6, No. 3, pp. 203-241.

Jones, F. A. J./Ward, D. A. (1993), Agents as Permanent Establishments under the OECD Model Tax Convention, *European Taxation* 33, No. 5, pp. 154-181.

Käbisch, V./Risse, R. (2014), Germany Report, in: IFA Cahiers Vol. 99a, *Cross-Border Outsourcing*, Rotterdam, pp. 325-342.

Kaeser, C. (2014), Seminar F: UN Matters – UN and OECD Differences in Model, TP etc.: Fokus auf technischen Dienstleistungen, *Internationales Steuerrecht* 19, pp. 708-711.

Kahle, H./Kindich, A. (2016), Begriff der Betriebsstätte nach nationalem Recht und DBA-Recht & Erfolgs- und Vermögensabgrenzung bei Betriebsstätten, in: Lübbehüsen, T./Kahle, H. (Eds.), *Brennpunkte der Besteuerung von Betriebsstätten*, 1st Edition, Herne, pp. 27-159, 213-372.

Kahle, H./Mödinger, J. (2010), Die Neufassung des Art. 7 OECD-MA im Rahmen der Aktualisierung des OECD-MA 2010, *Internationales Steuerrecht* 20, pp. 757-763.

Kahle, H./Ziegler, S. (2009), Betriebsstättenbegriff- Grundfragen und aktuelle Entwicklungen, *Deutsche Steuer-Zeitung* 22, pp. 834-847.

Kamath, S. (2013), U.K. Firm Not Taxable on Services for Indian Clients, Tribunal Rules, *Tax Notes International* 70, No. 10, pp. 961-963.

Kamath, S. (2014a), Treaties' Business Profits Article Prevails over Brazilian Law, AG Says, *Tax Notes International* 73, No. 9, pp. 772-773.

Kamath, S. (2014b), Booz India Is a Fixed-Place PE of Parent and Group Companies, AAR Says, *Tax Notes International* 73, No. 9, pp. 778-779.

Kaminski, B. (2012), Aktuelle Entwicklungen bei der Betriebsstättenbesteuerung, *Die Steuerberatung* 8, pp. 354-366.

Kane, M. A. (2004), Strategy and Cooperation in National Responses to International Tax Arbitrage, *Emory Law Journal* 53, pp. 89-169.

Kapur, R./Rawal, R. (2006), India Report, in: IFA Cahiers Vol. 91b, *The Attribution of Profits to Permanent Establishments*, Rotterdam, pp. 387-413.

Karzon, E. U. (1999), *Issue: Whether the United States Taxing Right Depends upon the Existence in the United States of a Permanent Establishment, a Mere Presence, or Evidence of Economic Activity, or a Combination of all Three*, Memorandum for William S. Tress, IRS Department of the Treasury, CAU-N-114393-99, 4 November 1999.

Kaufman, N. H. (1998), Fairness and the Taxation of International Income, *Law and Policy in International Business* 29, No. 2, pp. 145-203.

Kemmeren, E. (2006), Source of Income in Globalizing Economies: Overview of the Issues and a Plea for an Origin-Based Approach, *Bulletin for International Taxation* 60, No. 11, pp. 430-452.

Kemmeren, E. (2010), Legal and Economic Principles Support an Origin and Import Neutrality-Based over a Residence and Export Neutrality-Based Tax Treaty Policy, in: Editors: Lang, M./Pistone, P./Schuch, J./Staringer, C./Storck, A./ Zagler, M. (Eds.), *Tax Treaties: Building Bridges Between Law and Economics*, pp. 237-315.

Kerschner, I./Stiastny, M. (2013), The Experience with Advance Pricing Agreements, *Intertax* 41, No. 11, pp. 588-593.

Klein, M. (2009), Artikel 7. Gewerbliche Gewinne, in: Endres, D./Jacob, F./Gohr, M./Klein, M. (Eds.), *DBA Deutschland/USA Doppelbesteuerungsabkommen*, Munich, pp. 185-207.

Kleinbard, E. D. (2007), Throw Territorial Taxation From the Train, *Tax Notes* 114, pp. 547-564.

Knirsch, D./Niemann, R. (2008), Deferred Shareholder Taxation - Implementing a Neutral Business Tax in the European Union, *Accounting in Europe* 5, No. 2, pp. 101-125.

Kobetsky. M. (2011), *International Taxation of Permanent Establishments – Principles and Policy*, 1st Edition, Cambridge.

Konnov, O./Smirnov, E./Smith, H. (2012), Russia - Permanent Establishments, in: *IBFD Tax Research Platform, Topical Analyses: Permanent Establishments*, Access: September 2012.

Konnov, O./Smirnova, I./Smith, H. (2015), Russia - Permanent Establishments, in: *IBFD Tax Research Platform, Topical Analyses: Permanent Establishments*, Access: January 2015.

Korff, M. (2009), Die Rechtspechung zu § 12 AO in der internationalen Steuerplanung - zugleich eine Anmerkung zum BFH-Urteil vom 04.06.2008, I R 30/07, *Internationales Steuerrecht* 7, pp. 231-236.

Kosch, F. (2010), Der OECD-Betriebsstättenbericht 2008 im Vergleich zum deutschen Recht, *Internationales Steuerrecht* 2, pp. 42-45.

Kosters, B./Offermanns, R. (2013), Implementation of the Authorised OECD Approach by OECD Member Countries, in: Gutiérrez, C./Perdelwitz, A. (Eds.), *Taxation of Business Profits in the 21st Century – Selected Issues under Tax Treaties*, Amsterdam, pp. 273-306.

Krabbe, H. (2009), Vor Art. 1, in Debatin, H./Wassermeyer, F. (Eds.), *Beck'sche Steuerkommentare Doppelbesteuerung: DBA*, loose leaf (113th Suppl. Delivery 2011) Munich, pp. 1-82.

Krause, M. (2003), *Internationale Doppelbesteuerung - Ursachen und Lösungen*, ifst-Schrift No. 405, Bonn.

Krauß, S. (2014), Internationale Steuerausscheidung von Prinzipal-Gesellschaften in der Schweiz, *Internationales Steuerrecht* 15, pp. 548-553.

Krishnamurthy, V. (2015), Tax Aspects of Cross-Border Secondment of Employees to India, *Bulletin for International Taxation* 69, No. 2, pp. 100-110.

Kromer, C./Pumpler, R./Henschel, K. (2013), Tax Compliance, *Betriebs-Berater* 14, pp. 791-803.

Kroppen, H.-K. (2005), Neue Rechtsentwicklungen bei der Betriebsstätte nach Abkommensrecht, in: Gocke, R./Gosch, D./Lang, M. (Eds.), *Körperschaftsteuer, Internationales Steuerrecht, Doppelbesteuerung - Festschrift für Franz Wassermeyer zum 65. Geburtstag*, Munich, pp. 691-708.

Kroppen, H.-K. (2013), Internationale Aspekte einer Reform der Unternehmensbesteuerung, in: Jachmann, M. (Ed.), *Erneuerung des Steuerrechts*, 38. Jahrestagung der Deutschen Steuerjuristischen Gesellschaft e. V., Berlin, 9. und 10. September 2013, Cologne, pp. 259-279.

Kroppen, H.-K. (2014), Aufteilungen zwischen Stammhaus und Betriebsstätte auf Basis von Personalfunktionen?, *Der Betrieb* 38, pp. 2134-2135.

Kroppen, H.-K./Dawid, R./Schmidtke, R. (2012), Profit Split, the Future of Transfer Pricing? Arm's Length Principle and Formulary Apportionment Revisited from a Theoretical and a Practical Perspective, in: Schön, W./Konrad, K. A. (Eds.), *Fundamentals of International Transfer Pricing in Law and Economics*, Berlin Heidelberg, pp. 267-293.

Kruse, H. W. (2003), § 12 & § 13 AO, in: Tipke, K./Kruse, H. W. (Eds.), *Abgabenordnung, Finanzgerichtsordnung Kommentar,* loose leaf (125th Suppl. Delivery 2011), Cologne, pp. 41-55.

Kumpf, W. (1982), *Besteuerung inländischer Betriebsstätten von Steuerausländern*, 1st Edition, Cologne.

Kumpf, W. (1989), Ergebnis - und Vermögenszuordnung bei Betriebsstätten, in: Curtius-Hartung, R./Herzig, N./Niemann, U. (Eds.), *Steuerberater-Jahrbuch 1988/89*, Cologne, pp. 400-422.

Lang, M. (2002), Die Vermeidung der Doppelbesteuerung und der doppelten Nicht-Besteuerung als DBA-Auslegungsmaxime?, *Internationales Steuerrecht* 18, pp. 609-613.

Lang, M. (2004a), General Report, in: IFA Cahiers 89a, *Double Non-taxation*, Rotterdam, pp. 21 72.

Lang, M. (2004b), Vermeidung der Doppelbesteuerung und der doppelten Nicht-Besteuerung als Auslegungsmaxime für Doppelbesteuerungsabkommen?, in: Haarmann, W. (Ed.), *Auslegung und Anwendung von Doppelbesteuerungsabkommen*, Cologne, pp. 83-112.

Lang, M. (2009), 2008 OECD Model: Conflicts of Qualification and Double Non-taxation, *Bulletin for International Taxation* 63, No. 5, pp. 204-207.

Lang, M. (2011), Art. 3 Abs. 2 OECD-MA und die Auslegung von Doppelbesteuerungsabkommen, *Internationale Wirtschafts-Briefe* 8, pp. 281-294.

Lay, H./Stoecker, V. (2013), Die deutsche Verhandlungsgrundlage für DBA - Bewertung aus unternehmensteuerlicher Sicht, *Internationale Wirtschafts-Briefe* 11, pp. 368-377.

Le Gall, J. P. (2011), The Concept of Dependence in the Definition of a Permanent Establishment, in: Baker, P./Bobbett, C. (Eds.), *Tax Polymath – A Life in International Taxation – Essays in the Honour of John F. Avery Jones*, Amsterdam, pp. 79-94.

Lehner, M. (1998), Wettbewerb der Steuersysteme im Spiegel europäischer und US-amerikanischer Steuerpolitik, *Steuer und Wirtschaft* 2, pp. 159-173.

Lehner, M./Reimer, E. (2005a), Generalthema I: Quelle vs. Ansässigkeit- Wie sind die grundlegenden Verteilungsprinzipien des Internationalen Steuerrechts austariert?, *Internationales Steuerrecht* 16, pp. 542-551.

Lehner, M./Reimer, E. (2005b), Germany Report, in: IFA Cahiers 90a, *Source and Residence: New Configuration of Their Principles*, Rotterdam, pp. 311-336.

Lennard, M. (2014), Transfer Pricing Arbitration as an Option for Developing Countries, *Intertax* 42, No. 3, pp. 179-188.

Li, J. (2002), Global Profit Split: An Evolutionary Approach to International Income Allocation, *Canadian Tax Journal* 50, No. 3, pp. 823-883.

Li, J. (2012), The Great Fiscal Wall of China: Tax Treaties and Their Role in Defining and Defending the China's Tax Base, *Bulletin for International Taxation* 66, No. 9, pp. 452-479.

Liu, J./Eichelberger, J. (2013), China: Income Tax Treatment of Cross-Border Secondment, *Intertax* 41, No. 10, pp. 551-552.

Locher, P. (1995), Praktikabilität im Steuerrecht (unter besonderer Berücksichtigung des materiellen Rechts der direkten Steuern), in: Cagianut, F./Vallender, K. A. (Eds.*), Steuerrecht - Ausgewählte Probleme am Ende des 20. Jahrhunderts - Festschrift zum 65. Geburtstag von Ernst Hohn*, pp. 189-222.

Lorenzen, H./Feldtkeller, J. (2012), Verrechnungspreisfestsetzung mit Schwellenländern - Konfliktpotential durch zunehmende Bedeutung der BRIC Staaten, *Internationale Wirtschafts-Briefe* 12, pp. 452-456.

Löwenstein, U. W. (2011), Branchenspezifische Besonderheiten bei der Betriebsstättenbesteuerung, in: Löwenstein, U.W./Looks, C./Heinsen,O. (2011), *Betriebsstättenbesteuerung- Inboundinvestitionen, Outboundinvestitionen, Steuergestaltungen, Branchenbesonderheiten*, Munich, pp. 438-568.

Luckhaupt, H./Overesch, M./Schreiber, U. (2012a), The OECD Approach to Transfer Pricing: A Critical Assessment and Proposal, in: Schön, W./Konrad, K. A. (Eds.), *Fundamentals of International Transfer Pricing in Law and Economics*, Berlin Heidelberg, pp. 91-121.

Luckhaupt, H./Overesch, M./Schreiber, U. (2012b), Objektivierung der steuerlichen Erfolgsabgrenzung bei internationaler Geschäftstätigkeit, *Steuer und Wirtschaft* 4, pp. 359-368.

Lüdicke, J. (2008), *Überlegungen zur deutschen DBA-Politik*, 1st Edition, Baden-Baden.

Lüdicke, J. (2010), Exemption and Tax Credit in German Tax Treaties - Policy and Reality, *Bulletin for International Taxation* 64, No. 12, pp. 609-619.

Lungu, I. (2011), Russia Clarifies PE Tax Treatment Under Treaty With U.S., *Tax Notes International* 63, No. 11, pp. 790-791.

Lungu, I. (2013), Guidance Targets Interest Expenses Incurred by Nonresident's PE, *Tax Notes International* 72, No. 1, p. 33.

Luttermann, C. (2007), Normenklarheit im Steuerrecht und 'unbestimmte' Rechtsbegriffe?, *Finanz-Rundschau* 1, pp. 18-23.

Machado, C./Lagrasta, C./Dantas, J./Verboom, H./Dols, H. (2013), Recent Changes to Brazil's Transfer Pricing Legislation, *Tax Notes International* 70, No. 7, pp. 689-691.

Manolakas, C./Brown, C. (2008), Tax Discrimination and Trade in Services: The Search for Balance in Canada-U.S. Relations, *Georgetown Journal of International Law* 40, No. 1, pp. 3-66.

Mason, R. (2010), Tax Discrimination and Capital Neutrality, *World Tax Journal* 2, pp. 126-138.

Matchekhin, V. (2014), Russia Report, in: IFA Cahiers Vol. 99a, *Cross-Border Outsourcing*, Rotterdam, pp. 613-620.

Matchekhin, V. A./Vakhitov, R. (2006), Russia Report, in: IFA Cahiers Vol. 91b, *The Attribution of Profits to Permanent Establishments*, Rotterdam, pp. 543-554.

Mattern, O./Zimny, M. (2014), Germany, in: Reimer, E./Schmid, S./Orell, M. (Eds.), *Permanent Establishments – A Domestic Taxation, Bilateral Tax Treaty and OECD Perspective*, Alphen aan den Rijn, pp. 1-33.

McCaffery, G. C./McKewen, D. P./Farrah, G. R./Pskowski, H. W./Bassett, J./ Tanevski, T. (2011), *2011 U.S. International Tax Guide*, 2nd Edition, Arlington.

McDaniel, P. R./Ault, H. J./Repetti, J. R. (2005), *Introduction to United States International Taxation*, 5th Edition, New York.

Mclntyre M. J. (1994), Colloquium on NAFTA and Tradition: Commentary: The Design of Tax Rules for the North American Free Trade Alliance, *Tax Law Review* 49, pp. 769-793.

McLure, C. E. (1992), Substituting Consumption-Based Direct Taxation for Income Taxes as the International Norm, *National Tax Journal* 45, No. 2, pp. 145-154.

Metha, A. (2011), Dependent Agency Permanent Establishments - Judicial Developments in India, *Bulletin for International Taxation* 65, No. 10, pp. 561-572.

Metha, A. (2012), India - Permanent Establishments, in: *IBFD Tax Research Platform, Topical Analyses: Permanent Establishments*, Access: September 2012.

Metha, A. (2015), India - Permanent Establishments, in: *IBFD Tax Research Platform, Topical Analyses: Permanent Establishments*, Access: January 2015.

Miller, A./Oats, L. (2014), *Principles of International Taxation*, 2nd Edition, West Sussex.

Mitra, R./Almoula, M./Pardiwala, P./Haldia, G. (2012), Transfer Pricing Guide 2012: Part 2 Response, in: *Bloomberg Transfer Pricing Forum 9/2012*, pp. 74-79.

Mitra, R./Sen, A. (2012), Commentary on the Permanent Establishment Concept under the UN Model Tax Convention, in: *IBFD Tax Research Platform, Topical Analyses: Permanent Establishments*, Access: September 2012.

Mödinger, J. (2012), *Internationale Erfolgs- und Vermögensabgrenzung zwischen Stammhaus und Betriebsstätte nach der Neufassung des Art. 7 OECD-MA*, 1st Edition, Cologne/Lohmar.

Monsenego, J. (2014), Designing Arbitration Provisions for Tax Treaties: Reflections Based on the US Experience, *Intertax* 42, No. 3, pp. 163-168.

Morlock, G. (2011), Aktuelle Fragen aus dem Bilanzsteuerrecht und der Betriebsprüfung - II. Vertreterbetriebsstätte beim sogenannten Kommissionärsmodell, in:

Drüen, K.-D. (Ed.) *Jahrbuch der Fachanwälte für Steuerrecht 2011/12*, Herne, pp. 794-824.

Morse, S. C. (2010), Revisiting Global Formulary Apportionment, *Virgina Tax Review* 29, pp. 593-644.

Mössner, J. M. (2000), Das Welteinkommensprinzip, in: Tipke, K./Bozza, N. (Eds.), *Besteuerung von Einkommen - Rechtsvergleich Italien, Deutschland und Spanien als Beitrag zur Harmonisierung des Steuerrechts in Europa, Berlin*, pp. 253-269.

Mössner, M. (2006), Source versus Residence – An EU Perspective, *Bulletin for International Taxation* 60, No. 12, pp. 501-506.

Mui, M./Yam, A. (2014), China, in: Reimer, E./Schmid, S./Orell, M. (Eds.), *Permanent Establishments – A Domestic Taxation, Bilateral Tax Treaty and OECD Perspective*, Alphen aan den Rijn, pp. 1-24.

Müller-Gatermann, G. (2012), Aktuelle deutsche Abkommenspolitik, *Finanz-Rundschau* 21, pp. 1032-1037.

Munoz, M. A. (2010), Disposal of a Fixed Place of Business: A Further Erosion of the Residence State Principle?, *Tax Notes International* 59, No. 5, pp. 371-392.

Musgrave, P. B. (1984), Principles for Dividing the State Corporate Tax Base, in: McLure, C. E. (Ed.), *The State Corporation Income Tax – Issues in Worldwide Unitary Combination*, Stanford, pp. 228-252.

Musgrave, P. B. (1987), Interjurisdictional Coordination of Taxes on Capital Income, in: Cnossen, S. (Ed.), *Tax Coordination in the European Community*, Massachusetts, pp. 97-125.

Musgrave, P. B. (2000a), Interjurisdictional Equity in Company Taxation: Principles and Applications to the European Union, in: Cnossen, S. (Ed.), *Taxing Capital Income in the European Union – Issues and Options for Reform*, Oxford, pp. 46-77.

Musgrave, P. B. (2000b), Consumption Tax Proposals in an International Setting, *Tax Law Review* 54, pp. 77-100.

Musgrave, R. A./Musgrave, P. B. (1972), Inter-nation Equity, in: Bird, R. M./Head, J. G. (Eds.), *Modern Fiscal Issues, Essays in Honour of Carl S. Shoup*, Toronto, pp. 63-85.

Musgrave, R. A./Musgrave, P. B. (1989), *Public Finance in Theory and Practice*, 5th Edition, United States.

Neumark, F. (1970), *Grundsätze gerechter und ökonomisch rationaler Steuerpolitik*, 1st Edition, Tübingen.

Niehaves, D. (2010), *Die Vertreterbetriebsstätte - Konzeption und Einkünftezuordnung*, 1st Edition, Hamburg.

Niehaves, D. (2011), Die Gewinnabgrenzung bei Vertreterbetriebsstätten, *Internationales Steuerrecht* 10, pp. 373-379.

Nientimp, A./Ludwig, C./Stein, S. (2014), Die finale Betriebsstättengewinnaufteilungsverordnung (BsGaV) - Anwendung des Authorised OECD Approach in Deutschland, *Internationale Wirtschafts-Briefe* 22, pp. 815-826.

Nitikman, J. (2009), The Painter and the PE, *Canadian Tax Journal* 57, No. 2, pp. 681-707.

Nitikman, J. (2014), More on Services PEs – What Is a Connected Project?, *Tax Notes International* 76, No. 9, pp. 793-832.

Nouel, L, (2011), The New Article 7 of the OECD Model Tax Convention: The End of the Road?, *Bulletin for International Taxation* 65, No. 1, pp. 5-12.

O'Neill, J. (2001), *Building Better Global Economic BRICs*, Goldman Sachs, Global Economics Paper No. 66.

Obuoforibo, B. R. (2013), In the Name of Clarity: Defining a Dependent Agent Permanent Establishment, in: Gutiérrez, C./Perdelwitz, A. (Eds.), *Taxation of Business Profits in the 21st Century – Selected Issues under Tax Treaties*, Amsterdam, pp. 57-78.

OECD (2012), *OECD's Current Tax Agenda 2012*, Paris.

OECD Attribution of Income to PE (1993), *Attribution of Income to Permanent Establishments*, Discussion Draft, 26 November 1993, Paris.

OECD BEPS Action Plan (2013), *Action Plan on Base Erosion and Profit Shifting*, 19 July 2013, Paris.

OECD Developing Countries and BEPS (2015), http://www.oecd.org/tax/developing-countries-and-beps.htm, 04 December 2015.

OECD Discussion Draft BEPS Action 7 (2014), *BEPS Action 7: Preventing the Artificial Avoidance of the PE Status*, 31 October 2014-9 January 2015, Paris.

OECD Discussion Draft BEPS Action 10 (2015), *BEPS Action 10: Proposed Modifications to Chapter VII of the Transfer Pricing Guidelines Relating to Low Value-adding Intra-group Services*, 3 November 2014-14 January 2015, Paris.

OECD Discussion Draft BEPS Action 14 (2015), *BEPS Action 14: Make Dispute Resolution Mechanisms More Effective*, 18 December 2014-16 January 2015, Paris.

OECD Discussion Draft on the Attribution of Profits to PE (2001), *Discussion Draft on the Attribution of Profits to Permanent Establishments*, Public Discussion Draft, Paris.

OECD Discussion Draft on the Attribution of Profits to PE (2004), *Discussion Draft on the Attribution of Profits to Permanent Establishments*, Public Discussion Draft, Paris.

OECD Discussion Draft Transfer Pricing Comparability (2014), *Transfer Pricing Comparability Data and Developing Countries*, Paris

OECD Final Report BEPS Action 7 (2015), *Preventing the Artificial Avoidance of Permanent Establishment Status, Action 7 – 2015 Final Report*, 5 October 2015, Paris.

OECD Final Report BEPS Actions 8, 9 & 10 (2015), *Aligning Transfer Pricing Outcomes with Value Creation, Actions 8-10 – 2015 Final Reports*, 5 October 2015, Paris.

OECD MAP Statistics (2013), *Mutual Agreement Procedure Statistics 2006-2013*, http://www.oecd.org/ctp/dispute/map-statistics-2006-2013.htm, 04 December 2015.

OECD MC Commentary (2014), Model Tax Convention on Income and on Capital – Condensed Version: *Model Convention with Respect to Taxes on Income and on Capital & Commentaries on the Articles of the Model Tax Convention*, 15 July 2014, Paris.

OECD Partnership Report (1999), *The Application of the OECD Model Tax Convention to Partnerships*, Issues in International Taxation No. 6, Paris.

OECD Report BEPS Action 6 (2014), *Preventing the Granting of Treaty Benefits in Inappropriate Circumstances, Action 6: 2014 Deliverable*, 16 September 2014, Paris.

OECD Report E-Commerce (2003), *Are the Current Treaty Rules for Taxing Business Profits Appropriate for E-Commerce?*, Final Report, Paris.

OECD Report on the Attribution of Profits to PE (2006), *Report on the Attribution of Profits to Permanent Establishments*, December 2006, Paris.

OECD Report on the Attribution of Profits to PE (2008), *Report on the Attribution of Profits to Permanent Establishments*, 17 July 2008, Paris.

OECD Report on the Attribution of Profits to PE (2010), *Report on the Attribution of Profits to Permanent Establishments*, 22 July 2010, Paris.

OECD Report Safe Harbours (2013), *Revised Section E on Safe Harbours in Chapter IV of the Transfer Pricing Guidelines*, 16 May 2013, Paris.

OECD Revised Discussion Draft BEPS Action 7 (2015), *BEPS Action Plan 7: Preventing the Artificial Avoidance of PE Status*, 15 May 2015-12 June 2015, Paris.

OECD Revised Proposals (2012), *Revised Proposals concerning the Interpretation and Application of Article 5 (Permanent Establishment)*, Revised Public Discussion Draft, 19 October 2012-31 January 2013, Paris.

OECD Transfer Pricing Guidelines (2010), *OECD Transfer Pricing Guidelines for Multinational Enterprises and Tax Administrations*, 22 July 2010, Paris.

Oestreicher, A. (2000), *Konzern-Gewinnabgrenzung - Gewinnabgrenzung, Gewinnermittlung, Gewinnaufteilung*, 1st Edition, Munich.

Ott, S. (2009), *Die Vertreterbetriebsstätte nach OECD-MA*, 1st Edition, Frankfurt a.M.

Owens, J. (2002), Tax Administration in the New Millennium, *Intertax* 30, No. 4, pp. 125-130.

Owens, J. (2012), Trends and Challenges in the Tax Arena, *Bulletin for International Taxation* 66, No. 12, pp. 685-690.

Owens, J. (2015), The BRICS: An Overall Perspective, in: Brauner, Y./Pistone, P. (Eds.), *BRICS and the Emergence of International Tax Coordination*, Amsterdam, pp. 353-365.

Padmakshan, M. (2014), Hotel Rooms Used for Business Purposes Create PE in India, *Tax Notes International* 74, No. 3, pp. 246-247.

Palwe, S. S./Kumar, P. (2009), India's Position on OECD Tax Principles, *Tax Notes International* 53, No. 3, pp. 237-241.

Parada, L. (2013), Agents vs. Commissionaires: A Comparison in Light of the OECD Model Convention, *Tax Notes International* 72, No. 1, pp. 59-65.

Parillo, K. A. (2013), PE Profit Attribution Clarified Under Belgium-U.S. Treaty, *Tax Notes International* 71, No. 7, p. 619.

Parillo, K. A. (2015), A Destination-Based Corporate Tax: An Alternative to BEPS?, *Tax Notes International* 78, No. 4, pp. 315-320.

Parillo, K. A./Sheppard, L. A. (2014), OECD Addresses Artificial Avoidance of PE Status, *Tax Notes International* 76, No. 6, pp. 483-485.

Paulitsch, S./Eckerstorfer, M. (2014) Implementation of the Authorised OECD Approach: Case Study of Permanent Establishment Profit Determination under the

Austria-Germany Income Tax Treaty, *International Transfer Pricing Journal* 21, No. 3, pp. 185-188.

PE Decree (2014), *Verordnung zur Anwendung des Fremdvergleichsgrundsatzes auf Betriebsstätten nach §1 Absatz 5 des Außensteuergesetzes (Betriebsstättengewinnaufteilungsverordnung-BsGaV)*, BStBl. 2014 I, 13 October 2014, pp. 1378-1392.

PE Decree Draft (2013), *Entwurf: Verordnung zur Anwendung des Fremdvergleichsgrundsatzes auf Betriebsstätten nach § 1 Absatz 5 des Außensteuergesetzes (Betriebsstättengewinnaufteilungsverordnung - BsGaV)*, 5 August 2013.

Pellone, C. (2011), Tax Authorities Issue Circular on Interpretation of Double Tax Treaties, *International Transfer Pricing Journal* 18, No. 2, pp. 143-146.

Penn, O./Rinke, D. (2014), United States, in: Reimer, E./Schmid, S./Orell, M. (Eds.), *Permanent Establishments – A Domestic Taxation, Bilateral Tax Treaty and OECD Perspective*, Alphen aan den Rijn, pp. 1-26.

Perdelwitz, A. (2013), A Certain Degree of Permanence – Between Temporary and Everlasting Business Activities, in: Gutiérrez, C./Perdelwitz, A. (Eds.), *Taxation of Business Profits in the 21st Century – Selected Issues under Tax Treaties*, Amsterdam, pp. 27-55.

Persico, G. (2000), Agency Permanent Establishment under Article 5 of the OECD Model Convention, *Intertax* 28, No. 2, pp. 66-82.

Pickering, A. (2012), General Report, in: IFA Cahiers Vol. 97a, *Enterprise Services*, Rotterdam, pp. 17-60.

Pijl, H. (2006), The Zero-Sum Game, the Emperor's Beard and the Authorised OECD Approach, *European Taxation* 46, No. 1, pp. 29-35.

Pijl. H. (2008), Morgan Stanley: Issues regarding Permanent Establishments and Profit Attribution in Light of the OECD View, *Bulletin for International Taxation* 62, No. 5, pp. 174-182.

Pijl, H. (2013a), Agency Permanent Establishments: In the Name of and the Relationship between Article 5(5) and (6) – Part 1, *Bulletin for International Taxation* 67, No. 1, pp. 1-25.

Pijl, H. (2013b), Agency Permanent Establishments: In the Name of and the Relationship between Article 5(5) and (6) – Part 2, *Bulletin for International Taxation* 67, No. 2, pp. 62-97.

Piltz, D.J. (2004), Wann liegt eine DBA-Vertreter-Betriebsstätte vor?, *Internationales Steuerrecht* 6, pp. 181-187.

Pinkernell, R. (2014), *Internationale Steuergestaltung im Electronic Commerce*, ifst-Schrift No. 494, Berlin.

Pinkernell, R./Ditz, X. (2001), Betriebsstättenbegriff, Einkünftequalifikation und Gewinnabgrenzung beim Online-Vertrieb elektronischer Produkte (Teil I), *Finanz-Rundschau* 23, pp. 1193-1206.

Pinto, D. (2006), The Need to Reconceptualize the Permanent Establishment Threshold, *Bulletin for International Taxation* 60, No. 7, pp. 266-279.

Plansky, P. (2010), *Die Gewinnzurechnung zu Betriebsstätten im Recht der Doppelbesteuerungsabkommen*, 1st Edition, Wien.

Pleijsier, A (2001), The Agency Permanent Establishment: The Current Definition - Part One, *Intertax* 29, No. 5, pp. 167-183.

Pleijsier, A. (2015), The Agency Permanent Establishment in BEPS Action 7: Treaty Abuse or Business Abuse?, *Intertax* 43, No. 2, pp. 147-154.

Portner, R. (2014), Irrungen und Wirrungen beim Auslandseinsatz von Arbeitnehmern, *Internationales Steuerrecht* 12, pp. 435-443.

Protto, C. (2014), Mutual Agreement Procedures in Tax Treaties: Problems and Needs in Developing Countries and Countries in Transition, *Intertax* 42, No. 3, pp. 176-178.

Puls, M. (2005), *Die Betriebsstätte im Abgaben- und Abkommensrecht*, 1st Edition, Cologne.

Qiu, D. (2013), Permanent Establishment: An Evolving Concept Under China's Tax Treaties (1983-2013), *British Tax Review*, No. 3, pp. 274-306.

Rasch, S. (2011), Aktuelle Entwicklungen bei der Betriebsstättenbegründung - Renaissance des Kommissionärsmodells?, *Internationales Steuerrecht* 1, pp. 6-13.

Rasch, S./Dotterweich, S. (2014), Vertreterbetriebsstätte: Begründung durch Vertriebsstrukturen?, *Internationale Steuer-Rundschau* 2, pp. 65-72.

Rasch, S./Müller, C. (2014), Vertreterbetriebsstätte: BsGaV: Der ständige Vertreter und die 'Nullsummentheorie', *Internationale Steuer-Rundschau* 12, pp. 418-422.

Rasch, S./Tillmann, L. (2013), Base Erosion and Profit Shifting: Hat der Fremdvergleichsgrundsatz für die Bestimmung der Verrechnungspreise noch eine Zukunft?, *Internationale Steuer-Rundschau* 4, pp. 139-143.

Rautenstrauch, G./Binger, M. (2009), Dienstleistungsbetriebsstätten - Zukunft oder bereits Realität?, *Die Unternehmensbesteuerung* 9, pp. 619-627.

Rawal, R. (2004), *Attribution et al – Taxation of Permanent Establishment*, 1st Edition, Mumbai.

Rawal, R. (2005), Comparative Survey – India, in: Russo, R. (Ed.), *The Attribution of Profits to Permanent Establishments – The Taxation of Intra-Company Dealings*, Amsterdam, pp. 223-235.

Rawal, R. (2006), *Taxation of Permanent Establishments: An International Perspective*, 1st Edition, London.

Rehfeld, L./Goldner, H. (2013), Gewinnabgrenzung zwischen Stammhaus und Betriebsstätte: Nationale Umsetzung des AOA in§ 1 AStG n. F. durch das AmtshilfeRLUmsG, *Internationale Wirtschafts-Briefe* 16, pp. 548-554.

Reimer, E. (2014), Permanent Establishment in the OECD Model Tax Convention, Fundaments, Is There a Permanent Establishment?, in: Reimer, E./Schmid, S./Orell, M. (Eds.), *Permanent Establishments – A Domestic Taxation, Bilateral Tax Treaty and OECD Perspective*, Alphen aan den Rijn, pp. 3-30, 31-136.

Reimer, E./Schmid, S./Orell, M. (2014), *Permanent Establishments – A Domestic Taxation, Bilateral Tax Treaty and OECD Perspective*, 3rd Edition, Alphen aan den Rijn.

Remberg, M. (2006), Anmerkungen zu den OECD-Überlegungen zur Betriebsstättenbesteuerung aus der Sicht des Anlagenbaus, *Internationales Steuerrecht* 16, pp. 545-548.

Resch, R. W. (2002), *Public Finance – A Normative Theory*, 2nd Edition, San Diego/London.

Rigoni, J. M. (2014), A Brazilian View on Base Erosion and Profit Shifting: An Alternative Path, *Intertax* 42, No. 11, pp. 730-742.

Ring, D. M. (2002), One Nation Among Many: Policy Implications of Cross-Border Tax Arbitrage, *Boston College Law Review* 44, pp. 79-175.

Ring, D. M. (2012), United States – Permanent Establishments, in: *IBFD Tax Research Platform, Topical Analyses: Permanent Establishments*, Access: September 2012.

Ring, D. M. (2015), United States – Permanent Establishments, in: *IBFD Tax Research Platform, Topical Analyses: Permanent Establishments*, Access: January 2015.

Rocha, S. A. (2009), *Interpretation of Double Taxation Conventions – General Theory and Brazilian Perspective*, 1st Edition, Alphen aan den Rijn.

Rocha, S. A. (2012), Brazil Report, in: IFA Cahiers Vol. 97a, *Enterprise Services*, Rotterdam, pp. 155-167.

Rocha, S. A. (2013), Agency Permanent Establishment 'Brazilian Style': Taxation of Profits Earned Through Commission Merchants, Agents and Representatives, *Intertax* 41, No. 8/9, pp. 444-449.

Roeder, A./Friedrich, J. (2015), Regelungsmängel der Betriebsstättengewinnaufteilungsverordnung, *Betriebs-Berater* 18, pp. 1053-1057.

Rosalem, F. B. (2010), The Agent Permanent Establishment Reconsidered: Application of Arts. 5, 7 and 9 of the OECD Model Convention, *International Transfer Pricing Journal* 17, No. 1, pp. 12-33.

Rosenberger, F./Vitali, M./Ziehr, U. (2010), Die Dienstleistungsbetriebsstätte: Internationale Entwicklungen und ihre Rezeption im Internationalen Steuerrecht Deutschlands, Österreichs und der Schweiz, *Internationales Steuerrecht* Beiheft zu 18, pp. 1-36.

Roser, F. (2013), Ansatzpunkte und Fehlvorstellungen zur Dynamisierung steuerlicher Bestimmungen - unter besonderer Berücksichtigung der DBA, *Die Unternehmensbesteuerung* 1, pp. 37-45.

Roth, A. (2011), Die Gewinnabgrenzung bei der grenzüberschreitenden Überführung von Wirtschaftsgütern in eine Betriebsstätte unter steuerplanerischen Gesichtspunkten, in: Grotherr, S. (Ed.), *Handbuch der internationalen Steuerplanung*, Herne, pp. 75-96.

Roxan, I. (2012), *Limits to Globalisation: Some Implications for Taxation, Tax Policy, and the Developing World*, London.

Ruh, W./Beyer, W. (2010), Verschärfung der Quellensteuerpflicht für Dienstleistungen durch Einführung der Permanent Account Number in Indien, *Internationale Wirtschafts-Briefe* 17, pp. 642-646.

Runge, B. (2001), Der neue Betriebsstättenerlaß - Geregelte und nicht geregelte Fälle -, in: Piltz, D./Schaumburg, H. (Eds.), *Internationale Betriebsstättenbesteuerung*, Cologne, pp. 131-146.

Runkel, M. (2012), In Favor of Formulary Apportionment – A Comment on Kroppen/Dawid/Schmidtke: 'Profit Split, the Future of Transfer Pricing? Arm's Length Principle and Formulary Apportionment Revisited from a Theoretical and a Practical Perspective', in: Schön, W./Konrad, K. A. (Eds.), *Fundamentals of*

International Transfer Pricing in Law and Economics, Berlin Heidelberg, pp. 295-304.

Russo, R. (2006), Report on the historical development of article 7 of the OECD model, in: IFA Cahiers Vol. 91b, *The Attribution of Profits to Permanent Establishments*, Rotterdam, pp. 89-108.

Salzberger, W. (2013), I. Betriebsstätten und die Gewinnabgrenzung im Anlagenbau, in: Oestreicher, A. (Ed.), *Modernisierung des Unternehmenssteuerrechts*, Herne, pp. 137-148.

Sandford, C. (1995), Minimising Administrative and Compliance Costs, in: Sandford, C. (Ed.), *More Key Issues in Tax Reform*, Fersfield, Perrymead, pp. 89-104.

Sanghvi, S./Shaktawat, R. (2012), Taxation of Fees for Technical Services and Royalties, *Asia-Pacific Tax Bulletin* 18, No. 6, pp. 452-459.

Sasseville, J./Skaar, A. (2009), General Report, in: IFA Cahiers Vol. 94a, *Is There a Permanent Establishment?*, Rotterdam, pp. 17-63.

Schaumburg, H. (1995), Das Leistungsfähigkeitsprinzip im Internationalen Steuerrecht, in: Lang, J. (Ed.), *Die Steuerrechtsordnung in der Diskussion: Festschrift für Klaus Tipke zum 70. Geburtstag*, Cologne, pp. 125-151.

Schaumburg, H. (2013), Grenzüberschreitende Einkünftekorrektur bei Betriebsstätten - Verfassungs- und europarechtliche Aspekte, *Internationale Steuer-Rundschau* 6, pp. 197-202.

Schaumburg, H./Schaumburg, H. (2013), Steuergerechtigkeit in der Zeit, *Steuer und Wirtschaft* 1, pp. 61-71.

Scheffler, W. (2007), Rechtsform und Finanzierung einer Auslandsinvestition nach der Unternehmenssteuerreform 2008, *Steuer und Studium* 9, pp. 446-454.

Schindel, A./Atchabahian, A. (2005), General Report, in: IFA Cahiers 90a, *Source and Residence: New Configuration of Their Principles*, Rotterdam, pp. 21-99.

Schneider, D. (1992), *Investition, Finanzierung und Besteuerung*, 7th Edition, Wiesbaden.

Schnitger, A. (2012), Änderungen des § 1 AStG und Umsetzung des AOA durch das JStG 2013, *Internationales Steuerrecht* 17, pp. 633-645.

Schnitger, A. (2013), *Die Entstrickung im Steuerrecht*, ifst-Schrift No. 487, Berlin.

Schnorberger, S. (2012), Germany - Permanent Establishments, in: *IBFD Tax Research Platform, Topical Analyses: Permanent Establishments*, Access: September 2012.

Schnorberger, S. (2015), Germany - Permanent Establishments, in: *IBFD Tax Research Platform, Topical Analyses: Permanent Establishments*, Access: January 2015.

Schnorberger, S./Sassmann, J./Shekhovtsova, M. (2014), Betriebsstättengewinnermittlung nach dem OECD-Ansatz: Der Grundfall der Vertriebsbetriebsstätte, *Internationales Steuerrecht* 3, pp. 81-87.

Schön, W. (2002), Vermeidbare und unvermeidbare Hindernisse der Steuervereinfachung, *Steuer und Wirtschaft* 1, pp. 23-35.

Schön, W. (2009), International Tax Coordination for a Second-Best World (Part I), *World Tax Journal* 1, pp. 67-114.

Schön, W. (2012a), Zur Zukunft des Internationalen Steuerrechts, *Steuer und Wirtschaft* 3, pp. 213-224.

Schön, W. (2012b), The Permanent Establishment - One Word, Two Concepts, in: Kameda, K./Kawabata, Y./Miyamoto, T./Nakamura, S./Urahigashi, H./Tsuji, M. (Eds.), *Festschrift in Honor of Professor Tadashi Murai*, Osaka, pp. 437-442.

Schön, W. (2013), Leitideen des Steuerrechts oder: Nichtwissen als staatswissenschaftliches Problem, *Steuer und Wirtschaft* 4, pp. 289-297.

Schön, W. (2015), Neutrality and Territoriality - Competing or Converging Concepts in European Tax Law?, *Bulletin for International Taxation* 69, No. 4/5, pp. 271-293.

Schoss, N.-P. (2011), Betriebsstätte oder Tochtergesellschaft im Ausland, in: Grotherr, S. (Ed.), *Handbuch der internationalen Steuerplanung*, Herne, pp. 51-74.

Schoueri, L. E./Barbosa, M. C. (2013), Technical Services and the Application of Article 7 under Brazilian Treaty Practice: A Case Study, in: Lang, M./Owens, J./Pistone, P./Schuch, J./Staringer, C./Storck, A./Essers, P./Kemmeren, E. C.C.M./Smit, D. S. (Eds.), *Tax Treaty Case Law around the Globe 2013*, pp. 103-116.

Schreiber, U. (1994), Unternehmensbesteuerung im Europäischen Binnenmarkt, *Steuer und Wirtschaft* 3, pp. 238-254.

Schreiber, U. (2012), *Besteuerung der Unternehmen - Eine Einführung in Steuerrecht und Steuerwirkung*, 3rd Edition, Wiesbaden.

Schreiber, U. (2013), International Business Taxation and the Business Cash Flow Tax, *Review of Managerial Science* 7, No. 3, pp 309-326.

Schwinger, R. (1994), Konsum oder Einkommen als Bemessungsgrundlagen direkter Steuern?, *Steuer und Wirtschaft* 1, pp. 39-50.

Seeleitner, K./Krinninger, M./Grimm, K. (2013), Verschärfung der steuerlichen Herausforderungen durch den Authorised OECD Approach (AOA) bei Bau- und Montagebetriebsstätten?, *Internationales Steuerrecht* 6, pp. 220-227.

Seltenreich, S. (2006), Aktuelle Entwicklungen und Tendenzen im Bereich der Begründung einer Vertreter-Betriebsstatte gem. Art. 5 Abs. 5 OECD-MA, *Internationale Wirtschafts-Briefe* 6, pp. 247-258.

Shakow, D. J. (2013), The Taxation of Cloud Computing and Digital Content, *Tax Notes International* 71, No. 4, pp. 363-383.

Shaw, J./Slemrod, J. B./Whiting, J. (2010), Administration and Compliance, in: Mirrlees, J./Adam, S./Besley, T./Blundell, R./Bond, S./Chote, R./Gammie, M./ Johnson, P./Myles, G./Poterba, J. (Eds.), *Dimensions of Tax Design: the Mirrlees Review*, Oxford, pp. 1100-1162.

Shay, S. E./Fleming, J. C./Peroni, R. J. (2002), The David R. Tillinghast Lecture - 'What's Source Got to Do With It?' - Source Rules and U.S. International Taxation, *Tax Law Review* 56, pp. 81-155.

Sheppard, L. A. (2006), Revenge of the Source Countries, Part 5: Throwing BRICs, *Tax Notes* 111, No. 13, pp. 1455-1460.

Sheppard, L. A. (2010), Tweaking the Permanent Establishment Concept, *Tax Notes International* 57, No. 1, pp. 18-23.

Sheppard, L. A. (2011), Cross-Border Services and PE in Latin America, *Tax Notes International* 63, No. 1, pp. 10-15.

Sheppard, L. A. (2013), The Digital Economy and Permanent Establishment, *Tax Notes International* 70, No. 4, pp. 297-300.

Sherchan, P./Rao, S. (2010), Attribution of Business Income in India, *Tax Notes International* 57, No. 4, pp. 353-356.

Simpson, H. (2008), Investment Abroad and Adjustment at Home: evidence from UK multinational firms, *Canadian Journal of Economics* 45, No. 2, pp. 699-731.

Singh, M. K. (2014), Taxing E-Commerce on the Basis of Permanent Establishment: Critical Evaluation, *Intertax* 42, No. 5, pp. 325-333.

Skaar, A. A. (1991), *Permanent Establishment – Erosion of a Tax Treaty Principle*, 1st Edition, Deventer.

Skaar, A. A. (2012), Analysis Art. 5 OECD Model Convention, in: *IBFD Tax Research Platform, Topical Analyses: Permanent Establishments*, Access: September 2012.

Slemrod, J. B. (1995), Free Trade Taxation and Protectionist Taxation, *International Tax and Public Finance* 2, pp. 471-489.

Slemrod, J. B. (1996), Which is the Simplest Tax System of Them All?, in: Aaron, H. J./Gale, W. G. (Eds.), *Economic Effects of Fundamental Tax Reform*, Washington D.C., pp. 355-391.

Soares da Silva, D. R. (2011), *Brazil Tax Guide For Foreigners: A Comprehensive Guide to Investing and Surviving in One of the Most Complex Tax Systems in the World*, 1st Edition, Brazil.

Soares da Silva, D. R. (2012), A Look at the Court's Rationale in Brazil's COPESUL Case, *Tax Notes International* 67, No. 6, pp. 513-516.

Somare, M./Turcan, L./Zeiler, A. (2014), Case Studies on Construction Permanent Establishments and Related Taxation Issues, *Bulletin for International Taxation* 68, No. 4/5, pp. 224-228.

Spencer, D. (2014), Formula Apportionment Is Not a Panacea – Part 2, *Journal of International Taxation* 25, No. 5, pp. 35-48.

Spencer, D. (2014), Formula Apportionment Is Not a Panacea – Part 3, *Journal of International Taxation* 25, No. 6, pp. 31-42.

Spencer, D. (2014), Formula Apportionment Is Not a Panacea – Part 5, *Journal of International Taxation* 25, No. 8, pp. 33-64.

Spengel, C. (2003), *Internationale Unternehmensbesteuerung in der Europäischen Union*, 1st Edition, Düsseldorf.

Spengel, C. (2013), Neutralitätskonzepte und Anreizwirkungen im Internationalen Steuerrecht, in: Achatz, M. (Ed.), *Internationales Steuerrecht*, 37. Jahrestagung der Deutschen Steuerjuristischen Gesellschaft e.V. Linz, 10. und 11. September 2012, Cologne, pp. 39-70.

Spengel, C./Malke, C. (2008), Comprehensive Tax Base or Residual Reference to GAAP or Domestic Tax Law?, in: Lang, M./Pistone, P./Schuch, J./Staringer, C. (Eds.) *Common Consolidated Corporate Tax Base*, Vienna, pp. 63-92.

Spengel, C./Ortmann-Babel, M./Zinn, B./Matenaer, S. (2012), A Common Corporate Tax Base for Europe: An Impact Assessment of the Draft Council Directive on a CC(C)TB, *World Tax Journal* 4, No. 3, pp. 185-221.

Staringer, C. (2008), Requirements for Forming a Group, in: Lang, M./Pistone, P./Schuch, J./Staringer, C. (Eds.) *Common Consolidated Corporate Tax Base*, Vienna, pp. 117-136.

Staringer, C. (2010), Kommissionärsstrukturen im internationalen Konzernvertrieb, *Steuer und Wirtschaft* 9, pp. 407-413.

Strauß, J. (1999), Art. 12 Indien, in: Debatin, H./Wassermeyer, F. (Eds.), *Beck'sche Steuerkommentare Doppelbesteuerung: DBA*, loose leaf (113th Suppl. Delivery 2011), Munich, pp. 81-90.

Strunk, G./Wichmann, M. (2001), Germany, in: IFA Cahiers Vol. 86a, *Taxation of Income Derived from Electronic Commerce*, Rotterdam, pp. 409-438.

Susarla, K./Krishnan, C. (2014), Casenote - Delhi High Court Decision on Taxability of Offshore Supply and Services, *Asia-Pacific Tax Bulletin* 20, No. 6, pp. 433-437.

Tappe, H. (2011), Steuerliche Betriebsstätten in der 'Cloud' - Neuere technische Entwicklungen im Bereich des E-commerce als Herausforderung für den ertragsteuerrechtlichen Betriebsstättenbegriff, *Internationales Steuerrecht* 22, pp. 870-874.

Task Force (2006), Report of the Task Force on International Tax Reform, *Tax Lawyer* 59, No. 3, pp. 649-676.

Tipke, K. (2000), Der Grundsatz der Steuergerechtigkeit, in: Tipke, K./Bozza, N. (Eds.), *Besteuerung von Einkommen - Rechtsvergleich Italien, Deutschland und Spanien als Beitrag zur Harmonisierung des Steuerrechts in Europa*, Berlin, pp. 9-32.

Tittle, M. B. (2007a), *Permanent Establishment in the United States – A View Through Article V of the U.S.-Canada Tax Treaty*, 1st Edition, Lake Mary.

Tittle, M. B. (2007b), A Unified Approach to Permanent Establishment by Agent in the U.S., *Tax Notes International* 48, No. 6, pp. 597-612.

Toro, C. E. (2009), Different Methods of Attributing Profits to Agency PEs, *Tax Notes International* 53, No. 5, pp. 421-445.

Uckmar, V. (2012), Double Taxation Conventions, in: Amatucci, A. (Ed.), *International Tax Law*, 2nd Edition, Alphen aan den Rijn, pp. 161-193.

UN MC Commentary (2011), *United Nations Model Double Taxation Convention between Developed and Developing Countries*, New York.

UN Transfer Pricing Practical Manual (2013), Chapter 10.2: Brazil Country Practices, in: *United Nations – Practical Manual on Transfer Pricing for Developing Countries*, New York, pp. 358-374.

UN Working Paper (2008), *Proposal of the Amendments of the United Nations Model Double Taxation Convention between Developed and Developing Countries: Further Issues Relating to Permanent Establishment*, E/C.18/2008/CRP.3, Geneva, 20-24 October 2008.

US MC Technical Explanation (2006), *United States Model Technical Explanation accompanying the United States Model Income Tax Convention of November 15, 2006.*

USCIB Response (2012), *USCIB Response to the OECD Model Tax Convention: Revised Proposals Concerning the Interpretation and Application of Article 5 (Permanent Establishment)*, pp. 1-15.

US-Netherlands Tax Treaty Memorandum of Understanding (2004), *Understanding regarding the Convention between the Kingdom of the Netherlands and the United States of America for the Avoidance of Double Taxation and the Prevention of*

Fiscal Evasion with Respect to Taxes on Income, signed on 18 December, 1992 and Amended by Protocols signed on 13 October 1993 and 8 March 2004.

US-Poland Tax Treaty Explanation (2014), *Explanation of Proposed Income Tax Treaty between the US and Poland*, JCX-68-14, 17 June 2014.

Utescher, T. (1999), *Internet und Steuern: Electronic Commerce und Telearbeit*, 1st Edition, Düsseldorf.

Vacovec, K. J./James, T. S./Hoiberg, L. L. (2001), The U.S. Foreign Tax Credit for Corporate Taxpayers, *Bulletin for International Fiscal Documentation* 55, No. 9, pp. 397-406.

Vaillancourt, F./Clemens, J. (2008) Compliance and Administrative Costs of Taxation in Canada, in: Clemens, J. (Ed.), *The Impact and Cost of Taxation in Canada – The Case for Flat Tax Reform*, Canada, pp. 55-102.

Van Raad, K. (2000), Deemed Expenses of a Permanent Establishment under Article 7 of the OECD Model, *Intertax* 28, No. 4, pp. 162-167.

Van Raad, K. (2000), International Coordination of Tax Treaty Interpretation and Application, in: Kirchhof, P./Lehner, M./Raupach, A./Rodi, M. (Eds.), *Staaten und Steuern - Festschrift für Klaus Vogel zum 70. Geburtstag*, Heidelberg, pp. 1091-1103.

Van Wanrooij, J. S. A. (2009), Comments on the Proposed Article 7 of the OECD Model Convention, *Intertax* 37, No. 5, pp. 298-306.

Vann, R. (2012), IFA/OECD Seminar in Boston: Now You See It, Now You Don't - The Elusive Concept of Permanent Establishment, *Bulletin for International Taxation* 66, No. 9, pp. 1-2.

Vasutin, R. (2013), *Why Secondment Has Little Impact on Permanent Establishment in Russia*, Transfer Pricing Week, 12 September 2013, http://www.tpweek.com/Article/3254238/Why-secondment-has-little-impact-on-permanent-establishment-in-Russia.html, 04.12.2015.

Vogel, K. (1988), Worldwide vs. Source Taxation of Income – A Review and Re-evaluation of Arguments (Part III), *Intertax* 16, No. 11, pp. 393-402.

Vogel, K. (1993), Harmonisierung des Internationalen Steuerrechts in Europa als Alternative zur Harmonisierung des (materiellen) Körperschaftsteuerrechts, *Steuer und Wirtschaft* 4, pp. 380-388.

Vogel, K. (1994), Über 'Besteuerungsrechte' und über das Leistungsfähigkeitsprinzip im Internationalen Steuerrecht, in: Kirchhoff, P./Offerhaus, K./Schöberle, H. (Eds.), *Steuerrecht, Verfassungsrecht, Finanzpolitik: Festschrift für Franz Klein*, Cologne, pp. 361-376.

Vogel, K. (2003), Transnationale Auslegung von Doppelbesteuerungsabkommen, *Internationales Steuerrecht* 15, pp. 523-529.

Vogel, K./Rust, A. (2015), Introduction, in: Reimer, E./Rust, A. (Eds.) *Klaus Vogel on Double Taxation Conventions*, Alphen aan den Rijn, pp. 1-72.

Vollert, P./Eikel, C./Sureth, C. (2013), Advance Pricing Agreements (APAs) als Instrument zur Vermeidung von Verrechnungspreiskonflikten - eine kritische Betrachtung, *Steuer und Wirtschaft* 4, pp. 367-379.

Von Poser und Groß-Naedlitz, A. (1972), *Der Qualifikationskonflikt bei Doppelbesteuerungsabkommen*, 1st Edition, Munich.

Wagner, F. W. (1992), Neutralität und Gleichmäßigkeit als ökonomische und rechtliche Kriterien steuerlicher Normkritik, *Steuer und Wirtschaft* 1, pp. 2-13.

Wagner, F. W. (2005a), Steuervereinfachung und Entscheidungsneutralität - konkurrierende oder komplementäre Leitbilder für Steuerreformen?, *Steuer und Wirtschaft* 2, pp. 93-108.

Wagner, F. W. (2005b), Kann die Besteuerung vereinfacht werden, wenn die Rechnungslegung komplexer wird?, *Betriebswirtschaftliche Forschung und Praxis* 57, No. 6, pp. 528-545.

Wagner, F. W. (2006), Was bedeutet und wozu dient die Rechtsformneutralität der Unternehmensbesteuerung, *Steuer und Wirtschaft* 2, pp. 101-114.

Wang, H. (2008), Steuereffiziente Gestaltung deutscher Investitionen in China unter Berücksichtigung der chinesischen Unternehmenssteuerreform, *Internationales Steuerrecht* 7, pp. 242-254.

Wassermeyer, F. (2008), Die bilanzielle Behandlung der Entstrickungsbesteuerung nach § 4 Abs. 1 Satz 3 EStG und nach § 12 Abs. 1 KStG, *Der Betrieb* 9, pp. 430-434.

Wassermeyer, F. (2009), MA Art. 5, in: Debatin, H./Wassermeyer, F. (Eds.), *Beck'sche Steuerkommentare Doppelbesteuerung: DBA*, loose leaf (113th Suppl. Delivery 2011) Munich, pp. 1-143 (Article 5), 1-189 (Article 7).

Wehrße, M. (2011), *Grenzüberschreitende Besteuerung von Personengesellschaften im internationalen Vergleich, Qualifikationskonflikte - Doppel- und Nicht-Besteuerung - Reformüberlegungen*, 1st Edition, Cologne/Lohmar.

Wei, J. (2008), How to Determine a Permanent Establishment in China, *Tax Notes International* 52, No. 2, pp. 141-148.

Wei, J. (2013), Chinese Tax Risks on Employee Secondments, *Tax Notes International* 70, No. 8, pp. 722-725.

Weisbach, D. A. (1999), Formalism in the Tax Law, *The University of Chicago Law Review* 66, No. 3, pp. 860-886.

Welbers, H./Schulz, S. (2012), Betriebsstättenprobleme bei schweizerischen Prinzipalstrukturen?, *Die Unternehmensbesteuerung* 5, pp. 317-330.

West, P. R./Varma, A. P. (2012), US Taxation of Cross-Border Enterprise Services, *Bulletin for International Taxation* 66, No. 4/5, pp. 188-197.

Wichmann, M. (2005), Aktuelle Tendenzen der OECD-Arbeiten zur Betriebsstätte, insbesondere bei Vertretern und Dienstleistungen, in: Herzig, N./Gunkel, M./ Niemann, U. (Eds.), *Steuerberater-Jahrbuch 2004/2005, zugleich Bericht über den 56. Fachkongress der Steuerberater Köln, 12. und 13. Oktober 2004*, Cologne, pp. 93-108.

Wichmann, M. (2012), Seminar F: Kommt nach dem 'Anstreicher-Beispiel' die 'Subunternehmer-Betriebsstätte'?, *Internationales Steuerrecht* 18, pp. 711-713.

Wiesmann, F./Gerstner, H./Nast, S. (2013) Die Besteuerung von Betriebsstätten in Russland, *Praxis Internationale Steuerberatung* 4, pp. 104-112.

Wilke, K.-M. (2012), Die geplanten Änderungen in § 1 AStG -Referentenentwurf des JStG 2013 durch das BMF, *Internationale Wirtschafts-Briefe* 8, pp. 271-275.

Wilkie, J. S. (2012), Services Permanent Establishments and the Canada-United States Income Tax Treaty, *International Transfer Pricing Journal* 19 No. 3, pp. 179-185.

Williams, R. L. (2014), *Fundamentals of Permanent Establishments*, 2nd Edition, The Hague.

Wissenschaftlicher Beirat (1999), *Reform der internationalen Kapitaleinkommensbesteuerung*, Gutachten erstattet vom Wissenschaftlichen Beirat beim Bundesministerium der Finanzen, Heft 65, Bonn.

Wolff, U. (2004), Generalthema I: Doppelte Nicht-Besteuerung, *Internationales Steuerrecht* 16, pp. 542-549.

Wong, P. (2013), Staff Secondments and Taxable Presence for Nonresident Companies in China, *International Tax Journal* 39, No. 4, pp. 45-49.

Xavier, M. F. S. (2006), Brazil Report, in: IFA Cahiers Vol. 91b, *The Attribution of Profits to Permanent Establishments*, Rotterdam, pp. 199-214.

Yang, H. (2010), Taxation of Income from the Provision of Services-More Requirements, Less Certainty, *Asia-Pacific Tax Bulletin* 16, No. 3, pp. 247-255.

Zapata, S./Weiss, N./Ibarra, C./Martins, L. (2012), Brazil - Permanent Establishments, in: *IBFD Tax Research Platform, Topical Analyses: Permanent Establishments*, Access: September 2012.

Zapata, S./Weiss, N./Ibarra, C./Martins, L. (2015), Brazil - Permanent Establishments, in: *IBFD Tax Research Platform, Topical Analyses: Permanent Establishments*, Access: January 2015.

Zorn, N. (2001), Use of Foreign Losses in Tax Treaties with Exemption Method, *Steuer und Wirtschaft International* 11, pp. 456-465.

Zuber, B. (1991), *Anknüpfungsmerkmale und Reichweite der internationalen Besteuerung*, 1st Edition, Hamburg.

Judgments

AAR, 11 September 2009, Case No. 790 of 2008, *Ruling Pintsch Bamag Antriebs- Und Verkehrstechnik GmbH*, https://www.legalcrystal.com/case/1114664/pintsch-bamag-antriebs-und-verkehrstechnik-gmbh-vs-international-taxation, 04.12.2015.

BFH, 13 May 1958, Case I B 49/58 U, BStBl. III 1958, p. 379.

BFH, 17 March 1982, Case I R 189/79, BStBl. II 1982, pp. 624-625.

BFH, 29 August 1984, Case I R 154/81, BStBl. II 1985, pp. 160-162.

BFH, 20 July 1988, Case I R 49/84, BStBl. II 1989, pp. 140-143.

BFH, 29 July 1992, Case II R 39/89, BStBl. II 1993, pp. 63-67.

BFH, 3 February 1993, Case I R 80-81/91, BStBl. II 1993, pp. 462-467.

BFH, 28 July 1993, Case I R 15/93, BStBl. II 1994, pp. 148-150.

BFH, 23 August 2000, Case I R 98/96, BStBl. II 2002, pp. 207-210.

BFH, 14 July 2004, Case I R 106/03, BFH/NV 2005, pp. 154-156.

BFH, 4 June 2008, Case I R 30/07, BStBl. II 2008, pp. 922-924.

BFH, 17 July 2008, Case I R 77/06, BStBl. II 2009, pp. 464-471.

BFH, 23 February 2011, Case I R 52/10, BFH/NV II 2011, pp. 1354-1361.

BFH, 24 August 2011, Case I R 46/10, BFH/PR 2012, pp. 33-36.

FG Hessen, 26 March 1982, Case VIII 326/78, EFG 1983, pp. 34-35.

IRS revenue ruling, 1974, Case 74-330, CB 278, http://www.charitableplanning.com/document/668993, 04 December 2015.

IRS revenue ruling, 1977, Case 77-45, CB 413, http://www.charitableplanning.com/document/675359, 04 December 2015.

Index

M

N

O

P

Q

R

S

SERIES ON INTERNATIONAL TAXATION

1. Alberto Xavier, *The Taxation of Foreign Investment in Brazil,* 1980 (ISBN 90-200-0582-0).
2. Hugh J. Ault & Albert J. Rädler, *The German Corporation Tax Law with 1980 Amendments,* 1981 (ISBN 90-200-0642-8).
3. Paul R. McDaniel & Hugh J. Ault, *Introduction to United States International Taxation,* 1981 (ISBN 90-6544-004-6).
4. Albert J. Rädler, *German Transfer Pricing/Prix de Transfer en Allemagne,* 1984 (ISBN 90-6544-143-3).
5. Paul R. McDaniel & Stanley S. Surrey, *International Aspects of Tax Expenditures: A Comparative Study,* 1985 (ISBN 90-654-4163-8).
6. Kees van Raad, *Nondiscrimination in International Tax Law,* 1986 (ISBN 90-6544-266-9).
7. Sijbren Cnossen (ed.), *Tax Coordination in the European Community,* 1987 (ISBN 90-6544-272-3).
8. Ben Terra, *Sales Taxation. The Case of Value Added Tax in the European Community,* 1989 (ISBN 90-6544-381-9).
9. Rutsel S.J. Martha, *The Jurisdiction to Tax in International Law: Theory and Practice of Legislative Fiscal Jurisdiction,* 1989 (ISBN 90-654-4416-5).
10. Paul R. McDaniel & Hugh J. Ault, *Introduction to United States International Taxation* (3rd revised edition), 1989 (ISBN 90-6544-423-8).
11. Manuel Pires, *International Juridicial Double Taxation of Income,* 1989 (ISBN 90-6544-426-2).
12. A.H.M. Daniels, *Issues in International Partnership Taxation,* 1991 (ISBN 90-654-4577-3).
13. Arvid A. Skaar, *Permanent Establishment: Erosion of a Tax Treaty Principle,* 1992 (ISBN 90-6544-594-3).
14. Cyrille David & Geerten M.M. Michielse (eds), *Tax Treatment of Financial Instruments,* 1996 (ISBN 90-654-4666-4).
15. Herbert H. Alpert & Kees van Raad (eds), *Essays on International Taxation,* 1993 (ISBN 90-654-4781-4).
16. Wolfgang Gassner, Michael Lang & Eduard Lechner (eds), *Tax Treaties and EC Law,* 1997 (ISBN 90-411-0680-4).
17. Glória Teixeira, *Taxing Corporate Profits in the EU,* 1997 (ISBN 90-411-0703-7).
18. Michael Lang et al. (eds), *Multilateral Tax Treaties,* 1998 (ISBN 90-411-0704-5).
19. Stef van Weeghel, *The Improper Use of Tax Treaties,* 1998 (ISBN 90-411-0737-1).
20. Klaus Vogel (ed.), *Interpretation of Tax Law and Treaties and Transfer Pricing in Japan and Germany,* 1998 (ISBN 90-411-9655-2).
21. Bertil Wiman (ed.), *International Studies in Taxation: Law and Economics; Liber Amicorum Leif Mutén,* 1999 (ISBN 90-411-9692-7).
22. Alfonso J. Martín Jiménez, *Towards Corporate Tax Harmonization in the European Community,* 1999 (ISBN 90-411-9690-0).

23. Ramon J. Jeffery, *The Impact of State Sovereignty on Global Trade and International Taxation*, 1999 (ISBN 90-411-9703-6).
24. A.J. Easson, *Taxation of Foreign Direct Investment*, 1999 (ISBN 90-411-9741-9).
25. Marjaana Helminen, *The Dividend Concept in International Tax Law: Dividend Payments Between Corporate Entities*, 1999 (ISBN 90-411-9765-6).
26. Paul Kirchhof, Moris Lehner, Kees van Raad, Arndt Raupach & Michael-Rodi (eds), *International and Comparative Taxation: Essays in Honour of Klaus Vogel*, 2002 (ISBN 90-411-9841-5).
27. Krister Andersson, Peter Melz & Christer Silfverberg (eds), *Liber Amicorum Sven-Olof Lodin*, 2001 (ISBN 90-411-9850-4).
28. Juan Martín Jovanovich, *Customs Valuation and Transfer Pricing: Is It Possible to Harmonize Customs and Tax Rules?*, 2002 (ISBN 90-411-9888-1).
29. Stefano Simontacchi, *Taxation of Capital Gains under the OECD Model Convention: With Special Regard to Immovable Property*, 2007 (ISBN 978-90-411-2549-1).
30. Michael Lang, Josef Schuch, & Claus Staringer (eds), *Tax Treaty Law and EC Law*, 2007 (ISBN 978-90-411-2629-0).
31. Duncan Bentley, *Taxpayers' Rights: Theory Origin and Implementation*, 2007 (ISBN 978-90-411-2650-4).
32. Sergio André Rocha, *Interpretation of Double Taxation Conventions: General Theory and Brazilian Perspective*, 2008 (ISBN 978-90-411-2822-5).
33. Robert F. van Brederode, *Systems of General Sales Taxation: Theory, Policy and Practice*, 2009 (ISBN 978-90-411-2832-4).
34. John G. Head & Richard Krever (eds), *Tax Reform in the 21st Century: A Volume in Memory of Richard Musgrave*, 2009 (ISBN 978-90-411-2829-4).
35. Jens Wittendorff, *Transfer Pricing and the Arm's Length Principle in International Tax Law*, 2010 (ISBN 978-90-411-3270-3).
36. Marjaana Helminen, *The International Tax Law Concept of Dividend*, 2010 (ISBN 978-90-411-3206-2).
37. Robert F. van Brederode (ed.), *Immovable Property under VAT: A Comparative Global Analysis*, 2011 (ISBN 978-90-411-3126-3).
38. Dennis Weber & Stef van Weeghel, *The 2010 OECD Updates: Model Tax Convention & Transfer Pricing Guidelines - A Critical Review*, 2011 (ISBN 978-90-411-3812-5).
39. Yariv Brauner & Martin James McMahon, Jr. (eds), *The Proper Tax Base: Structural Fairness from an International and Comparative Perspective—Essays in Honour of Paul McDaniel*, 2012 (ISBN 978-90-411-3286-4).
40. Robert F. van Brederode (ed.), *Science, Technology and Taxation*, 2012 (ISBN 978-90-411-3125-6).
41. Oskar Henkow, *The VAT/GST Treatment of Public Bodies*, 2013 (ISBN 978-90-411-4663-2).
42. Jean Schaffner, *How Fixed Is a Permanent Establishment?*, 2013 (ISBN 978-90-411-4662-5).

43. Miguel Correia, *Taxation of Corporate Groups*, 2013 (ISBN 978-90-411-4841-4).
44. Veronika Daurer, *Tax Treaties and Developing Countries*, 2014 (ISBN 978-90-411-4982-4).
45. Claire Micheau, *State Aid, Subsidy and Tax Incentives under EU and WTO Law*, 2014 (ISBN 978-90-411-4555-0).
46. Robert F. van Brederode & Richard Krever (eds), *Legal Interpretation of Tax Law*, 2014 (ISBN 978-90-411-4945-9).
47. Radhakishan Rawal, *Taxation of Cross-border Services*, 2014 (ISBN 978-90-411-4947-3).
48. João Dácio Rolim, *Proportionality and Fair Taxation*, 2014 (ISBN 978-90-411-5838-3).
49. Paulo Rosenblatt, *General Anti-avoidance Rules for Major Developing Countries*, 2015 (ISBN 978-90-411-5839-0).
50. Gaspar Lopes Dias V.S., *Tax Arbitrage through Cross-Border Financial Engineering*, 2015 (ISBN 978-90-411-5875-8).
51. Geerten M.M. Michielse & Victor Thuronyi (eds), *Tax Design Issues Worldwide*, 2015 (ISBN 978-90-411-5610-5).
52. Oktavia Weidmann, *Taxation of Derivatives*, 2015 (ISBN 978-90-411-5977-9).
53. Chris Evans, Richard Krever & Peter Mellor (eds), *Tax Simplification*, 2015 (ISBN 978-90-411-5976-2).
54. Reuven Avi-Yonah & Joel Slemrod (eds), *Taxation and Migration*, 2015 (ISBN 978-90-411-6136-9).
55. Alexander Bosman, *Other Income under Tax Treaties: An Analysis of Article 21 of the OECD Model Convention*, 2015 (ISBN 978-90-411-6610-4).
56. John Abrahamson, *International Taxation of Manufacturing and Distribution*, 2016 (ISBN 978-90-411-6664-7).
57. Frederik Boulogne, *Shortcomings in the EU Merger Directive*, 2016 (ISBN 978-90-411-6713-2).
58. Angelika Meindl-Ringler, *Beneficial Ownership in International Tax Law*, 2016 (ISBN 978-90-411-6833-7).
59. Andreas Waltrich, *Cross-Border Taxation of Permanent Establishments: An International Comparison*, 2016 (ISBN 978-90-411-6832-0).

www.ingramcontent.com/pod-product-compliance
Lightning Source LLC
LaVergne TN
LVHW020001031026
849161LV00023B/807
9789041168320